Beyond Slavery

Beyond Slavery

Christian Theology and Rehabilitation from Human Trafficking

Chris Gooding

CASCADE *Books* • Eugene, Oregon

BEYOND SLAVERY
Christian Theology and Rehabilitation from Human Trafficking

Cascade Books
An Imprint of Wipf and Stock Publishers
199 W. 8th Ave., Suite 3
Eugene, OR 97401

www.wipfandstock.com

PAPERBACK ISBN: 978-1-6667-3515-4
HARDCOVER ISBN: 978-1-6667-9194-5
EBOOK ISBN: 978-1-6667-9195-2

Cataloguing-in-Publication data:

Names: Gooding, Chris, author.

Title: Beyond slavery : Christian theology and rehabilitation from human trafficking / Chris Gooding.

Description: Eugene, OR : Cascade Books, 2023 | Includes bibliographical references.

Identifiers: ISBN 978-1-6667-3515-4 (paperback) | ISBN 978-1-6667-9194-5 (hardcover) | ISBN 978-1-6667-9195-2 (ebook)

Subjects: LCSH: Slavery—Religious aspects. | Human trafficking—Religious aspects—Christianity. | Abolition of slavery.

Classification: HD4861 .G66 2023 (print) | HD4861 .G66 (ebook)

JUNE 1, 2023 8:18 AM

Contents

Acknowledgments

GIVEN THE FACT THAT this project involved fifty-four interviews and a trip all the way across the world, the number of debts I owe to those who helped make this research possible is substantial. A book in and of itself could be written to catalog the recognition that others deserve on this project, so I will try to keep things as brief as I can.

Thanks go first of all to all of my interviewees for being willing to provide the information that makes up the core of this project. Some interviewees even did more than sit for an interview. "Beth" laid the groundwork for the project in India. Her initial work was crucial during the proposal stage of this project. "Mallika" was kind enough to offer up her assistant, who coordinated a considerable chunk of my interviews in Mumbai. "Chitra" also helped establish a number of interview contacts, and helped me to get settled when I initially arrived in Mumbai. Thanks especially go to "Hannah," who likely invested more hours to this project than any other interviewee. She deserves credit for coordinating basically all of the interviews that occurred in Chennai. She also had by far the quickest turnaround of any of my NGO reviewers, and her constructive feedback (and effusive praise) on initial drafts was extremely helpful.

Since my competency in Hindi is limited and my competency in Tamil is nonexistent, this project also relied on a number of translators to make it possible. Thanks to Sunita Khursule, Mona Almeida, Muriella D'Silva, and "Auntie" Jai and "Auntie" Hoofritz for serving as translators for my Hindi-speaking survivors. Thanks to Aryan Timothy for serving as a translator for my Tamil-speaking survivors. All of my translators took to the work with such an impressive combination of exuberance and tact that it made speaking with survivors about potentially difficult topics considerably easier.

I have experienced struggles with housing discrimination every time I have lived in Mumbai. Such struggles would have likely posed an obstacle to research if it weren't for the amazing people at NLF Avatar Church in Mumbai. Thanks to Ara Daquinag and Michelle Bishop for allowing me to crash on their couch initially, Jimit and Hannah Mehta, Ishan Gupta and Philip for taking me in during periods of transition, and to Noble and Roju Philip for letting me rent a room in their apartment for the long haul. Avatar also served as a very welcoming church home away from home while I was in Mumbai. In the United States, a Mennonite among Reformed Evangelicals might be considered an oddity. In Mumbai, I was welcomed with open arms as an opportunity for edifying and lively discussion. Thanks especially to Noble Philip, Ravi Narain, and Erin Arendse for being thoughtful discussion partners.

Bharathy Tahiliani and Pranitha Timothy provided much-needed moral support at key times during my research. Both of them are by far the most seasoned professionals in the field of rehabilitation for survivors that I interviewed. And I can't tell you how much it meant to me that they, in their wisdom and experience, seemed to see the need for this research more than anyone I spoke to about the project. As such, several long conversations with them provided the energy and clarity I needed to push though my time in India. Both also provided extremely insightful interviews that formed key parts of several chapters that follow.

Moving from India to Milwaukee, special thanks go to Matthew, Mandy, Izzy, and Emma Bailey. The Baileys have been my housemates and support network for the past seven years as this project has moved from research to dissertation to book. As a grad student, they allowed me to occupy a room in their house while contributing what I was able in terms of food and rent money (which was extremely helpful, as I was living below the poverty line for most of my graduate studies). Norm and Candy Stolpe and Ethan Vanderleek were also briefly part of our little wannabe intentional community, and they offered day-to-day support as well. Thanks also go to Pascale Mayhorn (our landlord), who has continued to allow all of us to engage in this communal living experiment by providing us with an affordable place to stay.

Thanks also go to Milwaukee Mennonite Church for being my church home during the composition of this project. My church continues to impress me with their willingness to help others in ways great and small. Special thanks go to Ray Gingerich, for being a great resource on matters of restorative justice, and to Mandy Bailey, Matthew Bailey, Erin

Cassidente, Connie Evers, Ben Hochstedler, Matthew Keiser, Sarah Mast, Rachel Stolpe, and Barb White for transcribing portions of my interviews.

Thanks to Russell Johnson and Leatha Miles-Edmonson, who also served as transcriptionists.

On the Marquette side of things, thanks go to the folks who oversee the Smith Family Fellowship. The Fellowship gave me the funding I needed to finance this research. Thanks also to the folks who work at the Office of Research Compliance for making sure I conducted my research ethically and giving me pointers on how to go about the business of gathering informed consent. Thanks to Becky Long for helping me figure out how to code my interviews. Thanks to all the other doctoral candidates who walked alongside me at Marquette for helping me hone the theological thoughts that appear in these pages. Andy Alexis-Baker, Rick Barry, Christopher Brenna, Glenn Butner, Anne Carpenter, Nick Elder, Darin Fawley, Dallas Flippin, Tim Gabrielson, Joe Gordon, Kirsten Guidero, Chris Hadley, Drew Harmon, Jonathan Heaps, Ryan Hemmer, Darren Henson, David Horstkoetter, Erin Kidd, Dave Kiger, Andrew Kuzma, Nathan Lundsford, Alex Martins, Samantha Miller, Paul Pasquesi, Kyle Potter, Caroline Redick, Lincoln Rice, Jakob Rinderknecht, Gene Schlesinger, Luke Togni, Juli Vazquez, Jeff Walkey, Nathan Willowby, and Dominic Zappia all deserve recognition in this regard.

I could not have asked for a better dissertation committee. Many, many thanks to Willie Jennings, Steve Long, Bryan Massingale, and Kate Ward. Bryan contributed immensely to my competency in the theology of enslaved Christians in the antebellum period, and he served as a great conversation partner for a Mennonite considering a single vocation. Willie is infused with the virtue of joy, and his "Slavery and Obedience" course was the major inspiration for chapter 3. Kate is the best advocate a person could hope for. Even before this dissertation was submitted, she was promulgating this project for publication as a book to publishers far and wide. And Steve has struggled through every draft of this thing that I put in front of him, somehow managing to give speedy and deep feedback every time. He and his wife, Ricka, have also shown me immense hospitality in numerous ways throughout my time as a doctoral student. To a person, every member of my committee has given immensely valuable feedback. I suffer from an embarrassment of riches when it comes to mentors.

Thanks also go to Charlie Collier, Matt Wimer, George Callahan, and the rest of the editorial staff at Cascade. I found that not many publishers were willing to even consider a repurposed dissertation, and I am thankful for their willingness to walk with me through this process.

Finally, I'd like to thank my parents, Steve and Vona, and my sister, Jessi. Seventeen years ago, I told them that I was moving to India to try to help trafficking survivors. They have believed in and supported this project ever since.

I have almost certainly forgot to recognize someone in such a long list. I hope they can find it in themselves to forgive me for it.

INTRODUCTION

Is There Life after Slavery?

"JYOTHI" GREW UP IN a small village in rural Maharashtra. When she was in her early teens, her father sold her to a brothel keeper in Mumbai. Jyothi, like many girls who are trafficked into Mumbai brothels, initially resisted her captors. And, like many other girls who are trafficked, her will to resist was broken the first night she was left in a room alone with a paying customer. He had paid for her, and did not respect her pleas for him to stop. He raped Jyothi that night.

This soon became a frequent occurrence for Jyothi, as the brothel staff expected her to have sex with many men each night. They told her that she must do this to work off the "debt" she incurred when they bought her. Thankfully, the arrangement did not last much longer than a year before the brothel shut down, due to infighting amongst the management. As some of the money she had made there was sent back to her father, the brothel's closure meant that he suddenly experienced a significant drop in income. He soon figured out that the brothel had closed and he contacted Jyothi again. He told her that he loved her, and he pleaded with her to come live with him again. She accepted.

Soon after, her father sold her again, this time to a brothel that was little more than a dingy hellhole with tiny, cramped rooms, soiled beds, and a massive vermin infestation. Again, her owners expected her to have sex with many men each night for financial gain. Many of these men were horribly abusive to Jyothi. Sometime after she came to live in this brothel, she was rescued in a raid led by International Justice Mission (IJM), an anti-trafficking nongovernmental organization (NGO). They helped her move from the brothel into an aftercare home. While she was at the home, IJM staff asked her if she would be willing to testify against her traffickers. She enthusiastically accepted. Soon after, her father contacted her again. He pleaded with her not to incriminate him. He told her that he loved her. He told her that he had changed. He told her he was so sorry that he had ever sold her. He told her he would never do it again.

Jyothi wanted to believe her father. So, she resolved that she would testify against everyone involved in her trafficking. Everyone, that is, except her father. She would leave him out of the story. Unfortunately, by leaving out her father's role in her trafficking, her testimony became incoherent. All of her traffickers were acquitted, including her father. Sometime after the trial, she went back to living with her father once again.

Soon after returning to live with her father, he married her off to a very cruel and abusive man. Her new husband and her father decided that it was in their best interest to sell her to a brothel for the third time. Soon after she was re-trafficked, the staff at IJM were miraculously able to find her for a second time, and another raid was conducted. Jyothi was rescued and put in an aftercare home, where the home's staff soon discovered that Jyothi had AIDS.

Jyothi greatly disliked staying in the aftercare home, and soon returned to living with her father once again. Some months after she returned to her village, IJM sent a social worker up to check on her. When the social worker arrived, she found Jyothi lying in a corner of her father's house in a pile of rags and her own filth. Jyothi was almost comatose. She hadn't been taking her antiretroviral medication, and she hadn't been receiving adequate medical care. Her father responded to the social worker's outrage with indifference. He no longer told Jyothi that he loved her. He no longer pleaded with her. Once he had found out his daughter had AIDS, he had discarded her in that pile of rags in the corner. He wanted nothing more to do with her.

The social worker took Jyothi to the hospital, where she was admitted to hospice care. There, the nurses made her as comfortable as they could while she died. On her death bed, she thanked the IJM social worker for all that had been done for her. And despite all the rotten things that life had thrown at her, she could honestly say that she was departing this life in peace.

I never met Jyothi. She died some years before I would set foot in India for the first time. But nothing shaped my time working in India more than her story. I interned with IJM in Mumbai the year after I graduated from college. And during that year, it's fair to say that Jyothi haunted the small office building where I worked day in and day out. Every conversation about aftercare for survivors of sex trafficking had her story in the background. It was on the lips of our social workers so often that I learned it by rote within the first few months of my arrival in the office. How could something like this happen? And how could we avoid it in the future? Few of our stories were as devoid of justice as Jyothi's. And yet, the general situation was frightfully common. There isn't an anti-trafficking NGO in Mumbai that doesn't have a similar story in their case files. As I came to find out, the whole system of rehabilitation for sex trafficking survivors in Mumbai was based around one gnawing concern: that one day, the survivor would find a way to contact their former owner, that former owner would coax them to come back, and the survivor would walk back into a life of sex slavery.

In the last twenty years or so, the literature on human trafficking has exploded. This massive body of literature has brought significant public awareness to the issue. There are many excellent introductions to the topic that are available, all arguing forcefully that, despite what our political rhetoric and the way we narrate our own history have led to us to believe, slavery is still with us.[1] These works give accounts of different forms of human trafficking, recruitment methods, forms of abuse suffered by victims, the economics of modern slavery, and modern slavery's links to organized crime. There are even works now available that are comprised of direct testimony by survivors themselves, interviews or memoirs in which survivors describe their recruitment, sale, and abuse at the hands of their captors.[2] The assertion that slavery still exists and is a pressing problem in nearly every country on the globe is met with far less skepticism, scorn, and defensiveness than when I first got involved in anti-trafficking work over a decade ago. This is a very good thing: it means that more people are ready to address the problem of modern slavery.

And yet, amid this explosion of literature, it is extremely hard to find any treatment of the specific aspects of Jyothi's story that made it haunt the office of our NGO. What pushed Jyothi to run right back into enslavement not once, but *three times*? How many other formerly enslaved people end up returning to their masters? What can be done to

1. Kara, *Sex Trafficking*; Bales et al., *Modern Slavery*; Batstone, *Not for Sale*; Shelley, *Human Trafficking*; Bales, *Disposable People*.

2. Bales and Trodd, *To Plead Our Own Cause*; Lloyd, *Girls Like Us*.

minimize the chance that a case like Jyothi's will arise in the future? What does life look like after slavery? Is there life after slavery at all? Sources that even bring up these questions are difficult to find. When it comes to literature on aftercare, there are a few treatments of economic rehabilitation.[3] There are a few mentions of what life looks like after slavery in survivor memoirs.[4] But there is only one work I know of that directly addresses situations like Jyothi's: a phenomenal work on the pressures that often push former sex slaves back into the arms of their former masters.[5] Beyond this, resources are difficult to find. One of the social workers working with the aftercare department at IJM told me several years ago that they had recently done a literature review on best practices for the rehabilitation of trafficking survivors. They simply wanted to know if what they were doing to help survivors reintegrate (psychologically, physically, and economically) followed best practices. They found absolutely no literature on evidence-based best practices for rehabilitation for trafficking survivors. *Nothing.* Since I performed my interviews, I am aware of only one work on best practices that has been published (focused specifically on sex trafficking).[6] Granted, these social workers (and I) could have missed something. Inevitably, when you are trying to sift through a massive body of literature for something specific, some things fall through the cracks. And it could be written off as simply the nature of academic study of any sort. Inevitably there are going to be gaps in the literature. But in this case, this rationale doesn't seem to fit. After all, as I mentioned, the problem of returning to enslavement was so common in Mumbai that the whole aftercare system was practically crafted around that single problem. It seems bizarre that a problem that so many on-the-ground advocates are worried about in practice finds such little discussion in the literature.

The problem may be tied to a lack of interest in aftercare in general in anti-trafficking advocacy. Enforcement and prosecution of anti-trafficking laws simply capture the imagination much more easily at anti-trafficking rallies or in fundraising materials. Tales of exciting police raids

3. Kristof and WuDunn, *Half the Sky*. As we shall see in chapter 5, even these works are often limited by their economic perspective.

4. Richardson, *PHD to Ph.D.*; Rosenblatt and Murphy, *Stolen*; Hays, *Trafficked*. One should note here that these memoirs are all about sex trafficking. Memoirs from survivors of other forms of trafficking are considerably harder to find.

5. Lloyd, *Girls Like Us*.

6. Gerassi and Nichols, *Sex Trafficking*.

or taut courtroom drama seem to appeal to donors and attract young advocates to anti-trafficking work. Stories about helping a survivor get into a good therapy regimen or helping a survivor find a new profession don't inspire quite as much, even though they are absolutely necessary when it comes to avoiding re-enslavement. And then there is the sense that aftercare isn't *supposed* to be inherently exciting. Some advocates spoke to me off the record about a general pressure to make sure that aftercare isn't the part of the story filled with dynamic conflict. After all, if aftercare stories don't resolve in a neat, tidy, happy ending, donors might question what the use is in giving to your organization.

To cite one small example of how this works itself out, I received a postcard from IJM after my field interviews were completed in early 2015. The postcard had a picture on the front of a group who had just graduated from one of IJM's Freedom Trainings, an aftercare program the NGO runs for survivors of bonded labor (a particular species of human trafficking). The photo was taken from above, with the group looking up into the camera and smiling. The text on the back of the postcard emphasized the gift of newfound freedom that this group of bonded laborers had just received, and how it was only possible with the help of IJM donors like you. As I looked at the picture, I remembered my bonded labor survivor interviewees, all of whom had come from a class just like this one. I wondered how many of the people in the picture had acquired new debt, as one of my interviewees had (a sign that re-bondage might be on the horizon). I wondered how many of them dealt with alcohol abuse or domestic violence, as some of my interviewees had. I wondered how many of them suffered from "captive mentality"—the term social workers used to describe the various spiritual and emotional chains that continue to hold survivors captive, even after rescue—as some of my interviewees did. IJM wasn't being dishonest in what they presented, nor were they trying to silence the stories of individuals going through such hardships while rehabilitating. But I realized that what I held in my hand could easily be interpreted by most donors as exactly what they wanted. An unquestionably happy ending. It was, after all, what they paid for.

And isn't that what all of us want? For survivors of modern slavery to be free in the fullest sense? And beyond freedom for them, don't we want freedom for *everyone*? Don't we all want a world without slavery? There is always a temptation amid abolitionist fervor to close things down at the moment of liberation and not look into a survivor's life beyond that point. That way we can tell ourselves that the world we want has finally been achieved. Sometimes this desire for a world without slavery is based in a genuine care for the enslaved themselves. Sometimes it is based in more sinister motives. Some of our most ardent pundits and cultural commentators desperately *need* slavery to be over with, so that they can argue that their favorite economic, political, or religious system is the one that finally gets the credit for putting it to rest.[7] While they tout slavery's end, it continues in the lives of those like Jyothi. And Jyothi's enslavement didn't end after her first physical liberation. It didn't even end after her third. If we ever hope to move beyond slavery as a society, we must first talk about what it means to move beyond slavery in an individual human life. And that is not as easy a conversation to have as it might seem at first blush.

If discussion of the issues regarding aftercare is sparse, discussion of the ethics or theology of the various aspects of anti-trafficking work is even more so. This is particularly odd given the prominent role that Christians (and especially evangelical Christians) have played in popularizing anti-trafficking work. In fact, I am aware of only two book-length treatments on the ethics of anti-trafficking methods. One is an assessment of the (philosophical) ethics and economics of slave redemption (i.e., liberating slaves by paying for their release, as opposed to liberating them by say, performing a raid),[8] the other is a work of moral theology critiquing the sexual ethics that underwrites much of America's anti-trafficking advocacy.[9] Again, doubtless I've missed something. But I am sure that even if what I've overlooked were incorporated, there would remain a rich field of ethical topics left unexplored.

This book is an attempt to start a conversation at the nexus between those two largely forgotten worlds: it is a work of moral and political theology that attempts to address some of the common dilemmas faced by survivors of human trafficking during reintegration. As a Christian ethicist that remains haunted by Jyothi's story, it seemed only natural to explore whether the Christian tradition had the resources to begin to address situations like hers. But again, due to the gaps in the literature, I had few resources to go on. And I could not rely merely on anecdotal evidence

7. McCloskey, *Bourgeois Virtues*, 30. McCloskey argues that the skeptical academic clerisy that scoffs at capitalism should give up their scorn and embrace capitalism with open arms because it put an end to slavery. McCloskey needs slavery to be over with so that she can use it for apologetic purposes.

8. Appiah and Bunzl, *Buying Freedom*.

9. Zimmerman, *Other Dreams of Freedom*.

throughout what follows. So, I made an unusual choice for a theologian: I decided to do some fieldwork. As a part of this project, I conducted numerous interviews with both survivors who have been through the aftercare system and those who work with them on various rehabilitation issues. I used these interviews to construct a thick narrative of the dilemmas faced by survivors during the reintegration process. I then analyzed those dilemmas using insights from several conversations on similar issues that are currently going on in political and moral theology.

The Interviews

From September of 2014 to January of 2015, I conducted interviews in India with eleven women who had received aftercare for sex trafficking, ten individuals who had received aftercare for bonded labor, and thirty-four professionals who work with survivors in various capacities.[10] Of the eleven women who had received aftercare for sex trafficking that I interviewed, five were confirmed survivors of sex trafficking, three were suspected survivors of sex trafficking,[11] two were child brides,[12] and one was an "at risk" individual who entered into aftercare for prevention purposes and was never actually trafficked. In what follows, more weight is given to the testimony of confirmed survivors of sex trafficking than the other three categories. All ten individuals who received aftercare for bonded labor were from confirmed cases of bonded labor. All interviews involving bonded labor survivors or those who worked with bonded labor survivors were conducted in or around Chennai. All interviews involving sex trafficking survivors or those who worked with sex trafficking survivors

10. I also interviewed two professionals who work on prison ministry/reform in Mumbai. I had originally planned to incorporate some of these interviews into the material on victim-perpetrators in chapter 6.

11. This means that the agency providing aftercare could not confirm their trafficking with absolute certainty due to record keeping issues. However, given certain aspects of these survivors' case files, the agency providing aftercare heavily suspected that these women were trafficked at some point.

12. Whether child brides are included as sex trafficking victims or not is debated among anti-trafficking advocates. Some of the aftercare centers I went to included them in their definition of trafficking. Being forced to be a child bride can involve the same sorts of sale and abuse as other forms of human trafficking. However, there are some differences in the experience of child brides and sex trafficking survivors who are forced to act as sex workers. I have differentiated the two groups here due to this debate.

were conducted in Mumbai.[13] All interviews were completed in a single session[14] that lasted about an hour and a half on average.[15] All interviews were conducted in accordance with the informed consent guidelines laid out by Marquette University's Office of Research Compliance. Each survivor was allowed to choose their own pseudonym,[16] and no survivor's real name appears in what follows.[17] Professionals were given the option of using a pseudonym, their real first name only, or their real full name. For professionals who chose to use a pseudonym, the pseudonym is given in quotation marks (e.g., "Beth") the first time they are introduced. The vast majority of my professional interviewees were Indian nationals (with only a handful of American and Canadian nationals thrown in). Almost all of the survivors were Indian nationals.

Before giving an overview of what I learned from those interviews, a few questions about why these populations were approached for interviews need to be addressed. A few interviewees asked why India was chosen as a location for the interviews. Wouldn't it have been easier for me, as an American, to do these interviews in the United States? There are two reasons why India was chosen as a location for the interviews. The first is a pragmatic reason: I had already made the contacts necessary to do the research there when I was working with IJM in 2005–6. The second has to do with the depth of the conversation surrounding trafficking survivors. To put it bluntly, the state of the conversation among anti-trafficking groups in the United States is about twenty years behind the conversation going on in India. People frequently seem shocked when I say this, because the social services network in India is considerably thinner than it is in the United States, and mental health stigma

13. The only exception here is Pranitha Timothy, who has worked with survivors of both forms of trafficking and was interviewed in Chennai.

14. The only exception here is "Mallika," with whom I conducted a follow-up interview to clarify some details.

15. The shortest was forty-five minutes, the longest was more than three hours.

16. In most cases, *I* don't even know the survivor's real name—they introduced themselves to me using the pseudonym.

17. There are two exceptions to this rule among my bonded labor survivor interviewees: Raja and the unnamed couple. Raja works for an anti-trafficking NGO, and has given his testimony countless times before, so he is publicly known as a survivor of bonded labor. His real name is used. The unnamed couple are a husband and wife who refused to choose a pseudonym because they believed that they would be lying to you, the reader, if they did so. As an ethicist, I disagree with this conclusion, but chose to honor their difference of opinion. So they were never given a pseudonym.

is greater (though admittedly, the US still has considerable work to do in that arena). Hopefully two anecdotal examples here will suffice to illustrate what I mean. The first example comes from a conversation I had with a US-based women's shelter (run by a group of women religious) that offers services to trafficking survivors and other women looking to leave commercial sexual exploitation. The sisters informed me that the biggest obstacle that they faced in opening the center was getting a memorandum of understanding drafted with the city police department. It took a long time for the police department to concede that it was best to bring these women to the center rather than arrest them on vice charges (i.e., drug charges and prostitution charges), and much of the police department still isn't entirely comfortable with the memorandum. The second example is from a sex trafficking panel I sat on that was hosted by Catholic Relief Services at Marquette University. Of the four panelists (a prosecutor, an outreach worker, a survivor, and myself), I was the only one who opposed charging sex trafficking survivors with vice crimes. The issue in question in both examples is one that was solved very definitively on the Indian scene about twenty years ago. No, you absolutely should not charge survivors with vice crimes. Not only would doing so ignore the fact that they are victims, but having a rap sheet provides a plethora of unnecessary barriers to their reintegration. Enforcement agencies may be encouraged to charge those who *exploit* survivors, but certainly not the survivors themselves. Since many US-based agencies seem to remain stuck in preliminary conversations such as this, there is no talk going on of how to deal with deeper problems (such as captive mentality).

Why are Indian NGOs so much further along in this conversation? The likely reason is simply that NGOs on the Indian scene came to grips with the fact that trafficking is a problem in their country much quicker than American groups did. When I entered into this work more than fifteen years ago, I was told that the reason why IJM operates in other countries was because the American justice system was doing an adequate job combatting human trafficking. Fast forward fifteen years, and now American anti-trafficking advocates joke about the fact that for more than a decade we were simply listening to the TIP Report,[18] and we

18. The Trafficking in Persons (TIP) Report is an annual publication of the US State Department. It assesses the state of trafficking in as many countries as it can compile data for, and then assigns them one of three ranks intended to indicate how well that country is doing at combatting trafficking. In this report, the US is almost always ranked "Tier 1," which indicates that enforcement agencies are doing an adequate job of dealing with trafficking in that country.

never found it at all suspicious that we were evaluating ourselves and kept giving ourselves a passing grade. At least since the Polaris Project published its findings from the National Trafficking Hotline, it has been recognized that there is, indeed, a significant trafficking problem in the United States.[19] On the Indian scene, however, Indian NGOs readily accepted that trafficking was a problem nearly twenty years ago (government agencies, of course, were slower to recognize this, but eventually were forced to admit the problem). And because of this, there is a deep wisdom present in the conversation going on among Indian NGOs that is sorely missing in the United States, even if there remain things on the Indian scene that could be reformed. Thus, India proved a better location to do this research than the United States.

Some anti-trafficking advocates might hold that it is unwise to lump together bonded labor and sex trafficking survivors. The two forms of trafficking are different enough from each other that lumping them together simply invites overgeneralization. There is some truth to this, and it is the reason why there is one chapter in this work that focuses on problems experienced much more by sex trafficking survivors (chapter 4) and one chapter that focuses on problems experienced much more by labor trafficking survivors (chapter 5). But there are enough commonalities between the two forms of trafficking (because they are both species of enslavement) that the remaining four chapters deal with common threads between the two forms (chapters 1, 2, 3, and 6). It is my hope that by putting these two types of work in conversation with one another, it will be mutually illuminating for workers in both camps. My hope is also that the problems discussed will be general enough that workers from contexts other than India (say, in the US) can benefit from an analysis of the problems faced by survivors in India.

With those caveats out of the way, what follows are overviews of each of this book's six chapters.

19. The National Human Trafficking Hotline was started by the Polaris Project in 2007, and within five years, it was able to identify over nine thousand unique cases of human trafficking. These cases came from across the United States, and due to the fact that the hotline is still relatively unknown, this almost certainly is representative of only a fraction of the human trafficking cases that were going on during those five years. The Polaris Project provides a breakdown of reports made to the hotline by state and year at https://humantraffickinghotline.org/states. The National Human Trafficking Hotline is 1-888-373-7888. It is thirty-seven twice flanked on either side by three eights (if that makes it easier to remember).

Chapter Overviews

The first chapter ("Slavery Is Legion") addresses the question "What is slavery?" It is common to find a chapter that deals with this topic in many anti-trafficking works, but most of them are concerned with legal definitions of slavery in international or local legal instruments. This chapter considers enslavement from a legal, sociological, and theological standpoint, arguing that all three are ultimately necessary for a holistic account of slavery. My main concern in this chapter is to give a definition of enslavement that pays special attention to slavery's quickly evolving nature. Whenever anti-trafficking advocates employ a new method of intervention to emancipate victims, trafficking networks quickly shift tactics so that their slaveholding operations can continue. This seems to have been the case with past forms of enslavement as well: numerous historians have chronicled the evolution of slavery in the United States from chattel slavery to the convict leasing system after chattel slavery was legally abolished (such as W. E. B. Du Bois, Angela Davis, and Douglas Blackmon). This evolutionary aspect is not always considered in anti-slavery literature, leading to a naïve view of how easy it will be to put slavery to an end. For a more adequate characterization of enslavement that takes this evolutionary aspect into account, I turn to antebellum slave theologies in the US (which often characterized slavery as a demonic institution), putting them in conversation with the work of more recent biblical scholars on powers and principalities. I use this analysis to argue that slavery is a demonic power, one that evolves, reacts, submerges, and reappears in other forms, complicating advocates' efforts to fight it. This chapter acts as a keystone to the rest of the work, as the topics of the subsequent chapters all end up linking back to this initial theological definition of slavery in some shape or form.

Chapter 2 ("Chains of the Soul") discusses "captive mentality," a term the social workers I interviewed coined for a phenomenon that afflicts many formerly enslaved people. From the interviews, I have determined that captive mentality manifests in at least four levels. At its most basic level, captive mentality manifests in the inability to physically self-regulate one's own bodily functions (eating, sleeping, going to the bathroom, etc.) without explicit authorization from a master. At a deeper level, survivors with captive mentality become dependent on others to make even small decisions, or to cope with matters of daily life. They actively seek out new masters to make these decisions for them. At a still deeper level, survivors come under a condition strikingly akin to Stockholm syndrome, where they come to identify with their captors over and against those who might try to rescue them. These survivors display an extreme fascination with their captor and often attempt to return to situations of exploitation after rescue. Finally, at the fourth and deepest level of captive mentality, the fear and reverence with which the former slave regards their former master reaches its apex to the point that the formerly enslaved person will actually identify them as a god. By analyzing the phenomenon of captive mentality, I provide an account of the warped claims about the nature of love, justice, and God that lie dormant in the institution of slavery.

Chapter 3 ("An Abolitionist Theological Portrait") offers resources that are available to challenge the warped portraits of love, justice, and God present in slavery. In this chapter, I utilize theological and biblical resources to draw up alternative portraits of the nature of love and God, portraits that are rooted in the ministry of Jesus Christ, which culminates in the eschatological restoration of all things, and the liberation of all peoples from all forms of bondage.

Chapter 4 ("Prisons and Monasteries") discusses two models for aftercare homes for sex trafficking survivors that are common in Mumbai. One seems to be based on a monastic model (survivors are under a rule with heavy emphasis on the regulation of their time), while the other seems to be based on a prison model (the time regulation is present, but the perimeter is enclosed by thick stone walls topped with razor wire, and the residents are locked behind bars at night). The survivors I interviewed even openly referred to aftercare homes on this latter model as prisons. I probe the theological roots of both models (the monastic model and the prison model) and try to articulate why the difference between the two matters. Trying to articulate this difference is complicated by Michel Foucault's insight that the modern prison itself takes its logic and its discipline from pastoral and monastic practices: the modern prison is a monastery weaponized by the state. I rely on the insights of monastic theologians who were aware of the dangers of the uses of both monastic and prison models for rehabilitation to evaluate the ethics of both forms of institutionalization.

Chapter 5 ("Labor, Caste, and Obedience") critiques a common analysis of the economic plight of survivors after rescue: they were vulnerable to trafficking because of their poverty, and they are poor because they can only perform forms of "unskilled labor." Thus, aftercare workers must help survivors to gain proficiency in some form of "skilled labor" to raise them out of their poverty and prevent them from being re-trafficked. In the case of labor trafficking survivors near Chennai, it is simply false that survivors are not proficient in a form of skilled labor before trafficking. Oftentimes they are heavily exploited precisely *because* they possess highly specialized agricultural skills that are desirable for the owners of rice mills and other such businesses to acquire cheaply, and they are vulnerable to exploitation due to their position in the caste system. This means that full integration for these survivors will necessarily require some form of resistance to the caste system. I look at two avenues of resistance that have been common within Christian churches: community organizing and nonviolent direct action. I argue that a combination of the two can be of use for survivors in resisting caste oppression, and that since civil disobedience is an essential part of the Christian narrative, local churches can be of assistance in helping survivors understand the ins and outs of both types of resistance.

Chapter 6 ("Justice") deals with obstacles to restoration for those who cross the line between oppressor and enslaved at some point after their trafficking (a commonly overlooked subset of survivors). Many brothel madams arrested on anti-trafficking charges in Mumbai were trafficked themselves prior to becoming a madam. Once customers were no longer willing to pay their owners to sleep with them, these women were faced with two choices: beg on the street or go into a management position in the brothel (thereby participating in the trafficking of other women). In labor trafficking in Chennai, the focus is put on the *mestri* ("master workman"), an enslaved worker who serves as an overseer of other enslaved workers. An important part of the *mestri's* job is to help in trafficking other laborers for the master's benefit. Drawing on some of the insights of the restorative justice movement (and especially the theological principles articulated by Howard Zehr), I argue that a restorative justice approach would more adequately address two problems that the current system faces: (1) it would include survivors into the justice system in a much fuller and less intimidating way, and (2) it would extend rehabilitative services to this overlooked population of victim-perpetrators. This is the most speculative chapter, as I could find no organizations currently offering rehabilitative services to either of these populations, let alone offering restorative justice interventions to them. Instead, these survivors appear in the margins of many of my interviews.

Each chapter is meant to be an initial foray into each topic. They are by no means a comprehensive take on the given topic, and gaps will remain in the literature after this book is published. In fact, each chapter could itself be given a book-length treatment. My hope is not to definitively answer all questions about the difficulties of integration faced by survivors, but to simply broach conversation on these topics, since there is such a dearth of literature on them. Numerous questions will remain, some of which I have raised in the conclusion of this work. I encourage any interested scholar or activist to contest, refine, or build upon any conclusion I reach. So long as these needs start to be addressed, I will be happy with the results.

One final introductory note: the conclusions I reach in these chapters are my own. They are not necessarily representative of the positions of my interviewees (unless the quotations I have provided from those interviewees suggest otherwise). They should not face criticism or resistance simply because of a controversial policy that I suggest, or a controversial position that I occupy. Nearly every one of my interviewees (and the NGOs they are affiliated with) is bound to disagree with me on at least one thing in here, whether it be about biblical interpretation, nonviolence, restorative justice, LGBTQ inclusion, or some other topic. But though such disagreements may occasionally occur, I find it necessary to stress that the people I interviewed are my heroes. Some are even old friends. All of them, both survivors and professionals, have endured more than most people can bear for the sake of finding a lasting freedom. It is my hope that this book represents their motivations charitably, casts their words and thoughts accurately, and is finally of use to them in refining the work that they do. If I do nothing more than bring conversations they are having out of the hallways of their offices and into a wider world, I will have done my job. May all of them find the peace and endurance necessary to continue in the work laid out for them until the day that Christ finally loosens every chain, breaks every yoke, and sets the oppressed free—in body and in spirit.

Chapter 1

Slavery Is Legion

IN MAY OF 1865, the American Anti-Slavery Society met for what many members hoped would be the last time. The US Congress had officially approved the 13th Amendment back in February, formally abolishing slavery. Abolitionists in the society were euphoric. The May meeting of the society was to be the Society's official "Mission Accomplished" declaration. Many of its chief members—including William Lloyd Garrison, the president of the Society—moved to disband the Society in the wake of the Amendment's acceptance. But some members thought such a move would be horrendously short-sighted. They felt that the work of the Society was not yet done.

Frederick Douglass was one member of the Society who felt this way. In a plea he delivered for the Society not to disband, Douglass argued that the Amendment would not stop former slaveowners from continuing attempts to subjugate Black Americans. In a closing statement that would later be proven to be horrifyingly prescient, Douglass argued that slavery would try to reassert itself under a different face:

> They would not call it slavery, but some other name. Slavery has been fruitful in giving itself names. It has been called "the peculiar institution," "the social system," and the "impediment," as it was called by the General conference of the Methodist Episcopal Church. It has been called by a great many names, and it will call itself by yet another name; and you and I and all of us had better wait and see what new form this old monster will assume, in what new skin this old snake will come forth.[1]

1. Douglass, "Need for Continued Anti-Slavery Work," 579.

Slavery would return, Douglass claimed. The Society needed to be eternally vigilant in seeking out its newest incarnation.

When I ask anti-trafficking professionals about the challenges they face in their work, they often speak in these same terms. Slavery evolves. It responds to your efforts to combat it. It recedes, only to come back with a new face. I've heard this sentiment expressed by anti-trafficking advocates of all types, whether they be lawyers, social workers, investigators, aftercare home staff, or what have you. Take, for example, the following excerpt from an interview with "Chitra," an attorney who has worked on sex trafficking and bonded labor cases for over a decade:

> **Chris:** Where would you like to see [your organization's] strategy go in the future? Are there areas that you'd like to see change in, or see expansion in?
>
> **Chitra:** I think really nabbing the main traffickers. Really developing our strategies to the point where we're able to track these people and see how they operate and then expose that entire system of theirs. Actually being one step ahead of them. Right now (as I said), they know most of our strategies and the way we operate. We have to really re-think the way we do things.[2]

This feeling of being one step behind trafficking networks is a common one. Earlier in our interview, Chitra mentioned that her organization had seen a decrease in minors found trafficked into brothels in Mumbai's red light districts. Now traffickers were shifting the concentration of minors more toward call girl rings, presumably because, in call girl rings, victims are less exposed to the public and traffickers have more control over which customers see them. It was one way in which the tactics of trafficking organizations had evolved in direct response to the work of anti-trafficking NGOs in Mumbai over the past decade.

These statements by Chitra and Douglass raise an interesting question: When slavery arrives wearing a new mask, how do you identify it? US Supreme Court Justice Potter Stewart once said that he was unable to intelligibly define the kinds of material that fit under the category "hardcore pornography," yet when it comes down to it, "I know it when I see it."[3] Is slavery similar to pornography in this way? Even if we can't define slavery precisely, is it the sort of thing that we will simply be able to identify when we see it?

2. "Chitra," interview with the author, Mumbai, India, October 13, 2014.

3. Jacobellis v. Ohio, 378 U.S. 184 (1964).

Unfortunately, this test may not be enough. The precise reason why slavery switches up its appearance is to avoid detection. This is a strategy taken by many forms of social evil: as soon as it is named as an evil, it attempts to rebrand itself as something else to avoid further scrutiny. Thus, as prolonged solitary confinement becomes recognized as a human rights violation, it gets rebranded as "administrative segregation." Or, for similar reasons, waterboarding was touted by the Bush administration not as "torture," but as an "enhanced interrogation technique." Slavery, as Douglass has pointed out, has gone under several new names, often to avoid detection. We could add "teenage prostitution," "convict leasing," and "human trafficking" to the list of alternative names slavery has gone by in the last century and a half. Thus, while the debates over the core nature of slavery have been extraordinarily complex and long-standing, it will be necessary to weigh in, however briefly, on the question "What is slavery?" Our goal will not be to construct a bulletproof definition of what the phenomenon is, but to operate with a working definition that is fruitful in exposing new dimensions of the problem. In other words, a heuristic definition. Special focus will be put on two questions, both about return: Why does slavery keep coming back in new guises? And what draws people such as Jyothi back to slavery?

You could define slavery in a variety of different ways, depending on which discipline you represent. Most countries have legal definitions of various forms of modern slavery. There are also sociological definitions of slavery available, which attempt to get to the heart of the broader social problem of which all forms of human trafficking are subspecies. But this evolutionary aspect of slavery that Douglass and many modern abolitionists point to asks for a very different language. They describe slavery in terms of a monster: something that thinks, breathes, moves, and responds to threats to its continued existence. This is the language of the demonic. This is the language of the great beasts found in Daniel and in the Apocalypse of John. And this is where theology can enter in to give its own definition of slavery. What if there is something real to these descriptions? What if this language is used for reasons beyond the fact that it makes for effective oration?

I find that the perspective of all three of these disciplines (law, sociology, and theology) are necessary for a holistic response to slavery. As it happens, if we move through treatments of slavery in these three disciplines in this order, we also gain an understanding of slavery that moves from very specific forms of slavery to a more general understanding of slavery as a power (in the New Testament's sense of the term), a living, breathing, social system. An attempt to dissect slavery on all three of these levels is the focus of the present chapter.

Slavery in Legal Terms

The main concern of any law involving modern slavery is intervention (ideally intervention that is both victim-centered and effective). For this reason, it is actually not necessary for laws to give a terribly deep analysis of what slavery is, or indeed, to even use the term "slavery" at all. This may initially seem counterintuitive. How can you fight a social evil with laws that don't even name it? But oddly enough, the two major statutes that are used in India to combat bonded labor and sex trafficking don't mention the word "slavery." The Immoral Traffic (Prevention) Act of 1956 (also known as "PITA"), the main statute used to prosecute sex trafficking, doesn't even use the word "trafficking" to describe any of the offenses it lays down.[4] Instead, it criminalizes offenses such as "procuring, inducing, or taking [a] person for the sake of prostitution."[5] And this doesn't necessarily inhibit its use by modern abolitionist groups. Given that some of slavery's core aspects can undergo shift from iteration to iteration, sometimes it is easier to identify potential *indicators* of slavery. "Where there is smoke, there is fire," as the old saying goes. Anti-slavery laws focus on the smoke. So what are the most important indicators of slavery?

To talk about "human trafficking" is to talk about sale. "Trafficking" here is used in the same sense as it is in the terms "drug trafficking" or "arms trafficking," both of which describe illicit trade. In this case, the trade that is prohibited is the trade of human beings. The term does not necessarily imply movement across a political boundary, though that may be involved.[6] A common popular understanding of slavery is that slavery

4. The term only appears in the title and in the title of the "trafficking officer": a special police officer that the law specifies must be present on a raid.

5. The Immoral Traffic (Prevention) Act (1956), §5.

6. This is perhaps an older debate within the abolitionist community by now. Some abolitionists used the term "trafficking" to refer only to instances where human beings were moved across a political boundary, while others used the term to refer to any sort of trade in human beings. For an example of the former, see Bales et al., *Modern Slavery*, 35. For an example of the latter, see Kara, *Sex Trafficking*, 5. Most abolitionists now use the term in the latter sense.

is simply when one person exerts ownership over another person as he would over a piece of property. If that is the case, then to witness the sale of one person to another person would be one of the best indicators that slavery is occurring. I agree with the conclusion but not the underlying premise. Following the analysis of slavery given by Harvard sociologist Orlando Patterson,[7] I don't think that slavery is best understood in terms of property relations. The reasons for this are given in more detail below. For now, it will be sufficient to note that I *do* think that overt sale of one person to another is one of the best indicators that slavery has occurred. Another way to say this would be to say that human trafficking doesn't necessarily involve an overt sale of one person to another, but any time you do have an overt sale of one person to another, you very likely have an instance of human trafficking. In fact, the successful sale of one human being to another is, in and of itself, a form of exploitation. Chitra brought this fact to my attention during our interview:

> **Chris:** In cases where it's majors that are being forced, what are the requirements legally to prove that someone has been forced into prostitution? Is it only types of physical containment, or are there also other things that might count as inducement? Like, "twisting somebody's arm" and using their social circumstances to compel them?
>
> **Chitra:** Yeah. Right. In fact, most of our cases where majors have been detained, it's more often than not detention through other means, and not maybe physical detention. So, it could be anything from the girl being told that the trafficker who brought and left her there at the brothel was paid a certain amount of money (like maybe about a lakh),[8] and was paid that amount by the brothel owner, and now the girls have to earn that money and pay it back to the brothel owner to earn their freedom. So, the girls see no way out of this other than actually staying there and prostituting or doing whatever they are told.[9]

What Chitra is describing here is that aspect of slavery which may just be the most baffling to any free person. When a victim of trafficking is sold, they often accept that the transaction through which they are sold is valid without question. Why in the world would they do this? A fellow

7. Patterson, *Slavery and Social Death*.

8. The lakh is a common South Asian unit of measurement. It is equal to 100,000. In this case, 100,000 rupees.

9. "Chitra," interview with the author, Mumbai, India, October 13, 2014.

anti-trafficking advocate once expressed his confusion over this very issue in the following way: "If someone came up to me and said, 'Your traveling companion just sold you to me for 10,000 rupees and now you have to pay off that debt by working for me,' I would just say to that person, 'Well, I guess that means you just got ripped off. My traveling companion doesn't own me. It wasn't a valid transaction.'" But that is precisely the point. An enslaved person is liable to sale. A free person is not. The sale itself does not transform your social status; it may mark the official transition point from freedom to enslavement, but it can fail. And when it fails, it does so not due to a flaw in the performance of the sale, but precisely because the intended subject of the sale is situated socially in such a way that her freedom can be reasserted. Your ability to contest the sale of your person may very well be the best litmus test to measure whether you are free or not. And the gulf between those two responses is not one that is easily traversed.

This brings up an important caveat in our understanding of slavery: *slavery can still occur even if co-operation occurs between the enslaved and those who exploit the enslaved.* Thus, in cases of trafficking where overt sale occurs, it is of no consequence whether the enslaved person disputes their sale and is eventually brought to heel through physical violence, or if they comply with their new owner without question, accepting the debt foisted upon them. The success of the sale itself is sufficient to prove that enslavement has occurred. This will become extremely important as we consider the phenomenon my interviewees referred to as "captive mentality" in chapter 2.

Another primary indicator of slavery that is often brought forward is constrained freedom of movement. Kevin Bales, Zoe Trodd, and Alex Kent Williamson contend in *Modern Slavery* that perhaps the most important question to ask in order to determine if slavery is occurring is this: "Can this person walk away, or are they under violent control?"[10] I think this question is right, but that it actually combines two indicators: freedom of movement and violent control. Still, the "Can this person walk away?" test is a good one, and it has been used extensively in anti-trafficking laws.

To see this at work, it may be best to consider bonded labor more directly. Bales, Trodd, and Williamson give the following description of bonded labor:

10. Bales et al., *Modern Slavery*, 30.

> The most common form of modern slavery, this is where a person pledges him/herself against a loan of money, but the length and nature of the service is not defined, and their labor does not diminish the original debt. The work of the debtor may ostensibly be applied to the debt, but through false accounting or extortionate interest, repayment is forever out of reach. In many cases of debt bondage the slave's work (and his/her very life) becomes collateral for the debt. The debt passes from husband to wife and from parent to child, and since all the labor power of the debtor is the collateral property of the lender until the debt is repaid, the debtor can never earn enough to repay the debt by his/her own labor.[11]

This definition fits the situation of my bonded labor interviewees extraordinarily well. This isn't surprising, since South Asian bonded labor has long been considered the paradigmatic example of global bonded labor systems.

India's primary legal instrument dealing with bonded labor is the Bonded Labor System (Abolition) Act of 1976 (oftentimes just called "the Bonded Labor Act" or "the BLA"). According to the BLA, bonded labor can be identified in any situation where there is an obligation for a laborer to work for an employer, plus any of the following four indicators: (1) the laborer lacks freedom of movement, (2) the laborer lacks freedom of employment, (3) the laborer is paid below minimum wage, or (4) the laborer is restricted from selling goods in the marketplace.[12] Note that the first two of these criteria are related to the question, "Can this person walk away?" As these two criteria imply, the owner's control in these circumstances is commonly asserted by restricting the laborer's movement. Many bonded labor survivors testify that their owner never let them leave the work compound, even to travel home for the funeral of a loved one.[13] Likewise, they are not allowed to seek employment elsewhere to earn the money to pay off the debt owed to the owner.

The obligation and the BLA's last two indicators, however, are related to another general indicator of slavery: economic exploitation. In

11. Bales et al., *Modern Slavery*, 33.

12. "Ravi," interview with the author, Chennai, India, November 5, 2014; "Manav," interview with the author, Chennai, India, November 18, 2014; Bonded Labor System (Abolition) Act (1976), §1.

13. "Manav," interview with the author, Chennai, India, November 18, 2014; "Latha" and "Subramani," interview with the author, Chennai, India, November 10, 2014.

every single one of my interviews with labor trafficking survivors, there was an advance involved, either taken out by the interviewee or a member of the interviewee's family. It is this sort of advance that the BLA has in mind when it specifies "an obligation." Such advances are taken out for a variety of different reasons. Most commonly, advances are taken out to pay for medical expenses for a loved one, for basic subsistence reasons, to pay for the wedding of a son or daughter, or to clear other debts. The advance acts as an enticement to work for the employer. Once the laborer is employed, they often move to live on the compound in which they work. Then, as Bales, Trodd, and Williamson intimated, the owner uses various means to make sure the debt is never discharged, whether that means charging excessive interest, frequently deducting expenses from the laborer's meager pay, or simply by overtly changing numbers in the accounting books because the laborer does not know basic arithmetic and is unable to personally hold the owner accountable to a debt payment schedule.

Economic exploitation is likewise generally seen as the primary indicator used to identify instances of sex trafficking. In fact, sex trafficking usually goes hand-in-hand with what is more broadly called commercial sexual exploitation, a subspecies of economic exploitation. Commercial sexual exploitation occurs whenever the sexual activity of one person is exploited by another for financial gain. And that sexual activity itself may be forced upon the victim. PITA is often utilized by anti-trafficking advocates in Mumbai to highlight the existence of commercial sexual exploitation, even though the Act uses the language of "prostitution." And the Act has proved quite serviceable for anti-trafficking advocates, despite the fact that its use of the language of "prostitution" sets the average anti-trafficking advocate's teeth on edge.[14]

The concern with the term is that a "prostitute" is usually seen as an offender. Someone who is the object of "commercial sexual exploitation," on the other hand, is seen as a victim (more specifically, a victim of an identifiable form of economic exploitation). The debate over terminology is therefore extremely important because there is no worse piece of legislation than that which punishes the person who was wronged. One of the

14. The current preferred term is either "sex work" or "commercial sexual exploitation," depending on either context or ideological lens (or both). As can be seen above, I prefer to use "commercial sexual exploitation," and am aware that this puts me in a particular ideological camp. A great summation of the issues involved in selecting between these two terms can be found in Lloyd, *Girls Like Us*, 213–19.

major goals of the abolitionist movement as it pertains to sex trafficking has been to eliminate legislation that treats victims of sex trafficking as offenders guilty of the petty crime of prostitution. This is a rehabilitation concern as well as a justice concern because an arrest record is just one of many things which can stand in the way of a survivor's economic rehabilitation, given the way most individuals with an arrest record are treated by potential employers in many countries. The ideal for many "anti-prostitution" abolitionists is to produce legislation that decriminalizes "prostitution" (selling sex) while simultaneously holding pimps (those who profit from *someone else* selling sex) and solicitors (those who buy sex) accountable as offenders.[15] This is due to the fact that pimps and solicitors are the clear exploiters, while the women[16] selling sex are the ones exploited. I wholeheartedly agree with this school of thought but would subject it to a whole host of restorative justice caveats that will be explored in more detail in chapter 6.

Despite these (quite legitimate) concerns, PITA has generally not been used to penalize women who sell sex (though the wording of the act would suggest that it could be used for this purpose). Anti-trafficking advocates have used it very successfully against those who "live off of the earnings of prostitution"[17] (that is, pimps and brothel madams),[18] while avoiding charges for those who are victims of sex trafficking. The dividing line between those who exploit and those who are exploited is preserved. So long as the Act is not used to bring criminal charges against victims, it remains serviceable.

The final general indicator of slavery, violent control, is perhaps the most visible element in any situation of slavery. In situations of labor

15. "Pro-prostitution" abolitionists are those who see a hard line between "legitimate sex work" and "sex trafficking." The answer for pro-prostitution abolitionists is to legalize freely chosen sex work and submit it to industry regulation, while criminalizing sex trafficking as a form of slavery. "Anti-prostitution" abolitionists are those who tend to see prostitution as inherently exploitative (even in situations where it does not qualify as sex slavery), and claim that it is difficult to delineate when sex work is freely chosen and when it is coerced, given that most people in the industry choose it due to lack of options. There's actually a vast philosophical and theological difference between the two camps as to what constitutes a free choice. I would be classified as an anti-prostitution anti-trafficking advocate.

16. Or, in some cases, men or nonbinary individuals.

17. PITA, §4.

18. Holding "Johns" (men who solicit sex) accountable, however, is a different story. PITA has not been terribly effective at that ("Chitra," interview with the author, Mumbai, India, October 13, 2014).

trafficking, owners often use violent means of discipline to gain compliance from their victims, which may include rape, sexual assault, beatings, brandings, or other forms of physical mutilation.[19] Stories of burnings or brandings for behavior the master deems insubordinate (such as questioning orders) are frightfully common. In some cases, masters have beaten bonded laborers to death.[20] Similar means of gaining compliance are also used in situations of sex trafficking, whether it be for the purpose of disciplining the victim for perceived disobedience, or to "break in" the victim (i.e., make them a compliant subject). Numerous survivors testify that beatings, torture, rape, and sexual assault were a part of their "grooming" process.[21]

While it is possible that each of these four indicators (sale, restricted movement, economic exploitation, violent control) could be present in situations that would not constitute slavery, their presence in conjunction with one another presents a strong case that the situation constitutes slavery. It is also possible that some of these indicators could be absent in an instance of slavery (for example, sale would not necessarily be an indicator in a situation where the enslaved was born into bondage). Again, legal instruments generally aim at indicators rather than a deep social analysis of slavery because the main concern is intervention. But when addressing rehabilitation concerns for formerly enslaved people, it is necessary to probe deeper than slavery's surface indicators and into the social and interpersonal elements that underlie slavery. This is necessary because these elements can have a lasting effect on formerly enslaved people, even when the immediate bonds between enslaved people and their enslavers are severed. And to provide this deeper analysis of slavery, we need to turn to sociological treatments of the institution.

19. "Manav," interview with the author, Chennai, India, November 18, 2014; "Naveen," interview with the author, Chennai, India, November 12, 2014; K. Krishnan, interview with the author, Chennai, India, November 20, 2014.

20. Pranitha Timothy, interview with the author, Channai, India, November 11, 2014.

21. "Zara," interview with the author, Mumbai, India, November 29, 2014. See also Bales and Trodd, *To Plead Our Own Cause*. The sheer number of survivor testimonies in this work which mention this dynamic is staggering.

Slavery in Sociological Terms

Among sociological approaches to slavery, none has been more influential than Orlando Patterson's *Slavery and Social Death.* In this work, Patterson defines slavery as "the permanent, violent domination of natally alienated and generally dishonored persons."[22] Given the fact that Patterson's definition uses terms that are not widely used outside of his discipline, it may be helpful to further explain the main components of his definition. It has three major components: (1) natal alienation and social death, (2) honor capital, and (3) permanence.

Natal alienation and social death are related concepts. Natal alienation is a process, and social death is the social status that results from it. Natal alienation refers to the fact that an enslaved person is either violently uprooted from or is cast out of the kinship networks that would normally protect her by virtue of her birth. This includes the inability of an enslaved person to claim authority over her own children. Social death is the status which results from this alienation; an enslaved person belongs to no community and has no social existence outside of her master.[23] Patterson also describes this situation as "desocialization" or "depersonalization." To be human is to exist in community, and therefore the enslaved person is considered sub-human from within the slave system, because she belongs to no community. This is clearly the case in modern instances of slavery no less than ancient forms of slavery, as the induction process into either bonded labor or sex trafficking often includes some form of alienation from community and kinship bonds, either through force (as in instances of kidnapping), deceit (as in instances where a false job opportunity is presented), linguistic isolation (as in instances where the victim is taken to a location where he or she does not speak the language), or some combination of all three. However, as Patterson points out, slavery can also occur in situations in which an enslaved person "falls out of" a protective community network either through destitution or through a perceived social failing (or in some circumstances, where the former entails the latter). For instance, in bonded labor, the act of falling into debt by itself is perceived as a social failing. The act of falling into debt countenances any abuse that the bonded laborer might experience. An example of this can be seen in the testimony of "Maha," one of my

22. Patterson, *Slavery and Social Death*, 13.

23. Patterson, *Slavery and Social Death*, 38.

interviewees. Maha was a victim of generational slavery; she was bonded for her father's debt.

> **Maha:** Nobody used to respect us before because we are bonded laborers. Even my own family members, my sisters, everybody rejected us. Nobody used to give respect for us; they were all ignoring us very badly. But after rescue, we are so happy. We really would like to thank, from the bottom of my heart, the people who rescued me. And I would like to thank Jesus Christ, for these who rescued me.
>
> **Chris:** Okay. So, it sounds like there was some difficulty relating with family members before. Have some of those [difficulties] still continued on, after rescue?
>
> **Maha:** Now, everybody who rejected us before, they're all inviting us to their home. They're calling us and they're inviting us. But we are not going anywhere, we just want to live separately. We want to leave everyone, and me and my daughter want to live separately.[24]

Maha narrates a remarkable change in social recognition before and after her enslavement: before, her indigence was enough for her to be rejected by the rest of her family (and this was the case even though she was bonded not for her own debt, but for her father's). After liberation, there is a marked difference in how her family treats her. With the recognition that she is a free woman, she is now worthy of social recognition and her family wishes to re-establish the social bonds that used to constitute their relationship. Maha, however, interpreted this gesture as disingenuous. Those who previously marked her as socially dead did nothing to prevent her from acquiring this status, and so she has moved on to look for another community to form bonds with after coming out of slavery.

Similarly, in sex trafficking situations, social positioning is sufficient to result in social death. "Mallika"—a social worker who works with survivors of sex trafficking in Mumbai—expressed that this was clearly the case in cases of generational slavery in red light districts:

> **Chris:** I see. But it's not unusual to find a girl whose mother was also forced [i.e., into commercial sexual exploitation] before her in a forced situation.

24. "Maha," interview with the author, Chennai, India, November 6, 2014.

> **Mallika:** Yeah, because you know we've had a situation last year, we rescued three children from the red light area. They were all three children of sex workers. But the unfortunate part, which I have realized . . . because we don't work in the area itself. We are managing, handling trafficking cases. So, this is slightly different. But what I saw from it is because the child is a child of a prostitute, she's seen as a free commodity. Anybody can take advantage of her simply because she's the daughter of a prostitute. It's ridiculous. I mean, children! You know there's no sense of value or nothing. Married men, men with children of their own will take advantage of children simply because, "Oh, yeah, yeah, she'll eventually grow up to be a prostitute herself." It's just ridiculous.[25]

The children of trafficked women inherit the social death of their parents. For this reason, they can be bought and sold much as their mothers had been.

Historically, an enslaved person's social death has acted as an overt substitute for her physical death; the enslaved were taken from among war prisoners as an alternative to killing them on the battlefield.[26] Any claims that an enslaved person can make to belonging to a social order come solely through her master, meaning she is often referred to symbolically as either an "internal alien" or an insider who had fallen below the moral threshold for acceptance within their social world (as was the case with Maha). It is precisely this lack of ability to claim belonging to a community outside of the master that gives power to the master.[27] However, despite this alienated status, "there [is] almost a perverse intimacy in the bond resulting from the power the master claimed over his slave,"[28] and the enslaved are often referred to in familial terms, or even as part of the master's own body. One finds this tendency to refer to enslaved individuals in familiar terms especially in sex trafficking, where victims are often encouraged to refer to their owners as "mommy" or "auntie."[29]

25. "Mallika," interview with the author, Mumbai, India, September 17, 2014.

26. Patterson, *Slavery and Social Death*, 5. In the ancient world, commentators on slavery were particularly blunt about the practice of enslaving prisoners of war. One sees this for example in Augustine, *Civ.* 19.15 (pp. 874–75).

27. Patterson, *Slavery and Social Death*, 38.

28. Patterson, *Slavery and Social Death*, 50.

29. "Chitra," interview with the author, Mumbai, India, October 13, 2014; Jessica Gunjal, interview with the author, Mumbai, India, October 14, 2014; Penny Tong, interview with the author, Mumbai, India, December 19, 2014. See also the brothel

And this is the case even though the victim occupies a clearly subservient status, is liable to violent discipline, and can be sold to another owner at the current owner's whim.

This brings us to the second aspect of Patterson's definition: to be enslaved is to be a degraded person who lives within a system of "honor capital," where authority, power, and honor are closely related. In such systems, the enslaved are unable to accrue honor for themselves. Instead, their masters parasitically draw honor from their actions: the master gains honor and recognition from the degradation of the enslaved.[30] The one who is enslaved is rendered as a part of the master himself, and she becomes a means through which the master can extend influence and authority.

The residual effects of this loss of honor capital are something that social workers involved in the rehabilitation of survivors of sex trafficking see quite frequently. Here is how Mallika described the difficulties she encounters when trying to help survivors who grew up in a rural Indian setting reintegrate into their villages:

> **Mallika:** Families here, especially in our country, even if they were involved in selling their girl because of this whole honor and you know, "We are such honorable people" and things like that, they never, ever admit that they were involved in selling the girl. You know? They'll make out like they're just all innocent and all of that. And in fact if you ever told them that this girl was rescued from a sexually exploitative situation, they would reject the girl.
>
> **Chris:** So even if they're not involved in the trafficking, if they find out about it subsequently . . .
>
> **Mallika:** . . . they will reject the girl.
>
> **Chris:** They will reject them, like cast them out of the home?
>
> **Mallika:** Yeah, yeah. We've taken girls to be reintegrated to their homes, and then parents have put two and two together and . . . Because it's shame to the family. And we've had to bring the girls back to Bombay or take them to a shelter home. We've had many, many instances where girls have been rejected by their family, or there have been situations where we go to the village and the *entire* village will gather. And there is something called

---

situation described in Kristof and WuDunn, *Half the Sky*, 12–13.

30. Patterson, *Slavery and Social Death*, 79.

the village panchayat, which is like the whole group of influential, respected members of the village who manage the village affairs. We've had situations where they will all gather and ask us: Who are we? Where did we get this girl? Why have you brought her back here? Where has she been in the last two years, five years that she's been missing? And the village panchayat, takes a decision irrespective of what the family has to say. The village panchayat can take a decision to evict the girl from the village. And those instances are happening as well.

Chris: What were to happen in a situation like that if the family were to try to harbor her against the panchayat's decision?

Mallika: No, they cannot. They cannot because they are taken by the village elders. So, it's a decision that they have to abide by. And we've had such instances. And this whole—which I think is hypocrisy—the whole thing about honor, you know the honor of the girl, the girl is never, ever seen as a victim. Never. And so even when we've had to take girls back and even when we've had to bring girls back for legal cases, it's all . . . we can't tell them the truth. We never, ever tell the families that she was rescued from this situation. *Never.* We tell them always that the girl was rescued from a domestic abuse situation, she was working as a domestic maid—you know, a housemaid—and there was some amount of . . . whatever violence against her and we're an organization that works with these women. We never bring the sexual element in it, ever.[31]

In the case of sex trafficking victims, the loss of honor capital that occurs during their initial enslavement is particularly difficult to undo, since sex work is considered inherently dishonorable in a rural Indian context. If the survivor's village finds out about what happened during her bondage, it is likely that the village will cast her out. Thus, restoring the survivor's ability to accrue recognition for herself is particularly difficult. And if the community that raised her fails to recognize her, then she may end up returning to a situation of slavery simply because she has no other options. Because no human being can survive in isolation, a situation in which the recognition you accrue goes to someone else may be preferable to a situation in which you can accrue no recognition at all.

The third part of Patterson's definition, "permanence," does not rule out the possibility of eventual freedom (referred to as "manumission" in systems of legal slavery), but Patterson points out that true manumission

31. "Mallika," interview with the author, Mumbai, India, September 17, 2014.

is a far more complex phenomenon than simply "buying back one's freedom," "coming to own oneself," or even "becoming one's own master."[32] True manumission is an act of creation from the ground up, because it entails the reconstitution of the enslaved as a "socially living" entity once again. It takes a community's full recognition of an enslaved person to bring them back to life again, and that may be the most difficult task of all. Truly freeing someone from slavery is nothing less than an act of resurrection.

What are some of the upshots of defining slavery in this way? First, if Patterson is correct, slavery isn't defined by property relations. Patterson explicitly rejects the idea that slavery is limited to situations in which one person claims ownership over another.[33] However, he admits that claims of overt ownership are more likely to happen in situations in which slavery is occurring, simply because it is usually considered dishonoring to be likened to a piece of property.[34] This denial lies at the heart of most critiques of Patterson's analysis. Many individuals from a variety of disciplines think that slavery simply must be, at root, about one person claiming to own another person. It is not unusual to find this critique even among sociologists who have otherwise adopted Patterson's definition.[35] I think this critique is oversold, since Patterson himself admits

32. Patterson, *Slavery and Social Death*, 209–10.

33. Patterson uses an interesting counterexample to prove his point: professional football players. According to Patterson, NFL players are regularly rendered as property by others. They can be traded from franchise to franchise without much say in the matter. They undergo regular (usually annual) physical examinations to assess their capabilities and overall health, to see if they are still a good investment by the team (Patterson interestingly likens this to a privatized version of the physical inspection of the enslaved on the auction block). However, despite the protestations of the occasional sportswriter, *NFL players are not enslaved*. It is precisely their social status that differentiates them from people who are enslaved. Their ability to make claims to belonging in the social order outside their franchises and their ability to accrue (sometimes quite substantial) forms of honor capital in American society rules out any serious attempt to name NFL players as enslaved even though they are clearly rendered as the property of their franchise (Patterson, *Slavery and Social Death*, 24–25).

34. Patterson, *Slavery and Social Death*, 22.

35. See, for example, Garnsey, *Ideas of Slavery*, 1. Garnsey gives a three-point definition of slavery. The third point describes social death and is clearly indebted to Patterson's work. However, "a slave was property," is the first point, and "the slaveowner's rights over his slave-property were total," is the second, both of which Patterson identifies as the sort of statements that cause "inevitable confusions" (Patterson, *Slavery and Social Death*, 21). Patterson would, however, say that a slaveholder's *power* over an enslaved person was total (Patterson, *Slavery and Social Death*, 26). Note the shift from

that overt claims of ownership are often *sufficient* to prove that slavery is occurring, though they are not *necessary*. By making property relations a potential indicator of slavery rather than the centerpiece of a definition of slavery, Patterson can help us name certain relationships as slavery even when the issue of ownership is muted or absent. For example, the convict leasing system that existed in the United States from the close of the Civil War until World War II has been recognized as a reassertion of slavery since at least the work of W. E. B. Du Bois.[36] More recently, this claim has also been made in the work of Angela Davis and Douglas Blackmon.[37] In other words, convict leasing was slavery in a "new skin" (to use Frederick Douglass' idiom from the quotation given above). Convict leasing was heavily utilized by many of the same plantation owners who owned chattel slaves before the war,[38] the convicts were disciplined in much the same way chattel slaves were before them,[39] and the same population was press-ganged into convict leasing systems that served under chattel slavery (namely, Black people).[40] The only difference is that incarceration rather than direct ownership was the means of enslavement. Rather than directly rendering Black men and women as property and putting them up on the auction block, local law enforcement agents would round up Black men and women, charge them with "vagrancy" (which was essentially the inability to prove that one is gainfully employed at any given moment),[41] incarcerate them, then lease them to companies working in the coal and metalworking industries. Given the similarities to chattel slavery, clearly commenters like Du Bois, Davis, and Blackmon are right: convict leasing was a form of slavery.[42] And yet, it was a form of slavery

legal terms (rights) to social terms (power).

36. Du Bois, "Spawn of Slavery," 84–90.

37. Davis, "Prison of Slavery," 74–107; Blackmon, *Slavery by Another Name.*

38. Blackmon, *Slavery by Another Name*, 8.

39. Blackmon, *Slavery by Another Name*, 52. See also the accounts of the brutal whippings that occurred under convict leasing, described in Blackmon, *Slavery by Another Name*, 71, 154.

40. In some cases, the individuals caught up in convict leasing were enslaved under the antebellum system. For examples, see Blackmon, *Slavery by Another Name*, 143.

41. Davis, "Prison of Slavery," 100.

42. In some countries, convict leasing is still a prominent form of slavery. See for example the testimonies of survivors listed under the heading "prison camp slavery" in Bales and Trodd, *To Plead Our Own Cause*, 19–31. These individuals are survivors of China's "laogai" ("reform-through-labor") system. According to Bales and Trodd, the "crime" for which these individuals are incarcerated frequently boils down to

in which direct ownership was not asserted; the convict was simply a contract worker from the local prison. And indeed, part of the reason why this change occurred was precisely to keep slave systems going after chattel slavery had been legally abolished. Slavery rebranded to avoid detection. Indeed, when the US government tried to initiate a crackdown against convict leasing during McKinley and Roosevelt's administration, it found itself initially hamstrung by the fact that its anti-slavery laws were too specific. It had no laws on the books that could adequately be brought against businessmen and lawmen complicit in the convict leasing system.[43] Patterson's definition of slavery gives us the tools to identify slavery based upon an enslaved person's social death, rather than on the master's overt claims to ownership. And indeed, convicts in the convict leasing system were socially dead: they were snatched up out of the kinship systems that protected them and denied the basic legal protections that would have applied to anyone who had adequate social recognition (such as habeas corpus, the right to a fair trial, prohibitions on cruel and unusual punishment, etc.).

Second, if Patterson is correct, slavery isn't defined by labor relations. This is sometimes assumed by commentators who want to argue that capitalism and slavery are antithetical. For these commenters, slavery is illogical from an economic standpoint because it does not allow an enslaved person to maximize his utility. The slogan is that "free markets equal free people." To be sure, some sort of labor relation is present in many forms of slavery, but proscribing slavery to one particular *type* of labor relation proves problematic. As Gavin Wright has pointed out, a wide variety of labor relations can exist under the heading "slavery," to the point that it is sometimes quite difficult to delineate the difference between "slave labor" and "free labor" by considering labor relations alone. In fact, the net is so wide that slavery is not inconsistent even with the existence of negotiated contracts and collective bargaining.[44] This wide

belonging to a religious or ethnic minority.

43. Blackmon, *Slavery by Another Name*, 170–76.

44. Wright, *Slavery and Development*, 4–5. Wright canvasses a growing body of literature which documents instances in which enslaved workers entered into informal contracts and engaged in collective bargaining in the antebellum South. Patterson's analysis seems to implicitly agree with Wright's, in that (1) his definition makes no reference to labor relations, and (2) he critiques Hegel's slave-master dialectic precisely on the ground that Hegel's account of freedom requires the enslaved person to be not only a laborer, but more specifically a laborer whose work produces a physical object. Hegel believed that the beginning of an enslaved person's consciousness of their own

diversity of labor relations under slavery allows for a diversity of labor agreements, allowing for both the maximization of utility and a corresponding commodification of labor power (at least for enslaved persons with a certain skillset). Still less is it clear that slavery names a clear, distinct, or singular mode of production. There is a vast difference in mode of production between sex work and producing bricks, but one can find enslaved people filling both of those roles.

To cite an interesting historical example of the diversity of labor relations that occur under slavery, Douglas Blackmon notes that industrial slavery in the antebellum South did not take off until the eve of the Civil War, in order to boost iron production to meet the military demands of the Confederacy.[45] Prior to this, antebellum slavery was primarily a domestic (and therefore agricultural) phenomenon, and therefore when industries outside the plantation wanted to employ slave labor, they would do so not by purchasing enslaved people directly, but by contracting the labor of enslaved people who were privately owned. This is, in fact, exactly what happened to Frederick Douglass toward the end of his enslavement. While living in Baltimore with his master's brother, he was allowed to seek employment at the shipyard, where he gained considerable skill

freedom was that they would see their own mind and their own being through reflection on objects they had created. There are severe problems with this account. Here Patterson's critique is worth quoting at length: "Hegel is partly right and partly wrong in arriving at this conclusion. Ironically, he is wrong precisely where most commentators, including Marx and Kojève, have considered him most insightful. There is nothing in the nature of slavery that requires that the slave be a worker. Worker qua worker has no intrinsic relation to slave qua slave. This does not mean that the slave cannot be *used* as a worker. Indeed, his slaveness, especially his natal alienation, made possible his effective exploitation as laborer in conditions when no other kind of laborer would do. But this does not necessarily mean that slave necessarily implies worker. I have repeatedly stressed that most slaves in most precapitalist societies were not enslaved in order to be made over into workers; they may even have been economic burdens on their masters" (Patterson, *Slavery and Social Death*, 99 [emphasis in original]). Given the fact that this book deals with sex slavery, I share Patterson's concern here. It is not clear to me that a victim of sex trafficking's labor produces a physical object that she can look into and see her own mind and being. Perhaps some would argue that producing a child would serve this function. Such an account would be complicated by the fact that (1) children are not always produced because they are often seen by the master as an *undesirable* product of an enslaved person's labor (i.e., they are to be avoided through contraception or discarded through abortion), and (2) even when a child is produced through that labor, what the enslaved mother sees peering back at her is another enslaved person.

45. Blackmon, *Slavery by Another Name*, 21, 44.

as a caulker. Douglass recounts the measure of increased utility that this skill gave him in his first autobiography:

> [Mr. Gardner] took me into the ship-yard of which he was foreman, in the employment of Mr. Walter Price. There I was immediately set to calking, and very soon learned the art of using my mallet and irons. In the course of one year from the time I left Mr. Gardner's, I was able to command the highest wages given to the most experienced calkers. I was now of some importance to my master. I was bringing him six to seven dollars per week. I sometimes brought him nine dollars per week: my wages were a dollar and a half per day. After learning how to calk, I sought my own employment, made my own contacts, and collected the money which I earned. My pathway was much more smooth than before; my condition was now much more comfortable.[46]

By gaining a valuable skill, Douglass was able to commodify his labor power, freely entering into labor agreements in which he can negotiate higher wages, better hours, and better working conditions. And though Douglass was enslaved, his primary labor relationship occurred outside of the relationship he had with his master. Free markets do not necessarily equal free people. By avoiding a definition of slavery that focuses on labor relations, Patterson helps us skirt this issue.

Thirdly, and most importantly, the major advantage of defining slavery in terms of social death is that it makes far more sense of many of the issues encountered in the rehabilitation of people coming out of modern slavery. For instance, Patterson's categories of social death and honor capital are very helpful in analyzing survivor situations such as the one that Mallika described above: situations where lack of recognition or belonging within a social order push formerly enslaved individuals back into situations of slavery even after the immediate master-slave relationship is severed. If Patterson is right about the nature of social death that enslaved people undergo, then emancipating an enslaved person is extraordinarily difficult work, and must go far, far beyond simply the legal declaration that the enslaved person is her own master once more. Emancipation is a more drastic act; it is an act of social resurrection. It is nothing less than bestowing life upon that which is dead. Even if any situation in which one person exerts ownership over another person can be clearly identified as slavery (because only socially dead and dishonored persons would be in a position where they would be forced to suffer the

46. Douglass, *Narrative*, 215.

social indignity of another claiming ownership over them), emancipation is never quite so easy as simply legally transferring ownership of an enslaved person back into their own hands. Legal definitions which focus on the exploitation that occurs within the direct relationship between those who enslave and those who are enslaved don't always penetrate beyond to the broader social dynamics which allow exploitation of an enslaved person to occur even *after* the master-slave relationship is severed. In Patterson's treatment, it is much easier to see why an enslaved person would still be exploited even after this relationship is put to an end. The ways in which the domination of slavery can continue to exert force even after emancipation will be explored in greater depth in chapter 2.

Herein lies the definitive reason why a multi-disciplinary take on slavery is necessary. Legal definitions of slavery function better if they focus on the sufficient conditions to prove that slavery is occurring. This is, once again, because the focus is on intervention. How do you know when a situation of slavery is occurring so that you can mount some sort of intervention? A lack of freedom of movement is easy to identify during an investigation, or to prove in a courtroom. It would be much harder to establish in a legal proceeding that the survivor of slavery lacked any claim to belonging within a community at the time of her enslavement, or that the accused parasitically drew honor from her degradation. On the other hand, if Patterson's analysis is correct, then the internal logic of slave systems is highly symbolic, and symbolism isn't generally something that is easily established in a court of law. How would a prosecutor establish in court that a social status as symbolically laden as "social death" applied to the victim? Thus, legal definitions of slavery usually do not penetrate down into the social depths of the problem, which is why anti-slavery NGOs which focus on legal intervention often underestimate the depth of an enslaved person's social alienation, and therefore underestimate the extent of rehabilitative efforts that need to be undertaken. Hopefully, the ways in which this is so will become clearer as we move on to talk about the post-emancipation lives of the survivors of modern slavery in the chapters that follow.

Before we move on, however, it is important to clarify two things about Patterson's understanding of slavery. The first is that Patterson considered his definition of slavery to be a heuristic definition. He submitted it to the same caveats that I made for my treatment of slavery at the beginning of this chapter. Patterson's definition is meant to be a rule of thumb. It is fruitful for further analysis of slavery, but the definition is not meant to perfectly enfold all the myriad forms of social oppression that we might identify as slavery (and Patterson's study is immensely *wide*; part of its staying power has been that a single study of slavery on that scale has—to my knowledge—yet to be replicated). It is possible that a form of slavery exists that doesn't meet his criteria. But for our purposes, Patterson's definition fits both sex trafficking and bonded labor, and is fruitful in providing a deep understanding of both forms of slavery.

The second caveat deals with an objection to Patterson's understanding of slavery. Some have worried that "the permanent, violent domination of natally alienated and generally dishonored persons" is too general of a definition. There are many social practices that could be described as "violent domination," and could target alienated and dishonored persons. Based on this fact, some have pushed to add additional criteria to Patterson's definition.[47] This tendency ought to be resisted, because the broad character of Patterson's definition is a strength, not a weakness. While some modern sociologists have wished to produce an analysis of slavery that would draw clear lines of distinction between slavery and other social practices (especially incarceration), other social analysts have noted that this line is quite hard to draw in practice. Angela Davis pointed out decades ago that there is an odd species relationship between enslavement and incarceration that is captured perfectly in the legal caveat that exists in the middle of the Thirteenth Amendment: "Neither slavery nor involuntary servitude, *except as a punishment for crime whereof the party shall have been duly convicted*, shall exist within the United States." Incarceration is defined here as the only legal form of enslavement.[48] This is why, when white former slaveowners wished to reassert a system of racial enslavement in America, one of the first avenues they took was to direct the criminal justice system more explicitly toward the violent domination of African-Americans.

Ancient social commentators noticed similar connections. Throughout the biblical record and early church history, it is not unusual to find a clear species relationship between enslavement, incarceration, economic exploitation, and imperial occupation. All four social situations were subsumed under the category of "captivity." This is why biblical passages such as Isa 42:7 and Luke 4:16–21 can be translated as proclaiming release for either the incarcerated or the enslaved or even those under imperial

47. Again, this seems to be one reason why Garnsey added property relations to his definition. See Garnsey, *Ideas of Slavery*, 1.

48. Davis, "Prison of Slavery," 75–76.

occupation: the terms for "captives" could refer to people caught up in any of those social and political situations. In a similar vein (but with the exact opposite intent), one can find a thinker like Augustine of Hippo utilizing the same connection to argue that "the condition of slavery is justly imposed on the sinner," in *City of God* 19. Augustine argues that since the Babylonian captivity was justly imposed upon Judah because of the sins of Judah's people, so too the captivity of slavery is justly imposed upon others due to their sin.[49] Thus, whether the intent was to liberate captives or justify their captivity, one can see ancient thinkers of various sorts drawing connections between these four situations, both due to their material similarities (e.g., the use of chains in both enslavement and incarceration), but also due to the similarities in power relations that obtain under them, and in the justifications given for these practices.

I believe that the ancient analysis of these connections was more honest, though I would obviously prefer to take the path of Isaiah and Luke over the path of Augustine; seeing these connections should push us toward the abolition of these practices rather than toward their acceptance as just. Recognizing these connections help us to predict the sort of appearance slavery will take on as it tries to reassert itself in new forms. For example, it is not an accident that slavery has so often tried to rebrand itself through retributive justice interventions (as in convict leasing). I realize that recognizing these connections, however, may be disturbing to those who wish to limit their abolitionist commitments to slavery alone. For now, it will be sufficient to point out that the openness of Patterson's definition is another of its strengths.

Slavery in Theological Terms

If the focus of a legal definition of slavery is intervention, and the focus of a sociological definition of slavery is a deep analysis of the social and interpersonal relations which underlie slavery, what is the purpose of a theological definition of slavery? When Frederick Douglass warned that slavery would arise in another form, he personified slavery. He suggested that slavery was an ever-adaptable institution; it had a spirit capable of taking on different names and faces, one that would change shape or change names in response to efforts to outside pressure. Many readers look at Douglass' words now and assume that such language is simply

49. Augustine, *Civ.* 19.15 (pp. 874–75).

effective rhetoric. Douglass, as a master orator, simply knows the best way to make a mark on his audience.

But if you read the works of formerly enslaved people in Douglass' day, a different sort of picture emerges. Enslaved Christians in the United States were pioneers in the attempt to give a theological definition of slavery, and they described it in the language of the demonic. Various spirituals, for example, including "Jesus said He wouldn't die no mo'" and "Ride on, King Jesus," draw strongly from the portions of the Pauline corpus that proclaim that through the cross, Jesus conquers the demonic powers that hold this world in thrall. And chief among these powers is slavery.[50] According to Cheryl Kirk-Duggan, slaves in the "Invisible Institution" (i.e., the secret churches founded by enslaved Christians that dotted the antebellum United States) experienced slavery as an institution that was clearly helmed by demons, and composed the Spirituals as a way to exorcize and resist these demonic powers.[51] And in many ways, their language dovetails well with the language that modern antislavery advocates use. Both describe slavery in terms of a living, breathing social evil that makes strategic decisions and responds intelligibly to threats to its own existence.

Instead of dismissing such claims as superstitions or the vestiges of an archaic worldview, what if this aspect of their experience were taken seriously? To many modern readers, demons are silly things. This is likely because the word "demon" often conjures up images of little men wielding pitchforks and causing mischief, such as encouraging teenagers to sexually misbehave or listen to the wrong sort of music. And a concept like that is worthy of prompt dismissal. But the conceptualization of demons within Christianity changed quite a bit over the ages, and this image has little to do with the way in which the demonic was viewed in the first century. But over the past fifty years or so, biblical scholarship has gone far in attempting to recover what the various authors of the New Testament meant when they referred to "evil spirits," "demons," or "powers." Studies by Hendrikus Berkhof, William Stringfellow, Jacques Ellul, John Howard Yoder, Walter Wink, Ched Myers, and Amos Yong have been especially important in both excavating this concept from the New

50. Hopkins, "Slave Theology," 14–16.

51. Kirk-Duggan, *Exorcizing Evil*, 16. See also the way in which some enslaved Christians likened escape from slavery to escape from Satan's power or escape from hell (and using prayer to effect both) in Raboteau, *Slave Religion*, 305.

Testament and applying it to modern political struggles.[52] Against the modern tendency to bifurcate the material and the spiritual, these works unfold an ancient world that saw power in terms of a confluence between material and spiritual forces. Language of "powers and principalities" (or simply "the powers") could be used by New Testament authors to speak of local political rulers, angelic forces, or both at the same time. Such powers could be good or evil. In such a context, the word "demon" (or "unclean spirit") names a living, breathing, systemic evil. The demonic is neither fully reducible to human institutions, nor does it appear apart from them.

This is perhaps seen most clearly in one incident in the Gospel of Mark: the exorcism of the Gerasene Demoniac (Mark 5:1–20).[53] In this particular incident, Jesus comes across a man living in a graveyard who is constantly tormented by an unclean spirit. Jesus says to the spirit, "Come out of him!" and then asks the spirit for its name. The spirit responds, "My name is Legion; for we are many." At the spirit's behest, Jesus casts the demon into a herd of pigs, which charges headlong into the lake, only to drown.

As Ched Myers has pointed out, the spirit's name clearly links it to the *Roman* legion (the term which could be used to describe either a regiment of several thousand soldiers, or used as a shorthand to refer to

52. Berkhof, *Christ and the Powers*; Stringfellow, *Politics of Spirituality*; Ellul, *Ethics of Freedom*; Yoder, *Politics of Jesus*; Wink, *Naming the Powers*; Wink, *Unmasking the Powers*; Wink, *Engaging the Powers*; Myers, *Binding the Strong Man*; Yong, *In the Days of Caesar*. For a great literature review of this material, see Yong, *In the Days of Caesar*, 139–51. This is not to say that all of these authors agree on all details concerning the composition, origins, and final destiny of the powers. What follows is most indebted to Wink and Myers.

53. The association between Legion and the powers is often not overtly made in scholarly treatments of the powers (Myers being a clear exception to this trend). Wink even omits Mark 5:1–20 from his list of New Testament evidence for his theory in *Naming the Powers*. This could possibly be due to a lack of lexical ties to the more "established" powers and principalities passages, or it could be due to the fact that Wink didn't seem to intend for his list to be exhaustive. But conceptually, there are clearly ties between the depiction of Legion and the treatment of the powers elsewhere in the New Testament. And there is one feature of the passage that makes its omission fairly substantial: Mark 5:1–20 is the clearest example in the New Testament of a direct confrontation between human beings and a power. It is an "on the ground" account, as opposed to the much more theoretical treatment of the powers we find in the Pauline corpus. Thus, it serves as one of the most important passages for understanding how the powers actually manifest themselves.

all of Rome's military forces).[54] This is reinforced by the fact that the rest of the story unfolds using military imagery:

> The term for "herd" (*agelē*, 5:11)—inappropriate for pigs, who do not travel in herds—often was used to refer to a band of military recruits (Derret, 1979:5). Derret also points out that the phrase "he dismissed them" (*epetrepsen*) connotes a military command, and the pigs' charge (*ōrmēsen*) into the lake suggests troops rushing into battle (5:13).[55]

Further parallels include the fact that the pig was seen as emblematic of gentiles, and the rush into the lake recalls the drowning of Pharaoh's troops during the crossing of the Red Sea. This thing that Jesus converses with is the spiritual embodiment of Rome's military occupation of Palestine. Oddly enough, this aspect of the passage has been just as fraught with meaning for science fiction authors as it has for biblical scholars: Legion has become an allusion within science fiction to describe various forms of collective intelligence or "hive minds."[56] While the spirit represents the whole of the Roman legion, the Roman legion is obviously made up of individuals. This seems to make sense of Legion's vacillation between first-person singular and first-person plural pronouns in Mark's version of this exorcism ("*My* name is Legion; for *we* are many").

Walter Wink sums up the way in which the authors of the New Testament conceived of the demonic in these terms:

> [The New Testament's] "principalities and powers" are the inner and outer aspects of any given manifestation of power. . . . Every Power tends to have a visible pole, an outer form—be it a church, a nation, or an economy—and an invisible pole, an inner spirit or driving force that animates, legitimates, and regulates its physical manifestation in the world. Neither pole is the cause of the other. Both come into existence together and cease to exist together. When a particular Power becomes idolatrous, placing itself above God's purposes for the good of the whole, then that Power becomes demonic.[57]

54. Myers, *Binding the Strong Man*, 191.

55. Myers, *Binding the Strong Man*, 191.

56. Zelazny, *My Name Is Legion*; Wilson, *My Name Is Legion*; Taylor, *We Are Legion. We Are Legion* is also the name of a documentary about the anarchist "hacktivist" group Anonymous, so the association of the phrase with collectives that speak with one, unified voice is well established.

57. Wink, *Naming the Powers*, 5.

If Wink is correct, then slavery could be conceived as one of these powers that has turned demonic. Specifically, slavery is an economic demon; it is what one can expect to see when concerns of household order depart from the order of God's kingdom by allowing violence to permeate intimate relationships.

The suggestion that slavery is a power may meet with some immediate theological resistance since there are several different theologies of the powers that circulate, each with different political implications. The two major concerns could be summed up in the following two questions: (1) If slavery is a power, was it originally created by God for some divinely ordained purpose? (2) If slavery is a power, is it redeemable? The first question comes about due to a general trend in the Pauline writings that connects the powers with God's creative action. Numerous passages could be referred to in making this connection, but the clearest is generally considered to be Col 1:16–17:

> For in [Christ], all things in heaven and on earth were created, things visible and invisible, whether thrones or dominions or rulers or powers—all things have been created through him and for him. He himself is before all things, and in him all things hold together.

The second question follows from the first. If the powers have a divinely ordained purpose in God's creation, then it stands to reason that they will be redeemed in the new creation.

Answering either of these two questions with an unqualified "Yes" is not terribly appealing. Giving an affirmative answer to the first question suggests that slavery is a divinely ordained institution, in some way custom-made by God. Giving an affirmative answer to the second question could suggest that there is such a thing as "benign slavery" (exactly what many pro-slavery advocates during the Civil War era argued). I want to strenuously deny both of those conclusions. Slavery is not a part of God's purposes for the world, nor is it possible to produce a form of slavery that is in any sense benign. Slavery is an inherently violent institution.

But so too is Mark's Legion. It would be difficult to see either how Legion could be an entity that could have sprung fully formed from the mind of God in the form we find at Gerasa or how Legion could be considered divinely ordained in the sense that its current marching orders are in line with God's intentions.[58] Legion is the spiritual embodiment of

58. Wink himself points out that this problem obtains with *every* power once it is

the occupying Roman army whose explicit goal is to subjugate foreign peoples to spread the *Pax Romana*. "Roman" names a people group with an evolutionary history (not created fully formed by direct divine fiat), "army" names an institution that will be utterly purposeless in the new creation (because death and violence will cease), and the *Pax Romana* is a conception of peace that stands directly in conflict with the peace of Christ affirmed by the early church. If Legion is an entity whose existence is in some sense attributable to God's creative activity, then it must have undergone considerable (d)evolution to arrive at its current form. It could be considered derivative of regional governmental or administrative institutions which feasibly could have been instituted by God from the beginning for the common good, and could feasibly have a place after the eschaton. In other words, like any species that lives and moves and has being on the face of this earth, the powers evolve (or devolve).

In fact, such an evolution should be expected if Wink is right in the block quote given above: "Neither pole is the cause of the other. Both come into existence together and cease to exist together." This would mean that powers are never disconnected from human institutions, and all human institutions we encounter clearly undergo some evolution. An evolutionary history of powers should also be expected if they are some variety of collective mind, as in Mark's version of the Gerasene Demoniac. Legion is both one thing (the Legion) and many things (the soldiers who make up the Legion). If this is how powers are constituted, then it is possible for powers to change, disperse, collapse, merge, reform, split, or absorb other powers (much as we can imagine any institution undergoing such changes).[59] The unity (that which is indicated by "I" in Legion's

---

asserted that the powers are created by Christ in a direct way: "Throughout Christian history, the claim that the Powers have been created in and through and for Christ has all too easily been perverted into a justification of the status quo, a rationalization of every current evil, a legitimation of corrupt regimes" (Wink, *Naming the Powers*, 64). Thus, if "thrones" are created by God, then one could see how an argument for monarchy as a divinely instituted form of governance might proceed. Or if "the State" is a power, then one can see how an argument might proceed from the direct creation of the powers to the divine authorization of any particular state. I contend that all such arguments are illegitimate (in philosophical terms, they are all varieties of the naturalistic fallacy). Since human institutions (and powers) undergo substantial change over time, one cannot simply read God's will off of the face of the powers as they exist, even if all things owe their existence to God.

59. This may possibly put me at odds with Amos Yong's interpretation of the powers. Yong interprets the existence of the powers through Abraham Kuyper's concept of "sphere sovereignty," suggesting that every power operates within a distinct domain

speech) can stay stable while the plurality (that which is indicated by "we") changes, or vice versa. Thus, when it comes to asking whether the powers are created by God, one could answer "Yes, in the sense that all things are created by God," but that power could have undergone significant changes in both its constitution and its aims since its creation. Similarly, it may be possible for a power to be "redeemed," but perhaps not without complete collapse and reformation into something completely different. It may be possible for Legion to be redeemed, but it won't be as Legion.

This is why I suggested above that slavery is an economic power that has fallen. Every form of slavery justifies itself by identifying itself as a form of either love or justice. To put it another way, most forms of slavery are a perverse parody of an originally nonviolent household institution based in love. The family and the workplace are the most common institutions for slavery to imitate. In labor trafficking, the owner presents himself as a beneficent employer. "Have I not put a roof over your head?" he asks, "Have I not clothed you? Have I not fed you? Did I not give you an advance so that you could pay off your debts?"[60] In sex trafficking, the brothel madam presents herself as a caring mother, and the recruiter presents himself as a lover.[61] Of course, this is ultimately a farce; slavery is

---

of human life (see Yong, *In the Days of Caesar*, 162). I understand that this move is motivated by a dual desire to both (1) associate demons with human institutions, and (2) preserve *privatio boni* (the idea that evil ultimately has no substance, and therefore nothing God originally created is evil, an idea which is necessary to prevent ultimate metaphysical dualism). I think these are good commitments to have, and I hope that I have preserved them above. But the whole point of sphere sovereignty is that the spheres are relatively autonomous—they have their own dominions and logics. An evolutionary account of the powers might yield results that do fall neatly along the boundary lines (boundary surfaces?) of the spheres, but such a neat division could hardly ever be guaranteed. If powers do split and merge, then their dominions could cross sphere boundaries fairly easily.

60. "Ravi," interview with the author, Chennai, India, November 5, 2014; Pranitha Timothy, interview with the author, Channai, India, November 11, 2014; "Nisha," interview with the author, Chennai, India, November 7, 2014; Matthew Joji, interview with the author, Chennai, India, November 18, 2014. See also chapter 3 ("Just Like Family") of Choi-Fitzpatrick, *What Slaveholders Think*, esp. Choi-Fitzpatrick's summary of his findings on 48–49. Choi-Fitzpatrick conducted his own interviews among owners of bonded laborers in South India. A quotation from one such owner named Rahesh expressing these exact sentiments can be found on page vii.

61. Jessica Gunjal, interview with the author, Mumbai, India, October 14, 2014; "Lucy," interview with the author, Mumbai, India, September 9, 2014; "Lydia," interview with the author, Mumbai, India, September 11, 2014; "Megha," interview with the author, Mumbai, India, September 18, 2014.

always a severe perversion of what it claims to be, as violent control and the advancement of the owner through the degradation of the enslaved is presented as a normal part of these relationships. But there is just enough intimacy in the relationship mixed in with the violence that the idea that slavery is simply what real love looks like can take a deep hold of its victims. We shall discuss this more in the next chapter, which will explore the spiritual and mental bondage that results when an enslaved person begins to internalize these claims of love, or even to believe them. But for now, this analysis should help to show that identifying slavery as a power does not amount to a simple affirmation that slavery is divinely instituted or redeemable. If slavery (the power) is in any sense divinely instituted, it is as the *prior* institution that has been corrupted (family or work), not as slavery. Similarly, if slavery is redeemable, it must first undergo total collapse and the surviving pieces must be reconstituted into something far more akin to the prior institution.[62] Slavery is not redeemable as slavery.[63] Again, there is no such thing as "benign slavery."

Finally, the evolutionary nature of the powers and their linkage to human institutions should give us some idea of how they ought to be addressed. While many (more static) accounts of the origin of the powers may work to justify the idea that absolute power flows from the seat of government out toward the people, strongly connecting the powers to human institutions better corroborates the view of power found in the work of Gene Sharp. Drawing on a wide range of political thinkers,[64] Sharp formulates what he calls a "pluralistic-dependency theory" of power which he contrasts with a "monolith theory" of power.

> The "monolith theory" of power assumes that the power of a government is a relatively fixed *quantum* (i.e., "a discrete unit quantity of energy"), a "given," a strong, independent, durable (if not indestructible), self-reinforcing, and self-perpetuating force. Because of these assumed characteristics, it follows that in open conflict such power cannot in the last analysis simply be

62. "Something far more akin to" is not unnecessary hedging here. There are serious questions as to whether the family itself will survive the eschaton intact, given Jesus' treatment of it in his preaching (i.e., Matthew 22:30).

63. One recalls here Paul's statement that some people will only be saved "through fire" (1 Corinthians 3:15). Perhaps the same is true for some powers.

64. Sharp's source material encompasses everyone from Hobbes and Machiavelli to Gandhi and Tolstoy to MacIver and Jouvenal. Comte also features pretty heavily in *Power and Struggle*.

> controlled or destroyed simply by people but only by the threat or use of overwhelming physical might.[65]

"Pluralistic-dependency theory," on the other hand, is the idea that power comes from the consent of the governed; "[the idea] that governments depend on people, that power is pluralistic, and that political power is fragile because it depends on many groups for reinforcement of its power sources."[66] Power is thus strengthened or removed not through the possession of overwhelming force, but through reinforcing or removing its sources. If powers are composite entities that are in some sense one thing and in some sense many things, then it would make sense that the whole draws power from its constituent parts.

Sharp uses his theory of power to articulate the political power of nonviolent action, and his theory could help to guide modern resistance to slavery as well. Though anti-slavery laws are helpful for staging interventions, the idea that slavery can be undone simply by directing the overwhelming physical might of the state at it has some dire problems. These issues will be addressed later in chapter 5. Instead, slavery's power can only be broken by causing it to dry up at the roots.

Before closing our theological analysis of slavery, it is important to note that all forms of slavery are organized around a single implicit theological claim: the master is God. This aspect of slavery is brought home particularly strongly in US antebellum slavery, where the claim can be explicitly found in multiple forms. The slave catechisms themselves often overtly claim that the master acts as the mediator of the slave's salvation. Given the linkage between God and salvation in Christian theology, this quickly collapses into the claim that the master is God to the enslaved.[67] Since God is the author of salvation, salvation's mediators must in some way be divine themselves. Dwight Hopkins demonstrates the connection well:

> For example, a slave master caught his slave praying and demanded that the slave explain to whom he offered supplications. The slave replied: "Oh Marster, I'se just prayin' to Jesus 'cause I wants to go to Heaven when I dies." Belligerently and arrogantly,

65. Sharp, *Power and Struggle*, 9.

66. Sharp, *Power and Struggle*, 8.

67. One also has to remember that these claims were often made by slaveowning American Protestants who would frequently accuse Catholics of making Mary the fourth member of the Trinity due to her mediatory role between human beings and Christ.

> the Marster replied, "You's my Negro. I get ye to Heaven." Here we touch the heart of white Christianity and theology. The white man believed he filled the mediating and liberating role of Jesus Christ. As the anointed Jesus, to reach God, then, whites forced African Americans to accept the status of the white race as divine mediator.[68]

This theological claim sometimes even becomes accepted on the enslaved person's side of the relationship given the fact that the master's power over an enslaved person can seem absolute. And of course, no one possesses absolute power save God alone. One can see this manifest, for instance, in the *Narrative of the Life of Henry Box Brown*:

> I really believed my old master was Almighty God, and that the young master was Jesus Christ! The reason of this error seems to have been that we were taught to believe thunder to be the voice of God, and when it was about to thunder my master would approach us, if we were in the yard, and say, all you children run into the house now, for it is going to thunder; and after the thunder storm was over he would approach us smilingly and say "what a fine shower we have had," and bidding us look at the flowers would say how prettily they appeared; we children seeing this so frequently, could not avoid the idea that it was he that thundered and made the rain to fall, in order to make his flowers look beautiful, and I was nearly my eight years of age before I got rid of this childish superstition. Our master was uncommonly kind (for even a slaveholder may be kind) and as he moved about in his dignity, he seemed like a god to us, but not withstanding his kindness although he knew very well what superstitious notions we formed of him, he never made the least attempt to correct our erroneous impression, but rather seemed pleased with the reverential feelings which we entertained towards him.[69]

Brown goes on to describe how all the enslaved children on this plantation referred to his master's son as "Savior" and how he was eventually set straight by his mother, who informed him that the slaveholder and his

68. Hopkins, "Slave Theology," 9. Hopkins cites the testimony of two more enslaved people a mere three pages later that corroborate the same phenomenon. Here are his quotations collected from two slaveowners: "Ef I ketch you heah agin servin' God, I'll beat you. You havn' time to serve God. We bought you to serve us." Likewise: "The Lord rule Heaven, but [I] Jim Smith rule the earth" (Hopkins, "Slave Theology," 12–13).

69. Brown, *Life of Henry Box Brown*, 18.

son were not who Christians were referring to when they spoke of "God" and "Jesus Christ." Brown narrates this vignette as a part of a general trend within American slave religion: critiquing white slaveholding religion as something far removed from "the religion of Jesus Christ." Simply by dint of their position, Brown and other formerly enslaved Christians claimed, the master claims to usurp God's authority. This puts slaveowning clearly in the category of "idolatry."[70] Due to the claims of mediation and absolute power that are made in every slave system, their critique can be extended to *any* form of slavery. And Brown's experience of internalizing these claims to the point that he actually believed that his master was God is by no means unique. We will see this in the next chapter when we consider the testimony of formerly enslaved people in our time who came to very similar conclusions.

Given the fact that all forms of slavery implicitly make the assertion that the master is God, two things follow. First, this gives us a key theological insight into slavery's staying power. At least as far back as the composition of Gen 3, Jewish and Christian theologians have made the assertion that all forms of evil in the world are rooted in humanity's desire to be God.[71] "You will be like God" is precisely the promise that the serpent gives to the woman as she is considering eating the fruit of the tree of the knowledge of good and evil. The same temptation present in all forms of sin and evil lies at the heart of slavery, and that temptation

70. In this, Brown and other formerly enslaved Christians were drawing upon a thick theological tradition that goes all the way back to the antimonarchic strains of the Hebrew Bible. Samuel's critique of the monarchy in 1 Sam 8, for example, draws upon the conviction that Israel should have no king but God. To appoint a human king is to reject God as king. The underlying assumption is that once an individual starts to claim absolute power over another human being, they are simultaneously trying to usurp God's position.

71. There is, of course, a long tradition of deification in Christianity, traceable back to at least 2 Pet 1:4 ("he has given us his very great and precious promises, so that through them you may participate in the divine nature, having escaped the corruption in the world caused by evil desires"). I take it that this tradition of deification understands the process of "becoming God" differently than slavery does. Deification seeks to enter into and become a part of the divine life of the triune God. Slavery ignores or tries to actively displace the triune God and God's mediators. Further, slavery contains within itself a problematic understanding of what it means to be God in the first place. It misunderstands what the terms "God" and "power" mean in the first place. Deification, if articulated well, does not fall into this problem. The warped understanding of both God and power present within slavery (along with the alternative conception of God offered within the Christian tradition) will be explored in more depth in the next two chapters.

still calls to many a human being to enslave others even on a small scale. Second, this means that all abolitionist positions are at least minimally theological. To be opposed to the institution of slavery, one must be able to say what God is *not*. The master is not God.

This picture of what slavery is could be fleshed out in far more depth. But at this juncture, I believe we have at least the minimal framework necessary to understand slavery from a legal, sociological, and theological perspective. With this framework laid, we will turn to the experience of coming out of modern slavery more directly.

Chapter 2

Chains of the Soul

WHEN MY STUDENTS APPROACH the Torah for the first time, it's not unusual for them to be a bit baffled by the stories of Israel's wilderness wanderings. "If God truly did deliver the Israelites from slavery in such a visible manner, why do they immediately make their own god in the shape of a golden calf?" "If slavery in Egypt was so bad, why do they immediately long to go back to Egypt?" And certainly these students have picked up on something very important in the text: the theme of returning to Egypt—the place of slavery—is ubiquitous in the narrative. It is something the author wanted astute readers to pick up on. Perhaps the best statement of this theme in Exodus can be found in Exod 16:

> The whole congregation of the Israelites set out from Elim; and Israel came to the wilderness of Sin, which is between Elim and Sinai, on the fifteenth day of the second month after they had departed from the land of Egypt. The whole congregation of the Israelites complained against Moses and Aaron in the wilderness. The Israelites said to them, "If only we had died by the hand of the Lord in the land of Egypt, when we sat by the fleshpots and ate our fill of bread; for you have brought us out into this wilderness to kill this whole assembly with hunger." (Exod 16:1–3)

Unfortunately, one conclusion that has too often been drawn when Christians come across this theme is that the Israelites were either inherently foolish or inherently wicked as a people. Anti-Jewish or anti-Semitic readings have too naturally flowed from encounter with this theme. Any righteous or intelligent people group would have been happy to have been liberated by such an oppressive regime, but the Israelites desired to return to enslavement. Perhaps, some ancient commentators even mused, this means that they were in some way fit for slavery.[1]

But such an approach ignores the fact that slavery is a profoundly formative institution. It ignores the work that the master puts into making sure that an enslaved person is constantly dependent on him. To point to these dependencies post-liberation and claim that they are evidence that slavery naturally befits this enslaved person is like contracting someone to build a house without using mortar, then saying it is their fault that the brickwork is not terribly stable. There's something terribly disingenuous about this conclusion. No one born truly free longs for the warm (if suffocating) embrace of slavery, but given the right social formation, one can feel adrift apart from a state of bondage. No one is accustomed to bondage "by nature." That comfort is learned. And that comfort is shockingly common among the survivors of modern slavery. In fact, it is so common that the practitioners from my interviews have even come up with a name for the condition: "captive mentality."

When it comes to the Exodus narrative, biblical scholars still debate how much of the narrative reflects the actual history of Israel, and how much of it boils down to the repetitions, re-narrations, and figurative elaborations which are so characteristic of the Torah's "folkloric" genre.[2] While I don't imagine for a second that this settles the debate, it is this

1. Though Augustine does not cite this story directly, he may have had it in mind when he claimed that the Jews were relegated to the role of a slave to a Christian master in salvation history. Augustine claimed that it was the Jews' job to transmit the books of the Bible for the benefit of Christians, all the while failing to benefit from those books themselves: "In what sort of disgrace do the Jews find themselves? A Jew carries the book which is the foundation of faith for a Christian. Jews act as book-bearers for us, like the slaves who are accustomed to walk behind their masters carrying their books, so that while the slaves sink under the weight, the masters make great strides through reading" (Augustine, *Exp. Ps.* 56.9 [p. 110]). The charge that such punishments were heaped upon the Jews by God due to a history of moral failings on the part of Israel is a common one in the *Adversus Judaeos* literature (i.e., Christian works focused on anti-Jewish polemic). For an overview of this trend in portions of early Christianity (especially the work of John Chrysostom), see Simon, *Verus Israel*, 212–23.

2. For very different accounts of the relationship of the Exodus narrative to history, see Brueggemann and Linafelt, *Introduction to the Old Testament*; Dever, *Who Were the Early Israelites*, 7–21; Longman, *How to Read Exodus*, 68–94; Kaiser, *Old Testament Documents*, 109–18. For the best seminal work on the literary conventions of Hebrew folklore (the genre which Exodus falls under) and the complex interplay of fiction and history that seems to be the standard in this genre, see Alter, *Art of Biblical Narrative*, 25–54.

aspect of Israel's wilderness wanderings that smacks the most of realism to me.[3] When the Israelites "long for Egypt," they don't prove themselves to be particularly wicked or foolish. Their behavior is quite normal for formerly enslaved people who are in the process of reintegrating into society.[4] In fact, traces of captive mentality can be seen in many different forms of slavery across history. And so long as those who are trying to aid in rehabilitation see such behavior as rooted in some sort of character flaw, the help that they will be able to give will be substantially limited.

So, what is "captive mentality"? Simply put, it is the state that results when a formerly enslaved person's physical chains have been broken, but they are still bound by chains of the mind. It is their longing to "return to Egypt." When the professionals in my interviews use the term "captive mentality," they are expressing a phenomenon that seems to manifest itself in four ways:

3. It is important, however, not to cast this as a modern debate between "traditionalist" or "conservative" Christians and "liberal" Christians, and to assign me in the first camp. I do think I'm deeply in line with the tradition in my reading. However, I also think that those who think that not all of the stories in the Bible are historical are also deeply in line with the tradition. Scholars of early Christianity show an increasing awareness that most early Christians were comfortable with the idea that certain stories in the Bible "are not accurate historical accounts of actual events, but allegorical tales composed for the edification of readers" See Hart, *New Testament*, 336 n. q. Hart is here commenting on Paul's assertion in 1 Cor 10:11 that tales of destruction during Israel's wilderness wanderings (e.g., in Num 21:4–9) happened only "figuratively" (*typikōs*). True, ancient authors (such as Paul) did not use genre categories such as "folklore," but such a category is deeply in line with the tradition in that it helps readers distinguish between more thickly historical books of the Bible and more figurative books of the Bible while taking away some of that more arbitrary "pick-and-choose" feel that some ancient exegesis has. For example, readers approaching the flood story (Gen 6–9) can discern that it is figurative because the whole story bears the markings of the genre "myth" (i.e., it includes mythological creatures, unnaturally long lifespans, etiological explanations of natural phenomena, etc.). Readers approaching the resurrection of Jesus can discern that it is historical because it appears in a book bearing the markings of the genre "gospel" (i.e., it is a reconstruction based upon the testimony of direct eyewitnesses to the event). Neither judgment is based simply on whether the reader wants to believe the story is historical or not. For Evangelicals who might be uneasy about this exegetical strategy and would like to see an argument for it from an Evangelical perspective, see Bird, "Inerrancy Is Not Necessary," 149–54.

4. Christian survivors of trafficking frequently see the resonances here as well. The story of Israel's wilderness wanderings is frequently utilized by Rachel Lloyd in her work with survivors to describe the desire to return to a situation of bondage. See Lloyd, *Girls Like Us*, 189.

1. Captive mentality is a lingering connection to the daily rhythms of bondage; the survivor is physically habituated to slavery. Disruption of these rhythms through liberation may initially result in intense fear or anxiety. In severe cases, severing the connection may even trigger a severe psychosomatic reaction: the survivor suffers "withdrawal."
2. Captive mentality is the tendency to defer life decisions (either major or minor) and seek out a direct command from a surrogate master.
3. Captive mentality is a fascination with your former master; a fascination which manifests so strongly that you will resist outside attempts to sever your ties with the master.
4. Captive mentality is the (implicit or explicit) belief that your former master is god.

Not every enslaved person is bound by captive mentality. In this way, captive mentality could be compared to trauma. Not every person who goes through a traumatic experience winds up with PTSD. Just so, not every person who goes through enslavement exhibits forms of captive mentality. And those enslaved individuals that do exhibit captive mentality do not necessarily display it in all four of these ways. Nor do all enslaved people that exhibit captive mentality progress through these manifestations like stages. Nor are these ways necessarily organized in order of severity. While all of them are a testimony to the depth of the master's continued mental and spiritual grip on the enslaved, it does not necessarily take longer to unlearn the behavior or beliefs present in level 1 than it does to unlearn the behavior or beliefs in level 2. These levels are merely the four different ways in which the term "captive mentality" has been applied in my interviews.

Before discussing these four levels in more detail, a caveat is in order. Though this discussion of captive mentality includes the recommendation of a particular variety of therapy and references concepts such as trauma, PTSD, Stockholm syndrome,[5] and so forth, I am emphatically

5. "Stockholm syndrome" is what I initially referred to captive mentality as in my interviews; you can see me use the term in the block quotes below. However, as the interviews progressed, I realized this was the wrong lens through which to view the problem. It wasn't until I conducted my Chennai interviews that I encountered the far more fitting language of "captive mentality." It was already in use by the aftercare professionals that I interviewed. I adopted the term for later interviews.

not arguing that captive mentality is some sort of heretofore undiscovered mental disorder that needs to be added to the DSM VI. And this is the case not simply because I lack the credentials in psychology to tell the guild what they should put in the DSM VI (though that is definitely part of it). Rather, it is the case because I don't believe captive mentality is merely some variety of neurosis or delusion (though it does encourage certain delusions to the point where social workers sometimes dub it "brainwashing"[6]). It is instead a whole mode of spiritual and mental formation that is socially reinforced by the institution of slavery.[7] To put it in terms more germane to my own field (ethics), captive mentality is a complex of habits; habits that are organized with a very specific conception of love (*caritas*)[8] as their end. Or, to use more sinister terminology, ethicists have tended to speak of the sort of problem captive mentality represents in terms of "the formation of subjectivity." Captive mentality is the end result of a complex of social processes that are designed to form a certain sort of pliable, dependent subject. Additionally, this subjectivity persists after liberation in numerous forms. Further, the complex of social processes that produce captive mentality are unified not only in their implicit adherence to a particular conception of love, but they are also unified in their implicit adherence to a single dogma: the master is God. Finally, I

6. "Megha," interview with the author, Mumbai, India, September 18, 2014.

7. This also makes captive mentality a separate issue from trauma or PTSD. As Serene Jones points out, those who experience trauma symptoms describe them as an experience of "rupture" or "disorder." See Jones, *Trauma and Grace*, 19. Trauma is fundamentally chaotic. Survivors with PTSD may, for example, experience a disturbing memory that goes off like a psychological bomb in their head, suddenly overwhelming of the sufferer's capacity for language and memory. They forget commonly used terms and have difficulty recalling memories. Captive mentality is different: it is fundamentally ordered. It follows its own logic, and contains excavatable concepts of love, justice, and God. This is not, of course, to say that someone cannot suffer from *both* captive mentality and PTSD. Experiencing both at the same time may even occur more often than not, since those who are held as captives are frequently exposed to traumatic events. I merely wish to point out that these two things are distinct phenomena, and treatment options for them are at least theoretically distinct, even if they are conjoined in the same program (as is the case with TFCBT below). In what follows, I will focus much more on an analysis of captive mentality than on an analysis of trauma, as the issues survivors face relative to captive mentality emerged with greater clarity than the issues survivors face relative to trauma in my interviews.

8. *Caritas* was chosen here over any of the other love words (say, *amor*), because of its specific positioning in the tradition as a theological virtue. As I will elaborate as this chapter continues, slavery's implicit conception of love is connected to its implicit concept of God.

do not for a moment mean to suggest that captive mentality is unique to slavery. I readily admit that the phenomenon crosses over into situations which would not classify as slavery (such as domestic violence). But it must be addressed in any discussion of rehabilitation from the effects of slavery, because it is quite pervasive in survivors of slavery. Rehabilitation gets off on the wrong foot if it does not keep this phenomenon in mind. Thus, this chapter is an attempt to pull resources from the disciplines of psychology, ethics, and theology to address the chains of the mind that persist after an enslaved person is liberated from bondage.

Physical Habituation

Like any social arrangement, slavery has its rhythms. It disciplines its victims by giving them a time to rise and a time to sleep, a time to work and a time to rest, a time to love and a time to fear. Over time, the behaviors an enslaved person performs while caught in these rhythms crystallize into habits. They become physically habituated to slavery. Some survivors can get so habituated to slavery that the transition to freedom can be absolutely terrifying. Some may even perceive breaking the habit to be so daunting that they seek to return to bondage. As the saying goes, better the devil you know than the devil you don't.

One particularly visceral example of this connection was brought home during a training seminar I attended in Chennai that was led by Tammy Williams, who served as an aftercare consultant for IJM in South Asia in 2014. During the session, Williams referred to a "Crisis Period" that bonded labor survivors often go through soon after rescue. During this Crisis Period, survivors experience many acute mental and physical health problems, including malnutrition, overexertion, PTSD, and constant anxiety due to fear that their former owners will retaliate. In some cases, survivors may even go into shock. In a memo that Williams later forwarded to me, she lays out how many laborers express a desire to return to bondage during this period, as it seems to them to be the only way to alleviate this distress.[9] Immediate re-bondage presents itself as a paramount aftercare concern. In the same memo, Williams expresses a desire to incorporate a sort of "detox period"[10] into their rehabilitation

9. Tammy Williams, "Summary of Domains and Cross-Cutting Themes." Attachment in email message to author, November 18, 2014.

10. This is my own interpolation, not a direct quote from Williams.

schedule, where special services are offered to bonded labor survivors immediately after liberation and before returning them to their native place. These special services focused on meeting the immediate physical needs of former bonded laborers.

Why would return seem so appealing to a bonded laborer at that time? One social worker posited (outside of interviews) that it had to do with an inability to self-regulate. In many bonded labor situations, many victims' daily schedules are so intensely micromanaged that they are not allowed to eat, sleep, or even go to the bathroom without explicit authorization from their master. In the case of those born into slavery, they may have never known a situation in which they did not need to seek such authorization. As such, after these bonded laborers are emancipated, they may find that attending to these needs on their own takes some getting used to. Thus, some survivors of bonded labor go through forms of shock and anxiety immediately after liberation, as they learn to balance such needs on their own for the first time. If the task seems overwhelming, return to slavery may present itself as an easy out.

Another suggestion (not mutually exclusive with the preceding explanation) is desperation. Survivors come out of bondage almost completely dispossessed: no home, no bed, no food, no means of cooking.[11] They often find themselves necessarily in this situation, because abandoning a prior residence and moving onto the owner's property is an expected and normal part of their work contract. In fact, *all* of my survivor interviewees lived where they worked.[12] They were also frequently physically prevented from leaving the premises. For example, here is the testimony of a bonded labor survivor named "Latha":

> **Chris:** Okay. What was the situation that led you into bonded labor in the first place? Was it a debt that you took out, or . . . ?
>
> **Latha:** Yeah. It was because of my mother-in-law. She was sitting one day, and something from the roof fell on her head. She got a big cut above her eyes. And we took her to the hospital, and the doctors gave treatment. And then she went on coma. She went

11. "Hannah," interview with the author, Chennai, India, November 18, 2014; "Nisha," interview with the author, Chennai, India, November 7, 2014; "Kumar" and "Vijaya," interview with the author, Chennai, India, November 6, 2014.

12. There is one partial exception: Raja's parents were bonded, and he alternated between living with his parents and living with his grandmother (so that he could study). His parents, however, lived on the compound where they worked (Raja, interview with the author, Chennai, India, November 12, 2014).

> on coma stage. And then we were all in desperate need of money. So we couldn't do anything. At that moment, the owner—the rice mill owner—he comes to know about this. And he came up to us, and he said, "You could work for us. We will pay that money. We will pay the money for the medical treatment." And then he took us up, and he made us work in his rice mill. And then, within few days, my mother-in-law died. And even for the death, we were not allowed outside. We were not allowed for the final thing that we need to do. Formalities and everything [i.e., the funeral]. They didn't let us out.[13]

Taking out an advance (and thereby entering into bondage) was the way out of an economic tight spot in the past, and now the formerly enslaved person's economic, physical, and emotional distress is even more acute than it was before. Returning to bondage can look awfully tempting from the perspective of a survivor in this situation.[14]

In either explanation, habit takes hold of the survivor in an almost palpable way. The habit of asking for permission is so ingrained in the survivor that he feels he cannot manage the daily rhythms of life without it. Or the survivor is so used to turning to large advances to alleviate economic distress that he immediately takes out another loan. This even happened during one of my interviews: "Kumar" and "Vijaya" (mentioned in more depth below) had already taken out another loan of ₹50,000, even though this is one of the first things social workers caution their survivors against.[15] Do not take out another advance, they caution, it will lead back into slavery. Of course, from Kumar and Vijaya's perspective, the decision they made certainly seems unavoidable. They are among the poorest of the poor. Banks won't lend to them, and the government is slow in producing their rehabilitation money.[16] Where else will they get the money?

13. "Latha" and "Subramani," interview with the author, Chennai, India, November 10, 2014.

14. Again, it is necessary to note that this response is not uniform among former bonded laborers. Two survivors, Kadavul and Maha, told me some version of the following: "In bondage, the food was good. In freedom, the food is poor. But I'm still much happier in freedom than I ever was in bondage" ("Kadavul," interview with the author, Chennai, India, November 6, 2014; "Maha," interview with the author, Chennai, India, November 6, 2014).

15. "Kumar" and "Vijaya," interview with the author, Chennai, India, November 6, 2014. For social workers' advice against taking out loans: "Nisha," interview with the author, Chennai, India, November 7, 2014.

16. At the time of my interviews, under Indian law, all survivors of bonded labor

While the examples I found of this phenomenon in sex trafficking situations are not quite so drastic,[17] there are still indicators that sex trafficking survivors frequently become habituated to the rhythms of slavery and find it difficult to transition out of enslavement. For example, several aftercare professionals I interviewed testified that adjusting to a normal nine-to-five working schedule proved challenging for many survivors.[18] The survivors were used to sleeping during the day and working at night, the schedule the brothel set for them. Bharathy Tahiliani testified that some of the survivors she worked with even lost job opportunities due to their inability to transition between schedules.[19]

who received a release certificate were entitled to ₹20,000: ₹1,000 upon release, and ₹19,000 within three months of release. Under this policy, the Indian government was usually quite good at producing the initial ₹1,000. The other ₹19,000, however, took a lot of NGO lobbying to produce ("Kadavul," interview with the author, Chennai, India, November 6, 2014; "Kumar" and "Vijaya," interview with the author, Chennai, India, November 6, 2014; "Hannah," interview with the author, Chennai, India, November 18, 2014; "Nisha," interview with the author, Chennai, India, November 7, 2014; "Jaya," interview with the author, Chennai, India, November 10, 2014; unnamed couple, interview with the author, Channai, India, November 10, 2014). I believe Latha and Subramani were also waiting on this ₹19,000 amount, but they talked about so many government assistance programs during the interview that sorting out what money was owed from what source was a bit confusing ("Latha" and "Subramani," interview with the author, Chennai, India, November 10, 2014). In May of 2016, the Indian Central Government implemented the Central Sector Scheme for the Rehabilitation of Bonded Laborers. The Scheme increased the amount of rehabilitation money to ₹100,000 for adult male bonded laborers, ₹200,000 for female and child bonded laborers, and ₹300,000 for bonded laborers who are transgendered, commercially sexually exploited, trafficked, or disabled. However, disbursement of this money is contingent upon the conviction of the perpetrator, and the conviction rate for slaveowners in India is notoriously low. While the case is pending trial, survivors are entitled to ₹20,000 of the funds if they have a release certificate. This means that unless the conviction rate dramatically improves, the amount most survivors receive in practice will remain substantially unchanged from the amount survivors received in 2014.

17. By this, I mean that I could find no testimony of sex trafficking survivors going into shock after rescue. However, Bharathy Tahiliani did testify to a "crisis period" (the same words Tammy Williams used) to describe the period immediately post-rescue (Bharathy Tahiliani, interview with the author, Mumbai, India, January 2, 2014). I take it from her comments, however, that the crisis she described was less a physical reaction to a newfound life of freedom so much as it was a distress that the survivor's former masters were not present. As such, the crisis period she describes probably looks much more like the phenomena described under the "fascination" section below than it does the phenomena described in the section above.

18. Jessica Gunjal, interview with the author, Mumbai, India, October 14, 2014; Asha, interview with the author, Mumbai, India, September 9, 2014.

19. Bharathy Tahiliani, interview with the author, Mumbai, India, January 2, 2014.

Such transitional challenges may seem small to an outside observer, but they certainly do not seem that way to the survivor. Since many sex trafficking survivors have been told for years (or perhaps even decades) that they are not fit for anything other than sex slavery, every on-the-job challenge experienced during rehabilitation can seem insurmountable. It can be received by the survivor as one more pebble to add to a mountain of evidence that they cannot be anything other than a slave. Sunita, the director of operations for iSanctuary, an organization that employs sex trafficking survivors, described what this can look like on the job site during our interview:

> **Sunita:** Yeah, like just six months back, the girl [i.e., one of her employees] was sitting with me here . . . and she was working with me on some stuff iSanctuary. And she just came, full tears of eyes and sad face, and I didn't realize she's standing behind me, because I was so engrossed in checking my mails. And she was like, "I'm waiting here for last five minutes." So I looked back and was like, "Oh, I'm sorry." And she start crying, and said "I don't think so society has a place for me or I can ever better. I think the brothel is the best place for me." And I was like, "Oh God, give me the words to say to her. I don't know." So yeah. Even like, after long time also the trauma and the things that happen to them, that didn't go away. I feel like that stay for a longer time, specifically when they say the family does not support you, or they cannot do anything with the life. That's make them more discouraged than like, they gone through in that time that's okay I think. And then they're earning and they survive, but being here and doing something or try to do something and they cannot do, I think they feel discouraged with that.[20]

I later learned that the survivor Sunita is describing—the one who told Sunita, "I think the brothel is the best place for me"—was likely "Zara," one of my interviewees who works for iSanctuary. When I asked Sunita how many of her employees had expressed this sort of hopelessness during their transition, Sunita answered that about half of her employees had expressed similar feelings. Bharathy Tahiliani verified this trend of total hopelessness about rehabilitation among her clients as well:

> **Bharathy:** Yeah. And there's generalized hopelessness. So, you have to coach them, coach them, coach them, coach them, coach them . . . without breaking their dignity. . . . And a fatalistic

20. Sunita and Erin, interview with the author, Mumbai, India, October 1, 2014.

> attitude. And the *fear*. *Hanh*,[21] there is a fear that society will never accept them. So fear, shame, embarrassment, helplessness . . . very strong drivers. Very strong emotional drivers.[22]

When I asked Sunita what had triggered the outburst in the survivor she talked with, she was not sure. Perhaps it was an on-site challenge she experienced. Perhaps her parents or friends said something that shamed her or reminded her of her former life. Regardless, the feeling that a survivor simply cannot transition is common. A pervasive fear that transition is simply too daunting, too difficult, or "not for me" is a regular part of survivor experience. And a survivor may contemplate returning rather than dealing with the constant feeling of inevitable failure.

Human beings are extremely adaptable creatures, and so it should perhaps be no surprise to find that our bodies can become attuned even to the rhythms of an institution which seems so dead-set on the *breaking* of the human body. But this fact needs to be kept in full view when formulating a plan for rehabilitation. Becoming free is a matter of retraining the body.

Making Life Decisions

The dependence that an enslaved person develops toward their master can become so severe that, when the relationship between the two is severed, the survivor can feel adrift when it comes to making basic decisions. And this can be the case even if the enslaved person experiences their liberation as a relief. In such a situation, the most natural person for the survivor to latch onto is an outside party that assisted in their liberation.

I ran into a concrete example of this during my own field research. Before every interview I conducted, I was required to direct my interviewee through an informed consent process. During this process, I would explain who I was, why I was conducting this research, how I intended to use the information in the interview, and what risks and benefits the research could pose to the interviewee. Since most of the labor trafficking survivors I interviewed were illiterate, I gave the survivors this information in a presentation that was translated by my translator, Aryan Timothy.[23] At the end of this process, I would always ask the survivor

21. *Hanh* is "yes" in Hindi.

22. Bharathy Tahiliani, interview with the author, Mumbai, India, January 2, 2014.

23. Aryan translated all of my bonded labor survivor interviews. I acquired the

three questions: "Do you have any questions for me about anything I've said, or about the interviews in general?" "Do you understand everything that I have told you?" and "Do you still consent to participate in this interview?"

One afternoon, after attending a Monthly Meeting (a regular meeting that the social workers at an anti-trafficking NGO in Chennai hold with recent survivors to talk about unresolved aftercare issues), I sat down with two of the attendees—Kumar and Vijaya—who volunteered to participate in the interviews. I gave them the informed consent presentation, and had Aryan ask them the three questions. When Aryan got to the final question, a long back-and-forth ensued between Aryan and Kumar. I knew at that point that the answer could not have been a simple "Yes, I consent to this interview" or "No, I do not consent to this interview." Aryan then turned to me to translate.

"He literally said, 'Whatever my madam says, I'll do.'"

"Oh," I responded. Kumar didn't seem to be referring to his wife, who did not speak much and largely deferred to her husband throughout the interview. Aryan and I are both male, so he obviously wasn't referring to us. There was no one else around. I was confused. "Who is he talking about?"

Aryan turned back to Kumar and posed the question to him in Tamil.

"[Nisha] madam," Kumar responded, pointing to the social worker who had connected us for the interview.

This response posed a moral dilemma for Aryan and me. We explained to Kumar that participation in this interview was not required by his social worker or her employer. It was truly up to him and his wife whether or not they wanted to participate. After clarifying this, Kumar quickly affirmed, "Yes, *I* agree to talk." But questions about Kumar and Vijaya's free participation lingered between Aryan and me. Was this really a free decision on Kumar's part? Even if it was not, was giving consent in this circumstance a step forward for him, a necessary part of his growth toward freedom? Should I use this interview in my research, given his initial response? Especially disturbing was the title Kumar used for Nisha: "my madam." Nisha was his new master not only in fact, but also in name. Of course, this is not a position that Nisha desired to fill. Kumar

---

assistance of four separate translators (all of which were women who had some sort of prior working relationship with the survivors) for my sex trafficking survivor interviews.

simply was looking for a surrogate master to make the decision for him, and Nisha was the closest person that he could approach to fulfill that role. If an enslaved person has developed this form of captive mentality, he needs to learn new habits to come to a place where his decisions are truly his own.

At this point, a caveat may be in order. One could ask, "What is the problem here? Kumar has consented to the interview." Or one could object that, by my hesitancy to treat this as a free decision in the fullest sense, I am denying that Kumar possesses free will, and thus I am treating him as sub-human. A full discussion of the nature of agency is beyond the scope of this project, but for our purposes, I would like to clarify that the question is about neither consent nor about whether or not Kumar has free will. Kumar has given consent; I absolutely do not deny that he is capable of giving consent. Nor am I suggesting that he lacks free will, which has traditionally been seen as one of the primary theological indications that one is both human and created in the image of God. The question is rather about intention, one of many terms that could be used to describe the end that an agent is aiming for when she makes a decision. Consent is merely about the decision itself; it is about an agent's "Yes" or "No" and makes no reference to ends. Consent is a floor consideration; it is freedom in its most basic (but not its fullest) sense. It is possible to give consent and yet succumb to what G. W. F. Hegel called "alienation": the experience that one has given consent, but has not fully understood the issues at stake, or has consented in an attenuated, manipulated, resentful, or confused way.[24] Agency is thus deeper than, but on a continuum with, consent. And here, the concern is manipulation. Free agents have a diversity of intentions, and often possess multiple intentions when performing a single act. For example, I may choose to take a teaching job because (1) the community needs educators, and taking that job fills that need, (2) I need a paycheck, and (3) I find the work fulfilling. Those intentions are not mutually exclusive.

Slavery is an institution that aims at the destruction of intention. It does this by subsuming all intentions for action under a single intention: pleasing the master. But this is not the sole concern; an agent can be

24. This does not necessarily mean that I'm operating with a Hegelian theory of agency. Hegel simply takes a common experience and comes up with a good identifying term for it. I disagree with a good number of things in Hegel's account of agency, especially the view of the state and property rights that are entailed by Hegel's account.

"single-hearted" and still be free (i.e., alienation would not occur).[25] The problem is that slavery forcibly organizes intentionality this way through violence or threat of violence. One end is not seen as better than others, and thus made a focal point. Instead, all other possible intentions are either forcibly subsumed or quashed entirely. To use a common sight metaphor (an agent "sees the good" in her actions), the result is not that an enslaved person comes to see all goods as fulfilled through pursuing the good of serving the master, but rather that the enslaved person becomes blind to all other goods.[26] Since rationality plays a primary role in intentionality (we discern reasons for why we aim at certain ends—this is how we "see" an action or end as good), this is linked to the fact that slavery also aims at the destruction of rationality. Frederick Douglass articulated this connection ably back in 1845:

> I have found that, to make a contented slave, it is necessary to make a thoughtless one. It is necessary to darken his moral and mental vision, and, as far as possible, to annihilate the power of reason. He must be able to detect no inconsistencies in slavery; he must be made to feel that slavery is right; and he can be brought to that only when he ceases to be a man.[27]

And key to this annihilation of the power of reason, Douglass says, is the fear of death. When violence looms, thoughts of self-preservation take over, and a concern for life overtakes a concern for freedom. But when peace—even the relative peace of a slavery where the threat of violence is not immediately present—is present, thoughts of freedom creep back in. To make a "contented slave," you must try to destroy his rationality.

To sum up, the problem is that slavery produces alienation by institutionally manipulating rationality such that it proscribes intentionality.

25. "Singleness of heart" is typically used in monastic or spiritual formation literature to denote the practice of subsuming all ends under the end of friendship with God. However, a person could be "single-hearted" and subsume all ends to another sort of end. For example, you could organize your life in such a way that all decisions you make have the accumulation of more wealth as their ultimate end. This is typically considered a terrible way to live your life in monastic or spiritual formation literature, but simply because you live this way does not mean your agency is manipulated. You can freely live this way.

26. Hannah, one of my social worker interviewees, described this phenomenon as a failure of imagination ("Hannah," interview with the author, Chennai, India, November 18, 2014). The bonded labor survivors she worked with could not imagine a future for themselves or their children that was not doled out from above.

27. Douglass, *Narrative*, 216.

In Kumar's case, we find ourselves right up against this manipulated process of decision-making. Kumar was making decisions not as a free person, but as though he were someone still enslaved. The only difference was that his master was a different person. Kumar was even a bit confused as to why Aryan and I would find his stated reasons troubling. Under slavery, it is meritorious to have no intention save pleasing the master. He was trying to disclose that no other intentions mattered. As a researcher, I have a duty not only to garner Kumar's informed consent, but also to attempt to assure that his participation in my research is not alienating. Just as consent is the floor level of freedom, garnering informed consent is the floor level of moral obligation that a researcher owes to his interviewees.

Kumar's situation is by no means unique. The social workers themselves testified to routinely having to find ways to reduce the dependency and attachment that their clients would develop toward them. This proved to be no mean feat, and it was accompanied by a complex of new ethical dilemmas when it came to questions of survivor agency. For example, I later interviewed two social workers, "Nisha"[28] and "Sandeep," who informed me that their respective organizations found that they had to educate survivors of bonded labor about family planning methods.[29] This was because most survivors are both economically despondent and have a large number of children to provide for. In such a situation, an educational session on family planning is necessary simply from a survival perspective. However, when captive mentality enters the picture, that conversation must proceed *very carefully*. Both Nisha and Sandeep were aware that they had to present the information in a way that was taken as a suggestion, not a command, because their clients were already primed to discount all intentions aside from pleasing them. Both were concerned that, if a free decision is not made in the fullest sense, then the survivor is in some sense compelled or manipulated into getting a vasectomy. To return to our sight analogy, they would do it, but because they had been ordered to, not because they saw the good in it. Is the proper moral description of such a case "forced sterilization"? Certainly, this is the term we normally use for sterilization that involves compulsion. However, using the categories above ("consent" versus "agency"), this is probably too strong. The client would not be forced (against his will) to accept sterilization, but he would be unused to bringing the full resources

28. The same Nisha mentioned above.

29. "Nisha," interview with the author, Chennai, India, November 7, 2014; "Sandeep," interview with the author, Chennai, India, November 14, 2014.

of his rationality to the table when making a decision, and would thus leave them by the wayside. However, it is very possible that, in such a situation, the decision to get a vasectomy could be alienating. The result would thus still be less than optimal. Thus, the key to avoiding the Scylla of hunger on the one hand and the Charybdis of alienation on the other relies on a connection between will and rationality that most free individuals take for granted. Many survivors find themselves unpracticed in the full process of moral discernment, simply because moral discernment *requires* thick reflection utilizing this connection, whereas the institution of slavery aims at destroying it. Survivors thus often emerge from the institution of slavery with a strange sort of tunnel vision.

Survivors of sex trafficking exhibited the same sort of tunnel vision, but it often came intertwined with the next phenomenon on the list: fascination. So it is probably best to hold off on discussing how sex trafficking survivors exhibit this tunnel vision until fascination has been discussed more fully.

Fascination

Fascination with one's former captor(s) is perhaps the hallmark sign of captive mentality. Perhaps it is best to refer to the survivor in this stage as "enthralled," since the term in modern English usually means that one is mentally captivated by something, but in more archaic English, a "thrall" was simply a term for an enslaved person. Survivors who operate with captive mentality of this sort will try to reach out to their former masters once rescued, and they will often resist any attempts by outside agencies to sever their ties with their master. Survivors in this state often perceive attempts to interfere with this relationship to be invasive. The social workers, court officials, and law enforcement officers are the villains, and the master and his retinue are the support group trying to help the survivor. And many social workers testified that this can even reach beyond the initial, chaotic stages of a rescue. Here again is "Mallika" on the subject:

> **Chris:** How long do they generally try to reach back out to the perpetrators once they're in a home setting? Is it just the initial stages or does it go beyond that?

> **Mallika:** It goes beyond. It is very sad. It just breaks my heart. Because then for me that is a revelation of the amount of . . . I would say, psychological hold that the perpetrators have over the girls. You know, it's just heartbreaking because for me the biggest struggle, I feel, in all of this is the girls don't see themselves as victims. Worse, they see the perpetrators as their saviors. That is the worst thing. I cannot believe it. They don't see us or the shelter home situation or the fact that they are being rescued from an experience . . . they don't understand that at all! And that, I think, is deception of the highest skill. I can't believe the kind of manipulation or psychological hold. So they're choosing. . . . We've had so many girls choosing to go back to their traffickers, to their pimps, to their so-called husbands.[30]

The frequency with which survivors experience this level of captive mentality is difficult to ascertain. I had to rely on estimates to gauge prevalence, because (to my knowledge) no quantitative data exists on incidents of this level of captive mentality among sex trafficking or labor trafficking survivors, either globally or in India. In fact, one social worker told me (off the record) that an anti-trafficking NGO she had previously worked for could only account for about 7 percent of the sex trafficking survivors they had rescued after they were released from institutional aftercare. That means that 93 percent were unaccounted for after rehabilitation, and it is unclear what percentage of that 93 percent had walked right back into a situation of trafficking. However, there is reason to find this statistic deeply unsettling, as every aftercare worker I spoke to testified to a heavy prevalence of this level of captive mentality.[31] Additionally, each

30. "Mallika," interview with the author, Mumbai, India, September 17, 2014.

31. Asha and "Harit" both claimed that young survivors frequently desired to get in contact with their captors, even though they both estimated that re-trafficking or return was extremely rare (Asha, interview with the author, Mumbai, India, September 9, 2014; "Harit," interview with the author, Mumbai, India, December 19, 2014). Megha and Jessica Gunjal contended that nearly every survivor of sex trafficking experiences captive mentality on this level ("Megha," interview with the author, Mumbai, India, September 18, 2014; Jessica Gunjal, interview with the author, Mumbai, India, October 14, 2014). Sunita estimated that "about 50 percent" of survivors experienced captive mentality on this level (Sunita, interview with the author, Mumbai, India, October 1, 2014). Pranitha Timothy, who has experience working with survivors of both labor trafficking and sex trafficking, specified that this level of captive mentality was fairly common in *both* forms of trafficking, in her experience (Pranitha Timothy, interview with the author, Channai, India, November 11, 2014). All social workers who worked with labor trafficking survivors testified that this level of captive mentality was fairly common among survivors—in fact, these interviewees gave the phenomenon

aftercare organization's own internal best practices suggested that this level of captive mentality was assumed to be the norm for all survivors coming through the agency's casework. For example, all aftercare homes for sex trafficking survivors that I spoke to limited phone access to survivors, especially during the first few months of rehabilitation.[32] The social workers that I interviewed confirmed that this was a universal trend.[33] Why was this practice in place? To prevent survivors from calling their captors and identifying which home they were staying in. And phone monitoring trends continued in many of these homes beyond the initial stages of rescue.

The clear assumption here is that it is normal for enslaved people to see the initial intervention in their situation as threatening, and to reach back out to their captors as a defensive measure. For some survivors, this instinct only lasts for a matter of months, until the survivor can be assured that the intent of the intervention is not to permanently incarcerate them (thus exchanging one form of bondage for another). This is a worry that is by no means unfounded, because many survivors have firsthand experience with police corruption and brutality long before any sort of intervention occurs. It may even be the case that the very same officers involved in a rescue operation were guilty of committing an act of police brutality on the survivor at an earlier date. Numerous survivors of sex trafficking testify that their first interaction with police officers is generally not on the raid itself, but in the regular business of the brothel in which they are held. They may frequent the brothel as customers, stop by to receive kickbacks from those who manage the brothel, or even act as enforcers or informants for brothel staff.[34] In situations of labor

the name "captive mentality" in the first place.

32. Asha, interview with the author, Mumbai, India, September 9, 2014; "Harit," interview with the author, Mumbai, India, December 19, 2014; Jessica Gunjal, interview with the author, Mumbai, India, October 14, 2014.

33. "Megha," interview with the author, Mumbai, India, September 18, 2014; "Lucy," interview with the author, Mumbai, India, September 9, 2014; "Mallika," interview with the author, Mumbai, India, September 17, 2014; Bernie and Bennet David, interview with the author, Mumbai, India, December 31, 2014.

34. "Zara," interview with the author, Mumbai, India, November 29, 2014. See also the testimony of Rita in Bales and Trodd, *To Plead Our Own Cause*, 112–19. "Anita" testified that police officers tried to solicit her on multiple occasions, possibly outside of a brothel context ("Anita," interview with the author, Mumbai, India, November 29, 2014). "Aradhna" testified that a male police officer once offered her a place to stay at his house, but she was dissuaded by a female officer who was accompanying him, who warned that Aradhna would be subject to some form of sexual abuse if she took him

trafficking, bonded laborers find that the police are often willing to assist their masters in perpetuating their bondage. Pranitha Timothy and Hannah both testified that they have seen instances in their casework where slaveholders called upon local police to locate and return escaped bonded laborers and the police complied with the request.[35] Beyond this, however, many survivors of bonded labor are accustomed to frequent police harassment due to their position in the caste system. Once survivors come to see NGO staff or government officials as on their side, their desire to reach back out to their captors may dissipate.

For some advocates, the issues above bring into question whether the police are the best agency to stage rescues, given the problems they cause.[36] This is a very worthwhile topic to consider, especially as the practice of policing has come under heavy critique in recent years for related concerns.[37] However, the traumatic effects of police involvement in the rescue cannot solely account for the level of fascination many survivors experience. For some survivors, even a period of months spent in living conditions where basic needs are met and abuse is not present is not enough to convince them that anyone but their master has their best interest in mind. Even though their master has committed acts of abuse against them, they are determined to believe that their master truly exercises love or beneficence toward them. Take for example the testimony of "Savi" on her experience with counseling survivors of sex trafficking:

> **Chris:** Are you seeing any trauma bonds or Stockholm syndrome developing [in your clients]?

---

up on the offer ("Aradhna," interview with the author, Mumbai, India, December 29, 2014). For collaboration between police and traffickers in contexts outside of India, see Dina's testimony in Bales and Trodd, *To Plead Our Own Cause*, 103–6, and Rachel Lloyd's testimony in Lloyd, *Girls Like Us*, 120–23, as well as her summary of collaboration between police and traffickers in some of her client's cases on 124.

35. Pranitha Timothy, interview with the author, Channai, India, November 11, 2014; "Hannah," interview with the author, Chennai, India, November 18, 2014. Naveen likewise testified that police would sometimes tip off owners before raids ("Naveen," interview with the author, Chennai, India, November 12, 2014).

36. Harit's organization formally rejected police intervention in trafficking cases and preferred to extract sex trafficking victims from enslavement through either community interventions or redemption (i.e., literally "buying back" the enslaved person). They argued that involving the police simply opened the enslaved up to further trauma and failed to adequately dissuade the slaveholder from reclaiming the survivor anyway ("Harit," interview with the author, Mumbai, India, December 19, 2014).

37. See for example Vitale, *End of Policing*; Purnell, *Becoming Abolitionists*.

Savi: Actually, this most recent rescue, it seemed a lot like that. And one of our past social workers—we were roommates for a little while—she mentioned with one of her clients, it's just a total focus on the perpetrator, on the accused. It's not at all inwardly driven, it's all. . . . And this past client, I wouldn't say it was Stockholm, necessarily, but just a lack of introspection on, "Okay, this is me. This is what's happening with me right now. I need I need to focus on getting myself in a better place." It wasn't really that at all. Stockholm is a bit more serious than that.

Chris: But in those cases, there is some kind of fixation on the perpetrator? Desire to be with them again, that type of thing?

Savi: Yeah. And then just absolutely denying that they did anything. That "They beat me," or "They stabbed me," or that "They didn't give me any money." Everything was, "No, they took really good care of me," and "I had food to eat." It's two different stories. You know, it's "I had a roof over my head," and "I had food to eat," "I'm alive, so what did they really do that was so bad?" It's not, "They forced me to service 20 customers a night." It's the other side of "I'm safe. I had a place to be. So why would I ever say anything bad about them?"[38]

Such a fixation obtains no less in an American context than in an Indian one. Rachel Lloyd has given a similar assessment of the rose-colored glasses through which survivors she works with view their pimps. She gives an example that very well could have come straight from my interviews:

[Angelina's] still so stuck, physically free but emotionally tied; I know I can't push too hard. If I do I become the bad guy as she defends her love, her man, her experiences and feelings for the last three years. I try a different tack. "Why don't we make a list . . . of the good things and the bad stuff? The things you miss and the stuff you don't. Maybe it'll help sort through some of these feelings . . ."

It is, as always, a jarringly unequal list of pros and cons: *He told me he was my daddy*, plus; *He hit me*, minus; *He takes me on trips*, plus; *He makes me have sex with other men*, minus; *He gave me an STD*, minus; *He beat me with an extension cord*, minus; *He said I was a dumb bitch*, minus; *He told me he loved me*, plus, plus, plus.

38. "Savi," interview with the author, Mumbai, India, September 22, 2014.

As we sit together going over the list, there's an item on the pro side that I don't understand. Her tiny printed handwriting reads *Cheetos*. "Huh, what's this, Angie?"

"You told me to think of the times when he loved me, so there was this one time, when he got mad at something I did, I can't remember what, and he hit me some. And I was crying and shit and so then he left and that made me cry more cos he left me when I was crying. But then he came back and he'd gone to the store and he bought me Cheetos and a chocolate Yoo-Hoo milk."

I look at her a little blankly.

"Cos they were my favorites. And he knew they were my favorites and he got them for me to make me feel better." She smiles at this memory and I can picture her drying her tears—"Thank you, Daddy"—oh, so grateful for $1.25 worth of junk food from the corner bodega. "That's the main time I knew that he really loved me." She must mistake the look of sadness probably creeping across my face as incomprehension, as she explains again, "Cos they were my favorite and that was mad thoughtful of him."

As we continue to go through the list—*Set me up to get raped, Left me in jail*—I'm thinking how easy it is, how little it takes. A bag of Cheetos and chocolate Yoo-Hoo outweighed all the painful, awful, evil stuff he'd done. In the right circumstances, it didn't take much at all.

When someone has the power to take your life but doesn't, you feel grateful.[39]

It may be understandable at this point why I first conflated the phenomenon Lloyd is describing with Stockholm syndrome in the interviews. In hostage or kidnapping situations, the same dynamic is often present. The captor tries to establish their benevolence through what they *refrain* from doing. They could end the captive's life, but they do not. They could deprive the captive of food and allow them to starve, so even an underwhelming provision of food is seen as merciful. It's a predominantly negative concept of benevolence; it assumes the captor is able to take the captive's life at any time and is justified in doing so. Therefore, refraining from doing so is an act of grace. And in situations of Stockholm syndrome, the captor comes to accept this perspective. This is true no less of captive mentality.

39. Lloyd, *Girls Like Us*, 160–62.

This level of captive mentality was also a known phenomenon in US antebellum slavery. Take for example the testimony of Pet Franks, who was born into slavery on a plantation in Mississippi. Franks continued to live with his former masters after he was liberated. He exhibits many of the same attitudes that can be found in rehabilitating survivors of modern slavery. For example, he wholeheartedly accepts his former masters' claims to benevolence:

> I knows all about slavery and de war. I was right dere on the spot where it all happened. I wish to goodness we was back dere now, not in de war but in de slavery times. Niggers where I lived didn't have nothin' to worry about in them days.[40]

Franks admits that some enslaved people he knows had it quite bad (he even testifies that he witnessed one enslaved person die of exposure and another being ruthlessly tortured by his master), yet he assesses this situation in terms of the moral qualities of those masters.[41] Good masters make life easy for their slaves, Pet asserts. Those other enslaved people just had bad masters. However, like many modern survivors of slavery, he simultaneously downplays the violence he experienced while enslaved under "good" masters:

> We had a good overseer, his name was Marse Frank Beeks and he was as fine a white man as ever lived. I doan never 'member him whippin' one of his niggers, *leastways not real whippin's.*[42]

Formerly enslaved individuals who articulated opinions like Franks' were the object of a fair amount of vitriol from Black abolitionists, precisely because they gave proslavery whites ammunition in narrating slavery as a benevolent institution.[43] In fact, in the theologies of enslaved Christians and in Black abolitionist literature, one can find this phenomenon labeled directly as a desire to "return to Egypt" (drawing on the language

40. Pet Franks, quoted in Rawick, *American Slave*, 797.

41. Sanders, "Liberation Ethics," 77.

42. Franks, quoted in Rawick, *American Slave*, 795, emphasis added. See also Douglass, *Narrative*, 119, where Douglass speaks of Mr. Hopkins, whom the enslaved laborers considered a "good overseer," not because he refused to whip those who were enslaved, but because he took no joy in it when he whipped them (unlike other overseers).

43. See for example, Article 2 of Walker, *Appeal*. The entire article is a condemnation of the various ways enslaved Blacks help to bolster the ongoing existence of chattel slavery.

of the Exodus narrative). However, given the polemical context, they understandably identified this phenomenon as a clear moral failing on the part of the enthralled survivor. The captive mentality of other enslaved African-Americans made their own freedom far more tenuous. Given a shift in context, I am trying to move away from that negative moral evaluation in modern rehabilitative programs.

An alternative response was captured well during the period of American antebellum slavery by Frederick Douglass, who saw captive mentality at work (though he didn't call it by that name), and saw it as ultimately a very human response:

> It is partly in consequence of such facts [i.e., that enslaved people are punished for finding fault in their masters], that slaves, when inquired of as to their condition and the character of their masters, almost universally say they are contented, and that their masters are kind. The slaveholders have been known to send in spies among their slaves, to ascertain their views and feelings in regard to their condition. The frequency of this has had the effect to establish among the slaves the maxim, that a still tongue makes a wise head. They suppress the truth rather than take the consequences of telling it, and in so doing prove themselves a part of the human family. If they have anything to say of their masters, it is generally in their masters' favor, especially when speaking to an untried man. I have frequently been asked, when a slave, if I had a kind master, and do not remember ever to have given a negative answer; nor did I, in pursuing this course, consider myself as uttering what was absolutely false; for I always measured the kindness of my master by the standard of kindness set up among slaveholders around us. Moreover, slaves are like other people, and imbibe prejudices quite common to others. They think their own better than that of others. Many, under the influence of this prejudice, think their own masters are better than the masters of other slaves; and this, even when the very reverse is true. Indeed, it is not uncommon for slaves even to fall out and quarrel among themselves about the relative goodness of their masters, each contending for the superior goodness of his own over that of the others. . . . They seemed to think that the greatness of their masters was transferable to themselves.[44]

44. Douglass, *Narrative*, 127–28.

What Douglass is describing is a level of fascination whereby enslaved people not only come to see their masters as good, but also come to see their masters as a part of themselves.

Even if an enslaved person does not jump to the defense of their master as in the examples above, many are still "fascinated" in the sense that they have imbibed their master's concepts of love and justice wholesale. As strange as it may sound, a significant number of enslaved people do not see the various forms of violence that occur to them while bonded as forms of abuse. In fact, the overwhelming majority of bonded labor survivors *don't even know they are bonded* until they encounter someone who can provide them with a definition of bonded labor.[45] They don't see their situation as inherently unjust.

This explains in part why it is that sex trafficking organizations predominantly target teenage runaways from abusive families for induction into sex slavery, and why bonded labor organizations predominantly target people from oppressed castes for recruitment;[46] both groups are in some sense already socially primed to believe the claims to love and beneficence that their masters make. If a girl has been brought up to believe that love is fully compatible with acts of violence and degradation, then when she falls under the power of a master, it will make sense to her that he alternatively beats her and professes his love for her. Similarly, if a bonded laborer is told from birth that his degraded position within the caste system is for the good of society, then it will make sense to him that

45. Kadavul, Kumar, Vijaya, Maha, and the unnamed couple all testified that they had no idea that they were bonded ("Kadavul," interview with the author, Chennai, India, November 6, 2014; "Kumar" and "Vijaya," interview with the author, Chennai, India, November 6, 2014; "Maha," interview with the author, Chennai, India, November 6, 2014; unnamed couple, interview with the author, Channai, India, November 10, 2014). Hannah and Manav confirmed that they commonly hear this sentiment from bonded laborers in their work ("Hannah," interview with the author, Chennai, India, November 18, 2014; "Manav," interview with the author, Chennai, India, November 18, 2014). Naveen testified in 2014 that many government officials whose job description includes the enforcement of the Bonded Labor Act did not even know what bonded labor was, and they frequently denied that it occurred in their district despite abundant evidence to the contrary ("Naveen," interview with the author, Chennai, India, November 12, 2014). Public and governmental awareness of the issue has, however, increased in Tamil Nadu since Naveen gave his interview.

46. "Naveen," interview with the author, Chennai, India, November 12, 2014; "Nisha," interview with the author, Chennai, India, November 7, 2014; "Harit," interview with the author, Mumbai, India, December 19, 2014; Sunita and Erin, interview with the author, Mumbai, India, October 1, 2014. See also the statistics provided by Rachel Lloyd in Lloyd, *Girls Like Us*, 33–34.

his master alternatively beats him and professes beneficence toward him. The sense of duty toward the master may even increase in such situations if the care the master extends toward the enslaved person (when he is not subjecting them to abuse) exceeds that which they can normally expect to receive from family and society. The thinnest of loves can powerfully obligate when real love is in meager supply.

A particularly illuminating instance of how this takes hold can be found in Rachel Lloyd's own experience of reintegration. Soon after coming out of "the life," Rachel is hanging out with two new friends, David and Sonia. David and Sonia are married to each other and have two young children. The five of them are watching *The Little Mermaid* together, when the following scene unfolds:

> Toward the end of the afternoon, my entire worldview is shaken when David asks for a cup of tea. Sonia and I go into the kitchen, start chitchatting while she prepares some snacks for the kids, and we come back out sans tea. "Where's my tea?" David asks, and I steel myself, preparing for the scene that's about to come.
>
> Sonia, who has sat down, begins to rise. "Oh, I'm sorry, I forgot, honey." Any moment now. I'm waiting for the explosion.
>
> "It's OK, babe, I'll make it myself, don't worry about it," says David, and with that he smiles, rubs her shoulder, and trots off to the kitchen to make it himself.
>
> I'm stunned. Sonia is acting like everything is normal, but I'm having a hard time figuring this out. What just happened? What happened to the explosion, the anger, the disgust with her forgetfulness? I try to hold it, knowing somewhere in my head that my question is about to sound marginally crazy, but I need an answer.
>
> "Why didn't he hit you?" I whisper, worried David will hear.
>
> "Huh?" Sonia is confused.
>
> "I mean"—frustrated that she's not getting the obvious—"why didn't you get in trouble over the tea, why didn't he yell at you or something?"
>
> Sonia looks like she wants to laugh, but when she realizes that I'm serious, she looks horrified.
>
> "Oh, sweetie. That's not how we do things in this house. Ever. That's not how people should ever treat each other." Now she just looks sad.
>
> "Oh, OK." I feel bad that I've upset her and realize that I've betrayed exactly what I've been trying so hard to hide. I'm embarrassed.

> David comes back in with a tea for himself and one for me and one for her. This is just too much. He must be the nicest man on the planet. I'm completely thrown off.
>
> Sonia, guessing that we probably need to discuss this whole "Why doesn't he hit you?" thing a little more, tells him we're going into the kitchen for some girl talk. We spend the rest of the afternoon talking about love and abuse and how they're not the same thing. While I think I probably know this intellectually, at nineteen it's the first time that I've ever really begun to believe it. Putting this realization into practice will take a few more years.[47]

Lloyd goes on to mention exactly what this unlearning process requires. Even when a survivor reaches the point where she feels comfortable dating again, she may end up sabotaging relationships with men who don't hit her, thinking that they don't care enough about her.[48] They aren't "passionate" about her. Passion is equated with anger, and anger with physical abuse. If "passion" doesn't overflow to the point where it results in physical violence, then the wellspring must simply be very shallow. In this way of thinking, violence isn't merely compatible with love; love is *demonstrated* by violence.

As Lloyd mentions, this seems incredible to anyone raised in a stable, loving environment. And on some intellectual level, she knew that. She knew love mixed with violence was a farce. But prior to this incident, she has narrated so many instances where "boyfriends," pimps, and johns have alternately tried to beat her half to death and pronounced their love to her. Habit simply buries what she knows on a rational basis.

According to the conception of love embodied in most forms of slavery, love and violence are not incompatible. Indeed, on this way of thinking, violence (or threat of violence) is a necessary element of love, since violence (or threat of violence) is a necessary element of slavery. Without such violence, love is, in some sense, lacking. Lack of violence could indicate lack of intensity, lack of passion (as Lloyd expressed above). Or it could indicate lack of care or oversight, an abdication of the master's proper responsibilities as a benevolent father figure. "If he doesn't hit me,

47. Lloyd, *Girls Like Us*, 196–7.

48. Lloyd, *Girls Like Us*, 198–9. See also Lloyd's reflection on the connection between domestic violence and training sex trafficking victims in the chapter entitled "Family," 47–65.

how will I learn?" is a sentiment often expressed by survivors under the effects of captive mentality.[49]

What lessons are enslaved people meant to learn? This is typically difficult for survivors to put into words (aside from the general maxims "don't make the master mad" and "the master is superior"), because the violent discipline that defines slavery is a rather ineffective educational tool. Part of the reason for this is because violent discipline in slavery serves a double purpose. In many cases, punishment is doled out not because the enslaved person has violated some standard, but because the master perceives a need for his honor to be reaffirmed. Drawing on Patterson's definition of slavery discussed in the last chapter, a constituent element of slavery is that the master draws honor from the degradation of the enslaved. So, when a master abuses an enslaved person, he may be doing so to turn that person into a pliable subject, or he may be doing so simply because he needs a reaffirmation of his own honor and status. Thus, punishment can happen even when no standard has been violated, and it is impossible for most enslaved people to completely avoid punishment, no matter how obedient they are. Nevertheless, since the justification of the punishment is that it is educative, the enslaved person is often left with the inchoate sense that they have violated some standard, even in situations where it is impossible to identify any standard that has been violated. Confusion over a master's arbitrariness is a normal part of an enslaved person's experience, and it is reinforced by the breakdown of rationality that occurs in trauma. The enslaved person is actively dissuaded from recognizing inconsistencies in the master's behavior. Love under slavery is inherently arbitrary, rather than constant, because the master is arbitrary, rather than constant.

Violence becomes so normalized in contexts of slavery, that it is not at all uncommon for violence to "trickle down" into an enslaved person's other intimate relationships (even after rescue). For example, among survivors of labor trafficking, domestic abuse is shockingly common, and labor trafficking survivors in Tamil Nadu are shockingly frank about this:

> **Hannah:** Yeah. I would say our Tamil Nadu clients are very open with their trauma, for the most part. When you go to those rescues, a lot of them break down in tears, they're grabbing people's feet. . . . I see a lot of brokenness in those clients. They just let it out. They'll *openly* admit to substance abuse, they'll *openly*

49. See for instance Rachel Lloyd's conversation with a survivor named Tyria in Lloyd, *Girls Like Us*, 199–201.

> admit to domestic violence. I've had people proudly declaring that they beat their wives.[50]

Latha and Subramani (two labor trafficking survivors I interviewed who are married to each other), reported no domestic abuse in their immediate family, but claimed it was common in their post-rescue community, and even their extended family:

> **Latha:** My younger sister's husband, he's also one of the rescued bonded laborers. In the previous community, he used to live with us. And he is into drugs. He'd do all the drugs, he'd do injection, and he'll have sex with many women. . . . So, one fine day, my sister told me about this issue. And what happened is, he just randomly went into the community. He was trying to rape a small girl.
>
> **Chris:** Oh, wow.
>
> **Latha:** And my sister found out. My sister saw that, and she went and intervened. And she started fighting. And he was drunk. He was totally under the influence of alcohol. And he attacked my sister. He attacked my sister so badly that the blood was all over her face. And that's when she came up to me and told me all the problems she was going through. In fact, he was the one who had been supporting us and helping us a lot in [the] rescue and everything.[51] And we never know that he would be this kind of thing. And he used to sleep outside the home, and this problem was actually going [on] for many days. But we did not know this, and only after this thing happened, we came to know that all this kind of thing is going on there. That's when we decided to move.[52]

Hannah, a social worker I interviewed who works with survivors of labor trafficking, expressed the connection between captive mentality and trickle-down violence in the following way:

50. "Hannah," interview with the author, Chennai, India, November 18, 2014.

51. This may mean that Latha's brother-in-law was one of the initial informants to the NGO that rescued them. In any case, he seems to have been very involved with the rescue effort.

52. "Latha" and "Subramani," interview with the author, Chennai, India, November 10, 2014. Later in the interview, Latha also testified that "everyone had a problem after the rescue. But we never had a problem with our family." She was implying that substance abuse and domestic violence were rampant within her survivor community.

> **Hannah:** And also the other aspect of the captivity mentality is the violence you see. So, they're used to being beaten. The person who is in power is the one who beats them. And so, then if the husband is in power, he beats his wife. She's in power of the children, so she beats the children. And the children beat the animals.
>
> **Chris:** It just keeps going down?
>
> **Hannah:** It goes all the way down. Although, the women also beat the husbands. It's not that clear-cut. But violence *fills* their families. Because that is all they've seen for the past five, ten years. And they know no other way of solving problems or expressing frustration, because that's just what the person in charge does.[53]

Such trickle-down violence may be additionally reinforced by the effects of PTSD. In trauma literature, a compulsion to repeat violence is considered a common symptom of PTSD. Survivors with PTSD may recapitulate violence as a way of making sense of the violence inflicted upon them in a past traumatic event. Sometimes this is done in self-destructive ways (such as cutting), sometimes this is done by lashing out against others.[54] However, I do not believe trauma alone is sufficient to explain the commonality of violence Hannah and other social workers I interviewed reported. Not all who suffer from PTSD lash out in violent ways. And even if survivors are not suffering from PTSD, if violence is the only way they have learned to cope with household conflict, violence will continue to be the tool they turn to. But the common experience of trauma in survivor communities probably does not do much to help matters.

Pranitha Timothy—a social worker who has worked with survivors of sex and labor trafficking since the early 2000s—even claimed that, among bonded laborers suffering heavily from captive mentality, one often sees an *intensification* of violence. She had this to say about *mestris*, which are overseers of bonded laborers who are bonded themselves:

53. "Hannah," interview with the author, Chennai, India, November 18, 2014.

54. Jones, *Trauma and Grace*, 30. Judith Herman reports a case study which combines both elements. She tells the story of an incest survivor who tried to reenact the confrontation between herself and her abuser by playing chicken with male motorists on the highway. The result was obviously quite dangerous for both her and the other motorists, and the survivor did not seek help for this behavior until she caused an accident (thankfully, a non-fatal one). See Herman, *Trauma and Recovery*, 40, for a synopsis of the case.

Pranitha: I think as human behavior, [bonded laborers] begin to adapt, and they begin to see, "Yes, if I give in to the owner, he begins to give me power. He begins to give me the acknowledgment that I want. He begins to appreciate my work." And so, that give-and-take relationship begins to build. And many of them, from being victims, become the most trusted ally of the perpetrator. And then they begin to actually do the same things that the perpetrator did to the rest of the victims. And I have seen that pattern in almost *every* case. Like, if you take a rice mill, the most cruel person is a co-laborer who's won the heart of the owner.

Chris: Oh, I see. So the owner will put them over other bonded laborers . . .

Pranitha: [*agreeing*] Over the other laborers.

Chris: They're essentially a . . . in terms of legalized slave structures, they're a driver, a manager, a . . .

Pranitha: They become like them. So even if someone escapes, he uses them to track them down and bring them back. So, I guess it's in need of survival, as well as affirmation. Just the attention that the owner can give them. So, many of them end up trying to please him. And in many cases, the owner builds a trusting relationship with the victim.

Recall once again the honor dynamics that Patterson describes within any system of slavery. The situation that Pranitha describes makes perfect sense in light of these dynamics. The *mestri* intensifies violence because he realizes how precarious his situation is. By beating his fellow worker, he proves that he is the one who violently degrades, not the one who is violently degraded. By doing this, he receives recognition (what Pranitha calls "acknowledgement") from the master. He is attempting to move away from his enslaved status and ascend to master status. However, at the end of the day, he is still in bondage to the master. His movement is either slight or illusory. So, he redoubles his efforts, trying to reaffirm his position through increasing violence. Under slavery, violence is not only a necessary component of love, it is how one ascends.[55]

55. At this point, to be fair, I should mention that there was one interviewee involved in aftercare for bonded laborers who questioned the link between trickle-down violence and captive mentality. She argued that no causative connection had yet been established, and the high incidence of domestic violence among survivors could be due to a general culture of violence within India itself (I should probably add here

To what does such violence allow one to ascend?

The Master Is God

The final form of captive mentality involves the explicit or implicit recognition of the master as divine in some sense. When speaking on my research findings, this is generally the category that is received as the most outlandish. And yet it pops up in the strangest of places without prompting. Here, for example, is a segment of an interview I did with "Ravi," a researcher who works for an anti-trafficking NGO in Chennai:

> **Chris:** In that kind of a situation, have forms of Stockholm syndrome manifested?
>
> **Ravi:** Yes. There is a phenomenon. . . . This is one of the biggest challenges that we have. So, when we talk to laborers, there are some. . . . Like, there are a group of fifty laborers, out of which, forty of them want to liberate themselves from the situation of oppression. They want to seek—actively—help from someone, to desperately get out of this. But there'll be some ten people who will be so fearful, and they'll also have some undeserved loyalty towards their owners. So, because of that dependency, they are completely dependent for their next meal, everything is being provided by this person who's exploiting them. So, they create that kind of an affiliation towards the person [on] whom they're dependent. And they tend to see that person as a god. "This is a god-man who provides all my needs. So, whenever I am in need, I am going to this person, and this person is providing. How can I betray this person?"
>
> **Chris:** Will they actually express it in those terms? Seeing this person as a deity?

---

that this interviewee was Indian herself). However, she was an administrator, and not a direct service provider, and she pointed this out because she was worried about resource management for her organization. If domestic violence couldn't be shown to be directly caused by bonded labor, then the responsibility to "unlearn" that violence didn't fall to an organization providing aftercare to bonded laborers. Given Pranitha and Hannah's testimony based on services they've provided directly, combined with Patterson's heuristic analysis, it seems that there *is* a clear link between domestic violence and bonded labor. The latter may not serve as the sole cause of the former, but it certainly strongly reinforces it both as a good, proper, loving household management practice and a means to ascension to the head of household (the master's spot).

Ravi: Yes.[56]

While I introduced the topic in clinical terms, Ravi (and the laborers he is speaking of) found a theological term ("god") more illuminative of their relationship with their owners. At first blush, it may seem that what Ravi is describing might only be germane to a polytheist Hindu belief system, or perhaps a tribal belief system.[57] If the gods of this world are plural and immanent, then it makes sense that the master could be one of them. And we do see this in practice: in some areas of rural India, you can find the belief that those who are higher in the social hierarchy are the gods of their subordinates cropping up in several forms.[58] Some also might suggest that the Indian caste system is the real culprit behind the attribution of divinity to the master. Since the caste system encourages forms of absolute dependence, and the caste system is divinely reinforced, it is natural for someone caught up within it to refer to those who hold authority over them as "gods." And bonded laborers in India overwhelmingly come from low-caste groups. I believe there is some truth to this suggestion; the caste system certainly does reinforce this trend. But the fact is, I have seen this sentiment expressed among both American and British survivors of slavery, none of whom have any experience of India's caste system. Here again it is helpful to return to Rachel Lloyd's description of her relationship with her own captor:

> Omnipotent, omniscient, omnipresent. Even though it takes me years to actually be able to say omniscient properly—I'll call it omniscience—I know exactly what it means, both the dictionary definition, "having complete or unlimited knowledge, awareness, or understanding," and how it plays out in my real life. I know that he knows everything about me, past, present, and future. I know that he is all of the "omnis," he's all-powerful, all-knowing, and no matter where I go, he's there. Even when I run away, he finds me, like a part of my skin, he's in my bloodstream. When he tells me that even if I get married, have children, and

56. "Ravi," interview with the author, Chennai, India, November 5, 2014.

57. One cannot assume a Hindu majority for the Irular (as would be the case for India's population in general). Many Adivasi are adherents of tribal religions unrelated to Hinduism. However, some of my Irular interviewees were Hindu. One ("Maha") was a Christian.

58. For example, one can find rural Indian contexts where the belief that husbands are gods that must be worshipped by their wives is widespread. See Pandey, "Calling Your Husband by Name." Gavin Flood also points out that, in classical Hinduism, kings are seen as divine. See Flood, *Introduction to Hinduism*, 67–69.

> am gone for ten years, he'll find me, I believe him. When he says that I'll have no choice but to go with him, that I'll always belong to him, that I was born to be his, I believe him.
>
> No one knows what I've gone through like he does, largely due to the fact that he was there, putting me through it. During my first few months in the United States, almost three years since we'd last been together, as memories are stirred and trauma revisited, he'll be the only one I want to talk to. The only one who'll understand. I call him, ostensibly for closure but truthfully because despite all my progress, there is a part of me that is still glued to him. We talk until the wee hours and slowly I get sucked back into believing that we can be together, until one night when he asks me to wire him some money and I refuse. His reaction, angry, violent, threatening, is so familiar that even on the phone with him thousands of miles away in another state, I get on the floor and cover my head with my hands. I change my number the next morning.[59]

In Lloyd's case, reference to her pimp as God is explicit. She testifies to having learned the meaning and practical content of the primary attributes ascribed to God in Christian theology precisely through her relationship with her pimp. And if God is known precisely through the exercise of absolute power—of being able to dole out death on a whim, but mercifully refusing to—then there is no practical difference between God and one's master in the everyday life of an enslaved person. Lloyd is an evangelical Christian, and this is still the language that makes the most sense of the ongoing hold that her former master exercises over her life.[60]

The connection between Godhood and mastery reaches its apex in India when sex trafficking is conjoined with what is known as *devadasism*. *Devadasis* are girls dedicated to a god at a very young age (frequently the goddess Yellamma), and then formally inducted into temple prostitution.[61] They are then pimped out to various customers. Given

59. Lloyd, *Girls Like Us*, 185–6.

60. See also the passage written by Henry Box Brown that was quoted in chapter 1 for an even more direct attribution of Godhood to the master due to the power that he seems to wield. And once again, Brown is articulating this connection from within a Christian belief system, rather than a Hindu one.

61. Shankar, *Devadasi Cult*, 17. According to Shankar, the term *devadasi* itself means "female slave of the deity" (vii, 21). Shankar also notes that inductees into *devadasism* are frequently Dalit (18), and thus, the practice of *devadasism* can function as a form of caste oppression (vii). In Maharashtra (and other states), the dedication of

the young age at which they are inducted, the brainwashing aspects of captive mentality that my interviewees described (i.e., level three of captive mentality, above) have a particularly strong hold on *devadasis*. NGO staff who work with *devadasis* on rehabilitation testify that the *devadasis* themselves often see their sexual slavery as divinely ordained, and their slavery plays a role in the economy of salvation. In other words, they are called by God (or a god) to serve as a sex slave. Given the fact that their religious beliefs are so strongly tied to their enslavement, *devadasis* are often considered the hardest cases to rehabilitate in abolitionist circles.

In the regions in which I did my interviews, *devadasism* is uncommon (though its survivors do end up running into some of the NGO workers I interviewed from time to time).[62] However, sex trafficking survivors sometimes do express the belief that their bondage was divinely ordained, even if they were not *devadasis* during their period of enslavement:

> **Savi:** [In counseling sessions,] we usually don't talk about anything religious. . . . [However,] if she brings it up, then you address it, and you do it in a very wide, "God loves you, and this is not . . ." "If God is love, then . . ." "These things happen, but it's not something that God willed for you, or that God planned for this to happen to you." But that only ever comes out if the girl brings it out herself. That's not something that we bring up at all.
>
> **Chris:** Okay. So, you have had some interactions with girls where they've expressed feelings that they are in some way divinely ordained to occupy this particular position as a sex worker?
>
> **Savi:** [*nodding*] I did have somebody say that to me. She . . . Well, a lot of them are usually just angry. "Why did God let this happen? Why did God let this happen to me?" That's a question we've been asked. But another girl once told me, "If I didn't do this work, then maybe that man would have raped his daughter in his own home. So, it's better that he comes and sees me in a

---

girls as devadasis is illegal (157–58). However, several anti-trafficking NGOs in India testify that the practice is still common in rural areas, even in states where *devadasism* is formally illegal.

62. Sunita and Erin, interview with the author, Mumbai, India, October 1, 2014. Bernie and Bennet David, interview with the author, Mumbai, India, December 31, 2014. Two of my child bride survivor interviewees were from a caste and region among which *devadasism* is common, though it is not clear whether they were directly at risk of being forcibly inducted into *devadasism*. If they were at risk, it is clear that neither actually was successfully inducted.

> brothel than raping his daughter in his own house." So, it's a very warped way that they normalize the rape or the abuse.[63]

Pranitha Timothy verified this tendency:

> **Pranitha:** The cases I've worked with, survivors of sex trafficking. . . . Especially, there were two girls whose mothers sold them. They didn't even know that what the mother was doing was wrong until we began working with them. So, even the whole concept of right and wrong, and that. . . . They completely believed that this was the purpose of their life. That's why they're born. That's why girls are born.[64]

In other words, for some survivors, sex slavery is providential. They see it as their *calling.*

The root problem here is not only *who* is identified as God, but *how* God is identified. In what is described above, God is identified simply through the possession of absolute power. And that power is not only absolute, it is raw: raw in the sense that the power that identifies God lacks both specific methods and specific aims. There is no vision of goodness that limits how divine power is exercised, and there is no means by which God refuses to exercise this power. The problem here is that such a conception of God is not unique to systems of slavery. If enslaved people suffering from captive mentality are wrong in identifying their captors as God, why are they wrong? Is it merely because God has more power than their masters? Is God simply a slaveowner writ large?

Ultimately, I think the answer to that last question is "no." But I also believe that a more comprehensive answer can be given. But such an answer will have to retool not only the enslaved person's conception of God, but love and justice as well.

Recovery from Captive Mentality

Now that we have not only cataloged the manifestations of captive mentality but have also unearthed its conception of love, justice, and God, how do we deal with it? How does one expose such conceptions as false? How does one help loosen the mental and spiritual chains survivors find themselves bound by?

63. "Savi," interview with the author, Mumbai, India, September 22, 2014.

64. Pranitha Timothy, interview with the author, Channai, India, November 11, 2014.

One rubric that seems to be making a considerable amount of impact among sex trafficking survivors is a form of modified TFCBT (Trauma-Focused Cognitive Behavioral Therapy). This is what Savi guides her counselees through in Mumbai.[65] What Savi finds most effective about the rubric that she uses is that it focuses strongly on "psycho-education." In this context, psycho-education seems to encompass a basic education in: (1) forms of abuse, (2) trauma, (3) reproduction and sexual health, (4) emotional vocabulary,[66] and (5) coping mechanisms.[67] Each of these aspects of psycho-education is important, but for our purposes, the first (education in forms of abuse) is paramount when attempting to address

65. According to Savi, they actually use three different models of TFCBT (the rubric they use has been tailored quite extensively). What is described here is a general picture of the rubric.

66. Here's Savi's description of the emotional vocabulary sessions:

> **Savi:** *We teach them about the different kinds of emotions; it's not just "I'm happy," "I'm sad." There's a whole other plethora of emotions that we feel. Even "happy" can have layers of happy and your "sadness" has multiple layers of sadness. So, we do that: helping them to identify emotions that they might be feeling. Then we go over "Thinking." So, we teach them about the cognitive triangle . . . [Savi starts to draw the triangle in her notebook] in this part. So "Thinking" basically goes over positive and negative thought patterns. And then we teach them about the cognitive triangle, which basically talks about the relationship of your emotions, your thinking, and your behavior. So, your emotions usually affect the way you think, and then the way you think affects how you behave. And so, there's this whole. . . . And then that goes back to how you feel. So, this is like a very crucial part of therapy: trying to help them understand this whole cycle. But then, this is also one of the most difficult things to teach them, because most of our girls only have a very, very low literacy level. And there's very, very little emotional . . .*
>
> **Chris:** *. . . reflection?*
>
> **Savi:** *[said in a "that too, but that wasn't the word I was looking for" tone] . . . reflection . . . But for a lot of them, nobody's ever asked them, "How do you feel?" So, whenever you just ask them how they feel, "Oh, I'm happy." Even when you do activities with them. Like, you can do something as simple as a game, and then when you ask them, "How did you feel when you played that game?" everybody says, "I'm happy." "How was the game?" "It was good." That seems to be like the only level that they know and understand. So, it's very . . . like emotional . . . I don't want to call it "immaturity," but . . . just a lack of intelligence on that plane* ("Savi," interview with the author, Mumbai, India, September 22, 2014).

67. In this case, mindfulness, deep breathing exercises, and muscle relaxation are the primary coping mechanisms this rubric focuses on. The aim of teaching them coping mechanisms is to help deal with anger/anxiety/etc. that falls out of their trauma.

captive mentality. Here's Savi's description of what happens in a session that deals with forms of abuse:

> **Savi:** So, we have this little chart that's actually just all kinds of different abuse, but done on a little bit of a kiddie level. But for a lot of them, you can literally see this little light bulb going off in their head, because they're looking at the pictures, and then they realize, "Okay, this happened to me. That's one thing. Okay, this happened to me. That's another thing. This happened to me. Okay, that's a third thing. So, there are three major things that have happened in my life." And then, just the way you then deal with that realization, and you deal with that light bulb going off . . . that equips them to go ahead.[68]

Such sessions allow survivors to come to the conclusion that their former master was abusive on their own. Without the question of their loyalty at stake, as they learn what sorts of behaviors constitute abuse, they slowly associate past behavior with abuse, and begin to think that perhaps he was not, in fact, loving or benevolent toward them. This is the "light bulb" moment Savi is describing.

For survivors of labor trafficking, I could not find situations where clinical therapy methods were widely implemented.[69] However, some (but not all) of the objectives Savi lays out when she describes how TFCBT engages in psycho-education were met by sessions designed to educate survivors on the nature of their exploitation. The "Freedom Trainings" held by IJM mentioned in the introduction are one such educational program. Freedom Trainings are three-day-long programs that IJM provides for labor trafficking survivors shortly after rescue,[70] which aim to address various topics that are germane to the survivor's transition into freedom.

68. "Savi," interview with the author, Mumbai, India, September 22, 2014.

69. I could, however, find intermittent implementation. Nisha mentioned that she doesn't do much in the way of clinical therapies anymore, but at one time she was doing cognitive behavioral therapy with clients. Most of her work at the time I interviewed her involved appreciative inquiry to help them find alternative employment ("Nisha," interview with the author, Chennai, India, November 7, 2014). Likewise, Pranitha Timothy mentioned that she was experimenting with "logotherapy," a therapy regimen that comes from the work of the psychiatrist and Holocaust survivor Victor Frankl (Pranitha Timothy, interview with the author, Channai, India, November 11, 2014).

70. One interviewee claimed that these were offered thirty days after rescue, another claimed sixty days after rescue. It is not clear to me which is the case, but for our purposes here, the content of Freedom Training is more important than its exact timing.

The last session of Freedom Training is simply called "We Are Free." During the "We Are Free" session, social workers participate in various roleplays with the survivors. One scenario covered in the roleplays imagines the owner coming back to the community and demanding that the survivors continue to work for him.[71] Another scenario imagines community backlash against the survivors, accusing them of defrauding the owner. Both scenarios deal with a common way of narrating the situation that their former owners use to try to pressure them back into slavery: the survivors have defrauded the owner (and thereby taken advantage of his beneficence). The argument goes like this: The owner was kind enough to offer a loan to these workers to discharge their current debts. To pay back that debt, the owner allowed them to come and work for him to pay it off. He even provided them with food and shelter to accommodate this transition. And now these former workers are manipulating the legal system to unjustly discharge the debt they owe him, and they are walking off scot-free. What they are doing is the height of fraud and financial irresponsibility, and the justice system is rewarding them for this. If the owner convinces the community to view the situation in this way, various forms of backlash can occur. Worse, if the survivor comes to view things this way (which is especially likely if they are suffering from captive mentality), then they will return to a situation of slavery out of feelings of guilt and fear.

Educational sessions which directly address these claims help prepare survivors for situations in which such sentiments may be invoked to re-enslave them. Pranitha Timothy explained how she coaches survivors in how to respond to claims that they have defrauded their former master:

71. The prosecution rate for bonded labor cases in India is extremely low. Bonded labor is primarily seen as a labor issue in Southern India, rather than a human rights abuse. At the time of my interviews, IJM was trying to change the legal framework with which the issue is viewed from "labor violation" to "civil rights violation" in order to underscore the seriousness of the offense. Owners frequently are not prosecuted or are given "slap on the wrist" punishments. One such commonly prescribed punishment requires the owner to "stand until the rising of the court," which means that the owner must simply stand in the back of the courtroom until the court adjourns for the day. If the owner were charged with the criminal offense of holding slaves (IPC 370), the punishment would be much more severe, but as it stands, holding someone in a bonded labor situation is frequently dealt with legally by requiring the slaveholder to stand for a few hours. Thus, it is not at all unusual for the owner to be free to re-enter the survivors' village and harass the survivors after rescue (Ebenezer, interview with the author, Chennai, India, November 12, 2014).

> **Pranitha:** So, we teach them to say that, "It's not in your hands whether you get out of slavery or not. It's a legal proceeding. And the government came to rescue you. So, you shared what was happening there, and the government decided that it was a situation of bonded labor. And based on your statement, they sent you out. So, you don't have to feel guilty about anything." So, we talk them through those processes, and teach them how to respond to the community when they're accused of cheating the owner. When they feel guilty. And then we teach them, we show them how they owe the owner nothing. Because if we calculate the debt and the minimum wages that the owner did not give them, actually *he* owes *them* money. So, we have to dispel or actually crush or shatter all the lies that they told, in order for them to understand the truth. So, we shatter the lies one by one, we take the lies they believe in, and then we explained that, and then help them to see that they owe nothing to the owner.[72]

The argument Pranitha gives here is actually an expanded form of an argument given long ago by Thomas Aquinas. Aquinas held that, if anyone withholds that which is due to another, that person has committed a form of theft.[73] This has traditionally been extended specifically to wages in Christian ethics, and thus any employer who withholds wages (even in part) from a worker commits theft. Thus, owners who withhold wages from their laborers (thereby prohibiting them from paying off their debts) are engaged in an unjust practice.[74] On a related note, Aquinas also held that it was immoral to charge "usury" based on Exod 22:25.[75] In modern Christian circles, there is a debate between whether "usury"

72. Pranitha Timothy, interview with the author, Channai, India, November 11, 2014.

73. Aquinas, *ST*, II.ii.66.3, reply to objection 2.

74. Raja, one of my interviewees, testified that this occurred in his family's case: the owner of the brick kiln where his parents were bonded would purposefully hold wages from them. However, Raja saw an additional reason for why they did this that is not discussed above. Raja believes that the owner underpaid his parents so they could not pay for schooling for Raja and his siblings. And on days that Raja and his siblings did not go to school, they were working at the brick kiln. Thus, the owner underpaid them to get more workers for the day (Raja, interview with the author, Chennai, India, November 12, 2014).

75. Aquinas, *ST*, II.ii.78.1, sed contra. Exodus 22:25 reads, "If you lend money to my people, to the poor among you, you shall not deal with them as a creditor; you shall not exact interest from them." An almost exact parallel can be found in Leviticus 25:36.

means "charging excessive interest" or "charging any interest at all."[76] Either would apply in the case of most bonded laborers: their wages are generally so low that it is not difficult to charge just enough interest that it is impossible to pay it back with the worker's daily wage. The worker then gets deeper and deeper in debt, cementing their bondage into a permanent condition. Thus, owners who charge their workers (excessive) interest are engaged in an unjust practice.[77]

Though Aquinas does not go into the other conditions that legally qualify a labor situation as bonded labor under Indian law (i.e., restricting the survivor's movement, employment, or ability to sell goods in the marketplace), similar arguments could be advanced for why such practices are unjust. For example, many Hebrew Bible scholars argue that Exodus 22:25 and Leviticus 25:36 (Thomas' source material) were composed with the explicit goal of avoiding debt slavery.[78] According to Gregory Chirichigno, at the time of the composition of both of these laws, a widespread transition from tribal governance to more centralized governance (through palace and temple) was going on throughout Mesopotamia. As a centralized state apparatus began to form, it taxed the laborers, and laborers began to go into debt. Laborers sold their land or sold themselves into slavery to pay off rising debts. Kinship groups became increasingly unable to redeem alienated land or kin that were forced into debt-slavery after the land was lost. With this increasing economic hardship, incidents of debt-slavery dramatically increased. This arrangement benefitted wealthy landowners: their impoverished debtors would live on and work their land, providing them with a ready pool of cheap labor to exploit.[79] In other words, the economic situation faced by many ancient Israelites

76. From a historical perspective, however, the debate seems settled: I have never seen a historical scholar contend that Aquinas meant the former (i.e., "charging excessive interest"). He seems to have issued a blanket prohibition of interest (which seems to be the case in Exodus and Leviticus as well). However, given changes in banking practices between the medieval and modern ages, some (most?) Christians have argued for a moderation of the concept of usury. It is "excessive" interest that is prohibited. For a more nuanced take on this historical development that is in basic agreement with my conclusions here, see Finn, *Faithful Economics*, 32–33.

77. Maha testified that this happened to her. Her owner charged interest so excessive that neither she nor her father could discharge the debt ("Maha," interview with the author, Chennai, India, November 6, 2014). Recall from the last chapter that Maha was bonded for her father's debt, not her own.

78. Milgrom, *Leviticus*, 302; Meeks, "Economics in the Christian Scriptures," 17–18.

79. Chirichigno, *Debt-Slavery in Israel*, 30–54.

(who were periodically under the boot of these increasingly consolidating Mesopotamian city-states) was similar in some notable ways to the economic situation of my interviewees (i.e., not only were they forced into debt slavery, but landowners would *encourage* debt in order to enslave more people). Many of the economic practices outlined in Exodus and Leviticus (such as the Jubilee) are aimed at correcting these abuses. Thus, it is clearly in the spirit of these legal codes to put hedges around lending such that it is less easy to fall into bondage. This is, for example, why it is unethical for an owner to require that a laborer must pay off her debt by working specifically for the owner: it slides too easily into the practice of using debt to compel a person into bonded labor.

Explicitly spelling out the differences between just and unjust labor practices is important for survivors because they often lack the conceptual apparatus to even *see* the situation as unjust, let alone articulate exactly what is unjust about it. There are a few reasons for this: first, they have imbibed the slaveowner ethics of their masters. Under slaveowner ethics, the beneficence of the master obligates absolutely. The master has rescued the enslaved person from death by rescuing them from destitution, and by putting a roof over their head. For this reason, the master holds power of life or death over an enslaved person. Conversely, there are no obligations that the master owes to an enslaved person. Since the master has given the enslaved person his life back, obligation is a one-way street.[80] Second, as mentioned before, many bonded laborers in India are Irular, and are thus from tribal backgrounds that still operate on a barter system. To these survivors, loans are a foreign concept. Sometimes even *currency* is a foreign concept.[81] If many survivors are struggling just to understand the economic reality in the first place, how much more will they struggle to work out how to ethically regulate that reality?

By offering a fleshed-out counter-conception of just labor practices, social workers in Tamil Nadu help survivors to advocate for themselves in the event that their former master returns, or in the event that others come and try to compel them back into a situation of bondage. And these social workers do so precisely by providing the survivors with new ways

80. The ethics of the caste system can also serve as reinforcement for this. Theologically, the one-way street of obligation (from laborer to owner, but not vice versa) could be justified by way of either dharma or karma.

81. "Ravi," interview with the author, Chennai, India, November 5, 2014.

of understanding concepts like love (beneficence) and justice, allowing them to read their situation out of a new framework.[82]

Another session that comprises Freedom Training is "House of Freedom." For this session, survivor families are broken into two groups: adults and children. Each group then goes through a slightly different iteration of the session (separately). During "House of Freedom," social workers speak with survivors about the dynamics of a healthy household. They stress that healthy households are non-abusive, thus providing survivors with a basic education in abuse (much like the TFCBT model discussed above). They stress that healthy households are based upon the equality of the husband and the wife. They also explain what a negative coping mechanism is, and they try to get survivors to identify their negative coping mechanisms (such as alcohol or spousal abuse). In these ways, social workers attempt to address the trickle-down violence that is learned through the institution of slavery and is bolstered by slavery's conceptions of power and love.[83]

In many cases, however, it is not sufficient to simply present the survivor with new *information* concerning love and justice. The method of delivery is also of paramount importance. I am convinced that a therapeutic approach is necessary to combat many cases of captive mentality, precisely because survivors are not blank slates. If the analysis that I have given is even remotely correct, then survivors often enter rehabilitation with well-reinforced concepts of love (a love compatible with extreme violence), justice (a justice that is best served through their subjugation), power (the one who holds absolute power over their life/death is god), and obedience (they ought to be grateful to the one who has not chosen to destroy their life, and obey him/her). Such concepts are not easily dislodged, and they may even be reinforced by direct confrontation. If a

82. Some NGO workers also mentioned that issuing a release certificate helps reinforce this as well (Ebenezer, interview with the author, Chennai, India, November 12, 2014; "Naveen," interview with the author, Chennai, India, November 12, 2014). The release certificate is the legal indicator that the state recognizes their claims to justice. However, without the ability to articulate alternative claims to justice, and without the resources to mobilize according to those claims as a community, a release certificate alone is hardly an impervious shield against re-bondage.

83. Other sessions involved in Freedom Training include sessions on money management, family planning, future employment plans, basic self-advocacy methods, and other topics. But for our purposes here, the "We Are Free" and "House of Freedom" are the sessions that most directly aim at retooling the survivors' concepts of love and justice, and thus attempt to address the problem of captive mentality.

social worker presses the point too hard ("His behavior toward you was unjust"; "He doesn't really love you"; etc.), the survivor suffering under captive mentality will simply rush to their master's defense ("But he gave me a roof over my head"; "But he bought me my favorite food"; etc.).

Instead, many survivors must be gently moved to the "light bulb" moment described by Savi, Timothy, and Lloyd at various points above. When a form of abuse is presented and named as abuse without naming specific actors, the survivor is allowed to piece together the picture themselves. This technique is precisely what I mean by a therapeutic approach: any method that forgoes direct confrontation of contrary values and beliefs in favor of setting up an alternative picture of those same values and beliefs, thereby rendering the prior picture unnecessary. This method can be deployed even outside of clinical settings;[84] Ludwig Wittgenstein's philosophical method was famously described as "therapeutic" in this sense.[85] Likewise, labor organizers frequently utilize a "therapeutic" approach to allow a worker to come to their own conclusions about the need to band together with other workers to bring about change in their workplace (as opposed to just giving them advice or telling them what to do).[86] In the case of survivors struggling with captive mentality, the alternative picture of love, justice, and abuse must be described and laid out in front of the survivor for evaluation. Inevitably, the survivor will lay that picture alongside their own experience, even without prompting. In laying this new picture beside their inherited picture, survivors are given the space to come to conclusions on their own; the assumptions and flaws present in the old picture will be exposed to their view, perhaps for the first time. As Savi described, they will begin to see a certain class of behaviors as abusive, and they will identify their former masters as engaging in those behaviors. They will come to conclusions such as "he did not love me," "he was not benevolent toward me," and "he abused me" on their own.[87] By presenting survivors with a basic education in abuse,

84. This is of course not to suggest that clinical expertise not be sought in cases of captive mentality. It is only to suggest that, even where clinical expertise is lacking, some work can still be done.

85. See for example, Hector, *Theology without Metaphysics*, 28–29. Hector describes his own philosophical approach as "Wittgensteinian" because it is therapeutic in the sense outlined above.

86. See for example the approach to having organizing conversations recommended in Bradbury et al., *Secrets of a Successful Organizer*, 52–58.

87. By providing this space, I also believe that it helps correct some of the work slavery does to disassociate rationality and intention delineated above. By being able

TFCBT provides this opportunity. And by presenting survivors with a better picture of what a loving and just household looks like, as well as helping bonded labor survivors to name the abuse present in their former bondage, educational programs like Freedom Training provide for this as well.

Or perhaps more accurately, these two methods provide at least a window into what real love looks like on the ground. I add this caveat because I'm haunted by Lloyd's description of how long it takes for such lessons to take hold. The revelatory moment she experienced at Sonia and David's house was merely the beginning of her rehabilitative journey. If an alternative picture of love is not reinforced on a regular basis, slippage back into captive mentality is likely, and perhaps inevitable. Lloyd even called such moments "relapse"; the old picture reasserts itself as though the survivor is addicted to it. Thickly reinforced conceptions of love, justice, and God cannot be undone in a session, in a week of sessions, or even in several months of sessions. Unseating the old picture requires sustained presentation of a new picture.[88] My greatest worry (a worry I'm sure the social workers I interviewed in Chennai share) is that the lessons learned at programs like Freedom Training will be forgotten amongst the hustle and bustle of life back with the tribe, and the survivors who attended it will not retain its lessons over time.[89] After all, at the time of my interviews, there were only a handful of social workers working with survivors of bonded labor in the region, and the ones I interviewed all had individual caseloads of more than 100 people. And they were expected to

to come to the conclusion that certain actions taken toward them were abusive, it helps them connect these two, even if it is in regard to the intentions of another toward them, rather than in regard to their own intentions.

88. Serene Jones has a quite beautiful description of this: survivors require what she calls a "healing imagination," a sustained presentation of different "thought stories" that help survivors make sense of their experience (Jones, *Trauma and Grace*, 20). And a healing imagination requires a stable community that lives and tells such stories. And stable communities are exactly what the social workers I interviewed are struggling to create (or find).

89. During my interviews, Jaya, Kumar, and Vijaya all had difficulty articulating concepts that were presented at the educational sessions they attended ("Jaya," interview with the author, Chennai, India, November 10, 2014; "Kumar" and "Vijaya," interview with the author, Chennai, India, November 6, 2014). Was this an indication that they felt "put on the spot," or was it evidence that a handful of sessions were not sufficient to allow for adequate retention of an alternative understanding of justice? It is difficult to say.

graduate them out of the program in an extremely short period of time.[90] And most of the time they spent on their clients involved advocating with the government to produce benefits and services (such as rehabilitation money and land pattas) that the survivors were owed by law.[91] I do not wish in any way to downplay the value of the work that they are doing, but that schedule does not leave a lot of space or time for a thoroughgoing re-education program. Similarly, the social workers I interviewed who worked with sex trafficking survivors testified that post-relocation therapy (i.e., therapy after a survivor returns to her village in rural India) is practically nonexistent.[92] That concerned them. If a survivor goes back to her village, will the gains made in TFCBT sessions simply vanish within a few months? After all, living in a way consistent with a new vision of love and justice is not merely a matter of cognition, but a matter of habit. Refusing to respond to domestic conflicts with violence is a matter of habit. Overcoming substance abuse is a matter of habit. It isn't enough for survivors to know what they ought to do and ought not to do; they need to put it into practice. Throw a lot of trauma into the mix from years of horrid abuse, and the reeducation process becomes even more daunting.

Ideally, therapy rubrics like the form of TFCBT given above would be widely implemented. However, I did encounter some resistance to the idea during my interviews. Some aftercare workers (working with both labor trafficking survivors and sex trafficking survivors) saw counseling as a Western imposition that directly competed with what was called "family counseling."[93] Family counseling, in this case, seems to refer to practices of advocacy, advice, and care that are practiced within family structures. This came out the most clearly in my interview with Dr. K. Krishnan of the National Adivasi Solidarity Council (NASC). When I

90. "Nisha," interview with the author, Chennai, India, November 7, 2014; "Naveen," interview with the author, Chennai, India, November 12, 2014. In the case of one NGO, survivors were expected to complete the training in only six home visits which were carried out within a two-year period.

91. "Nisha," interview with the author, Chennai, India, November 7, 2014; "Naveen," interview with the author, Chennai, India, November 12, 2014.

92. Bharathy Tahiliani, interview with the author, Mumbai, India, January 2, 2014; "Mallika," interview with the author, Mumbai, India, September 17, 2014. To be fair, these social workers also said that there is a gap for most services for survivors once they go back to their village. About the only exception seems to be HIV treatment.

93. "Harit," interview with the author, Mumbai, India, December 19, 2014; K. Krishnan, interview with the author, Chennai, India, November 20, 2014.

asked him how counselors in his organization were trained, he responded with the following:

> **Krishnan:** Historically, in India, this counseling is part of our culture.
>
> **Chris:** Okay.
>
> **Krishnan:** Yeah, we have . . . Because you know, India lives with the family-type. See, family . . . There's one good thing in this country, in this culture of the country, family is a part of counseling. In the family process. In foreign countries, they don't have that habit. In the family, for example, if a child is beaten by a father, immediately, grandmother, grandfather, they take the child and give them counseling and support and everything. That's how the family goes in India. Always, somebody is there to take care of. Actually, many people criticize, "Oh, family—joint family—very big! Everybody you have to fear!" Like that. But it's a good support . . . counseling . . . social . . . psychosocial counseling, the family gives very good. So that way, the training is there.[94]

This was one of many indicators in my interviews that different interviewees used "counseling" in drastically different ways. I couldn't assume a shared understanding of the word, and I would have to ask the interviewee qualifying questions about what method of counseling was used.

In such cases, I don't think the interviewee was aware of the methods used in TFCBT or its benefits. It was simply something "Western," and therefore unnecessary. Given its colonial history, I can understand why many Indians would be worried about the imposition of "Western" therapy. The tendency to view native forms of culture, language, and governance as inferior simply because they are Indian is something that the country has lived under for quite some time. I've even seen examples of this sort of mentality in my experience working for an anti-trafficking NGO that brought together Americans and Indians in the same working environment.[95] There are times, however, that labeling something as

94. K. Krishnan, interview with the author, Chennai, India, November 20, 2014.

95. As referenced in the introduction, about fifteen years ago, it was common among US anti-trafficking groups to assume that anti-trafficking work was necessary in India but not in the US because our criminal system was adequately dealing with the task, but theirs was not. The assumption essentially was that the Indian criminal justice system needed to become more American. Two things now reveal this view to be essentially ethnocentric: (1) the realization that the US has had a very prominent

"Western" can serve simply to dismiss something that fills a need that is improperly understood. In this case, it would be a matter of using post-colonial concerns (which are legitimate) to proliferate stigma against mental health resources (which is illegitimate). Additionally, the comparison of what Krishnan calls "family counseling" to therapies such as TFCBT is a matter of comparing apples and oranges. This is not a matter of comparing a Western method and an Indian method that both address the same problem, and then finding the Indian method to be substandard. This is a matter of two different methods addressing different sets of problems that occur within the field of aftercare. I would be happy to concede that forms of therapy such as TFCBT (due to its origins in England) could be replaced with some other (more Indian) rubric, provided that rubric allowed for both a basic education in abuse and coping mechanisms, and that rubric was carried out by people trained to identify and deal with various forms of trauma (as detailed in the description of TFCBT above). If alternatives do not address these problems, however, I think that implementation of forms of therapy such as TFCBT is still ideal, but that such forms of therapy would not have to replace "family counseling." One can still give sage advice as a surrogate family member without feeling the need to oppose TFCBT due to its place of origin.

Helping to allay such worries is Savi's own testimony about how her team developed their TFCBT rubric: the rubric as they received it was not culturally sensitive. The educative sessions and examples had to be heavily edited by Indian counselors to make it sensitive to an Indian (and especially *rural* Indian) context. This is an absolutely crucial part of the process. No one is arguing that a therapeutic model implemented in the US or the UK should serve as some sort of infallible script that must be implemented as is without (sometimes significant) changes.

Another objection is that therapy rubrics like TFCBT are too resource intensive. The average aftercare home in India simply doesn't have the funds to afford the care, precisely because TFCBT is only known and practiced by a handful of specialists. Things like beds and food come first, therapy comes later (if there are funds left over). I'm sympathetic to this concern: the damage that slavery does often outstrips the resources we put in to correct it, and therapy requires stability if it is going to be effective. If a survivor isn't sleeping (because they don't have a place to sleep) and

(and growing) trafficking problem for quite some time, and (2) the growing focus on how the US criminal legal system is used as a mechanism of social control against people of color (who are more likely to be victims of trafficking than white people).

is suffering from malnutrition (because they don't have sufficient food), then they aren't likely to get much out of therapy sessions, even if they are offered. Maslow's hierarchy of need was cited several times among aftercare workers in Chennai as to why they spent so much of their time trying to spur a lethargic government to action rather than moving on to setting up counseling services for survivors.[96] Additionally, the specialized knowledge required simply is hard to find. India has professional counselors, but it is in desperate need of more. Several of my interviewees (most of whom were Indian) testified that mental health services were under a lot of stigma in India, and therefore India suffers from a dearth of trained counselors.[97] It will take time for that stigma to be overcome and for people to be trained up with the specialized knowledge of how to deal with trauma. In the immediate future, it is not possible to conjure more counselors out of thin air.

But here, too, NGOs such as IJM may have supplied a pragmatic answer to the problem: they still provide "freedom training," even if they can't provide specialized therapy. In the absence of specialized training on dealing with trauma, it is still possible to give survivors a basic education in forms of abuse and coping mechanisms, and to try to retool their sense of love and justice.

However, this emphatically does *not* mean that an organization should forgo training service providers in trauma-informed care. Trauma-informed care differs from TFCBT in that TFCBT is a form of trauma-specific intervention. For those unfamiliar with the difference, trauma-informed care trains service providers to be sensitive to the effects of trauma and to avoid exacerbating trauma in survivors. It can be provided in a crash-course training format.[98] Trauma-specific intervention specifically targets trauma and tries to help a survivor deal with it. It requires specialized training. If you compare a survivor's trauma to a field full of land mines, the difference between the two is essentially that one method teaches individuals how to avoid stepping on land mines while

96. "Nisha," interview with the author, Chennai, India, November 7, 2014.

97. Bharathy Tahiliani, interview with the author, Mumbai, India, January 2, 2014; "Savi," interview with the author, Mumbai, India, September 22, 2014; Bernie and Bennet David, interview with the author, Mumbai, India, December 31, 2014.

98. It is usually best if you can have a group that organizes trainings in your region give a presentation to your organization. However, if none is available in your region, a good online repository of resources can be found at https://www.traumainformedcare.chcs.org/trauma-informed-care-basics.

walking through the field (trauma-informed care), while the other method gives a survivor the tools and techniques necessary to start de-mining the field (trauma-specific intervention).[99] It's considered preferable to provide trauma-specific intervention if you can, but trauma-informed care is a necessary measure if the specialized knowledge for intervention is unavailable.[100] NGOs (such as IJM) who are aware of the difference and the gap in resources have implemented such trainings for their service providers.

Additionally, even though I have given a defense of the practices given above, I have my doubts about whether either of them will serve as a sufficient response to the reality of captive mentality by themselves. Some of my interviewees share these doubts. For example, Hannah, at the end of our interview, mentioned that she realized how many of her organization's rehabilitative goals would come together if adequate community structures existed to help them. Thus, community development needed to be a bigger focus for her organization. If a community can advocate for itself, it could meet more of its own physical needs, and more outside resources could be spent on psycho-social issues. Hannah also mentioned that the church might be an even better help in providing this kind of community rehabilitation than the government, if a very careful

99. Some might argue that there are limits to this comparison. It could be taken to suggest trauma can be completely healed, which is a bit of a controversial proposition amongst experts on trauma. It may be the case that sometimes the best you can hope for is that survivors learn how to cope with the aftereffects. Some academics who study trauma, such as Shelley Rambo, seem to resist any sort of language that implies completion in favor of a language of "remaining" (see Rambo, *Spirit and Trauma*, 6–8). The rationale for this is that such language pushes too quickly past the myriad forms of lingering suffering that survivors face. Other individuals dealing with survivors contend that completion language such as "moving on," "healing, "reconciling," or "redeeming" is absolutely necessary as a part of their work (see for example, Yoder, *Little Book of Trauma Healing*, 45–69). Savi also stressed the necessity of such language ("Savi," interview with the author, Mumbai, India, September 22, 2014). Individuals in this latter camp would argue that one of the needs of survivors is to "re-story" their lives in the wake of trauma (Yoder, *Trauma Healing*, 25). Continually dwelling in the murky middle created by trauma and refusing forward movement is a refusal to re-story. I find myself agreeing far more with the latter camp, but (like Yoder and Savi), I realize that some forms of trauma are generational, and are not neatly summed up in the sufferers' lifetime.

100. This is an important caveat even for aftercare organizations based in the US. I have asked US aftercare providers in the past whether or not they provide TFCBT, and they have responded, "Yes, we provide trauma-informed care," not realizing that those are two very different things.

and non-invasive way can be designed to "adopt" the community.[101] I would add that community development (including offering survivors trainings on how to organize for power themselves) would help to reinforce an alternative picture of love and justice internally, rather than keeping all reinforcement sporadic and external.[102] We will return to this topic in chapter 5.

I would also advocate for expansion of the sorts of training that survivors are receiving. Sessions on peacebuilding and nonviolent conflict transformation would likely go a long way to helping survivors unlearn practices like domestic violence, helping to bring them further out of the conceptions of love and justice that typify slavery. I am uncertain whether adequate resources exist for this in Tamil or Hindi, but in English, there is a Little Books of Justice and Peacebuilding series that might be helpful for service providers.[103] Additional resources could be found at the Kroc Institute for Peace Studies at the University of Notre Dame,[104] and the Center for Justice and Peacebuilding at Eastern Mennonite University.[105]

At this point, it seems clear that all rehabilitative programs will require least some minimal portrait of love, justice, and God that can be offered up as an alternative to the portrait of love, justice, and God offered up by slavery. Without a grand vision that animates on-the-ground rehabilitative practices, the portrait offered up by slavery will still hold sway over survivors, even after they have been physically separated from their enslavers. Fleshing out this grand vision will be the primary objective of the next chapter.

101. "Hannah," interview with the author, Chennai, India, November 18, 2014.

102. A great example of what this might look like could be found in my interview with Latha and Subramani. Latha was serving as a leader in her community after rescue, and she was able to strongly articulate how it was that her and her husband's previous owners had been unjust to them. She even managed to advocate with the government for some free services for her community (such as electricity), which would be a daunting task for any survivor suffering heavily from captive mentality ("Latha" and "Subramani," interview with the author, Chennai, India, November 10, 2014). Fostering community leaders like Latha would likely help make local anti-trafficking NGOs jobs easier.

103. Examples would include Yoder, *Little Book of Trauma Healing*, and Lederach, *Little Book of Conflict Transformation*.

104. http://kroc.nd.edu/.

105. http://www.emu.edu/cjp/.

Chapter 3

An Abolitionist Theological Portrait

ELIZABETH PHILLIPS ONCE POIGNANTLY observed that "at the heart of all other issues in political theology is the issue of the relationship between the church and the political."[1] However, many attempts to resolve this issue in the history of theology have subtly changed the terminology used for the two realms. Is the goal to figure out the relationship between "church" and "state"? "Church" and "world"? "Nature" and "grace"? "Religion" and "politics"? "The sacred" and "the secular"? In most cases, those sets of terms cannot be taken as simply synonyms for the same realities, so which set is chosen as a starting point can genuinely make a difference in the analysis that follows. Arguably the most common set to run into in the United States is "religion" and "politics," with a considerable number of individuals (both Christian and non-Christian) assuming that the goal is to keep the two absolutely separated. Many "non-religious" folks insist that people of faith must keep their religion out of their politics, and many Christians have attempted to draw up ironclad dividing walls to prevent their theological beliefs from informing their political stance.

If the latter claim seems overstated, consider for a moment the sheer number of theological terms clearly borrowed from political and social life that circulate in Christian circles but no longer have any clear bearing on the political and social arenas they are borrowed from. "Redemption" is a term clearly borrowed from a specific economic and social context: slavery. It originally refers to the practice of buying back a loved one who

1. Phillips, *Political Theology*, 57.

has fallen into enslavement, freeing them from bondage (this is why in English you can redeem both people and coupons). "Salvation" is another term with an originally political meaning: it referred to the act of liberating a people from an occupying military force. And yet in many Christian circles (though by no means all), both of these terms are now relegated to describing spiritual realities that are utterly disconnected from the concerns of those under occupation or in bondage in our time. Or consider Christopher Marshall's rather astute observation that Paul's "extreme skepticism about the ability of an external law-code to control human wrongdoing,"[2] which is a central feature in Protestant accounts of justification by faith alone, is rarely ever used as a critique of retributive justice systems. In other words, it is not unusual to meet Christians who think that, when it comes to the law of Moses, the law has no power to make human beings righteous and merely increases awareness of sin (Rom 3:9–20), but when it comes to criminal law, harsh penalties and enforcement are an effective and necessary means of deterring people from wrongdoing and forming them into good citizens.

As we shall see later, there are good reasons to hold that some theological terms that began as political terms ought not be interpreted "literally" when they are applied directly to God (as opposed to the realities of human life). And, given a global history that includes colonialism, the Crusades, and the use of imperial power to enforce religious conformity, there are good reasons to try to draw up boundary lines that will prevent one religious group from taking a position that will allow them to dominate others. Both concerns are often cited by people who advocate for a thick dividing wall between "politics" and "religion." The problem is that this way of dividing things up simply cannot function meaningfully in human social life. Theological beliefs inevitably end up influencing political realities and vice versa. We saw this briefly in the last chapter: a set of beliefs about how God is identified led survivors of slavery to develop the belief (implicitly or explicitly) that the enslaver is God (or a god). This means that, in these cases, any program committed to rehabilitation must make at least a minimal theological claim: no, the enslaver is not God. In a later chapter, we will explore how one of the primary social realities affecting bonded labor in India (caste) has religious and theological moorings. As long as religious beliefs affect human behavior, no bright line can ever be drawn between the religious and the political.[3] This claim

2. Marshall, *Beyond Retribution*, 11.

3. For a more in-depth defense of why "politics" and "religion" cannot be held

is likely to make some social workers working in the field with survivors uncomfortable. In India, many Christian anti-trafficking organizations can only operate with the government's approval under the condition that they do not proselytize survivors. And for many reasons, it would indeed be unethical for a Christian social worker to pressure survivors to undergo a religious conversion while offering services. If an evangelical Christian social worker pressured a survivor to pray the Sinner's Prayer or "make a decision for Christ," the result would not be genuine conversion, it would be greater alienation, and could provide a major setback to rehabilitation. Fortunately, regardless of the theological outlook of the social workers I interviewed, all of them seemed to agree that conversion was not a goal of their work.

I doubt I would be able to adequately advise social workers giving direct care how to differentiate between appropriate and inappropriate theological conversations to have with survivors. But what I may be able to do briefly is sketch a theological portrait that would bolster rehabilitation efforts. I can't recommend that it be actively taught to survivors of all faiths, but perhaps it will help Christians offering direct services to understand the theological grounds for why they are doing what they are doing. Some aspects of this portrait could be affirmed by individuals of many different faiths. For example, the affirmation that God is not a being among beings, but rather Being itself (an idea utilized in the portrait of God below) is a belief common to Christians, Muslims, and monotheistic Hindus.[4] And so, perhaps occasionally, if difficult conversations with survivors arise, aspects of this portrait might be referenced for therapeutic purposes rather than for proselytization purposes. In other words, if a survivor's intuitive theological beliefs are contributing to ongoing bondage, the social worker might ask something to the effect of, "Does it need to be the case that God is that way? Isn't it possible that God is this way instead?"

---

absolutely separate from one another, see Phillips, *Political Theology*, 2–3. There is also the rather interesting argument that Bill Cavanaugh makes in *Migrations of the Holy* that the beliefs about salvation and the practices of devotion once aimed at God within the church have "migrated" such that in the modern era they are now aimed at the nation state (see Cavanaugh, *Migrations of the Holy*). If Cavanaugh is right, modern states actually depend on religious devotion to command the allegiance of their subjects, not through adopting an official state church, but rather by forming a national religion that attempts to mask its existence as a religion for ideological reasons (as is the case with American civil religion).

4. Hart, *Experience of God*, 107–8.

Here we can take some inspiration from the work of Howard Zehr, one of the primary voices in the restorative justice movement. To dispel the myths about justice that lead to abusive practices in criminal legal systems, Zehr proposed an "alternative lens" through which justice could be viewed. Similarly, to dispel the myths about love, justice, and God perpetuated in slave systems, it will be necessary to view love, justice, and God through alternative lenses. Or, to use a slightly different metaphor borrowed from the visual arts, it will be necessary to provide alternative portraits for comparison. I will have to defer a full account of God's justice until chapter 6 (where questions of justice for victim-offenders will be discussed). In this chapter, I will attempt to provide alternative portraits of love and God that might bolster rehabilitative practices such as TFCBT and the Freedom Trainings described in the last chapter. We will start with an alternative portrait of love.

An Alternative Portrait of Love

The greatest point of contrast between the portrait of love offered up in slave systems and the portrait of love offered up in TFCBT concerns the compatibility of love and violence. As mentioned before, in the portrait of love offered up by enslavers, love and violence are not only compatible, violence is a necessary component of love. The enslaver proves the intensity of their love for the enslaved *through* their violence toward the enslaved. In contrast, the portrait of love offered up by TFCBT assumes a fundamental incompatibility between love and violence. Put simply, real love is nonviolent.[5]

For Christians, the idea that love is ultimately incompatible with violence has clear theological roots. God's love for the world is shown most palpably in the birth, ministry, death, and resurrection of Jesus Christ. Jesus' ministry is characterized by the call to love all, even one's own enemies (Matt 5:43–48; Luke 6:27–28). And it is what Jesus says about what love looks like toward this extreme group (enemies) that demonstrates the incompatibility of all forms of love with violence in Jesus' teaching. "Don't react violently against the one who is evil,"[6] he commands his

5. I take it that "violence" here also covers any form of abuse, whether physical, emotional, or spiritual.

6. This translation is from the Scholars Version, and it was chosen following Walter Wink's criticism of the typical rendering. See Wink, *Jesus and Nonviolence*, 9–12. David Bentley Hart's rendition from his recent translation of the New Testament ("Whereas

disciples (Matt 5:39), a command he abides by in his own ministry. He refuses to call down fire on a Samaritan city that opposes his ministry (Luke 9:51–56), he discourages other Jews from engaging in armed resistance against their Roman occupiers (Luke 13:1–5),[7] he rebukes the disciple who leaps to his defense by attacking those who have come to arrest him in the Garden of Gethsemane (Matt 26:50–52), and he ultimately bears the cross as the ultimate demonstration of his nonviolent love toward his enemies, even going so far as praying for their forgiveness as they are crucifying him (Luke 23:34). To paraphrase Drew Hart, whatever else loving one's enemies might mean, it certainly means refusing to destroy them.[8] And if violence and love are incompatible when it comes to your enemies, how much more so are these two things incompatible when it comes to those who share your home and your labor?

Numerous Christian theologians have further claimed that the nonviolent conception of love advocated by Jesus finds its origins in the life of the triune God.[9] The triune God is a God of peace, a community of persons who possess distinct wills, yet are unified in both being and purpose. "Harmonious" is a good word to use when describing this relationship, as harmonies are composed of different musical lines which unite into a coherent and pleasing whole. The relation between these persons has been described as "self-giving" or even "self-emptying" ("kenotic"), but not in such a way that any one of them is subject to violence or abuse

---

I tell you not to oppose the wicked man by force") reflects the same criticism, but I chose the Scholars Edition because it makes it clear that the problem is specifically *violent* force (see Hart, *New Testament*, 9). The common translation found in many Bibles—"Do not resist an evil person"—is too broad. The word that Jesus uses that is often translated "resist" (*antistēnai*) is a form of *stasis*, which means specifically *violent* resistance. For example, this same term is used to describe the charge that is brought against Barabbas (Luke 23:19). As will be discussed above, Jesus is not forbidding all types of resistance to evil, only violent resistance to evil. If Jesus forbade all forms of resistance to evil (including nonviolent resistance), then there are a great many actions Jesus takes in Matthew that would be inconsistent with his words in the Sermon on the Mount, not least of which is his cleansing of the temple (Matt 21:12–13).

7. And this is in spite of the fact that the hope for Israel's liberation is stated quite strongly elsewhere in Luke (e.g., Luke 1:68–74). However, for Jesus, this did not in any way preclude participation in nonviolent resistance against Roman rule.

8. Hart, *Who Will Be a Witness?*, 356.

9. See for example, Dear, *God of Peace*, 43–51; Cunningham, *These Three Are One*, 237–69. Cunningham's work traces the presence of this theme in the works of Tertullian, Gregory of Nazianzus, Jürgen Moltmann, and Leonardo Boff.

from either of the other two. Within the life of the Trinity, just as much as within the ministry of Jesus, love and violence are incompatible.

Unfortunately, Christian theologians have not always maintained this incompatibility. To take perhaps the most prominent example, Augustine of Hippo maintained that love and violence were not incompatible. While Augustine assiduously held throughout his career that Christians are forbidden in engaging in violence if *vengeance* is the motive, he repeatedly argues that Christians are authorized to use violence if the motive for doing so is love and correction.[10] This distinction is crucial to his argument that a Christian can kill while serving as a soldier in a just war,[11] his argument that it is allowable for a Christian magistrate to enact judicial torture on a suspected criminal,[12] and his argument for why it is allowable for the Roman state to use violence to force the Donatists to rejoin the Catholic Church.[13] This is specifically to try to

10. This seems to fit well into Augustine's theology of the Two Cities: the Heavenly City and the Earthly City. The Earthly City is oriented toward the love of self to the neglect of love of God, the Heavenly City is oriented around love of God to the neglect of love of self (Augustine, *Civ.* 14.28). Importantly, for Augustine, the two cities employ the same means of governance and are intermixed, but the difference in orientation makes all the difference between them. Applying this to the situation at hand, violence isn't absolutely ruled out for a Christian. However, a Christian must use violence with a different end in mind than a pagan (i.e., for love rather than vengeance).

11. Augustine, Letter 138 (p. 14); Augustine, Letter 220 (p. 8). He makes a similar argument in Augustine, Letter 189 (p. 6) without directly coming to the conclusion that it is possible to love someone while using the sword against them.

12. Augustine, Letter 133 (p. 2). Here he commends Marcellinus, a Christian magistrate (more specifically, a military tribune), for showing paternal love toward accused criminals who appear before him. According to Augustine, his love toward them is shown by the fact that he does not torture them with hooks, as other magistrates would, in order to secure a confession. Instead, he coaxes confessions out of them by beating them with rods, just as a loving father would beat a misbehaving child. The amount of violence permissible when administering judicial torture is lessened (at least theoretically), but Augustine's example still distressingly assumes that it is morally acceptable to beat a confession out of a suspect.

13. Augustine, Letter 173 (p. 2). This is perhaps the most bizarre of Augustine's deployments of the distinction. In a letter to Donatus (a Donatist priest in prison), Augustine argues that incarcerating and torturing Donatists until they rejoin the church is morally acceptable because the infamous practice of kidnapping influential Christian monks and submitting them to incarceration until they agree to serve as bishops is *also* morally acceptable. His argument to the incarcerated Donatist priest can be paraphrased as follows: "You object to the way you are being treated because you believe that no one should be forced to accept what is good for him. But the church, when she encounters influential Christians who do not wish to be bishops, arrests them, locks them up, and submits them to unpleasant treatment until they come

honor Jesus' command to love your enemies while simultaneously opening up the possibility that you can harm or kill those enemies.[14] One may object that Augustine had in mind a very different circumstance than we are considering: he thought that love and violence could be compatible with regard to one's (political) enemies, but not with regard to more intimate relationships (i.e., those who share home or labor). But there is a decent amount of evidence in his writings that this admixture of love and violence bled back into the domestic sphere quite readily for him, since he (like most Greco-Roman intellectuals) did not conceive of a thick dividing wall that stood between public and private spheres.[15] Further, a domestic violence metaphor is assumed in every single argument Augustine makes in favor of the use of political violence above (usually that of a father beating a child in order to discipline him).[16] Since it is

to see that it is good for them to become a bishop. If this practice is acceptable, what we are doing to you right now is definitely acceptable!" This suggests that, contrary to some commentators on Augustine's political theology, Augustine's stance during the Donatist controversy is *not* a blind spot in Augustine's political thought, but a natural entailment of one of his central ethical tenets.

14. It is worth noting that, on all three of these points, Augustine is directly opposing almost four hundred years of church tradition that preceded him.

15. Some commenters on Augustine reject this reading. For instance, see Elshtain, "Augustine," 39. Here Elshtain argues, "Nor does Augustine analogize from the rule of fathers in households to political rule." I'm a bit puzzled by this statement, since Augustine seems to do exactly that: "Now a man's house ought to be the beginning, or rather a small component of the city, and every beginning is directed to some end of its own kind, and every component part contributes to the completeness of the whole of which it forms a part. The implication is quite apparent, that domestic peace contributes to the peace of the city—that is, the ordered harmony of those who live together in a house in the matter of giving and obeying orders, contributes to the ordered harmony concerning authority and obedience obtaining among the citizens. Consequently it is fitting that the father of a household should take his rules from the law of the city, and govern his household in such a way that it fits in with the peace of the city" (Augustine, *Civ.* 19.16 [p. 876]). Unlike most modern Western intellectuals, the ancient Greeks and Romans saw the family as the most basic political unit (sort of like the most local branch of government), rather than as something quite separate from political life. The family was also a microcosm of the whole political system, such that the best practices for running a family were also the best practices for running an Empire (and vice versa). As can be seen from the quotation in this footnote, Augustine seems to whole-heartedly agree with this way of thinking.

16. This is the explicitly the case in Augustine, Letter 138 (p. 14) (concerning killing in war) and Augustine, Letter 133 (p. 2) (concerning judicial torture). It is implicit in Augustine, Letter 220 (p. 8) (concerning killing in war). Again, the metaphor in Augustine, Letter 173 (p. 2) (concerning forced conversion of the Donatists) is the forced episcopate.

licit for parents to exercise violence against their children for the sake of their correction in the domestic sphere, Augustine argues, it is also licit for Christian officials to exercise violence for the correction of others in wider political spheres. In fact, in *City of God*, Chapter XIX, the domestic violence metaphor used to justify the legitimate use of political violence and dominion by Christians is slavery itself.[17] It seems clear, then, that love looked the same for Augustine in both spheres.

Certainly, love is internally diverse. In this book I have talked about romantic love, familial love, beneficence, and *caritas* (the love that is a theological virtue). Theologians have often given a fourfold distinction of love based on an ancient Greek schema: *eros*, *philia*, *storge*, and *agape*.[18] I don't object to such differentiations. But in all of its forms, love must be unified around a few core similarities. It is not arbitrary that we call both romantic love and familial love "loves"; there is a species connection. And one of these unifying characteristics must be its nonviolence. Violence is as inappropriate in romance as it is in *caritas*.

Insisting that love and violence are ultimately incompatible is important because there really is no other adequate way to differentiate authentic love from the false love that an enslaver claims he has for the enslaved. One could say many other things about love. For example, one could say that love is the desire to give oneself away for another. It is "self-giving" or "self-emptying." This is true, but such language is easily integrated into the love language that slavery uses. From the master's perspective, a virtuous enslaved person will give herself away for her master. Her master will also wax lyrical about how much he gives himself away for her (though there are obviously limitations to this that are not present from the enslaved person's side): he puts a roof over her head, he feeds her, he provides for her physical needs. But as we have seen, slavery also requires violence or threat of violence to maintain the relationship of domination. If it does not destroy an enslaved person's intentionality, how will it preserve harmony? If it does not allow for beatings, how will the master affirm his self-worth and gain recognition? If it does not allow for violent discipline, how will an enslaved person learn what is right? Slave systems could never truly affirm a love that is inherently nonviolent. Slavery is always an inherently violent institution.

17. Augustine, *Civ.* 19.15–16. John Rist correctly notes that slavery serves as a "test case" for Augustine's political theology in City of God. See Rist, *Augustine*, 236–39.

18. That is (roughly), romantic love, friendship, familial love, and theological love, respectively.

At this point it is probably worth clarifying that when I say that love is nonviolent, I am implying something positive as well as something negative. Nonviolence is both the refusal to resort to violence or abuse (the negative), but it is also the commitment to positive forms of conflict resolution (the positive). It is not merely "being a doormat." To return to Jesus' ministry, while Jesus did not retaliate against his enemies in going to the cross, it was his resistance to evil that led him there. There is no cross without the cleansing of the temple (Matt 21:12–17; Mark 11:15–19; Luke 19:45–48; John 2:13–16), which serves as the clearest example of nonviolent resistance in Jesus' entire ministry.[19] In the cleansing of the temple, Jesus nonviolently[20] occupies the temple, protests its unjust economic practices, teaches the people, and then vacates the premises after a few days. What he does falls in the same general category of nonviolent resistance as the Nashville sit-in campaigns: nonviolent occupation. Note that the account is so important that it occurs in all four Gospels. Without this action, the local authorities and the Romans would likely have ignored him. One cannot understand the crucifixion without this demonstration. This helps us to see that while authentic love does not resort to violence, it also does not allow abuse to continue unchecked. A love that tolerates and justifies abuse from the party with power is just

19. Not that it is the only example of nonviolent resistance in Jesus' ministry. I follow the interpretation of the controversy about paying taxes to Caesar (Mark 12:13–17; Matt 22:15–22; Luke 20:20–26) which identifies Jesus' response as evidence that he advocates (and practices) tax resistance against Rome. Tax resistance is a classic form of nonviolent resistance. For a recent defense of this reading, see Kraybill, *Apocalypse and Allegiance*, 150.

20. Some argue that in John's account, Jesus *does* occupy the temple violently. This is because he makes a whip of cords, and it is grammatically unclear in Greek whom Jesus whips with it. I think this is a bad reading. John is clear that Jesus uses the whip to drive the animals, not to assault the people in the temple grounds. Hence the NRSV's rendering: "Making a whip of cords, he drove all of them out of the temple, *both the sheep and the cattle*" (John 2:15, emphasis added). In other words, John clarifies that it is the *animals* Jesus is using the whip on, not any human beings in the temple. For a thoroughgoing exegetical defense of this understanding of this verse, see Alexis-Baker, "Violence, Nonviolence, and the Temple Incident," 88–92. The position that Jesus *did* whip human beings in the temple runs into an additional historical difficulty: if Jesus assaulted guards, priests, or worshippers in the temple, how is it that, at his trial, his accusers have difficulty bringing (truthful) legal charges against him (Matt 26:59–60; Mark 14:55–59; Luke 23:1–5; John 18:29–38)? Assaulting temple guards or staff could have easily been rendered as a prosecutable offense, and yet Jesus' accusers never charge him with this in any account of his trial before the Sanhedrin or before Pilate. Driving a sheep or a cow out of the temple grounds, however, would have been more difficult to name as a prosecutable offense.

as inauthentic as a love that tolerates and justifies abuse from the one without.

This is the sort of love that is assumed in TFCBT or in Freedom Training. And it is the sort of love that must be at least implicitly embraced by any rehabilitative program for survivors of slavery. It is a love that teaches survivors to name forms of abuse. It is a love that pushes survivors to embrace nonviolent means of sorting through their problems.[21]

An Alternative Portrait of God

As with false love, the best way to be rid of a false god is not by attacking its image, but by providing a better alternative portrait to set alongside it and expose its flaws. What is needed is a portrait of God who operates nonviolently toward creation, refusing to exercise power over creation like a slaveholder exercises power over an enslaved person.

Some have argued that this is exactly where the portrait of God offered up in the Christian Scriptures fails to be useful for abolitionist purposes. And on first blush, it is easy to understand why some have come to believe this. Indeed, the master-slave analogy even occurs with disturbing frequency in the New Testament itself. Authors of the New Testament epistles frequently introduce themselves as "a slave of Jesus Christ" (e.g., Rom 1:1; Phil 1:1; Jas 1:1; 2 Pet 1:1). "Slaves of God" is also an occasional designation for Christians in general (e.g., 1 Pet 2:16; Rom 6:22). Slaveowners even likely act as stand-ins for God in some of the parables of Jesus.[22] Slavery is frequently used in the New Testament to illumine not only the relationship between human beings and God, but also to explain what occurs in the Incarnation (e.g., Phil 2:7; Christ's "taking the form of a slave"). The authors of the New Testament also found slavery to be a particularly apt point of comparison to Christ in his passion, since he

21. Though I have given an explicitly Christian defense of nonviolent love, it could very plausibly be defended from other religious traditions. Buddhists, for example, can likewise give an argument for why love is inherently nonviolent based on the self-defeating nature of violence. See for example, Rosch, "Peace is the Strongest Force," 142.

22. See for example, Matt 18:21–35. I insert "likely" here because I want to resist the tendency to always assume that any slaveowner that shows up in Jesus' parables is automatically God. In some cases, this seems to me far from clear (e.g., Luke 16:1–13, the parable of the shrewd steward). I suspect that the general belief that God is designated primarily by power (and therefore God is always the person with the most earthly power in the parable) exercises too much interpretive influence in such cases. Nevertheless, it seems likely to me that, in at least a few parables, the master is meant to stand in for God.

became a victim of the sort of violent discipline that normally characterizes an enslaved person's existence (e.g., 1 Pet 2:18–25). Jesus died the death of an enslaved person; he was crucified.

Such passages have been taken by some to indicate that God does hold the same sort of power that slaveowners hold over enslaved people, and that the exercise of this type of power is a necessary part of the identity of the Christian God. However, I believe that the New Testament actually lays the groundwork for the idea that God not only operates nonviolently toward creation, but that God also eschews power of the sort that slaveowners wield, exposing it as a false form of power. Thus, the passages cited above must be qualified by four considerations: (1) Christian beliefs concerning how analogies function in speech about God, (2) the nature of God's revelation in the person of Jesus Christ, (3) Jesus' teachings about the nature of power and authority, and (4) an often-ignored abolitionist trajectory in the narrative of Scripture itself.

Regarding the first consideration, throughout the history of Christian theology, it has been held that God is ultimately ineffable. Human language can fruitfully be used to describe God, but all statements about God will be, in some sense, inadequate. God can never be fully "captured" in human language.[23] Therefore all language concerning God is analogous: it helpfully illumines some aspect of God, but also contains the possibility for distortion if taken too literally or in the wrong way.[24] For example, feminist theologians have long pointed out the possibility (and reality) of distortion that exists in calling God "Father." The analogy can

23. Scare quotes are inserted here to draw attention to the fact that this too is an analogous use of language. I don't think that language actually "captures" anything to which it refers. There are some thinkers who seem to take the analogy in an overly literal fashion and think that language can actually bind things and do epistemic violence to them. I am not suggesting that this is the case here.

24. I am only here advocating for the linguistic use of analogy, without committing myself to any particular rendering of the metaphysics of analogy (e.g., that there is an "analogy of being" or *analogia entis* between God and creatures). The latter debate has been notoriously controversial among theologians in the modern era, and often constitutes a line of division between Protestants and Catholics. It may also constitute a line of division between Catholics and other Catholics, who disagree on what sort of "analogy of being" obtains, even if they uphold the *analogia entis*. See for example Long, *Saving Karl Barth*, 169n88. Karl Barth famously called the *analogia entis* the invention of the anti-Christ. However, even as he spoke these words, he still held that to call the First Person of the Trinity "the Father" is an analogous use of the term. God the Father isn't a "father" in the same sense a human father is and does not sexually generate the Son. It is in this more ecumenical (or perhaps baseline) sense that I intend to use the concept.

fruitfully be used to describe either the relationship of the First Person of the Trinity toward the Second Person of the Trinity or the relationship between human beings and God. This is because the analogy highlights things like care, dependence, love, etc. However, overuse or too literal use of the analogy can reaffirm (and has reaffirmed) structures of patriarchy.[25] Or, to take a concern more germane to the church fathers, too literal use of the analogy of God as "Father" can produce a crass belief that the Father literally generates the Son through sexual reproduction (much like human fathers generate human children through sexual reproduction).

Analogical language contrasts with univocal language. If language about God is univocal, then an expression concerning God finds a perfect parallel in the world. This is what most people mean when they say that language applies "literally" to God. Zero distortion is present. In the example above, if calling the First Person of the Trinity "Father" necessarily implies that he generated the Second Person of the Trinity through sexual reproduction, then use of the term "Father" when describing God is univocal.

Holding that all language that applies to God is analogous helps assuage some of the difficulties we encounter when confronted with slaveholding analogies in the New Testament, though admittedly not all difficulties. On the one hand, it means that the analogy contains distortion. The kind of power God holds over believers is *not* the same as the power a master holds over an enslaved person. This can be fruitfully seen in the fact that there is one situation that has been theologically imagined within Christianity in which the term "slave of God" *would* apply univocally, and it is not the situation in which the New Testament uses this term.[26] That situation is this: the term "slave of God" would ap-

25. See for example, Johnson, *She Who Is*, 33–41; Ruether, *Sexism and God-Talk*, 53.

26. The only possible exception to this is Matt 18:21–35. Here the term "slave of God" is not used, but eschatological judgment is described in terms of an unmerciful slave being handed over to "the jailer to be tortured, until he should pay back all he owed." However, other constituent parts of the picture are not present (i.e., the eternality of the punishment, that the punishment is done for the glory of God), so even this is not entirely a perfect fit. Additionally, the nonviolence that Jesus commands of the disciples in Matthew (a nonviolence that imitates God's nonviolence; see Matt 5:43–48) contrasts so jarringly with some of the violent descriptions of eschatological judgment in Matthew that it invites an analogical interpretation of those very scenes of eschatological judgment. The scene described in Matt 18:21–35 is still disturbing, however, I don't believe that God will literally return to do violence against any human being (for reasons I will get into above). For a more in-depth argument for taking

ply univocally to a person if it referred to an individual in hell, where hell is conceived of as a place where sinners suffer eternal violence and alienation from others, and *where God accrues glory from their suffering.*[27] Recall that, under Patterson's definition of slavery, a situation where one person accrues honor from the violent domination of a natally alienated person is slavery. God would hold *that* sort of power over a human being—the sort of power that a master holds over an enslaved person—only in a situation where hell is conceived in exactly the way described above. However, there are a diversity of views on final judgment within Christian theology, so Christians are not forced into affirming that this situation ever obtains, least of all from any reading of the books that comprise the New Testament itself.[28]

On the other hand, even if the language of "slaves of God" is analogous, it is still disturbing because it uses an unjust situation to illuminate God's relationship to humanity. Does use of the analogy imply approval of slavery? Do we need to observe enslaved individuals in day-to-day life to understand the analogy? Does the use of the analogy make slavery's presence necessary for the practice of Christian spirituality? I believe the answer to all three questions is "No." This is because, in his parables, Jesus

violent eschatological language in the New Testament canon as analogical or metaphorical rather than literal or univocal, see Hays, *Moral Vision*, 173–75.

27. One of the most famous examples of this teaching is Jonathan Edward's "Sinners in the Hands of an Angry God," where Edwards depicts God as almost gleefully holding the damned over a raging fire (among other things). See Edwards et al., *Sinners in the Hands*, 33. Though I have cited Thomas Aquinas favorably up until this point, even he may ultimately fall into this camp, as he claims that God reprobates some to hell for the sake of his glory (*ST* I.23.5 reply to objection 3).

28. For example, annihilationists and universalists would easily avoid the belief that God ever holds enslaved people in this (univocal) sense. Additionally, those who believe in a "hell" that is essentially non-eternal and remedial would avoid this troubling implication. For those who would reject all such beliefs as aberrant or heterodox, it is important to remember that a very wide diversity of beliefs concerning "hell" obtained in Christianity before the doctrine was formalized as a place of eternal, conscious torment in the early middle ages. Even Jesus' use of terms such as *Gehenna* in no way indicate that he believed in a place of eternal, conscious torment, let alone one where God derived glory from the abuse being heaped upon its occupants. For the exegetical issues involved with "hell" terms, see David Bentley Hart's notes on his translation of the New Testament in Hart, *New Testament*, 537–48. Hart argues that *aiōnios* (the word used to designate the duration of the punishment) is frustratingly inexact, and can confusingly mean both "eternal" and "temporary." Likewise, *Gehenna* is more frequently associated with temporary and remedial punishment than it is with eternal and retributive punishment.

frequently uses unsavory characters to explain God's relationship with humanity. In Matt 24:43, Jesus likens God to a thief.[29] In Luke 19:11–27, Jesus compares God to a king that he explicitly characterizes as a murderous tyrant. In Luke 18:1–8, Jesus compares God to an unjust judge. Do these analogies entail approval of theft, tyranny, murder, corruption? Do they require the presence of people who practice these things for Christian spirituality to remain viable? Clearly Jesus didn't think so, as he advocates that his disciples imitate God in eschewing such things (e.g., Matt 5:48; Luke 6:36). This suggests that, while Jesus thought that even the lives of horrendously unjust human beings could be used as a conduit of revelation, God is still very unlike the examples Jesus brings forward.[30]

One final indicator that "slaves of God" is not intended in a univocal sense in the New Testament is the fact that Christians are called both "slaves of God" and "children of God." In the New Testament, adoption frequently serves as a metaphor of the relationship between the believer and God. In Greco-Roman terms, these are mutually exclusive social roles; one cannot be a child and be enslaved at the same time. Reading these phrases analogously is the only way to read Romans in a way that doesn't entail that Paul's thought is self-contradictory, since Paul says *both* that Christians are slaves of God (Rom 6:22) and that Christians are *not* slaves of God (Rom 8:15) in the same unit of discourse. Given the emphasis on adoption in early Christian theology, and the subsequent emphasis on salvation being a matter of incorporation into the divine life of the Trinity, the enslavement analogy is shown to encompass the greater disanalogy: Christians are "slaves of God" in a metaphorical sense only. They aren't enslaved in any real sense.[31]

29. See also 1 Thess 5:2; 2 Pet 3:10; and Rev 16:15.

30. Here, an insight by Dale Martin is helpful. Martin points out that it is extremely odd that early Christians chose slavery as a *positive* metaphor for salvation. He astutely asks, "If the institution of slavery was as oppressive as it seems to have been, and if Greeks and Romans so feared slavery and despised slaves, how could slavery portray salvation positively for early Christians? Why, in other words, would any person of that society want to be called a slave of Christ?" (Martin, *Slavery as Salvation*, xiv). Believing that there must be some sort of sociological explanation behind this positive deployment of the metaphor, Martin goes on to make the rather controversial argument that, in some instances, slavery could be an avenue for upward social mobility in the Roman Empire (see esp. Martin, *Slavery as Salvation*, xxii, 1–49). Regardless of whether or not Martin is correct in his analysis, his initial questions are quite astute. Only if we take into account the "topsy-turvy" power relations that obtain in Jesus' preaching about the kingdom of God (discussed later) can such a positive deployment of the metaphor even begin to make sense.

31. Hans Urs von Balthasar once claimed that this particular shortcoming in the

In fact, to call God "Lord" may be the most distortive of all analogies. Jesus never consciously tries to upend his disciples' conceptions of fatherhood, motherhood, or judgeship before comparing God to a father, a mother, or a judge, even though distortion exists in these analogies. He largely trusts them to know where such distortion lies. But here (and only here), he raises a red flag. He tries to completely upend their conception of "lordship" before applying the term to either himself or God. For the "God Is Lord" analogy to have any positive purpose, in order for it not to be completely distortive, the disciples have to completely change their understanding of what "lordship" is.

Before moving on to the second consideration, a final caveat is in order: nothing I have said above should be taken as an attempt to rehabilitate the use of the phrase "slaves of God" for a modern context. In fact, I would argue *against* its use in modern contexts, because the possibility for distortion is too great. All I am trying to do here is assure that the analogy doesn't work to obscure the portrait of God presented by the authors of the New Testament. In some cases, a misunderstanding of how analogy functions has led readers of the New Testament to the wrong sorts of conclusions about God. I am trying to assure that the phrase doesn't obscure our portrait of God; I am not trying to rehabilitate the phrase.

Regarding the second consideration, since the beginning, Christians have held that the highest, most complete revelation of God is found in the person of Jesus Christ. There is no God "behind" Jesus. The life of Jesus Christ is not a temporary performance that God must "get over" to get to God's true agenda. Christ is the apex revelation of God's character and of the nature of God's salvation for humanity. One never sees—and never *can* see—God more clearly than in the face of Jesus Christ.

This is important to affirm, because Christian groups have tried to find a God behind Jesus Christ at various points at history. Christians have tried to say things like, "Jesus once came in humility, but later he will come in glory." "Jesus once came preaching a message of nonviolent enemy love, but later he will come to slaughter all of his enemies." Another variation of this would be "Jesus once came to die the death of a slave,

---

analogy was exactly why the Servant-Lord language so present in the Hebrew Bible is challenged in Jesus, and ultimately gives way to the language of mutual glorification in the New Testament: each person of the Trinity glorifies those they adopt into the divine life, just as those they adopt glorify each person of the Trinity. For Balthasar's extended argument on how this shift occurs (especially in the Gospel of John), see Balthasar, *Glory of the Lord*, 239–63.

but now he comes to make others his slaves" (i.e., to suffer for his glory eternally in hell).

In contrast to this, it must be said that Jesus' humble itinerant ministry (culminating in his crucifixion on a Roman cross) is not a temporary performance that Jesus performs so that he can get back to the real business of being God. Jesus in his earthly ministry already reveals divine glory in its fullest (as is blatantly obvious in the Gospel of John).[32] In the Sermon on the Mount, Christ offers not a temporary ethic to be overturned at some time in the future, but an invitation into the divine life itself, a life that eschews judgment, hatred, violence, separation, and worry. There is no God that Christians can ever hope to see, now or at any point in the future, that does not look like a homeless, itinerant, nonviolent radical Jew from the backwater of Galilee. This is the only thing Christians can ever claim to see of God clearly. Anything else entails approaching God with a veiled mind.[33]

This brings us to the third consideration, Jesus' teachings on the nature of power and authority. The centerpiece of Jesus' teaching on power and authority is a passage that is found in all of the Synoptic Gospels. Here's Mark's version:

> Jesus called them together and said, "You know that those who are regarded as rulers of the Gentiles lord it over them, and their high officials exercise authority over them. Not so with you. Instead, whoever wants to become great among you must be your servant, and whoever wants to be first must be slave of all. For even the Son of Man did not come to be served, but to serve, and to give his life as a ransom for many." (Mark 10:42–45; cf. Matt 20:25–28)

32. For an overview of this theme in the scholarship on the *krisis* (judgment) and glory revealed in Jesus' (first) coming in the Johannine Literature, see Hays, *Moral Vision*, 149–50.

33. The analogy was first used by Paul to describe reading the Torah non-Christologically (2 Cor 3:15–16). He was contending that the contents of the Torah could foster deep confusion in Christian readers if they were not reading it in the light of the life, death, and resurrection of Jesus Christ. I'm suggesting that this is a fruitful way for Christians to read the Torah, but Christians have often not carried the conclusion far enough. Not only is Genesis difficult to understand without this lens, but so is Revelation. Anything said in the New Testament could be distortive if it is not read through the life, death, and resurrection of Jesus Christ. Hence if one comes at the White Rider in Revelation as though it were a stable image of who Jesus is, without considering the poor Galilean, that person will fundamentally misunderstand who Jesus is, and will therefore misunderstand who God is.

The contrast Jesus is giving is between lordship as it is practiced in "the nations" (or "among the gentiles") and his own lordship. Among the nations, the one with power is the one at the top. Jesus says his power—real power—is found in the hands of the folks at the bottom. The one who is enslaved is more powerful than the one who claims to be master. Luke's version of this teaching is worth laying aside Mark's, because it heightens the unexpected nature of this revelation:

> A dispute also arose among them as to which one of them was to be regarded as the greatest. But he said to them, "The kings of the Gentiles lord it over them; and those in authority over them are called benefactors. But not so with you; rather the greatest among you must become like the youngest, and the leader like one who serves. For who is greater, the one who is at the table or the one who serves? Is it not the one at the table? But I am among you as one who serves." (Luke 22:24–27)

This is despite the fact that Luke's most common title for Jesus is "the Lord."[34] At every turn in Luke (and the other Synoptics), Jesus is contrasting his lordship to the lordship of the rulers of the nations, though if you read this passage in isolation (and without any hint of irony), you might come away with the impression that Jesus' question ("For who is greater, the one who is at the table or the one who serves? Is it not the one at the table?") is a concession that the more conventional conception of lordship is the correct one. But the very next statement gives the expected answer the lie: "I am among you as one who serves."

The clear message is rather that disciples of Jesus should completely upend their understanding of what power is. The answer to the question Jesus asks seems obvious. But that answer is wrong. Jesus is often taken in these passages as setting an ethical rule that people who have power should follow. If you have power, you should not "lord it over others." You should use your power to serve others (let's call this "the command reading"). But what if Jesus is trying to redefine what power *is*? Recall Gene Sharp's distinction between a "monolith" theory of power and a "pluralistic-dependency" theory of power (mentioned in the first chapter). "Monolith" theory holds that power flows from the person on top down to the people below. "Pluralistic-dependency" theory holds that power flows in the opposite direction. If pluralistic-dependency theory

34. For an in-depth treatment of the frequency and significance of this title in Luke's Gospel, see Rowe, *Early Narrative Christology*.

is correct, lords depend on their subjects, not the other way around (as is commonly thought). This is because

> by themselves, rulers cannot collect taxes, enforce repressive laws and regulations, keep trains running on time, prepare national budgets, direct traffic, manage ports, print money, repair roads, keep markets supplied with food, make steel, build rockets, train the police and army, issue postage stamps or even milk a cow.[35]

Map these theories of power onto the distinction Jesus makes (where "the lordship of the nations" = monolith theory and "the lordship of Christ" = pluralistic-dependency theory), and a very different reading is produced (let's call this "the power analysis reading"). On the power analysis reading, Jesus is pointing out that power as the nations see it is parasitic. A gentile lord is dependent on his subjects for power. But God is transcendent (i.e., not dependent upon anything in the world, including its power structures). If Jesus is God-With-Us, if Jesus ushers in the kingdom of God, if Jesus wields the power of God, then he cannot be dependent upon the world's sources of power.[36] On this analysis of power, if Jesus were to simply take a place higher up the chain of command than these lords of the nations, he would actually be *more* dependent than the lords below him.

One can see this critique of worldly power at subtly play in all of the Gospels. The two most powerful men in the Gospel narrative are Herod and Pilate, both of whom are regularly portrayed as no more than puppets (usually to the will of the people). According to Mark, Herod has John the Baptist executed not because he wants to, but because his wife and daughter manipulate him through a foolish oath he makes (Mark 6:17–29). Pilate is revealed to be a man without principle, a man who

35. This quotation frequently circulates in the literature on nonviolent resistance, and it is frequently credited as coming from Sharp, *Politics of Nonviolent Action, Part One*. However, I have been unable to locate this quotation in this source, even after several readthroughs. I first encountered it in Popovic and Mimoun, "How to Beat the Islamic State." Regardless of whether or not this quotation comes from Sharp's work, it is a good summary of his thought.

36. In John, Jesus makes much the same point: "My kingdom is not from this world. If my kingdom were from this world, my followers would be fighting to keep me from being handed over to the Jews. But as it is, my kingdom is not from here" (John 18:36). If Jesus wielded power as the lords of the nations wielded power, then he would command an army against his enemies. But power on the world's terms is weak. Or ineffectual. Or just plain alien to the reign of God. Or all of the above.

will execute even those he finds innocent if it pleases the crowds (Luke 22:13–25). On the other hand, Jesus the peasant's very words have an immediacy and power that the crowds all inherently recognize (Matthew 7:29), and he is the one who emerges victorious over even death itself.

Why is this re-evaluation of where true power lies important for our purposes here? The answer lies in how we identify God. It is a common belief that God is identified primarily through the possession of raw power. Even if one does not believe omnipotence is possible, they may still believe that if you put all entities that exist in the same room with one another, the one who possesses the most power could be addressed as "god." In this sense, if Superman were real, you could call him a "god." More contextually, if a master holds power of life or death over you, then he is your "god," but may not be the "god" of someone else (over whom that power is not held).

The problem is that this is a fundamentally "gentile" (and polytheist) concept of divinity, and one that rests on what Jesus points out is a "gentile" concept of lordship. The God of Israel is neither a "god" nor an "entity" in this sense at all.[37] Perhaps the clearest story in the Hebrew Bible that calls attention to this is the story of Elijah meeting God at Horeb:

> Then the word of the Lord came to him, saying, "What are you doing here, Elijah?" He answered, "I have been very zealous for the Lord, the God of hosts; for the Israelites have forsaken your covenant, thrown down your altars, and killed your prophets with the sword. I alone am left, and they are seeking my life, to take it away." He said, "Go out and stand on the mountain before

37. Hence Brad Gregory is correct when he argues, "The difference between Christian and other ancient views of God (or gods) is more fundamental than is often recognized, and goes far beyond a distinction of monotheism and polytheism. According to this Christian view, God is not a highest, noblest, or most powerful entity within the universe, 'divine' by virtue of being comparatively greatest. Rather, God is radically distinct from the universe as a whole, which he did not fashion by ordering anything already existent but rather created entirely ex nihilo. God's creative action proceeded neither by necessity nor by chance but from his deliberative love, and *as* love (cf. 1 Jn 4:8) God constantly sustains the world through his intimate, providential care. Although God is radically transcendent and altogether other than his creation, he is sovereignly present to and acts in and through it. There is no 'outside' to creation, spatially or temporally, nor is any part of creation independent of God or capable of existing independently of God" (Gregory, *Unintended Reformation*, 29–30). It is important to add, however, that because God is transcendent, even descriptors of God's power such as "sovereign" are analogies. If God is transcendent, then the statements "the king is sovereign" and "God is sovereign" cannot be utilizing the adjective "sovereign" in the same way.

> the Lord, for the Lord is about to pass by." Now there was a great wind, so strong that it was splitting mountains and breaking rocks in pieces before the Lord, but the Lord was not in the wind; and after the wind an earthquake, but the Lord was not in the earthquake; and after the earthquake a fire, but the Lord was not in the fire; and after the fire a sound of sheer silence. When Elijah heard it, he wrapped his face in his mantle and went out and stood at the entrance of the cave. Then there came a voice to him that said, "What are you doing here, Elijah?" (1 Kgs 19:9–13)

Here we see that powerful, terrifying, and flashy natural phenomena (great winds, earthquakes, and fire) are explicitly *not* to be identified with God. God is instead identified in "a sound of silence," a confusing and much debated phrase, but surely an unexpected place to find God however it is rendered.

Finding God is not merely a matter of seeking out the person who wields the most power (at least, in a conventional sense). Even if you can find someone who can move mountains at a whim, you can't be entirely sure you've found what you're looking for.[38] God can never be identified through the sheer exercise of power.[39] How then is God to be identified? Multiple ways have been proposed, many of which could be considered complementary. Two are worth mentioning here: (1) God is identified as the one who fulfills the promises God made to Israel.[40] (2) God is the ground of all Being; the source of all that is.[41] The first identifies God by way of a history, one that refers to both past and future events (and as

38. This is precisely why the claim that Jesus is God was controversial in the first century (and beyond) even among those who recognized that Jesus performed miracles. Casting out demons, healing all forms of illness, and even raising the dead do not serve as proof of divinity in the Jewish theological world. They don't even necessarily prove divine authorization; the source of the power could come from elsewhere (see for example, the accusation Jesus faces in Mark 3:20–22 and its parallels).

39. On a related note, this is precisely the problem with the continual assumption that when Jesus places a master or a rich landowner in a parable, that person represents God. Simply because that person has the most earthly power in the parable doesn't automatically make them a divine stand-in.

40. Many Jewish scholars would likely back this description (minus the references to events in the New Testament). Among Christian scholars, N. T. Wright stands out here. Wright contends that this plus the miracles was what convinced a group of Jews in the first century that Jesus was God, not simply the miracles alone (Wright, *Challenge of Jesus*, 106–20).

41. This is an explicitly Thomist way of rendering the matter.

such, it has an aim). God is identified as the one who frees the Israelites from slavery; the one who calls Abram out of Ur; the one who raised Jesus from the dead; the one who will put an end to sin, death, and evil once and for all. The second identifies God as perpetual gift; as that which continually gives being to all that is out of a perpetual excess that flows out of the life of the Trinity.

I have already alluded to how God's history with Israel, especially in the person of Jesus Christ, questions the portrait of power and godhood assumed in systems of slavery. Jesus' analysis of the authority of the nations reveals the sort of power that masters seek as weak, derivative, dependent, parasitic, false. Ultimately, Hegel was right when he claimed that the slave-master relationship results in a false form of recognition because the master receives recognition from the one who is enslaved, but does not give that enslaved person recognition, while the one who is enslaved gives recognition to the master but does not receive recognition from the master. This means that it is the one who is enslaved who is independent and it is the one who claims to be the master who is dependent, meaning that the one who is enslaved is in a very real sense more powerful than the one who claims to be master.[42] Hegel simply didn't take matters far enough: this is what happens any time one tries to climb some sort of dominance-based hierarchy in order to claim power. It simply ends up reaffirming dependency.

The second way outlined above helps us to see that God is not so much the most powerful entity in existence, but is rather the ground or possibility for all that exists (including all exercises of power). "Omnipotence" is a fine word to use to describe God's relationship to power, so long as one realizes that it (like all language for God) is analogical. Omnipotence ("all powerful") can, however, be distorting because it can give one the sense that God exercises power in the same way that human beings do. Here, Rowan Williams has offered a helpful corrective:

> Creation is not an exercise of divine power, odd though that certainly sounds. Power is exercised *by* x *over* y; but creation is

42. Hegel, *Phenomenology of Spirit*, 116–17. What Hegel got precisely wrong here was his conviction that God needs to go through this abortive form of recognition to become God. That fundamentally falls into the exact mistake currently under critique: that "God" simply names the entity with the most power. Hegel's God is ultimately a shadow of a human lord, because Hegel's God, like a human lord, needs to ascend. But such an ascension simply reveals the lord's dependence, rather than proving his independence.

> not power, because it is not exercised *on* anything. We might, of course, want to say that creation presupposes a divine potentiality, or resourcefulness, or abundance of active life; and "power" can sometimes be used in those senses. But what creation emphatically isn't is any kind of imposition or manipulation: it is not God imposing on us divinely willed roles rather than the ones we "naturally" might have, or defining us out of our own systems into God's. . . . Creation in the classical sense does not therefore involve some uncritical idea of God's "monarchy." The absolute freedom ascribed to God in creation means that God *cannot* make a reality that then needs to be actively governed, subdued, bent to the divine purpose away from its natural course. If God creates freely, God does not need the power of a sovereign; what is, is from God. God's sovereign purpose *is* what the world is becoming.[43]

"Omnipotence" becomes a distorting descriptor for God when it is taken to mean simply that God has acquired enough power to bend any possible competitors to God's will, whatever that will might be. This is completely unnecessary, because, as Williams points out, the relationship between God and the world is not one of competition. God is not a thing in the world, and therefore does not compete with anything in the world. Similarly, God's "sovereignty" is not a matter of God exercising governance over the cosmos as a human king exercises governance over his territory, for if it were, then God would be dependent upon creatures for God's omnipotence, because the exercise of God's power would be dependent upon human obedience to the divine will. This is because human political power is not self-generating; it depends on the obedience of the governed toward the sovereign. God's power is rather a power of "donation," "animation," or "vivification." God gives all things their motion. "Source" is perhaps a better term than "lord" with respect to God because human lords depend on their subjects for their power. A source, however, does not depend on what it powers for its power.

This may explain why, in the *Summa Theologica*, Thomas Aquinas did not list "power" or "omnipotence" among God's attributes.[44] Instead,

43. Williams, *On Christian Theology*, 68–69, emphasis in original. Part of me wants to quibble with Williams' language here in his contention that all power is power *over*, but really, the point seems moot because Williams himself admits that we use the language of power in rather fuzzy ways. What is important is that I emphatically do agree with Williams' conclusion: God does not impose upon or manipulate creation.

44. God's attributes are listed in Aquinas, *ST* I.3–11. Those attributes are simplicity, goodness, perfection, infinity, omnipresence, immutability, eternity, and unity.

Aquinas lists "power" among God's "operations,"[45] and it is specifically an "external" operation, that is, one ordered to creation.[46] The other two operations are knowledge and will, and they are both "internal" to God.[47] God's power is God's activity proceeding from God's knowledge and will toward creatures. Power, then, is not something God exercises over Godself, because God does not serve as a "cause" of God. Given the fact that God's power proceeds from God's knowledge and will, there is also no disconnect or "gap" in its exercise. In any relationship of dominance, there is a disconnect that obtains between that which dominates and that which is dominated, and between will and the exercise of power. In God there is no such separation between will and power. Thus, "power" in reference to God names both an end and a set of means. It is neither "sheer" nor "arbitrary" (as the power of a master is). It is always aimed toward that which is good, it is always aimed toward a giving of oneself out of a life so abundant that even perpetual giving does not result in decrease. God's power is also not separate from the perfect, and ever-giving love that flows out of the community of divine persons that is the Trinity. The name for both the purpose of God's power and the means God's power utilizes is "peace."[48] This means that God cannot enslave people, for slavery is antithetical to peace. It is antithetical to the nonviolent love of God. In violently dominating another, in gaining glory from the suffering of another, God would be untrue to Godself. God would prove to be arbitrary, false, dependent, weak, parasitic on creation. God can become incarnate in "the form of a slave" and stay true to Godself, because enslaved people are not parasites. God cannot become incarnate in the form of a slaveholder and stay true to Godself, because slaveholders *are* parasites.

This brings us to the fourth and final item that should ground a Christian portrait of God. By centering Jesus' critique of "gentile"

45. Aquinas, *ST* I.14–26.

46. Aquinas, *ST* I.25.

47. The terms "internal" and "external" here are likewise distorting. The terms suggest limits or boundaries, both of which are specifically denied by naming "infinity" among God's attributes. Here a clarification made by Steve Long is helpful: "The expressions 'internal' and 'external' are not about space or location; they signify what God must be to be God (internal operations) and what God can do in God's freedom as God (external operations)" (Long, *Perfectly Simple Triune God*, 34).

48. Mahatma Gandhi called his philosophy of nonviolence *satyagraha* to point out that truth is always the aim of true nonviolence, and nonviolence was always the means through which truth expressed itself. As Truth, I am claiming the same thing for God.

lordship, it is now considerably easier to discern an abolitionist trajectory in the narrative of Scripture that runs far deeper than the slaveholding metaphors. And this is what we should expect to find if the power of God explicitly repudiates the power of all "gods" and "masters." I have given an account of this abolitionist trajectory in Scripture elsewhere,[49] but I will try to briefly restate the main points of this trajectory in what follows.

The story of the people called Israel truly begins with the Exodus. Having formed an ethnic identity through enslavement in the Egyptian Empire, the Hebrews are liberated by the God of their ancestors through the mediation of Moses, Aaron, and Miriam. As Israel is in the process of coming out of Egypt, God gives Israel a blueprint for a new tribal society that stands in contrast to the Egyptian Empire. This blueprint is referred to as the Torah. In stark contrast to the Empire built on slavery that God liberated the Israelites from, the new society that the Hebrews are tasked with founding puts a heavy emphasis on economic equality.[50] Some key distinctives of economic life in this new society include mandatory weekly periods of rest for workers (e.g., Exod 20:8–11), the institution of protections for economically vulnerable populations (e.g., Exod 23:9; Lev 19:33–34; Num 15:15; Deut 10:17–19), the abolition of charging interest on loans to the poor (e.g., Lev 25:36), prohibitions on exploiting laborers through robbing them of their wages (e.g., Deut 24:14–15), and the institution of a massive recurring program of wealth redistribution (e.g., the famous Jubilee legislation of Lev 25). In fact, the explicit goal of Israelite society was to become a classless society with no distinction between rich and poor (Deut 15:4). All of these distinctives are important for assuring economic justice on their own, but for our purposes here, it is important to note that collectively, these are the societal safeguards that would have been necessary in the ancient Near East to prevent Israelites from falling into debt slavery. In other words, the explicit goal of a Torah-based society is to prevent its most vulnerable members from slipping back into slavery.

As such, the appearance of mass slavery in the land of Israel was the ultimate sign of the abandonment of the way of life prescribed in the Torah. Since Israel had been set free from slavery in Egypt by God, God gives repeated instructions to the Israelites not to return to slavery. Returning to slavery is frequently referred to as "returning to Egypt" in

49. See Gooding, "Judgment."

50. Brueggemann, *Prophetic Imagination*, 6–9.

the Torah (e.g., Num 14:3–4; Deut 17:16; cf. Hos 8:13). But "returning to Egypt" also has a dual meaning: Israel is forbidden both from resubmitting themselves to bondage to the Egyptians and from structuring their society like Egypt. In other words, they are forbidden from attempting to become yet another Empire built upon the backs of enslaved people.

When the people appoint a king in Israel, it represents the ultimate abandonment of the Torah's vision of a new society.[51] This is because Israel's monarchs attempted to fashion Israel into an empire built upon slavery, just like all of the other empires of the world. The palace and military administrations instituted by the kings were funded by a regressive taxation scheme that drove the poor into massive debt and dispossessed them of their lands. This caused a significant portion of Israel's population to fall into debt slavery.[52] Samuel even predicts that this will occur in detail when Israel asks him to appoint a king in 1 Sam 8. Samuel's prophetic word to Israel culminates with the ominous prediction that the king will enslave the Israelites. This prediction comes horrifyingly true when Solomon uses the labor of enslaved people (including enslaved Israelites) to build the Jerusalem temple, his palace, and the walls surrounding Jerusalem (1 Kgs 9:15; 1 Kgs 11:28).[53] The Israelites go to Solomon's son Rehoboam and request that he "lighten the harsh labor and the heavy yoke" put on Israel by Solomon. Instead, Rehoboam vows to intensify the practice of inducting Israelites into slavery. Incensed by his response, the Northern Tribes rebel, and the once unified kingdom of Israel divides into the northern kingdom of Israel and the southern kingdom of Judah (1 Kings 12:1–19). The kings of both the northern kingdom and the southern kingdom continue to try to fashion their kingdoms into empires, ignoring the tenets of economic justice laid out in the Torah. God decides that if these kingdoms aspire to become slaveholding empires, then God will not protect them from sharing the fate of all slaveholding empires. Thus, the independent kingdoms of Israel and Judah came to an end the same way that all ancient empires did: they eventually got taken

51. Brueggeman, *Prophetic Imagination*, 22–23.

52. Chirichigno, *Debt-Slavery in Israel*, 113–20.

53. First Kings 9:20 asserts that the Israelites were *not* forced into slavery build the temple. Rather, it was the Canaanite peoples surrounding Israel who were enslaved and forced to build the temple. However, 1 Kgs 11:28 directly contradicts this assertion by stating plainly that the Northern Tribes were inducted into forced labor soon before Solomon's death, and the ensuing rebellion against Rehoboam occurs because he intensifies (rather than eases) his father's practice of utilizing forced Israelite labor (1 Kgs 12:1–19).

over by a larger empire. Israel is conquered by the Assyrian Empire, and Judah is overtaken by the Babylonian Empire and forced into exile. In other words, the refusal to build a society that protects its most vulnerable members from being enslaved results in a judgment that splits the nation, robs Israel and Judah of peaceful coexistence, and eventually ends with their captivity to greater empires. No economic justice, no provision of peace and protection.

The transition of Israel into a slaveholding empire is a constant point of social critique for the pre-Exilic Prophets (especially Amos, Hosea, Isaiah, and Micah).[54] For the Prophets, it is not just any violation of the many dictates of the Torah that accrues God's judgment. There is a reoccurring theme in the Prophets that the exile results specifically from Israel's abandonment of monotheism and its abandonment of economic justice. And even then, there is a recurring theme in the Prophets that adherence to the Torah's guidance on matters of economic justice is far more important in God's eyes than adherence to its guidance on right worship (e.g., Hos 6:4-11; Isa 1:11–17; Jer 7). Prophetic diatribes that contend that calamity comes upon Israel and Judah precisely because the Torah's standards of economic justice have been abandoned include Isa 3:14–15; 58:2–7; Jer 22; Ezek 18:1–13; 22:23–29; Zech 7:9–13; Amos 4:1; 5:11–12; 8:4–6 and many others. In fact, for Isaiah, the point of the entirety of the Torah is the liberation of all people from captivity of all kinds, whether it be the captivity of slavery, the captivity of prison, or the captivity of subjugation by the empires. Here, Isa 58 is worth quoting in full, simply because of its abolitionist fervor:

> Is not this the kind of fasting I have chosen:
> to loose the chains of injustice
> and untie the ropes of the enslaved,
> to set the oppressed free
> and break every yoke? (v. 6)

Fortunately, for the Prophets, the exile is not God's last word on the matter. The Prophets began to predict the coming of a Messiah: a king that would not be like the kings of the nations, a king who would uphold the Torah and lead people back to its original vision for a just society. This would be a king that would end the unjust reign of the empires that subjugated Israel and would liberate its people from all forms of bondage (Dan 7:1–14). As I mentioned in chapter 1, the Prophets seemed to see

54. Chirichigno, *Debt-Slavery in Israel*, 125–28.

a species relationship between incarceration, enslavement, and occupation by the empires. All of these were forms of "captivity," and when the Messiah came, he would put an end to them all. This is why passages such as Isa 42:6–7 and Zech 9:9–12 can be translated as proclaiming release for either the incarcerated or the enslaved or even those under imperial occupation.[55]

Jesus clearly embraced this understanding of the Messiah's mission. In Luke 4:16–21 he states clearly that the mission of his ministry is to "proclaim release to the captives" and "to let the oppressed go free." And like the Prophets, Jesus prioritizes economic equality in his message. This is perhaps nowhere more obvious than in Jesus' repeated admonitions to his disciples to regularly and radically redistribute their wealth, much as the Jubilee asked Israel to regularly and radically redistribute their wealth (Matt 19:21; Mark 10:21; Luke 12:22a; 14:33; 18:22; cf. 19:8). In fact, Luke presents the Jerusalem church as a foretaste of the ideal eschatological classless society envisioned in Deut 15:

> All the believers were one in heart and mind. No one claimed that any of their possessions was their own, but they shared everything they had. With great power the apostles continued to testify to the resurrection of the Lord Jesus. And God's grace was so powerfully at work in them all that there were no needy persons among them. For from time to time those who owned land or houses sold them, brought the money from the sales and put it at the apostles' feet, and it was distributed to anyone who had need." (Acts 4:32–35; cf. 2:44–45)

In other words, the Gospel writers (and Luke especially) anticipate that the societal safeguards necessary to prevent individuals from falling into slavery will be fully present when the kingdom of God that Christ has inaugurated comes in its fullness.

But here one more note about the abolitionist trajectory in Scripture is necessary. I have contended above that the idea that God's justice ultimately requires a large chunk of humanity suffering eternal conscious torment in hell borrows too much from the logic of slavery and is antithetical to an abolitionist understanding of justice. I have alleged that the belief that God consigns people to eternal conscious torment for the sake of his own glory essentially puts God in the role of a slaveowner

55. Again, for a deeper look at the species connections between enslavement, incarceration, and imperial occupation in both the ancient world and in the work of modern abolitionists, see Gooding, "Judgment."

and the damned in the role of the enslaved. Thankfully, many authors of the New Testament seem to have little sympathy with the idea of eternal damnation themselves. This may be a contentious claim for some. Given the predominance of the theology of Augustine (who argued thoroughly for the existence of a hell of eternal conscious torment in *Civ.* 21) it was once assumed in most parts of Western Christianity that belief in a hell of eternal conscious torment was shared by all of the authors of the New Testament as well as the majority of the church fathers. But a slow reassessment of both the church fathers and the New Testament over the past century has revealed that there is good reason to think that a belief in the universal restoration of all things was more common than previously admitted. In other words, the biblical narrative culminates with the affirmation that, in the end, God saves everyone. This is an idea frequently referred to as universal salvation. Universal salvation entails that Christ's death and resurrection were sufficient to bring salvation to all, even without regard to whether an individual manifests faith in Christ in this life (as is assumed in 1 Tim 4:10). Belief in universal salvation is not incompatible with a belief in hell or a final judgment (many adherents of universal salvation believe in both), but on a universalist reading, hell is temporary and restorative (rather than a place of eternal torture). Eventually, those who enter it will be redeemed, and hell will be empty.

Belief in universal salvation was a conviction shared among early Christian theologians such as Origen of Alexandria, Gregory of Nyssa, Theodore of Mopsuestia, Clement of Alexandria, Isaac of Nineveh, and Evagrius Ponticus. Even such theological heavy hitters as Athanasius of Alexandria, Basil the Great, and Maximus Confessor make arguments in their writings that seem to assume universal salvation as a given.[56] Among the New Testament writings, affirmations of universal salvation show up in the Johannine literature (esp. John 3:17; 17:2; and 1 John 2:2), in Luke-Acts (esp. Luke 16:16), in Hebrews (esp. 2:9), and in other Catholic epistles (esp. 2 Pet 3:9). But by a fairly wide margin, the New Testament author who refers to universal salvation the most is Paul. Numerous passages could here be cited, but the most significant are Rom 5:12–21 and 1 Cor 15:21–28. In both locations, Paul presents the death of Christ as straightforwardly undoing the sin of Adam. Just as through

56. An assessment of all of these thinkers would be impossible here, but for those who are interested, the most in-depth treatment of early Christian universalism is Ramelli, *Christian Doctrine of Apokatastasis*. For a defense of universal salvation that is accessible to lay Christians, I would recommend Hart, *That All Shall Be Saved*.

Adam's action sin comes to permeate all of humanity, so through Christ's action salvation comes to all of humanity: "Therefore just as one man's trespass led to condemnation for all, so one man's act of righteousness leads to justification and life for all" (Rom 5:21–28). The scope of the liberation that Christ brings extends to all of humanity, and even to the ends of the cosmos in Paul's writings.

The passage from 1 Cor 15 is even more germane for our purposes here. There Paul affirms that Christ will bring life to all "after he has destroyed all dominion, authority, and power" (v. 24). Again, the affirmation is that all forms of "lordship" and "captivity" are done away with when Christ comes again in power. The result is that all humanity is given life, all of creation is liberated from all forms of bondage, and "God will be all in all" (v. 28). Here then is the final abolitionist word in the Christian narrative: the kingdom of God aims at the full abolition of all varieties of human bondage, whether that bondage is slavery, prison, imperial occupation, economic exploitation, or even hell itself. Justice and liberation in eternity cannot be fundamentally different from justice and liberation in the here and now.

And this is precisely where the portrait of God I am offering up may experience the most resistance. Many Christians in the modern anti-slavery movement are willing to fight for the abolition of slavery, but many are not yet ready to push for the abolition of prisons, fully repudiate the legacy of colonialism, work for the abolition of class and caste, or affirm universal salvation. The modern anti-slavery movement has often prided itself on the fact that it has found an issue everyone can agree upon. Everyone agrees that slavery is a moral abomination. Affirming abolitionist views of other sorts might be considered controversial or divisive. In the end, this may also be why biblical scholarship on slavery in Scripture often completely ignores the abolitionist trajectory I have just sketched: the Messianic abolitionism in Jesus and the Prophets may be seen as so radical that many Christian readers have simply assumed they cannot seriously have meant what they claimed. The "everys" and "alls" in "break every yoke," "Christ will destroy all dominion, authority, and power" and "all will be given life" have been taken as merely rhetorical flourishes, nothing more. However, there have always been Christians that have been willing to take the calls to loosen every chain and break every yoke at face value, and to draw connections between species of abolitionism.[57]

57. Concerning Christian arguments for prison abolition, I would heartily recommend Dubler and Lloyd, *Break Every Yoke*; Logan, *Good Punishment?*; and Taylor, *Way*

Their witness has already had a decided impact on the historic coalition against slavery, whether we wish to admit it or not.

It is the hope and confession of every Christian that one day, all "gods" and all "masters" will die. The form of power that is parasitic on others will pass away. All that will remain is God and those caught up in the triune life. But until that day comes in its fullness, it is the calling of those who worship this God to look for ways to extricate others from this form of power. We turn next to what that might look like in the day-to-day lives of sex trafficking survivors.

of the Cross. For Christian arguments for police abolition, I would recommend Purnell, *Becoming Abolitionists*. Unlike the others in this list, Derecka Purnell is a lawyer rather than a theologian. But she makes her Christian faith commitments clear in her writings and public speaking engagements.

Chapter 4

Prisons and Monasteries[1]

IN MUMBAI, THERE ARE two basic types of institutional aftercare for sex trafficking survivors: prisons and monasteries. That statement may seem a touch overdramatic to some readers, but it comes from the testimony of the survivors I interviewed. I could, perhaps, be accused of importing the concept of "monasteries" onto their testimony (it isn't language that they use themselves), but as this chapter unfolds, I will maintain that it is a fairly accurate description based on the testimony given by my interviewees. The same accusation cannot be made concerning the language of "prisons" or "jails": those are terms my interviewees used directly.

> **Muskan:** I was in Devnar (that's a government home). There were 150 girls there with me. The home was okay, but sometimes we would get enough food, and other times we wouldn't. There were times we found bugs in the food. There was almost always some kind of issue with the food. While I was in Devnar, most of the time I felt like I was in jail. If someone came they could not leave, and you didn't have the freedom to do what you wanted to. They were saying, "You're free from where you were," but we weren't free. We were still encaged in those four walls.[2]

1. The relationship between prison and monastic discipline (and especially Benedictine discipline) was first presented to me in a course called "Slavery and Obedience" taught by Willie Jennings at Duke Divinity School in the Spring of 2011. Much of what follows in this chapter is an extended reflection on the themes Willie presented in that class amid my interview experience in Mumbai.

2. "Muskan," interview with the author, Mumbai, India, November 29, 2014. Another survivor interviewee ("Seema") testified that the transition was so sudden and

Institutionalization is a common method of aftercare for sex trafficking survivors, especially when the survivor is a minor at the time of rescue. After all, when survivors come out, they are often staggeringly alone and lacking in resources. They need food and shelter, and (unlike in bonded labor situations) often have no prior ties to others enslaved alongside them. They do not come out of bondage with a ready-made social support network. It is also common to find that their families were somehow involved in their trafficking (often even directly selling them into slavery), so it often is not safe to send them back home. Additionally, given the topic discussed in chapter 2, survivors often need a safe space that will offer them the services to truly see their bondage for what it was: a form of abuse. Otherwise, they may be tempted to return. For all these reasons, institutionalization seems to be the most natural remedy.

However, the practice of institutionalization is hardly morally neutral.[3] There are better and worse ways to deal with institutionalization; better and worse institutional philosophies. Additionally, both of the two institutional models cited above (prisons and monasteries) have thick theological roots. As of yet, I have been unable to find any piece of writing that evaluates the ethics of institutionalization for sex trafficking survivors, let alone the theological logic that might stand behind various institutional models. It is this lacuna in the literature that this chapter will attempt to address (at least in part). Since institutionalization is not regularly used as an aftercare tactic among the bonded labor survivors I interviewed, this chapter will solely deal with rehabilitation for sex trafficking survivors (unlike the previous chapters, which dealt with common threads in both sex and labor trafficking).[4]

---

the living conditions so chaotic, that she initially thought she had been taken to a "mental asylum." The term tends to conjure up prison-like conditions in India (as it often does in the US). In actuality, Seema had been placed in a government aftercare home by the police after rescue ("Seema," interview with the author, Mumbai, India, December 15, 2014). The police did not inform her where she actually was, why she was there, or how long she would be staying.

3. This is perhaps especially important to remember in our historical context. As the historian Pieter Spierenburg points out, institutionalization is a far more common solution to most major social problems (whether dealing with criminal justice, mental health, public health, poverty, or in dealing with displaced populations) in modern states than it was in the seventeenth through nineteenth centuries (see Spierenburg, *Prison Experience*, 10). Given the fact that institutionalization has become almost a knee-jerk reaction in the modern world, it is especially valuable to question its appropriateness before prescribing it.

4. In my interviews, rehabilitation for bonded laborers was typically

Ultimately, both institutional models aim at forming new habits in survivors through the regulation of time. Monasteries often do this through the institution of a rule. More specifically, this monastic innovation is usually credited to Benedict of Nursia, the founder of the Benedictine order, who for theological reasons made the strict regulation of time a part of the rule he initiated.[5] Prisons likewise institute strict rules which serve to regulate inmates' schedules. In fact, the French philosopher Michel Foucault claimed that prisons implemented the same technique of power that is used to run a monastery. This essentially means that a prison is a monastery that has been weaponized by the state. What then makes for the difference between the two? Arguably, sometimes the difference can be somewhat slim. There is no one monastic model, and some models have *explicitly* crossed the line between monastery and prison, drawing on monastic rules to run monastic prisons.[6] However, there do seem to be some clear lines that can be drawn between monastic and prison discipline, even if it is easy for the former to shift into the later if extreme care is not taken.

To briefly summarize the argument that will follow, monastic discipline shifts into prison discipline when discipline ceases to be a "way"

"community-based." Since tribal connections existed between bonded labor survivors prior to bondage, and since survivors were rescued in large groups, survivors would often be re-settled into an area previously occupied by the tribe. However, I should note that some labor trafficking aftercare specialists that I interviewed *are* interested in incorporating institutionalization into their rehabilitative schemes (at least partially). The most common way in which this was proposed was to remove the children from the community and place them in hostels that would allow them to focus on their education. This proposal was considered controversial among aftercare specialists. Since the proposal is only tangentially addressed in the interviews I recorded, and since I did not interview any survivors who had tried this rehabilitation route personally, I don't feel fully equipped to evaluate it myself. I think from an ethical standpoint, very different questions would be involved. In the case of sex trafficking survivors under consideration, there often aren't many alternatives to institutionalization, since the community often contributes to the victim's trafficking, or is otherwise unfit to care for the survivor. In the case of children who were bonded with their families, the situation is often quite different. Community rehabilitation may still be a live option in many such cases, and my pre-critical inclination is to try to exhaust all community rehabilitation options before attempting institutionalization. Still, I lack the knowledge at this point to make any presumptive case against it. Perhaps a good case could be made for the hostel policy.

5. Unless otherwise noted, all passages quoted from the Rule come from Fry, *RB 1980*.

6. For some rather unsettling examples of what happens when this line is crossed see Lehner, *Monastic Prisons*.

and becomes a "technique." The difference between the two has to do with how the method of discipline links up with the moral vision of the community, as well as how discipline becomes quantified. A technique simply works: the overarching moral vision of the community has little to do with its operation, and as such, it can be applied by anyone to guarantee compliance by inmates of the institution. The character of the directors using the technique makes little difference. A technique also heavily quantifies discipline: it involves very precise controls placed upon an inmate's living space and daily schedule, it involves submitting the inmate to very precise evaluation schema, and it involves invasive surveillance over the inmate. A way puts much heavier emphasis on the character of the people within the community who are aiding in the formation of the character of the inmates. The character of instructors of the way is not a matter of indifference. Likewise, a way resists heavy quantification of discipline: a way recognizes that invasive surveillance, intense evaluation, and strict control of a person's schedule and living space can be detrimental to the type of formation the way seeks to inculcate in those under its charge.

Before exploring how fitting it is to use monastic forms of discipline in rehabilitative schemes for sex trafficking survivors, it will be necessary to give a history of the development of monastic discipline, and how it was adopted and transformed by state institutions into a technique for social control.

Monastic Discipline

There is no one monastic model. Throughout church history, mendicants, cenobites, anchorites, stylites, and other monks have all practiced very, very different forms of monasticism.[7] There is a world of difference between the way of life embodied in Benedictine and Franciscan forms

7. Mendicants are monks who own no private property (either individually or collectively) and beg for a living. Mendicants are often itinerant, though some have organized themselves into communities. Cenobites are monks that live in community. They do not own private property individually, but do exercise ownership over private property collectively: they share what they own with everyone in the monastery. Anchorites are monks that withdraw from the world to live in a cell to fast and pray (often this cell is attached to a church). Stylites are monks that vow to spend the rest of their life atop a pillar. Stylites are basically extinct: they could be found in the Byzantine Empire, but I know of no Christians that still practice this particular (and peculiar) form of monasticism.

of monasticism. About the only thing that unites all forms of monastic living is a call to simplicity and celibacy.[8] For our purposes here, it is best to begin with Benedictine monasticism, since the Rule of St. Benedict is generally taken as the document which perfects the method of discipline which underwrites many modern models of institutionalization and rehabilitation.[9]

Benedict of Nursia (ca. 480–547) is a figure about which very little is known. The only history of his life comes from Saint Gregory's later work *The Dialogues*, which was written about half a century after Benedict's death, and is hagiographical.[10] At the very least, it can be determined that Benedict was born in the village of Nursia in the Apennine Mountains, went to Rome to receive a classical education, became disillusioned with that education and retreated from the world to become a hermit in Subiaco, left Subiaco to start a community at Monte Cassino, then presided over that community until he died of a fever in 547. He is credited with writing a single work—the Rule of St. Benedict—which was intended to govern the monastery he founded. From there on, the testimony of his life has had quite an interesting and tumultuous reception. His Rule became quite famous in the West, but Gregory's account of his life did not.

8. In fact, the English word "monk" comes from the Greek word *monachos*, which simply means "single." And in this case, "single" has a double meaning and encompasses the two senses above (celibacy and simplicity). Monks are "single" in that they are not married, and monks are "single" in that they are single-minded or single-hearted: they put aside other concerns to focus solely on (the work of) God.

9. Benedict is also sometimes called "the founder of Western monasticism," but I find even this a bit too sweeping. Without a doubt, Benedict's influence has been extremely far reaching. But again, there is still quite a difference between the sort of community described in the Rule and (for example) the mendicancy model which has been so influential for Franciscans for much of their history (and Franciscans have made no small impact on the history of Western monasticism). In fact, Benedict even singles out the "gyrovagues"—a group of monks who wandered and begged much like some mendicant orders—as the worst sort of monk (see Rule of St. Benedict, 1.10–11). This seems to have continued even into the modern period, as Cassinese Benedictines threatened monks with excommunication if they received a monk from a mendicant order into their monastery (see Lehner, *Monastic Prisons*, 34). As we will discuss later, stability is essential to the Benedictine vision of moral formation, and it seems that this caused many Benedictine orders to view most mendicants as inherently morally malformed simply because they refused to adopt a rule that required stability.

10. Smith, "Benedictines," 63. Hagiographies are saints' lives. The difficulty in using them for historical inquiry is that hagiographies are often rooted in history, but exaggerate their subject matter to a greater or lesser degree. The point of a hagiography is often to give you a saint to look up to, not to give an accurate biography of that saint's life.

However, in the East, Gregory's account of his life became quite famous, but his Rule did not.

Benedict has become something of a hot topic in political theology in the last several decades. His monastic model is often credited with having saved "Western civilization" (or "Christian Europe") from immanent collapse in the face of the Dark Ages.[11] The contention is usually twofold. First, by withdrawing into the forest and starting a monastic community, Benedictines created a safe space where manuscripts that preserved classical education and culture could be kept and copied. Second, Benedict provided a new disciplinary model that could be replicated by all sorts of institutions. Cities sprung up around the monasteries Benedict founded, and the residents of these cities turned to the monastery for education, basic medical care, spiritual advice, and administrative wisdom. For this, he is often remembered as the patron saint of Europe. Thus, there are those who have turned to Benedict's institutional model to accomplish one of two tasks. We could call the first task "cultural preservation," and the second task "disciplinary innovation." These two tasks are frequently confused. It will be necessary to disentangle them because both represent two very different *partial* appropriations of the Benedictine vision that can (and have) led to rather unsavory results. They are incomplete appropriations of Benedictine spirituality for purposes Benedictine spirituality was not designed to carry out.

To give an example of someone who turns to Benedict to engage in cultural preservation, consider Rod Dreher. In his book *The Benedict Option*, Dreher claims that Benedict withdrew into the forest to start his project because he was appalled at the moral chaos that gripped Rome in the wake of its fall to the Visigoths led by Alaric I. Dreher posits that a new Dark Ages is descending upon post-Christian America, one in which a secularized pseudo-Christianity threatens American Christianity from within (akin to the moral chaos Rome experienced internally) and assaults on "religious freedom" and the "traditional family" threaten American Christianity from without (akin to the Germanic invaders Rome battled externally). Dreher's answer to this crisis is to encourage American Christians to withdraw from mainstream culture and establish a vibrant Christian counterculture (as Benedict did).[12] Dreher sees

11. For references to this view, see for example MacIntyre, *After Virtue*, 263; Coulter et al., *Encyclopedia of Catholic Social Thought*, 24–26; Chittister, *Rule of Benedict*, 15.

12. Alasdair MacIntyre is the explicit inspiration for Dreher's project. See Dreher, *Benedict Option*, 16–18. However, MacIntyre has explicitly expressed regret for the

Benedictine spirituality as a vessel that will help preserve Western culture through a coming deluge.[13]

I use the word "vessel" because Dreher's appropriation is of Benedictine spirituality in its broad strokes. The specific content of the vessel does not seem to be particularly important to Dreher, and it seems to be readily replaceable. Most of the chapters of *The Benedict Option* (apart from chapter 3) do not seem particularly focused on the Benedictine form of life. Most of his chapters deal with topics such as liturgical formation, sex and the family, and technology. The Rule only deals with the first topic, and again, Dreher never actually advocates adopting the Rule in even a modified form. He merely advocates for a liturgical revival among "non-liturgical" churches.[14] Even when he does deal with the Benedictine tradition explicitly, his focus seems somewhat arbitrary. He could have used many other voices in the Christian tradition for inspiration on

---

comments that inspired Dreher's project, and does not share Dreher's political agenda. MacIntyre is both a Thomist and a Marxist, while Dreher seems to be a staunch Republican (despite some critique of his party). In addition, Dreher turns to a number of communities as examples in his book that I suspect would likewise find his political views appalling. Chief among them is Reba Place in Evanston, Illinois. I have had some contact with this community, and its members hardly seem interested in either the Republican Party or in "culture wars" Christianity.

13. Dreher explicitly contends on one occasion that he is not "trying to save the West" (Dreher, *Benedict Option*, 53–54). However, he spends an entire chapter (chapter 7) advocating for the adoption of "classic Christian education," which is predominantly a Great Books program aimed at "immers[ing] the young in the history of Western civilization" (152). He advocates this program because "we cannot understand the West apart from the Christian faith, and we cannot understand the Christian faith as we live it today without understanding the history and culture of the West. If future generations fail to learn to love our Western cultural heritage, we will lose it" (153). That statement seems to tie Christianity pretty tightly to one very specific cultural form (which must also be preserved if Christianity is to be finally preserved).

14. Dreher simply advocates that readers adopt *any* liturgy that rejects the "worship as entertainment" model (113), adopt some sort of fasting regimen (114), and "tighten church discipline" (115). The only example he gives of what he means by the last prescription involves a story about a church that seriously considered excommunicating a divorcee, but it is not even clear whether or not Dreher is encouraging his readers to follow the exact same procedure as the church in the story (117). "Non-liturgical" is in scare quotes above because it is language that Dreher uses, but it is also a term that tends to be used to paper over a whole host of issues. All churches (even the most non-denominational) follow liturgies. That doesn't mean that liturgical critique is never fruitful; liturgics are a very valuable part of the study of theology. However, there does seem to be an inherent power play present in claiming that some churches follow "the liturgy" (as though there existed, at some point in time, an orthodox and catholic liturgy that all Christians agreed upon) and others do not.

such topics as a theology of work, a theology of sex, a theology of community, etc. In short, Dreher seems interested in Benedictine *goals* (or at least, a particular interpretation of them) but not Benedictine *method.*

The disciplinary innovation task could be seen as the flip side of the cultural preservation task. Those who see the Rule as a disciplinary innovation deal with its specific methods of moral formation but strip the Rule of its explicit goals. In particular, some commentators find in the Rule the advent of a new technique of discipline that has come to pervade many institutions in "the West": the formation of a pliable subject through constant observation and rigorous regulation of their schedule. Chapters 8–20 of the Rule are aimed precisely at the deconstruction of an old self and the construction of a new self through time regulation.[15] They give a detailed account of the "Work of God"; a daily office comprised of eight periods of prayer scheduled throughout the day and night. The times for the office strike many modern readers of the Rule as odd. For example, the Rule dictates that the monks must rise in the middle of the night for the first office ("Vigils").[16] Why do the hours of the Rule begin so early? The whole point seems to be to remove the monk from the control of the time regulations of the outside world and to reset his rhythms; to recreate his world through a new rendering of time. This is the core disciplinary innovation of Benedict's Rule. His Rule is noteworthy not because he was the first to give his monks rules to follow. He was not. His Rule is innovative because it aims all of its rules toward a particular vision of time. It attempts to create holy *people* by painstakingly incorporating them into holy *time.*

The results here can be positive or negative depending on your view of the outside world. Supporters call this "liturgical formation," and argue for its necessity. The world is full of various forms of evil, both personal and social, and liturgical formation helps purge the monk of the sinful desires of this world and focus solely on Christ alone. The monastery is, after all, "a school for the Lord's service."[17] Detractors, however, have called this part of "the production of docile bodies," noticing that this can be quite a powerful technique of control; a skilled director could essentially use the Work of God (or something akin to it) to mold someone in their own image. Since the technique has no necessary relationship to

15. This constitutes the longest contiguous section on a single topic within the Rule, so its importance cannot be understated.

16. Rule of St. Benedict, 8.

17. Rule of St. Benedict, Prol. 45.

Christian doctrine or ethics, it can be uncoupled from them and used to serve other purposes. The production of docile bodies actually requires a second "technique" in order to be terribly effective: surveillance.[18] Surveillance suggests a combination of both watching and evaluation. The subject is constantly seen, and the subject is constantly being judged. The Rule could be seen to embrace this technique as well. Chapter 7 of the Rule (the chapter immediately preceding the detailed description of the hours of the daily office) is an extended discourse on humility, and the first step of humility is as follows:

> The first step of humility, then, is that a man keeps the *fear of God* always *before his eyes* and never forgets it. He must constantly remember everything God has commanded, keeping in mind that all who despise God will burn in hell for their sins, and all who fear God have everlasting life awaiting them. While he guards himself at every moment from sin and vices of thought or tongue, of hand or foot, of self-will or bodily desire, let him recall that he is always seen by God in heaven, that his actions everywhere are in God's sight and are reported by angels at every hour.
>
> The Prophet indicates this to us when he shows that our thoughts are always present to God, saying: *God searches hearts and minds*; and again he says: *The Lord knows the thoughts of men.*[19]

The placement of this section before the hours seems quite deliberate. The monk is to remember that God is always monitoring his thoughts and actions. The monk is also to remember that God is always judging his thoughts and actions. The hours are the mechanism by which this constant sense of being surveilled by God becomes internalized in the life of the monk. Thus, later on in chapter 7, Benedict describes this transformation as follows:

> Now, therefore, after ascending all these steps of humility, the monk will quickly arrive at that *perfect love* of God which *casts out fear*. Through this love, all that he once performed with dread, he will now begin to observe without effort, as though naturally, from habit, no longer out of fear of hell, but out of love for Christ, good habit and delight in virtue.[20]

18. Foucault, *Discipline and Punish*, 187.

19. Rule of St. Benedict, 7.10–15.

20. Rule of St. Benedict, 7.67–69.

The monk starts with fear of hell (the sense that God is always watching and judging him), and gradually progresses to love of Christ (the freedom from judgment that comes from a transformed self). It seems that Benedict considers God's surveillance necessary to the process. And while Benedict puts it positively, detractors have noted that one starts this process with a certain set of desires and ends it with the desires of the one in control of the hours. This is a process that produces bodies which are malleable, docile, easy to control. When loosed from its monastic moorings, this technique would be used by other institutions to a much more sinister purpose (which will be explored more in depth in the next section).

What are we to make of these two appropriations of the Benedictine tradition (for cultural preservation and for disciplinary innovation)? First of all, to claim that Benedict "preserved" Western culture strikes me as a bit odd. In fact, the claim seems to run counter to Gregory's account of his life. According to Gregory's account, Benedict withdrew to Subiaco to become a hermit not because he was appalled at the "moral chaos" that followed in the wake of Rome's fall, but because he thought the classical education he received was inherently morally bankrupt:

> He was born in the district of Norcia of distinguished parents, who sent him to Rome for a liberal education. But when he saw many of his fellow students falling headlong into vice, he stepped back from the threshold of the world in which he had just set foot. For he was afraid that if he acquired any of its learning he, too, would later plunge, body and soul, into the great abyss. In his desire to please God alone, he turned his back on further studies, gave up home and inheritance and resolved to embrace the religious life. He took this step, well aware of his ignorance, yet wise, uneducated though he was.[21]

There is absolutely no indication in this narration that the "moral chaos" had anything to do with Rome's decline, or with the invasion of Rome by Germanic peoples.[22] In fact, it seems very in line with the general dis-

21. Gregory the Great, *Dialogues*, 55–56.

22. Thus, in Dreher's narration of Benedict's life, he adds two key sentences: "We know few particulars of social life in barbarian-ruled Rome, but history shows that a general loosening of morals follows the shattering of a long-standing social order. Think of the decadence of Paris and Berlin after World War I, or of Russia in the decade after the end of the Soviet empire" (Dreher, *Benedict Option*, 14). In order to read a decline narrative that is not present in the Dialogues back onto Gregory's account, Dreher appeals to an assumed truth that all good students of history know

dain for Roman education that characterizes hagiographical accounts of monks' lives going back to Athanasius' *Life of Antony*.[23] This is just what a classical education does to you: it makes you "fall headlong into vice." In Gregory's account, Roman culture and education are not some treasured repository that need to be preserved from decay, they are the *problem*. Better to be uneducated than educated by Rome. Hence the aspects of Dreher's narration, which imagine a more pristine past which needs to be preserved from decay, seem to severely twist the traditional narrative of Benedict's life. It is perhaps the height of irony that Dreher calls a project that heavily relies upon the preservation of a classical education[24] "Benedictine." Additionally, I find it ironic that Dreher turns to Benedict's project to preserve "the traditional family." If Benedict believed in any such thing, he certainly did not see it as worth preserving. According to the Rule, when a monk enters the monastery, he completely severs his former ties to his family. He cannot even speak with them if they visit the monastery unless the abbot permits,[25] and if a family member sends him a gift, the abbot is free to redistribute the gift to anyone in the monastery.[26] The monastery always takes precedence over family. Benedict's program does not seem particularly conservative when it comes to either its views on family or its views on education.

The second appropriation is harder to dismiss so easily, and it relates far more directly to the situation most sex trafficking survivors in Mumbai find themselves in. The second appropriation is also stronger because it focuses on what seems to be a specifically *Benedictine* innovation (namely, the reformation of a subject through a strict timetable). However, I also think that (oddly enough), the ancient monks might have anticipated something like the critique of this appropriation advanced by thinkers like Foucault. John Cassian (who most historians agree clearly influenced Benedict) famously refused to draft his own rule for monastic life precisely because he was worried it would become too rigid and

---

about cultures in transition, then imports this assumption back into Benedict's mind, and reads his revulsion at his education through this imported assumption.

23. Athanasius, *Vit Ant.* 72–80. One notes that Anthony turned to monasticism in the third century, well before the sack of Rome. This is before Roman culture declined, according to Dreher's narrative.

24. See Dreher, *Benedict Option*, 144–75 for his advocacy for a return to classical forms of education.

25. Rule of St. Benedict, 53:23–24.

26. Rule of St. Benedict, 54.

inflexible.[27] In fact, the fear of applying over-rigid standards that would destroy neophyte Christians rather than build them up was a common worry in the monastic sources Benedict drew upon. For example, as the institutional church became more and more rigid in its penitential structures (requiring four years of penance for offenses such as fornication),[28] the Desert Fathers and Mothers circulated stories such as this:

> A brother came to consult Poemen and said, "I have committed a great sin, and I will do penance for three years." But Poemen said to him, "That is a long time." The brother said, "Are you telling me to do penance for one year then?" Again he said, "That is a long time." Some of the people who were nearby suggested, "A penance of forty days?" Again he said, "That is a long time." Then he added, "I think that if someone is whole-heartedly penitent, and determined not to sin that sin again, God will accept a penance of even three days."[29]

In other words, the Desert Fathers and Mothers quietly defied the institutional apparatus of the church by forgiving sins without requiring extreme acts of penance. The monks were well aware of the sorts of burdens such strictures could place upon each other and upon the world that watched them, whether such strictures were imposed as monastic rules or as penitential acts. Thus, though the possibility that a rule might become unhinged from its moorings and be used for more sinister purposes may not have been directly considered by the monks, it is also not completely beyond the scope of their concerns.

Still, while many historians of monasticism point to these concerns in the sources Benedict used to draft the Rule (which also would have been a part of the daily intellectual diet of his community),[30] it is surprising to see how little such concerns are directly reflected in the Rule. For example, the Rule punishes even minor acts of tardiness during the Work of God with rather grandiose forms of public humiliation:

> On hearing the signal for an hour of the divine office, the monk will immediately set aside what he has in hand and go with utmost speed, yet with gravity and without giving occasion for frivolity. Indeed, nothing is to be preferred to the Work of God.

27. Smith, "Benedictines," 63.

28. See for example Basil of Caesarea, Letter 198, Canon 22.

29. Ward, *Desert Fathers*, 98–99.

30. See for example, Rule of St. Benedict, 42.3, which calls for regular meditation on other monastic works.

> If at Vigils anyone comes after the "Glory be to the Father" of Psalm 94, which we wish, therefore, to be said quite deliberately and slowly, he is not to stand in his regular place in choir. He must take the last place of all, or one set apart by the abbot for such offenders, that they may be seen by him and by all, until they do penance by public satisfaction at the end of the Work of God. We have decided, therefore, that they ought to stand either in the last place or apart from the others so that the attention they attract will shame them into amending.[31]

What sort of "satisfaction" is imagined here? The Rule goes on to proscribe prostration at the feet of all the brothers and the abbot for serious faults for "satisfaction," until the abbot releases him.[32] It suggests that a lesser satisfaction might be appropriate for a lesser offense, but it does not detail what that means.[33] Whatever it is, it is public in nature, so it may include prostration as well. Such public humiliation contrasts profoundly with the *Sayings of the Desert Fathers*, in which the Desert Fathers and Mothers frequently advocate the bearing of another's public humiliation as a method of critiquing the one who doles it out:

> A brother who had sinned was turned out of the church by the priest; Abba Bessarion got up and went with him, saying, "I too, am a sinner."[34]

In fact, the Rule of St. Benedict may even be invoked to *punish* Bessarion's gesture in the saying above.[35] The two takes on judgment seem to be drastically opposed. Benedict sees this sort of judgment as necessary to reform the monks' passions, to turn them toward the love of Christ. The

31. Rule of St. Benedict, 43.1–7.

32. Rule of St. Benedict, 44.1–8.

33. Rule of St. Benedict, 44.9. Later Benedictine tradition drew a distinction between the "major ban" and the "minor ban," but it is not clear to me that this distinction is helpful to shore up the difference between the punishment for lesser offenses and major offenses in these chapters.

34. Ward, *Desert Fathers*, 42. It is sometimes pointed out that the Rule of St. Benedict does encourage the abbot to be gentle and reserved in doling out public humiliation as a punishment. However, if an abbot were tempted to abuse power, the admonition to be gentle does very little to check this temptation. It is easy to rationalize that one is "doing only what is necessary (and no more)" in the midst of an abuse of power. The Desert Fathers and Mothers seem to realize this, and seek to disrupt public humiliation and judgment on a deeper level.

35. See for example Rule of St. Benedict, 69, which calls for the punishing of a monk who presumes to defend another monk.

Desert Fathers and Mothers see this sort of judgment as a socially dangerous gesture that cuts against Jesus' admonition not to judge others.[36]

I cannot help but think that the Desert Fathers' and Mothers' concerns are warranted. A friend of mine who left a Benedictine monastery after a long period of living under the Rule once told me that he still found himself waking up in the middle of the night to perform the office after he came out. The body has been trained to do the office, and it still responds to the office's hours. He also testified to a profound feeling of guilt; he was no longer performing the all-important Work of God, and he felt condemned for it. The judgment implicit within the process of formation remains, and Benedictine formation leaves a powerful mark on the body and soul when it is abandoned. If this is what occurs after abandoning Benedictine formation, what occurs when this technique is unrooted from the moorings Benedict intended for it? What happens when the Rule points to something other than love of Christ?

From Monasteries to Prisons

In *Discipline and Punish*,[37] Michel Foucault gives a narration of the transition from premodern forms of criminal punishment to modern criminal punishment; from public executions to incarceration.[38] He introduces

36. Matt 7:1–5; Luke 6:37–42. "Non-judgment" is such an important theme in the *Sayings of the Desert Fathers* that the *Verba Seniorum* (a Latin version of the sayings which is organized topically) organizes sayings on this theme into an entire chapter (chapter 9).

37. The original French title of the book is actually *Surveiller et punir*. The French verb *surveiller* is generally not translated "surveil" because it has a wider range of connotations. However, as Foucault's later analysis shows, it *is* meant to include the idea of surveillance, which we touched on above.

38. It is important to note from the outset that a considerable number of Foucault's central historical claims concerning the development of modern prisons have been decisively refuted by criminal justice historians. Chief among them is the claim (suggested but not fully argued in the sentences above) that there was a rapid change in which prisons replaced capital punishment in Europe in the 1800s. In fact, modern prison structures can be found much earlier than Foucault thought. Pieter Spierenburg's *The Prison Experience*, for example, establishes the existence of a fully developed prison system in Central Europe by the seventeenth century (i.e., *before* the execution of Damiens that serves as the contrast point for Foucault's narrative). However, Foucault is remembered primarily as a philosopher (not a historian), and many consider his power analysis of prisons fruitful even if his account of historical development could be considerably shored up. In fact, Ulrich Lehner's *Monastic Prisons and Torture Chambers*, which considers a drastically overlooked part of this history, could actually

this change by first describing the brutal drawing and quartering of Robert Damiens in 1757 (for charges that certainly did not seem to merit execution),[39] and moving rapidly to describing the timetable that your average prisoner lived by in a detention center in Paris in 1837.[40] Foucault does this to raise a question: Is this shift the progressive, humane, and gentle development its advocates take it to be? Students of Foucault are quick to clarify that he never denies that the refusal to rip prisoners to pieces is a step forward.[41] What Foucault is questioning instead is whether Western civilization has abandoned something unspeakably brutal and replaced it with something physically gentler but far more psychologically manipulative. An improvement, to be sure, but one with a dark side that must be taken into account: a desire for total control of the one to whom discipline is applied, in both body and soul. In Foucault's mind, modern punishment aims not at simple retribution, but at conversion: for those of us who live in a world formed by the monks, "the soul is the prison of the body."[42] Control the soul, and you control the body.

By focusing on a timetable, Foucault is implicitly referencing Benedict's innovation, even though Benedict is not referenced by name in

---

be used to strengthen some of Foucault's claims about the relationship between monastic discipline and discipline in modern prisons. Even when it comes to Foucaultian power analysis, however, I find it wise to abide by a maxim advanced by Willie Jennings (which I will unfortunately have to paraphrase here since I forgot to write down his exact wording while taking his classes): "Foucault is like salt. Sprinkle him on a historical situation, and he brings out some very interesting flavors. However, if you live on nothing but Foucault, you will become a very sick person."

39. Damiens was executed for regicide, even though he did not actually kill the king. He approached Louis XV with a knife and inflicted a light wound, then surrendered without a fight. He claimed that he only meant to frighten the king, not kill him.

40. Foucault, *Discipline and Punish*, 3–7.

41. See for example, Gutting, *Foucault*, 80. As a counterpoint, however, see Glazek, "Raise the Crime Rate." Glazek is an ardent prison abolitionist who advocates a massive return to the death penalty as an alternative to continued use of prisons in the United States. Glazek never cites Foucault directly, but he could be taken as someone who takes an analysis like Foucault's, and accepts a rather extreme policy change as a corrective to the problem. Interestingly enough, Glazek became a prison abolitionist largely because he believes the racial disparity in American prisons cannot be corrected by any set of reforms, but he never seems to consider the racial disparity in capital punishment in the United States, let alone what horrors might result if his proposal were adopted before that disparity is addressed.

42. Foucault, *Discipline and Punish*, 30.

Foucault's analysis.[43] He simply credits "monastic communities" with the innovation:

> The *time-table* is an old inheritance. The strict model was no doubt suggested by the monastic communities. It soon spread. Its three great methods—establish rhythms, impose particular occupations, regulate the cycles of repetition—were soon to be found in schools, workshops and hospitals. The new disciplines had no difficulty in taking up their place in the old forms; the schools and poorhouses extended the life and the regularity of the monastic communities to which they were often attached. . . . For centuries, the religious orders had been masters of discipline: they were the specialists of time, the great technicians of rhythm and regular activities. But the disciplines altered these methods of temporal regulation from which they derived.[44]

The timetable is then filled with tasks or exercises, including mandatory waking times and sleeping times, prayer times, work times, household chores, etc. This too is a monastic inheritance that was picked up by prisons. And in monastic circles, all of these activities are given a theological cast. Commenters on the Rule often point out that work is a sacred task for Benedict. Work is sacramental because it is a way in which human beings join with creation in giving praise to God.[45] As such, in the Rule, work tools are given the same reverence as the adornments of the altar.[46] The work performed (as well as the precise rendering of time allotted to it) becomes a means of grace. Taken out of a monastic setting, however, they can also become a means of subjection:

43. Again, it has often been pointed out that Foucault's genealogies are quite sweeping and not always very nuanced. "Christianity" sometimes seems to be a fairly monolithic entity for him, and the division between different Christian groups are often elided. The same is often true concerning the differences between different forms of monasticism. Foucault has a tendency elsewhere to call this shift an exercise in "pastoral power," which originated within Christianity, but has since been taken up by the state (see Foucault, *Power*, 333).

44. Foucault, *Discipline and Punish*, 149–50.

45. In the words of the Benedictine monk and priest, Martin Bernhard, "Creation gives praise to God. We give praise to God through Creation, through the material world, and into our areas of work. Any time we take something neutral, something material, and we make something out of it for the sake of giving glory to God, it becomes sacramental, it becomes a channel of grace" (quoted in Dreher, *Benedict Option*, 61).

46. Rule of St. Benedict, 31.10.

> Perhaps it was these procedures of community life and salvation that were the first nucleus of methods intended to produce individually characterized, but collectively useful aptitudes. In its mystical or ascetic form, exercise was a way of ordering earthly time for the conquest of salvation. It was gradually, in the history of the West, to change direction while preserving certain of its characteristics; it served to economize the time of life, to accumulate it in a useful form and to exercise power over men through the mediation of time arranged in this way. Exercise, having become an element in the political technology of the body and of duration, does not culminate in a beyond, but tends towards a subjection that has never reached its limit.[47]

In other words, when one takes this time regiment and unhooks it from praise of the Creator, work becomes merely useful to the overseers of the institution. It becomes alienating to the worker. The timetable also becomes its own end, submitting the inmate to "a subjection without limit."

Foucault does not spell this out explicitly, but he may have in mind two things. The first is the labor regimens which characterize many prisons. Labor in the prison becomes merely useful for the prison, or to outside contractors. For the inmate, it may at best prove that she has taken the effort to reform. But it is most certainly not a means of grace. The sense of "salvation" gained through the work itself has taken a complete change in cast. We have moved from praise of God to "productive member of society." The second thing he may have in mind is that the timetable can become its own end in the prison. Mandatory waking and sleeping periods, mandatory work periods, mandatory free times, etc., come to shape the inmate without limit. Much like those who leave the discipline of the Rule behind, those who come out of prison frequently testify to following its rhythms long after release: they wake at the time the prison requires, even without the prison requiring them to do so.

However, as Foucault points out, it is not *simply* the timetable that constitutes the innovation in punishment in modern prisons. Three other things characterize the discipline of modern prisons: (1) surveillance, (2) evaluation, and (3) a precise rendering of physical space. Nor have modern prisons adapted the monastic model without some noticeable changes. There is simultaneously organic unity and disturbing innovation in the transition from monastic discipline to prison discipline. It is to those innovations we will now turn.

47. Foucault, *Discipline and Punish*, 162.

It is difficult to treat these three items separately, as they are often operating in conjunction. Take the rendering of physical space, for example. Foucault points out that the cell is likewise a monastic innovation (one that predates Benedict); prison cells are modeled on monastic cells.[48] "Solitude," Foucault writes, "was necessary to both body and soul, according to a certain asceticism: they must at certain moments at least, confront temptation and perhaps the severity of God alone."[49] The cell then, is a combination of these three things. It is a *particular rendering of space* where one is *watched* by God, and one is *judged* by God. Prisons have taken this basic idea and modified all three aspects. The cell becomes incorporated into Jeremy Bentham's panopticon,[50] a prison layout where all cells are set in circle facing inward. In the center of the circle is an observation tower. It is set up such that the occupant of the tower can easily see into any of the cells, but the occupants of the cells cannot see into the cells of their neighbors. This sets up the sense that the inmates in the cells are both individuated (preventing collaboration or revolt) and under constant observation. The tower is also set up such that the inmates in the cells cannot always see into the tower to see if it is staffed (by putting blinds on the windows or using tinted glass). This is so that the inmate always perceives that she is being observed, even if no one is staffing the tower. The tower is always visible, but whether observation is occurring or not is unverifiable. A simple architectural structure makes the prison authorities seem omnipresent and omniscient. And under

48. In the United States, the Quakers are usually credited as the primary group who developed the modern prison. They utilized modified forms of monastic discipline and gave an explicit theological rationale for a turn to incarceration in the criminal justice system. Here James Samuel Logan's analysis is helpful: "It was under Quaker influence that Philadelphia's Eastern State Penitentiary, arguably the first modern American prison, was opened in 1829. Earlier Quakers, who were 'anxious to find an effective substitute for brutal flogging and the lopping off of ears . . . instituted the solitary confinement plan.' They believed that places of detention and penitence should replace those of unchristian retributive punishment. . . . The penitentiary was the place 'where the offender could ponder his sins in solitude, and then reform as he did penance.'" See Logan, *Good Punishment?*, 18–19. Logan's quotations come from Wilkinson, *Realities of Crime and Punishment*, 12. However, Quakers over time have come to realize that the penitentiary did not end up as the nonviolent criminal justice reform they had hoped for. In the hands of the state, prisons increasingly became centers of violent social control. As such, the Quakers are now one of the leading Christian denominations advocating for prison abolition. See Van Ness and Strong, *Restoring Justice*, 14.

49. Foucault, *Discipline and Punish*, 143.

50. Foucault, *Discipline and Punish*, 201.

this constant supervision, the inmate becomes a "subject"; one who self-regulates according to the demands of the perceived observers.

> A real subjection is born mechanically from a fictitious relation. So it is not necessary to use force to constrain the convict to good behaviour, the madman to calm, the worker to work, the school-boy to application, the patient to the observation of regulations. . . . The efficiency of power, its constraining force have [*sic*], in a sense, passed over to the other side—to the side of its surface of application. He who is subjected to a field of visibility, and who knows it, assumes responsibility for the constraints of power; he makes them play spontaneously upon himself; he inscribes in himself the power relation in which he simultaneously plays both roles; he becomes the principle of his own subjection.[51]

This is a powerful means of control, and one that can operate without continued supervision. Are prisons, then, aimed at reform? Or are they aimed at continued existence in a prison? This question becomes even more disturbing when one considers Foucault's suggestion that prison discipline had come to permeate many institutions (schools, the military, factories, etc.). The panoptic model—the model of constant observation and evaluation—is in effect even when the specific architecture of the panopticon is abandoned. It turns out that many different ways of rendering space can be germane to the same sort of control exercised by the panopticon. We live, he claimed, in a "carcerial archipelago."[52]

This constitutes a final difference between the implementation of a rule in a monastic setting versus the implementation of a rule in a prison setting. Prisons turn rules into what Foucault called a "technique." The panopticon is designed to do a particular sort of work on inmates no matter who occupies the observation tower. In fact, the panopticon works best when the relationship between the observer and the inmate is left completely mysterious. This could never be true when it comes to the use of the Rule in monastic communities. All authorities within a monastery who follow or enforce the Rule must be of a certain character. This is as true of the abbot as it is of the cellarer and the porter. The Rule is a bare-bones guideline in a monastic setting. It is not meant to operate regardless of who is at the helm. It is also not meant to be overly rigid. It encourages the communities that take it up to modify its requirements as necessary. As Joan Chittister—a Benedictine sister who has lived under

51. Foucault, *Discipline and Punish*, 202–3.

52. Foucault, *Discipline and Punish*, 297.

the rule for quite some time—puts it, "Benedictine spirituality offers more a way of life and an attitude of mind than it does a set of religious prescriptions."[53]

The idea that the Rule could be turned into a technique is often considered disturbing by the religious who live under its dictates because this runs completely counter to the Benedictine concept of stability. Benedictines are required to take a vow of stability before joining the monastery; they commit their lives to a particular location (i.e., a particular monastery), and spend little time away from that place. Stability is seen as important in both the work of the monastery and in the transformation of the monks in the monastery. If a person is constantly moving from place to place, Benedict suspects that that person cannot build anything that lasts, and that person will always simply be at the mercy of their own whims. The person who embraces stability masters his desires. The person who rejects stability has his desires master him. The idea that just anyone could sweep in and helm the disciplinary mechanisms the Rule prescribes would likely seem to Benedict an entirely foreign concept.

To use the language that Chittister uses above, to use the Rule as a "way" presupposes a particular vision of community life. This includes a vision of character development that pervades the community and is linked to a particular vision of communion with God. To use the Rule as a "technique" does not presuppose a particular vision of community life, nor does it connect the development of character to a particular vision of communion with God. Techniques simply work: they procure obedience and docility regardless of the particular community that utilizes them, and independently of the character of the operator at the helm. This should not necessarily be taken as a critique of Benedictine spirituality as a whole. I have not lived in a Benedictine community for any length of time, and thus lack the insight to see how the Rule is actually adapted and applied in the context it was intended for. And even if I had such experience, one Benedictine community might adapt and apply the Rule differently from another. Nevertheless, lacking this context, it is easy to see how the overall vision of Benedictine spirituality could be forgotten, and how the Rule could be taken as proposing a particular technique. There's a certain relentlessness to how the Rule attempts to reclaim holy time. As I mentioned in the section above, sometimes it is so relentless that it seems to bypass salient advice on communal living prized in generations of monasticism before it, especially concerning the nature of judgment.

53. Chittister, *Rule of Benedict*, 15.

In the face of living Benedictines, it is possible that this relentlessness could be moderated by other concerns. Absent the right sort of community, however, its relentlessness can break down human beings very quickly. It can become a tool whose only goal is to produce obedience. Additionally, I have some reservations about the vision of how God and the angelic hierarchy relate to the work of the community in the Rule. As mentioned above, the role that God plays in the Rule is one of surveillance, and the angels function merely to report the monks' misdeeds to God.[54] Benedict relies almost exclusively on biblical metaphors in which God's omniscience and omnipresence reinforce God's judgment. He ignores almost entirely passages of Scripture in which God's omniscience and omnipresence are meant to reassure or protect.[55] The effect is that God can end up seeming much like a prison warden in the Rule, with the angels as his prison guards. Likewise, the fear of eternal damnation is what motivates transformation in the Rule, rather than a vision of the goodness of a life transformed under the Rule's way. If this is the predominant understanding of the hierarchy of the universe (and how the community links up with it), it is easy to see how monastic discipline could slide into prison discipline. Again, perhaps these concerns could be moderated in Benedictine communities whose theological resources include monastic theologians who have diverse views on final states,[56] who do not view God predominantly through surveillance metaphors, and who offer a vision of a transformed life as a motivator as opposed to the fear of hell. Here the Desert Fathers and Mothers commend themselves yet again, as they emphasize non-judgment because Christ practiced it first, they emphasize beatific visions of God as opposed to a God that constantly surveils, and they offer up brief vignettes about the lives of the monks as positive models to emulate.

Having given an overview of both the Benedictine model and its appropriation by prisons, let us turn to a much more direct question: how

54. Rule of St. Benedict, 7.10–13. See also 7.26–30.

55. Two ready examples would be Exod 3:7–10, where God reassures Moses that God has seen and heard the cry of the Israelites in bondage (indicating that God will act to deliver them), and Matt 18:19–20, where Jesus assures the disciples of his ongoing presence within the church in order to give them the courage to deal with difficult disciplinary decisions.

56. I.e., Monastic theologians who do not believe "hell" is a place of eternal, conscious torment. As mentioned in the last chapter, there are a diversity of positions on this present throughout Christian history, and good reasons to prefer a vision of final judgment aimed at the universal restoration of all things.

might this analysis inform institutional rehabilitation for sex trafficking survivors? Since (as mentioned above) there are two models on offer in Mumbai (the prison model and the monastic model), we will need to look at how this analysis applies to each model separately.

Institutional Aftercare: the Prison Tradition in Mumbai[57]

Devnar[58] is a government-run aftercare facility in Mumbai. It only houses minors. The vast majority of sex trafficking survivors in and around Mumbai who are minors at the time of their rescue end up there at some point, due to the fact that survivors are mandated by law to spend the initial part of their rehabilitation in a government home. Devnar has a

57. The following account mostly follows Muskan's testimony, but its details were corroborated off the record by multiple outside sources who, for various reasons, asked not to be identified. And my own experience visiting Devnar at least partially collaborates Muskan's testimony. Upon reviewing my dissertation (which included a version of this chapter), IJM asked me to include the following statement: "*While the government-run aftercare programs were under-resourced in the past, IJM has been working closely with these institutions to improve minimum standards of care, and as of 2019 we are much more confident in their ability to provide quality support to survivors of sex trafficking.*" Some of the changes IJM itemized were quite extensive construction changes (including plumbing renovations that provide water to every dormitory for the first time), and some were very necessary staff training items (such as education in trauma-informed care for all staff social workers at Devnar). Both of these things are clearly steps in the right direction—the first improves quality of life at the facility, and the second may help to educate staff on why it is wrong to resort to the forms of discipline outlined in Muskan's testimony. However, I continue to have three items of concern. First, Devnar retains its prison architecture. Second, it is not clear that any of the changes address its high staff turnover, which could undo the gains made through trauma-informed care trainings (as trained staff leave and are replaced by new staff). Third, only one renovation addresses any of the myriad food issues Muskan names above (the provision of a new kitchen), and I'm not sure that is enough. Improving conditions is a very good thing, but the rendering of the space and the stability of the workers must be directly addressed. Without doing so, it is possible that Devnar social workers will slide back into prison methods of discipline. And prison methods of discipline come with high costs for survivors. Muskan required years of therapy at Oasis to overcome the complex trauma caused by suffering through conditions at Devnar *after* suffering through the conditions of her trafficking. As such, I believe the analysis provided based on Muskan's testimony is still quite fruitful for facilities such as Devnar, even taking into account the changes have been instituted.

58. Also sometimes spelled "Deonar." I have decided to predominantly use the "Devnar" spelling because the most common pronunciation of the word in Mumbai does include a hard "V" sound.

high turnover rate, as survivors are constantly being cycled out of the home and into more long-term aftercare placements. However, for some, Devnar *is* a long-term placement. This was the case for Muskan; she was there for three years.[59]

In the eight years that had passed between my days working for an anti-trafficking NGO in Mumbai and my return to India to do this research, Devnar had moved. I remember upon approach that you were greeted with high steel walls topped with rather intimidating razor wire. Now the walls are stone and topped with barbed wire, but the wire is significantly less intimidating: it is old and rusted. Nevertheless, when survivors call it a jail or a prison, it is easy to see where they come up with this idea. It looks like one. Nav Jeevan, the government facility for majors in Mumbai, has a similar setup, and they even have gates with bars on them that stand between the women's dormitories and the home's public spaces. The survivors are locked behind these gates at night. The ostensible reason given for why the high walls with barbed or razor wire exist around the perimeter is always security. It is there to protect the survivors. The same goes with the bars and gates that stand between private and public areas. While it is true that sometimes those who once held survivors captive do seek them out (sometimes because the survivor reached out to them first, as was mentioned in the discussion on captive mentality in chapter 2), this rationale has always seemed a bit suspicious. Those aftercare homes that will be discussed later as more "monastic" version of the Benedictine model seem to be able to provide adequate security without the high walls, the gates, and the bars. To the survivors in the home, it often seems very much like such barriers are in place to keep them *in* rather than to keep those who might harass them *out*. Escape attempts are, after all, quite common.[60] It seems very much like, as in a

59. Muskan also noted that Devnar was desperately overcrowded during her stay there, due to its position as a mandatory starting location for aftercare:

> **Muskan:** *In the beginning, when I arrived in the aftercare home, I was very nervous. I didn't know where I was, but I knew I was very far from home. I also wasn't used to there being so many people. I'm from a small family and there were so many girls in the aftercare home. I didn't know how I was going to adjust to having so many people around. As time went on, I started to like the place, but there were some things I enjoyed, and there were other things I would never get used to. . . . There were 150 girls there with me* ("Muskan," interview with the author, Mumbai, India, November 29, 2014).

60. Bharathy Tahiliani, interview with the author, Mumbai, India, January 2, 2014.

prison, a precise rendering of physical space is implemented to maximize control over the inmates of the institution.

The extent of the physical barriers is especially noteworthy given the otherwise poor physical conditions that exist in facilities like Devnar. Muskan testified that the home was overcrowded and the food was frequently either insufficient (as in, there was not enough for the residents) or rotten (sometimes even infested with maggots or bugs). Even just walking around the grounds, one can see that a significant amount of the furniture is stamped with the name of various NGOs. "Donated by Save the Children International" is a frequent sight on items like lockers or desks. If an NGO donates an electrical appliance (say, an air conditioner), that NGO may be later called upon to provide service for the appliance when it breaks down. Even though Devnar is a government facility, and by law the mandatory starting place for minors that are newly rescued in the Mumbai area, the state and city governments do not seem to care at all about properly funding the facility. Local NGOs have shored up the severe shortfalls in Devnar's operating budget through frequent donations. The very fact that strong bars, high walls, and barbed wire have been prioritized over clean beds, fresh food, and regular maintenance speaks volumes.

Government-run homes such as Devnar and Nav Jeevan have also adopted strict timetables for their inmates. Survivors living in such homes have mandatory waking and sleeping times (recall that at some such facilities, they are locked in at night, which also entails a mandatory "lights out" time), mandatory job skill training times, mandatory chore times, mandatory education times, etc. In other words, they rely on Benedict's innovation. Again, this may be necessary for the survivors' rehabilitation, for reasons we will explore more fully later. However—as in Foucault's analysis of prisons in general—these timetables are sometimes combined with observation and evaluation methods that the residents quite rightfully find problematic. For instance, Muskan testified that home staff during her stay at Devnar would frequently use shaming tactics to enforce discipline:

> **Muskan:** [The staff think they] are really good. They have a good background, good family, and they're more respectable than the girls.
>
> **Sunita:** So, you felt like you didn't receive enough respect, is what you're saying?

> **Muskan:** They pretty much just judge us. How much good character they think I have, and how bad I am. They say, "You've done this," and "You've done that." "We know everything that you've done."
>
> **Chris:** Oh, they like, throw it back in [your] face?
>
> **Sunita:** So, that's why she's saying, there's no time when we could make good relationship with staff, or even with the girls. Because she had been there for three years. She had seen like, "if I share my feelings with this one, she will go to the next one, and she will go to the next one," and they'd start talking about what she had done.[61]

If a survivor does not comply with the rules of the home, Muskan is saying, then home staff would bring up the survivor's sexual history as a way of shaming them into compliance. "You think you know better than me? You're just a whore." Evaluation is both public and extremely judgmental. In some cases, corporal punishment is even implemented. Muskan testified that she was struck or slapped on a few occasions by home staff.[62]

Observation is likewise ubiquitous in government homes like Devnar. Survivors are under constant supervision when they are allowed to move freely about, whether it is by monitors, police officers, or social workers. It is difficult to live in such a situation and not feel as though you are being constantly watched. Again, the justification is often that the residents are watched for their own safety. And if we recall the discussion of captive mentality from the last chapter, extensive monitoring may be necessary for the initial period after rescue (the period in which the survivor may be especially tempted to reach out to their former captor and return to bondage).

It is easy to see how such programs are aimed at control. It is difficult to see how such programs are aimed at rehabilitation. However, I wish to make it clear that I do not believe that these governmental homes became prison-like intentionally. I truly believe that they began with rehabilitation as the goal. But then such institutions faced budgetary restrictions and found little help from the government to shore up the difference. So, facilities cut back on quality of life investments and funneled money solely into overwhelming security measures. Then staff turnover rates

61. "Muskan," interview with the author, Mumbai, India, November 29, 2014. Sunita served as my translator for this interview.

62. "Muskan," interview with the author, Mumbai, India, November 29, 2014.

became quite high,[63] which led to ill-trained staff members resorting to measures such as striking and shaming in order to maintain control.[64] Herein lies the problem: if the Benedictine model is not implemented with extreme care by knowledgeable practitioners who are well aware of both its goals and its dangers, it is possible for those using a version of the model to rapidly cross the line from understandable rehabilitative measures to measures that are blatantly aimed at total control of inmates. In other words, institutions that implement a rule can end up slipping into the institutional mindset that Foucault critiques not because they wish to gain total control over an abused population, but because many of the differences between a prison rule and a monastic rule have to do with their very different *ends*. The danger of crossing the line becomes immediately present once both the original goals and the vision of rehabilitation that lies implicit within the model are removed. Again, monastic rules are meant to be implemented as a *way*, not a *technique*. And once the line from monastic rule to prison rule is crossed, the effects can be devastating for survivors. When Muskan was eventually transferred from Devnar to Oasis (a private Christian aftercare facility), she needed extensive counseling to recover from the compound trauma of both being held in sex slavery and of being held in Devnar:

> **Muskan:** I was relocated to Oasis India. As I entered that house, I felt alive. I felt really good. Everyone there was standing at the door to welcome me, like I was a member of their family. It was like I had been traveling far away for three years, and they were standing there to welcome me home. I had smiles on their faces, they were hugging me, and they were talking to me. I felt alive, like I could live my life now, like there was no life before. I had so much trauma from before, in my past life, and from my time in Devnar. So I had so much trauma and different issues. [*Muskan laughs as she is speaking*] So, if someone would start talking to me and saying nice things, I couldn't hear that. I feel like I was deaf at that time. I could only hear what I thought was right. I would start fighting, yelling, and saying things that

63. Bharathy Tahiliani, interview with the author, Mumbai, India, January 2, 2014.

64. It is unlikely that any of the staff members Muskan remembers when she describes being struck or being shamed are still employed by the home. Nevertheless, that does not necessarily mean improvement, as turnover is still high, and that fact alone is not good for a population that needs some stability in their rehabilitative programs.

> I shouldn't. So, they immediately put me in counseling. They hired a counselor.[65]

Certainly not all aftercare homes for sex trafficking survivors in Mumbai operate like prisons. Some are remembered quite fondly by the survivors I interviewed. However, these aftercare homes were almost always private homes, usually run by a religious organization or local NGO. Such organizations usually follow the monastic model much more directly, without some of the disturbing modifications that characterize life in the government homes. However, the placement of survivors on a Rule still raises a few notable (though perhaps not insurmountable) concerns. It is to how the Rule functions in these homes that we will now turn.

Institutional Aftercare: The Monastic Tradition in Mumbai

Sr. Asha is a Carmelite nun who serves as the superintendent of Advaith, a closed[66] private home that is located just outside of Mumbai. In addition to Sr. Asha, there are three other Carmelite nuns who serve as live-in staff members. Despite this fact, however, Sr. Asha informs me that the home is not affiliated with the Carmelites. I think it is probably less controversial to say that the home is affiliated with the Catholic Church (although this of course does not mean that it only takes Catholic residents). The grounds are rather picturesque: Advaith is located in a set of gated bungalows on the top of a hill, and the Advaith facility is noticeably cleaner and more upscale than most of the bungalows that surround it.

The first thing that you notice as you approach the facility—especially after visiting Devnar—is the lack of Devnar's characteristic prison features. Though the home is gated, it is distinctly not surrounded by high stone or steel walls topped with razor wire. The walls are low enough that an Indian teenager of average height (i.e., most of the residents of Advaith) would have little trouble climbing over the wall. Additionally, there are no bars that separate private and public spaces. The residents are not locked in at night. Technically, there is not much that is physically keeping the residents there.

65. "Muskan," interview with the author, Mumbai, India, November 29, 2014.

66. "Closed" in this case seems to mean two things: the home is not open to male visitors (with the exception of priests?) and the residents are not allowed to leave unescorted.

Again, monitoring may be necessary for a time to ensure that the survivor does not try to reach back out to her former captors. But I cannot help but think the lack of a prison-like rendering of space is anything but an improvement. Advaith reported no severe security concerns when it came to visitors to the home that might mandate building higher, more intimidating walls. And while it is true that survivors may occasionally be tempted to run away from the home, leaving open that possibility may be better for the long-term rehabilitative needs of the survivor than re-working the space such that they essentially become incarcerated in the home. Quality of life seems much higher at homes like Advaith than at Devnar, whose own social workers reported a constant concern that survivors were going to attempt suicide.[67] As hard as it is to accept that survivors may be tempted to return to slavery even after years of living in an aftercare home, leaving this possibility open seems far more humane than turning a survivor into a prisoner (and far more conducive to the goal of rehabilitation). As painful as it may be to those who devote their lives to the work of rehabilitation, the fact remains that no one can be forced to be free.[68] As was argued in chapter 2, if a survivor is persuaded that life with their captor is better than life without, then the only acceptable way forward is to present the survivor with a better alternative picture of what life can be like.

As I sit down to interview Sr. Asha, I realize that her residents are on a rule. When I ask her what the biggest challenge for survivors is, she responds, "To discipline them is the biggest problem. To correct them is not easy."[69] It quickly becomes obvious that what Sr. Asha means by "discipline" is the same thing that many monks mean by the word: that is, the imposition of a rule. Survivors find it difficult, Asha claims, to wake up at 5:30 every morning and do yoga (a sort of interfaith replacement for the Work of God). They find it difficult to sit for a class for an hour

67. A group of Devnar social workers disclosed this to me off the record during a visit to Devnar.

68. During my interview with Jessica Gunjal of Oasis India, she mentioned that rehabilitative plans for her organization are always drafted with the survivor present. Her reasoning behind this? "We believe that we won't force any one of them in what we think they should do. It should come out of their own choice, because then they will persevere in it" (Jessica Gunjal, interview with the author, Mumbai, India, October 14, 2014). The same goes for their presence at the aftercare facility in the first place: any rehabilitative schema that the survivor perceives as an outside imposition will ultimately be unsuccessful.

69. Asha, interview with the author, Mumbai, India, September 9, 2014.

each day, or to show up for job skill training at the mandatory time. And there is a reason for this: the schedule their former captors put them on just so happened to facilitate control over them. Sex trafficking victims are frequently required to work in the evenings and sleep during the daytime, given the timeframe that most solicitors visit brothels or utilize escort services. Victims are taken off of the rest of the world's time in much the same way Benedict took monks off of the rest of the world's time. Since many individuals caught up in sex slavery live on the premises where they work, showing up to work on time isn't generally an issue. But when a survivor comes out of sex slavery and starts a rehabilitation rubric, this suddenly becomes a very necessary consideration to factor back into the equation. Multiple social workers testified that survivors lost job opportunities due to a combination of these two factors: (1) they did not know how to prioritize showing up to work on time,[70] and (2) they had difficulty adjusting to a schedule where they would be working during the daytime and sleeping at night.[71] The schedule a survivor is submitted to under slavery is a way in which the captor can reinforce the idea that the survivor is not good for anything besides sex work. Thus, the management of their timetable in the aftercare home is not merely to help give the survivor a needed structure, but to also undo a form of control that is still active upon them.

The reworking of a survivor's schedule is often considered so necessary that most nongovernmental aftercare homes place survivors on some variety of rule. However, many of these facilities would strongly eschew the sorts of judgment and observation detailed in the previous section. Public shaming and corporal punishment are not only harmful to the survivor, but counterproductive to any rehabilitative plan. Corporal punishment is counterproductive because it simply reconfirms the idea that physical force is acceptable within intimate relationships (a problem discussed in the last chapter), and public shaming is counterproductive because it only serves as a push factor that threatens to drive the survivor back into slavery. Jessica Gunjal[72] and Sunita[73] both testified that a large part of their work with helping survivors on the job site was

70. Bharathy Tahiliani, interview with the author, Mumbai, India, January 2, 2014; Mona Almeida, interview with the author, Mumbai, India, December 15, 2014.

71. Jessica Gunjal, interview with the author, Mumbai, India, October 14, 2014.

72. Jessica Gunjal is the project leader for Oasis India's rehabilitation programs.

73. Sunita is both the Director of Operations for iSanctuary and the translator for my interviews with iSanctuary survivors.

simply encouraging them to stick with it. Survivors carry so much shame with them already, and they are constantly haunted by the fear that they are good for nothing other than sex slavery. Utilizing shame as an enforcement mechanism in a situation where they are already constantly thinking about abandoning their rehabilitative plan could simply serve as the tipping point that convinces them to return to slavery. Regular periods of encouragement are thus incorporated into the form of the rule that operates in most nongovernmental aftercare homes by necessity.

Stability is another crucial Benedictine emphasis that is preserved in many of Mumbai's nongovernmental homes (and frequently absent in government homes). As noted above, Advaith's staff lives in the home, and is comprised entirely of Catholic religious that are dedicated to the work. Both their commitment to stay in a particular location (rather than move from job to job or from site to site) and their singleness are crucial elements in their provision of stability for survivors. The provision of stability is of primary concern in institutional aftercare, because (as discussed in the last chapter), stability is an essential component of most counseling programs. To do the slow work of replacing the master's views on love, justice, and God that have taken root in the survivor, the survivor needs to trust the counseling staff that are providing her with an alternative picture. For trust to take root, the survivor must have some assurance that the counseling staff is not likely to simply pack up and leave anytime soon.

Although the institution of a rule in nongovernmental aftercare homes in Mumbai is far less problematic than it is in governmental aftercare homes in Mumbai, there remain some troubling ethical questions involving implementation in the nongovernmental homes. For example, are monastic rules good for any purpose other than becoming a monk? Does it ever make sense to put someone *temporarily* on a rule for rehabilitative purposes? There certainly is a sense in which Benedict wanted to "rehabilitate" the people who came to his community to become monks. He wanted to remove the habits of this world from his monks and replace them with a set of habits that would orient them toward the love of Christ. But there is certainly nothing temporary about his Rule. Instead of putting monks into an incubation state before they could join the community, prospective monks were simply thrown headlong into the community. True, initiation happens in degrees in the Rule, but prospective monks are at no time held separate from the community that they are meant to join. To make the concern more specific to trafficking survivors, the worry here is that survivors may become institutionalized, that the aftercare home may become the new normal for survivors, and survivors may have trouble transitioning out of it. Does placing them on a rule make them fit into the aftercare community, but neglect to form them for a community that they will join *after* the aftercare home?

The reality of this danger was nowhere clearer in my interviews than in the case of "Khushi." Khushi is a survivor who spent seven years in Asha Sadan. At the time of our interview, she had only been out of institutional aftercare for three months, and she was quite obviously having difficulty with the transition.

> **Khushi:** I left Asha Sadan. Asha Sadan was okay, because I didn't have to work for anything. I used to get everything. But now after leaving and staying away from the home, it's tough . . .
>
> **Chris:** So, it was kind of hard transitioning from . . .
>
> **Khushi:** Yes. That time, because everything [was] easy, everything fell into your hands, but now. . . . That time, we didn't value what we received. [*Khushi giggles*] Now we are realizing the value.
>
> **Chris:** So, where do you live now? Where did you transition into?
>
> **Khushi:** I stay in [REDACTED] hostel. Ladies' hostel.
>
> **Chris:** A ladies' hostel, okay.
>
> **Khushi:** Everyone in their own world: nobody bothers to ask or talk about, "What it is?" "How you are?"
>
> **Chris:** So, you don't have much of a relationship with the other ladies at [REDACTED]?
>
> **Khushi:** Yes. When I was in Asha Sadan, if you are sick or anything, there used to be a nurse or doctor, they would take care. Now, if you have fallen sick, you have to go on your own. Nobody is looking after you. You have to look after yourself. I feel very lonely. When I'm here [at work], it's okay. I don't feel lonely. But once I go . . . I don't know how the time passes, but once I leave from here . . .[74]

Khushi remembers rebelling against every aspect of the rule that governed the home. She initially felt it was too extensive, too invasive. There

74. "Khushi," interview with the author, Chennai, India, November 6, 2014.

seemed to be a rule for everything. But her perspective had changed in the seven years between her entrance into Asha Sadan and our interview.

> **Khushi:** When we are staying in a home and all, it's so beautiful, but we think that staying out would be much better. Because of all the rules and regulations. But my experience now tells me that, when you're out, it's really terrible. Your home was better. That home, that place that you were staying, it's very good. I want to tell all the girls that, as long as you are in that home, take the full advantage of that home, not to be like me, be rebellious.[75]

Khushi was very obviously depressed.[76] In fact, she reported that she had considered committing suicide when she was informed that it was time for her to leave Asha Sadan.

> **Khushi:** When they started telling me that I had to leave and go, that was a time that was very tormenting. Because I really felt like doing something to myself.
>
> **Chris:** "Doing something to myself" means . . . ?
>
> **Khushi:** Suicide. After I left from there, I was feeling so terrible that there's no place over there. There you feel very nice. So early in the morning, I went and sat down, whole day I sat there only. I didn't get up from there. From six to eight in the night, I was there only. Sitting in that place. I was feeling so horrible that my friends from the hostel, they kept some food for me, but I didn't feel like eating that. I didn't get sleep, but I was just lying down.[77]

Not all survivors who share Khushi's experience will necessarily contemplate suicide. But if a survivor feels adrift—without a community—after her release, then it may seem extraordinarily tempting to return to the last community that did accept her. And that can be extraordinarily dangerous (for reasons addressed in chapter 2).

Fortunately, this problem is gaining recognition among aftercare professionals in the Mumbai area. For example, I spoke with "Lydia," the CEO of an NGO that essentially provides post-aftercare aftercare to survivors of sex trafficking. Because Lydia requested that her NGO remain

75. "Khushi," interview with the author, Chennai, India, November 6, 2014.

76. Somewhat ironically, "khushi" is the Hindi word for "happiness." Like all of my survivor interviewees, Khushi chose the name for herself. I have never been able to figure out whether the choice was aspirational, or if she simply liked the name.

77. "Khushi," interview with the author, Chennai, India, November 6, 2014.

anonymous in this research, I will simply refer to her NGO as "NGO X." NGO X works with "case-free" survivors, which means that there is currently no protective order issued by a court that legally mandates the survivor to be in protective care. In most cases, this means that the survivor started in protective care in one of the non-governmental homes for minors, but they have since turned eighteen (which means they have to transition out of the home).[78] However, some survivors at NGO X are referred from other organizations—they may never have had protective orders in the first place.

> **Lydia:** The intent is for us to be a transitional step for them from whatever shelter home they came from previously to independent, reintegrated life. So, we get referrals from other aftercare homes for minor girls who are here in Mumbai and then we will do an interview and intake process with the girl to see if our homes are a good fit for her as she is majoring out of another home. So, our homes themselves are intended to be like a family-style home. So, they're not on a compound, they're all spread out, and are just apartment buildings. So, they're like, two-, three-bedroom apartments. We have a maximum of six girls staying in each home and they have a house mother who is there full-time. So, the group homes themselves are just like a family home where girls have duties there for cooking and cleaning and things like that.[79]

There are still house rules that residents must abide by (such as "no hitting other residents," "no drug use," "residents must sign in and out when they leave," and so on). In fact, the organization explicitly draws upon Matt 18:15–22 as a guideline for dispute resolution within the home.[80] Residents also still have schedules and obligations (such as work or class schedules and chore rotations). So, a form of internal discipline is still present. But survivors in NGO X residences are not on such a stringent timetable as the survivors who are in court-ordered protective care.

78. At least, this is theoretically what is supposed to happen. Practically, not every survivor is considered fully rehabilitated at eighteen, and many that turn eighteen don't have any other place to go. I ran across many homes that kept survivors on after eighteen, even if their in-house best practices said otherwise.

79. "Lydia," interview with the author, Mumbai, India, September 11, 2014.

80. This passage has a long history of use as a disciplinary rule in Christian settings. It has seen usage in Anabaptist churches, American churches during the controversy over slavery, monastic groups, the Unitas Fratrum, and the early Wesleyan movement.

> **Lydia:** We try to model it like a family-style setting. What kind of rules would you have in a family? What kind of freedoms would you have in a family? And how do you manage those well, so that when they do go to reintegrated, independent life, to not have to jump from no freedom to complete freedom, and "Now what do I do with that?" We try to gradually give freedom in a safe environment so that they're learning how to handle that freedom responsibly in a place that is safe.[81]

Just as most families are not living on some variant of the Rule, so survivors in NGO X residences are not living on a variant of the Rule. Again, Benedict's innovation was not just giving residents rules, but focusing those rules largely on time management, and attaching that time management to an observation and evaluation schema. NGO X does not employ a rule that seeks to transform survivors through the strict management of their time. It seeks to get residents to relate in healthy ways to each other, to their respective communities, and even the technology they use, but it does not aim at creating holy time. This is precisely because adopting holy time in a Benedictine fashion throws them off of the time of the society that they wish to reintegrate back into.[82]

What community are survivors being prepared for then? For Lydia's organization, the most readily available community is the Indian church.

> **Lydia:** We have what we'll call an "aftercare pipeline," which is kind of our strategy for elements of aftercare we want to implement: housing, education, therapy, job readiness, and community. And we as an organization can do those first four (housing, education, therapy, job readiness). The community piece is what we feel is the most important part to successful reintegration. And the way that we are trying to address that is by partnering with the local Indian church; to leverage them to be a community for girls who have reintegrated. Right now, we

81. "Lydia," interview with the author, Mumbai, India, September 11, 2014.

82. This is not a critique of all attempts to render holy time. Liturgical calendars and the observation of feast days are the lifeblood of many Christian communities. And many laypeople have incorporated at least a moderated form of the daily office into their spiritual lives. However, Christians have long figured out how to live by such calendars while still interacting in deep ways with the world outside the church. The problem here is that Benedict's rendering of holy time in the Rule seems to be purposely designed to interfere with full integration into the outside world. This is less of a problem if a divide between laity and religious is in place, but again, most sex trafficking survivors are not on a path to adopting Catholic religious life (nor would any aftercare professional I've ever met wish to pressure them into that route).

are partnering with [REDACTED] and working with them and their congregations to try to build up a network of people who are ready and trained and engaged to be able to accept these girls into their community (regardless of what the girl herself believes). But that there is already a natural system of support, because many of these girls don't have family to go back to.

Chris: Right.

Lydia: And in an Indian context, especially here in Mumbai, you *have* to have family to be successful in community. Women don't live independently, single women very rarely live together. . . . So, we are trying to leverage the local Indian church to envelop and enfold these girls after they have left our homes. We, [NGO X], our mission is to be a bridge for girls: a bridge to hope, freedom, and independence. And part of being that bridge, it means that you don't stay on a bridge forever. So, the girls aren't . . . We don't *want* them to be with us forever because our goal for them is reintegration.[83]

When I asked what it looks like for the church to "enfold" survivors, she quoted a common maxim used by aftercare specialists: rehabilitation looks different for every survivor. At the time of our interview, NGO X had only graduated six survivors out of its program, and so the nature of interaction with the Indian church community is still evolving. But Lydia mentioned that survivors who had graduated out of the program were in a variety of different living situations—from living in hostels to living with family members to living with single roommates—and there were a variety of different relationships that they had with Mumbaikar churches. Some rented from church members, some would meet regularly with church members for meals, some would have members of the church community informally check in with them on a regular basis to see how things were going. That may seem like a small gesture to American readers, as Americans are increasingly becoming more and more used to fragmented community structures. But in Mumbai, it is quite significant. One of the biggest difficulties in rehabilitation for sex trafficking survivors in Mumbai is a sort of family hegemony that hangs over the city (which Lydia alludes to in the quote above). The family is such a necessary gateway to all sorts of things in Indian culture that it is not in American culture (including housing). Those who are estranged from their families are especially disadvantaged, and they require an alternative community

83. "Lydia," interview with the author, Mumbai, India, September 11, 2014.

that is willing to look out for them. The important piece Lydia highlights is the fact that the NGO does not conceive of itself as that community. It is organized around the idea of being a "bridge" to rehabilitation.

Lydia admitted that there remain some tensions between the two focal images that NGO X employs: it is difficult at times to see how NGO X could be both "family" and "bridge." But at the very least, there is recognition that the monastic model that closed aftercare homes utilize requires some modification. It cannot be conceived of an end in itself unless it is asking survivors to actually take on a monastic calling. With this piece absent, at best it can only be a link in the aftercare chain. But if that is the case, what are the other links supposed to look like? This question is still in the process of being worked out, and answering it will have to take into account the role of family as a community mediator in Indian culture.

The Adaptation of Monastic Discipline: An Evaluation

Now that we have looked at the advantages and drawbacks of various attempts at aftercare that have drawn inspiration (intentionally or unintentionally) from a monastic rule, what sort of conclusions can we come to as far as acceptable and unacceptable adaptations? First and foremost, any aftercare home implicitly based on a model of monastic discipline must constantly reassess its basic commitments and ends on a regular basis. Many of the more disturbing uses of discipline in rehabilitative centers above have taken shape not out of malice but out of inertia. The success of the implementation of any monastic model hinges on it remaining a "way" rather than a "technique." The model cannot be thought to work on its own regardless of its operators. Instead, the operators must be distinctly woven into the life of the community, constantly being re-trained in certain virtues by the community's norms. As mentioned before, one of the primary virtues that should be inculcated by that community is stability. Rapid turnover leads to chaos in any institution established for rehabilitative purposes. Rehabilitation is a calling, and a quite necessary one at that.

Can an aftercare home truly embody stability if each link in the aftercare chain is only temporary?[84] Does stability always require vowed,

84. Formulating a comprehensive aftercare chain of this nature was heavily emphasized by both "Mallika" and Lydia in their interviews ("Lydia," interview with the

lifelong membership? Who would be required to commit to stability? Only social workers and other professionals? Professionals and all survivor residents? Professionals and only *some* survivor residents? These questions are by no means unique to communities of care for trafficking survivors. In the Christian tradition, similar questions about the nature of stability arise when any intentional community is formed (and especially within those that draw inspiration from monastic theology).[85] To see this, it may be helpful to turn to two Christian communities that were formed out of social concern, even though their charisms[86] deal with different social issues: the Catholic Worker Movement and L'Arche. The Catholic Worker Movement was founded in the 1930s by Dorothy Day and Peter Maurin. According to Day, the movement was comprised of three interrelated projects: (1) publishing a newspaper that would apply the teachings of Jesus Christ and Catholic social teaching to contemporary events, (2) establishing houses of hospitality where people would come together to live in communities based around the works of mercy, and (3) organizing communitarian farms where members would live off of the land.[87] The overarching concern of the Catholic Worker has always been how to deal with poverty. However, the movement is animated by a conviction that many social programs oriented toward alleviating poverty do not do enough to overcome the root issues that divide individuals into rich and poor. For example, the houses of hospitality consciously did not want to operate by the same model that many homeless shelters in the United States do, with a thick division between those providing care and those receiving care.

---

author, Mumbai, India, September 11, 2014; "Mallika," interview with the author, Mumbai, India, September 17, 2014).

85. David Janzen's working definition of "intentional Christian community" is "a group of people deliberately sharing life in order to follow more closely the teachings and practices of Jesus with his disciples. The more essential dimensions of life that are shared—such as daily prayer and worship, possessions, life decisions, living in proximity, friendship, common work or ministry, meals, care for children and elderly—the more intentional is the community" (Janzen, *Intentional Christian Community Handbook*, 12). Janzen himself is a part of the wider intentional community movement often known as the New Monasticism. Its best-known advocates in the US are probably Shane Claiborne and Jonathan Wilson-Hartgrove.

86. *Charism* literally means "gift" (as in, gift of the Holy Spirit). In this case, charisms are linked to a community's call or mission. A community is gifted specifically for service (cf. 1 Cor 12:4–7).

87. Day, *Loaves and Fishes*, 7.

L'Arche was founded in the 1960s when Jean Vanier invited Raphael Simi and Philippe Seux (two men with intellectual disabilities) into his home.[88] Vanier had done extensive visits to asylums for those with intellectual disabilities and disorders in France, and he was horrified at the conditions he saw. L'Arche was founded to provide an alternative way of dealing with disability, in a way that was neither exploitative nor abusive. And as with the Catholic Worker, L'Arche wished to find a way to incorporate those with disabilities into communities that did not draw such thick dividing lines between those providing care and those receiving care. As such, Vanier tends to put a lot of emphasis in his writings on the mutual dependence that core members (those who have disabilities) and assistants (those who do not have disabilities) discover that they have for each other in L'Arche communities.[89] The core members obviously depend upon the assistants for various types of physical care. But the core members also reveal both the presence of Christ in weakness and the weaknesses of the assistants in unique ways. And the assistants need such things revealed to them. Thus, there is a mutual dependence that both groups discover in the midst of community.

It is likely that the core tension that both L'Arche and the Catholic Worker have struggled with arises when any social division is addressed institutionally. Will the institution mimic the divisions present in the society that produced the problem in the first place, or will those divisions be overcome by producing a new community? A related question is whether participation in the institution itself will be temporary (considering rehabilitation a matter of "adjustment") or if the institution envisions itself as a long-term solution, a new form of life together. The virtue of stability is related to these tensions. From a close look at the struggles of these two communities, it seems that the nature of the virtue of stability is defined

88. It is worth noting that shortly after this chapter was originally published, credible allegations of sexual and spiritual abuse against Vanier were disclosed to the public. In a press release, L'Arche USA reported the following: "Jean Vanier himself has been accused of manipulative sexual relationships and emotional abuse between 1970 and 2005, usually within a relational context where he exercised significant power and a psychological hold over the alleged victims." All of the victims were adult women who sought out Vanier for spiritual direction, rather than residents of L'Arche communities (see O'Loughlin, "Sexual Misconduct"). This news is incredibly distressing, but L'Arche is (and always was) more than Vanier. I believe they still stand as a good example of community done right, despite the sins of the organization's founder.

89. See for example, Vanier, *Essential Writings*, 100–101.

largely by the nature of the community's charism.[90] Catholic Worker communities have rarely asked stability of the unemployed individuals who stand in their bread lines, the transients who come to their houses of hospitality for a season, or the refugees that they help transition. They do, however, often rely on a committed core of members to run the business of the houses of hospitality, and sometimes these core members are living out of a common purse, which makes it difficult to simply pull up and leave. In L'Arche communities, on the other hand, the core membership is made up of those who come to the communities for aid. These members are often stable out of necessity: their disabilities do not afford them particularly high mobility. While assistants are asked to make long-term commitments to the community, there is always a shortage of assistants who stay in L'Arche communities for the long haul.[91] However, this does not prevent the communities from taking in new assistants for the short-term, anyway. What stability looks like varies in the two communities, and yet both communities are still able to perform their mission.

Perhaps stability looks different in different communities because stability is a somewhat paradoxical virtue: to embody it, you must leave one community and join or start another.[92] It asks you to leave in order to be stable, because stability is linked to mission. In most intentional communities (unlike in Benedictine monasteries), stability also does not mean that a person is required to stay in the community for the rest of their lives. They may need to leave to facilitate the community's mission, or to follow another calling.[93] For these reasons, it would probably be best to specify what stability would look like in different contexts. For closed aftercare homes like Advaith and Devnar, there is no real question

90. This should not be at all surprising to students of modern virtue theory. The content of the virtues is fleshed out in the midst of a tradition, which is a "historically extended, socially embodied argument, and an argument precisely about the goods which constitute that tradition" (MacIntyre, *After Virtue*, 222). Virtues are given shape in communities constituted by a shared narrative.

91. See for example, Vanier, *Essential Writings*, 105.

92. Benedict, Jean Vanier, and Jonathan Wilson-Hartgrove all emphasize this in their writings. To be a stable member of one community, one must simultaneously be called out of a former community (see Vanier, *Community and Growth*, 39–41; Wilson-Hartgrove, *New Monasticism*, 86). Benedict's emphasis on severing family ties when joining the monastery has already been treated above.

93. David Janzen even has a whole chapter in *The Intentional Christian Community Handbook* entitled "When People Leave," and it deals largely with his family's decision to move from one intentional community to another even after becoming covenanted members of the first community (240–50).

of stability for residents; they are placed in such homes by a custody board decision immediately after they are liberated from slavery. This is because the only other place they can go is back into slavery (or back into the home situation that sent them into slavery in the first place). These homes are in a position similar to L'Arche, where there is no real question of the stability of individuals *receiving* care. The question is stability on the part of those *giving* care. At Advaith, dedicated nuns live out this virtue extremely well: given the nature of their religious vocation, they can live in the community and provide stable supports that the survivors can rely upon in uncertain times. At Devnar, no such commitment is expected of the social workers who live there, social workers do not live in the community as a part of it, and staff turnover is high. Stability is nonexistent. As such, it seems that there must be some core group of individuals giving care who commit to investment in the community for the long-term, ideally some form of live-in caregivers that are themselves part of the community. It need not be for life, but at least for long enough to help survivors transition. Survivors themselves are in such placements for often no more than five years (although exceptions to this rule do exist). For open homes for case-free survivors (i.e., "after-aftercare homes" like those run by NGO X), conclusions will have to be tentative, because not many homes have tried to fill this link in the aftercare chain yet. NGO X itself is focused on transitioning survivors rather than on stability, but they have been able to embody greater stability than homes with frequent staff turnover. This is because the core of the community is the survivors themselves, and each home has live-in housemothers who are present at the home in half-day shifts. At this point in the aftercare chain, houses could spring up that are closer to the Catholic Worker model: a core group of survivors (and non-survivors) who live in and administer a house where other survivors are more transient. Perhaps these houses could have church affiliations and ties (such as the Catholic Worker) that allow community members to come to the house for different events to "enfold" survivors into the community, as Lydia mentioned. Such a house would have a concept of stability that looks slightly different than a closed aftercare facility.

Adding stable intentional communities made up of both survivors and non-survivors late in the aftercare chain would likely have the added effect of challenging a social system that divides people strongly in terms of family ties. If communities are formed where people who are related neither by blood nor by marriage become more socially acceptable, it will help address some of the problems survivors without family ties face in India. Further, intentional communities often do not run around a rule in the same way Benedictine communities do, so some of the difficulties associated with life under the Rule would not apply. On the other hand, I know of no intentional communities that incorporate the kind of therapy regimens that would be desirable for trafficking survivors, so a full-scale turn to this sort of model may not be desirable early in the aftercare chain (i.e., in closed homes). Earlier steps in the aftercare chain will likely need to embody stability differently than steps later in the chain. What that might mean is that closed aftercare is utilized for a time, followed by life in community. It is even possible that the current system could in some way be blended with the intentional community model followed by the Catholic Worker or L'Arche. However this looks, it is clear that returning to the survivor's community of origin is often neither plausible nor desirable. They must either be incorporated into a new community or help construct a new one themselves. If the monastic model is only employed temporarily (i.e., no stable "Catholic Worker for Trafficking Survivors" is formed), this needs to be taken into account by the organization. How is the home going to pass off the survivor to the next link in the chain? How is the home going to prepare the survivor for transitions? What does a home need to provide to a survivor like Khushi? Does an organization like NGO X exist that can be there during the transition?

Secondly, it is important to remove all disciplinary measures from the community that are based in shame or corporal punishment. The reasons for this were given above. The survivor is awash in shame already, and piling more on could simply push her back into the community that exploited her. Surveillance techniques should be used especially sparingly. While it may be necessary to monitor a survivor's movements and behavior for a time to make sure that the survivor does not immediately return to her former captors, long-term surveillance used for disciplinary purposes could easily bleed into the sense of ubiquitous judgment the survivor experiences from within and from without. Survivors need a Bessarion who will walk with them in their shame far more than they need a Benedict who will submit them to deeper scrutiny. Additionally, corporal punishment serves to reinforce the correctness of the same disciplinary regimen slavery uses. To avoid these two forms of discipline, the last point (the formation of all members of the community) is paramount. Both the non-survivor members of the community and the survivor members of the community must be trained in nonviolent forms of conflict transformation if they are to have any sense of how to avoid trying to compel others to comply with their wishes through coercive means. It is understandable that overworked, undertrained professionals resort to slaps and public shaming to compel assent. It is the wrong thing to do, but it is also a human thing to do. Training helps overcome that.[94] For resources that can facilitate such training, see the list given at the end of chapter 2.

Thirdly, "prison space" has to be abandoned. There are aftercare centers out there that have established that it is possible to maintain security without utilizing architecture that mimics a prison. Their wisdom should be sought in any situation in which a newly-established facility fears that they will not be able to maintain security. Oasis, Advaith, and other homes which do not utilize such architecture are proof of that. Of course, this does mean that aftercare facilities must be open to the possibility that survivors will run away; that captive mentality may finally claim some survivors. But this will happen regardless. As Jessica Gunjal and others have pointed out, there is no scenario in which high steel walls can force a person to be free of the emotional chains that bind them. You cannot coerce freedom; the means is simply incommensurate with the ends.[95]

Finally, the sacramental nature of the work that survivors are engaging in needs to be reclaimed. There are already some extraordinarily encouraging ways in which rehabilitative organizations in Mumbai are starting to do this. As will be discussed more in depth in the next chapter, there is some doubt among aftercare professionals about the current

94. The same basic insight was realized by Jim Lawson when he trained student groups in nonviolent protest methods in the American South. When he organized the Nashville sit-in campaign, he realized that it took a certain amount of character formation not to strike back when struck. So, he organized roleplays among his students with some students playing the role of the person sitting in, and other students playing the role of the angry mobs that would oppose them. This taught them resources to utilize when bystanders would curse at them, throw food on them, or strike them (see Ackerman and Duvall, *Force More Powerful*, 313–17). The same basic principle applies to nonviolent conflict transformation in any community: for it to be successful, community members require training in nonviolent ways to handle conflict. They need to develop peacemaking as a virtue.

95. To take this concern further, it would be a good idea for an aftercare institution to constantly reevaluate the relationship between its architecture and its rehabilitative goals. As Foucault pointed out, prisons have become masterful at using space to control a population. How do you set up an aftercare facility to use space to heal a population?

efficacy of job skill training programs for survivors of human trafficking.[96] The concern is that a lack of job skills is clearly not the only factor that leads to sex trafficking, and the acquisition of job skills in many cases does not lead to gainful employment, financial stability, or protection from further exploitation. This has led several aftercare facilities to the conclusion that they need to rethink how they view work more generally. iSanctuary is one such organization which is trying to incorporate a thicker theology of work into its training programs, while keeping in mind survivor financial needs. iSanctuary is an organization that teaches survivors to make hand-made jewelry. And while these survivors can use this skill to make a living, the expectation is not that those involved in iSanctuary are going to become jewelers.

> **Sunita:** I don't think so they choose jewelry-making as their job skill training—job—for the future, but they try iSanctuary as a step up a CV, where they can work here part-time, continue their education, or I think at least get more . . . better? . . . at understanding the world of people, and get wise how they—whom they need to trust. Or how they need to behave in the society, or what is the more mannered way. Those are the basic skills we really have to build. And if girls have an interest to do *anything*, more than jewelry, we always try to support that.[97]

But iSanctuary doesn't simply focus on inculcating basic job skills that have an application beyond making jewelry. They also see the act of work itself as therapeutic.

> **Erin:** Before [survivors come to our workshop], we go to the homes, so there are actually girls in our office here who are in charge of teaching jewelry-making classes in the homes. And they're in charge of leading those classes. And I heard Stephanie described it as "more like arts and crafts time," so it's not like . . . You were talking about how child labor is not a *job*, per se, it's an opportunity for them to participate in . . . you could call it occupational therapy, if you want to. So, they can earn some money on the side which is then available to them when they become old enough to access it. So . . .

96. The discussion in chapter 5 specifically deals with economic rehabilitation for bonded labor survivors, but similar concerns apply in economic rehabilitation for survivors of sex trafficking.

97. Sunita and Erin, interview with the author, Mumbai, India, October 1, 2014.

> **Sunita:** Yeah, yeah. At the same time, I think during that time, we just not teach them how to make the jewelry, but we do small chart how we are doing, and if child happen to be open, we encourage them like that. Whenever we have the session come, whenever we start the programs, our focus is to be more open and more friendly with the child or the girls who's working with us. So, if they happen to feel free and feel confident to talk things out loud and share with us, we can have somewhere in those areas, and we always try our best.[98]

iSanctuary staff members are very aware that work is not a matter of acquiring transferrable "skills" which allow a survivor to simply plug into a given economic order like interchangeable parts in a machine. Work makes us a part of a social order in unique ways. And it is the sense of social belonging and the healing of old wounds that are especially emphasized by iSanctuary. This is the kind of fertile ground in which the Benedictine theology of work as a sacrament could easily take root. Such a theology already dovetails nicely with iSanctuary's core values, since iSanctuary already sees work as valuable beyond simple considerations of economic utility. Work knits people together. Work can heal old wounds. Work is an act of partnering with God in creation. It is easy to see how these pieces of a theology of work could easily fit together.

Unfortunately, work can also the area of our lives where we as human beings experience exploitation in the most visceral ways. If the dignity of labor is not upheld, survivors can find their work after enslavement not as means to liberation, but as yet another dead end that pushes them back into slavery. How can aftercare agencies help assure that survivors find themselves empowered in their new work after emancipation, rather than re-exploited through their new profession? It is to this question that we now turn.

98. Sunita and Erin, interview with the author, Mumbai, India, October 1, 2014.

Chapter 5

Labor, Caste, and Obedience

IF YOU WERE TO look at the bibliography of Nicholas Kristof and Cheryl WuDunn, long-time correspondents for the *New York Times*, you might find yourself a bit puzzled. Kristof and WuDunn are responsible for penning both one of the most celebrated popular works on combatting sex trafficking[1] and one of the most celebrated apologies for sweatshops.[2] How can the same authors be so in favor of one form of exploitative labor and so against another?

The answer has to do with an assumption that is made in orthodox economic theory: A lack of labor skills is the root of all sorts of bondage. Skilled labor allows for a comparative advantage in the market. Those who lack such skills must find some other kind of competitive advantage. And according to Charles Wheelan,

> *The comparative advantage of workers in poor countries is cheap labor*. That is all they have to offer. They are not better educated; they do not have better access to technology. They are paid very little by Western standards because they accomplish very little by Western standards. If foreign companies are forced to raise wages significantly, then there is no longer any advantage to having plants in the developing world.[3]

Unskilled laborers in poor countries then have one of two choices: they can either starve or they can submit to some form of exploitative labor.

1. Kristof and WuDunn, *Half the Sky*.
2. Kristof and WuDunn, "Two Cheers for Sweatshops," 70–71.
3. Wheelan, *Naked Economics*, 288 (emphasis in original).

And it seems that the majority of the people on this planet will eventually choose the latter. Survival trumps free and equitable working conditions. And so, the apologists for sweatshops argue, it is preferable to be caught in sweat labor rather than slavery because sweat labor offers some hope for advancement. And so sweat labor ought to be embraced by the West rather than fought against. Slavery, however, still ought to be fought against. In fact, many apologists for sweatshops argue that we are left with a choice of one or the other. We either support sweatshops or we end up supporting slavery. Here again is Charles Wheelan:

> Nor does it make sense that we can make sweatshop workers better off by refusing to buy the products that they make. Industrialization, however primitive, sets in motion a process that can make poor countries richer. Mr. Kristof and Ms. WuDunn arrived in Asia in the 1980s. "Like most Westerners, we arrived in the region outraged at sweatshops," they recalled fourteen years later. "In time, though, we came to accept the view supported by most Asians: that the campaign against sweatshops risks harming the very people it is intended to help. For beneath their grime, sweatshops are a clear sign of the industrial revolution that is beginning to reshape Asia." After describing the horrific conditions—workers denied bathroom breaks, exposed to dangerous chemicals, forced to work seven days a week—they conclude, "Asian workers would be aghast at the idea of American consumers boycotting certain toys or clothing in protest. The simplest way to help the poorest Asians would be to buy more from sweatshops, not less."
>
> You're not convinced? Paul Krugman offers a sad example of good intentions gone awry:
>
> "In 1993, child workers from Bangladesh were found to be producing clothing for Wal-Mart and Senator Tom Harkin proposed legislation banning imports from countries employing underage workers. The direct result was that Bangladeshi textile factories stopped employing children. But did the children go back to school? Did they return to happy homes? Not according to Oxfam, which found that the displaced child workers ended up in even worse jobs, or on the streets—and that a significant number were forced into prostitution."
>
> Oops.[4]

4. Wheelan, *Naked Economics*, 288–89. Wheelan's two citations are from Kristof and WuDunn, "Two Cheers for Sweatshops" and Krugman, "Hearts and Heads."

So, there it is: don't fight for better wages for sweat laborers and don't boycott goods made in sweatshops. Both options will simply cause people to fall into slavery. If you oppose slavery, support sweatshops.

The problem is, this argument makes *massive* value judgments without fully disclosing them, and those implicit value judgments, in turn, distort the picture that apologists of sweat labor draw of poor laborers. First, why is sweat labor preferable to slavery? Apologists for sweat labor claim (implicitly or explicitly) that it is because sweat labor allows for advancement. But apologists for slavery have historically claimed that slavery is morally justified because it too allows for advancement. Many advocates argued that it offered spiritual, moral, cultural, *and* economic advancement; slavery was a school for virtue for those who were unvirtuous *and* it made their lives better off.[5] Make no mistake: many pious, compassionate human beings were able to convince themselves that slavery was the "development economics" of the New World. It was horrible in practice, they thought, but it was ultimately for the betterment of others. As we discussed in chapter 2, many modern slaveowners employ similar arguments, even if public opinion has changed such that the majority of academics, politicians, and cultural critics in most modern nations find such arguments disingenuous. Are Western advocates of sweat labor on a better footing? Is slavery obviously a bad tool for advancement whereas sweat labor is obviously a good tool for advancement? Apologists for sweat labor would doubtless say so. Like Wheelan, they argue that "a rising tide lifts all boats." Sweat labor makes a whole country richer. When a whole country gets richer, the median income rises. When the median income rises, the poor benefit along with everyone else. But is this truly what happens? Slavery made countries richer, too. But rather than "lifting all boats," it created a permanent underclass, such that in countries like America (where a history of slavery significantly

5. For the various ways in which ancient thinkers argued that slavery was a form of beneficial training for slaves, see Garnsey, *Ideas of Slavery*, 23–52. For a disturbing account of how Prince Henry the Navigator's chronicler (Gomes Eanes de Zurara) wept upon seeing the suffering of slaves at auction while simultaneously drafting a theodicy that justified their suffering (i.e., that their captivity would lead to their conversion, and therefore their salvation), see Jennings, *Christian Imagination*, 15–20. The way in which Zurara cries tears for the violence done to African slaves while giving a moral justification for why such violence was necessary for the salvation of their souls is disturbingly reminiscent of the way in which Wheelan, Kristof, and WuDunn lament the violence done to sweatshop workers while giving a moral justification for why such violence is necessary for their economic salvation.

contributed to economic development), there still exists a caste system that advances whites over against non-whites (and especially over and against Blacks). Are we so sure that the same thing does not happen under cases of sweat labor? Are the sweat laborers themselves able to get job skills that help them get a better job? Are their kids more likely to gain an education? Does that education guarantee them a better future? This is exactly where the evidence is wanting. Few longitudinal studies exist that follow generations of sweat laborers to show whether such advancement is likely to happen, and they would likely need to be done in multiple contexts to prove compelling. In fact, some research suggests that what happened under slavery is happening under sweatshops. Most evidence in the developing world shows industrialization contributing to vast wealth gaps, showing that not all boats are being lifted. Worse, the development models on offer often leave developing countries at the mercy of richer countries due to protracted debt accrued during the development process. Even the "Asian tigers" (which are often cited as the success stories of industrialization and globalization) have shown signs of uneven and dependent development.[6]

From within the Christian tradition, such wealth gaps cannot come to be seen as natural. This is because a religious tradition with documents such as the Gospel of Luke in its canon cannot see questions of just distribution of wealth as a tertiary issue. Luke's Gospel deals with the topic of money and possessions more than any of the other three Gospels,[7] and Luke provides a gradually unfolding vision for how wealth

6. Surin, *Freedom Not Yet*, 104. This is why some critics of the trickle-down argument allege that it is based on faith rather than historical precedent. Take, for example, the pertinent rhetorical questions of Terry Eagleton: "Though [capitalism] has had a long time to demonstrate that it is capable of satisfying human demands all around, it seems no closer to doing so than ever. How long are we prepared to wait for it to come up with the goods? Why do we continue to indulge the myth that the fabulous wealth generated by this mode of production will in the fullness of time become available to all?" (Eagleton, *Why Marx Was Right*, 10). There is a bit of a utopian eschatological hope to the trickle-down argument that seems difficult to justify historically in the face of an ever-widening wealth gap.

7. Luke contains every passage on possessions found in Mark, most of the passages on possessions found in Matthew, as well as a slew of passages on possessions that are unique. Luke Timothy Johnson helpfully gives a list of these unique passages. They are 1:51–53; 3:10–14; 6:24; 8:1–3; 10:1–16; 10:38–42; 11:41; 12:13–21; 14:12–14; 15:8–10; 15:11–32; 16:1–9, 14, 19–31; 17:28–30, 32; 18:9–14; 19:1–10; 21:34–36; 22:35–38 (see Johnson, *Sharing Possessions*, 13). As long as this list is, it does not include all the references to possessions, money, or economic matters in Acts.

redistribution should occur. It begins with the disciplining of desire such that one does not try to acquire more than one needs (hence John the Baptist's advice to Roman tax collectors and soldiers in Luke 2:12–14), proceeds to a willingness to significantly divest oneself of wealth for the good of others (hence Zaccheus' actions when he comes to believe that Jesus is the Messiah in Luke 19:1–10), and culminates in participation in a community that encourages common ownership of resources and is able to justly redistribute the proceeds of those who are willing to divest themselves (hence Luke's description of the church in Acts 2:42–47 and Acts 4:32–35, and the warning he gives through the story of Ananias and Sapphira in Acts 5:1–10).[8] However, Luke's economic vision does not stop there. In Acts, Luke goes on to detail the journeys of Paul, who proves to be a gigantic disruption to Rome's economy wherever he goes. In Philippi, he casts a spirit of divination out of an enslaved girl, thereby making her unprofitable for her owners. This gets him thrown in prison (Acts 16:16–40). In Ephesus, his evangelism and miracles cause the local populous to give up sorcery in droves, leading to a massive burning of books on sorcery (Acts 19:11–20). Luke notes that the value of these books is "fifty thousand drachmas" (v. 19), which was an obscene amount of money in ancient Rome. Later, the Ephesian silversmiths organize a riot against Paul on the grounds that his preaching encourages people to give up idols, which is in turn having a negative economic effect on the lucrative silver trade (Acts 19:23–41). Clearly Luke's economic vision calls, then, for both the redistribution of wealth and for a cultural clash with any system based on an unjust or profligate distribution of wealth. Thus, from a Christian perspective, wealth gaps are not a matter of indifference. In heavily developed nations, problems of radically unjust

8. I am aware that some commenters have argued that Acts 2 and Acts 4 present an idealized picture of the church. Even if this is true (and I'm not sure that it is: the New Testament presents us with various models of how to "do church," and, to my knowledge, we lack countervailing evidence that would suggest that the Jerusalem church was not actually on a communitarian model in the early days), it makes little difference to the church's economic ethics. Even if the church in Acts is an ideal, proclaiming the ideal issues a call that many Christians throughout history have responded to with very concrete gestures. Despite all the squeamish hermeneutical gymnastics that Christians have used throughout the history of interpretation to dull the force of that ideal, its proclamation still produced Saint Antony, the Benedictines, the Poor Clares, the Brothers and Sisters of the Common Life, the Hutterites, the Bruderhof, the Amish, the *Kleine Gemeinde*, the Catholic Worker Movement, Base Christian communities, the Simple Way, Koinonia Farm, Reba Place Fellowship, and many, many others. And the proclamation of that ideal *will continue* to produce such groups.

distribution of wealth are already at crisis levels,[9] and this has arisen largely because questions of economic distribution have been completely forgotten in favor of exclusive focus on questions of economic growth (the two are implicitly seen as antithetical in many orthodox models).[10] In any sufficient account of economic justice, *both* must be considered.

Is sweat labor assumed to be less violent than slavery? That could be an interminable debate. Sweat laborers work under unsafe conditions, just like enslaved workers. They work long hours, just like enslaved workers. They often sleep in the compounds where they work, just like enslaved workers. They are often subject to physical and sexual abuse, just like enslaved workers. They sometimes die of overexertion, just like enslaved workers.[11] Is sweat labor less violent than slavery? On this note, perhaps the best answer we could procure is "it depends on the situation." This is not a promising start, since enslaved people in various eras have noted that there is also a wide range in the expression of physical violence from slaveholder to slaveholder. As such, the spectrum of physical violence in sweat labor and the spectrum of physical violence in slavery itself seem

9. Piketty, *Capital*, 255–65. Piketty ominously points out that income inequality levels in the United States today are comparable to those that obtained in France just prior to the French Revolution. Today, US income inequality is at even greater levels than when Piketty's work was first published, especially given the rise of "mega-billionaires" after the emergence of COVID-19.

10. Piketty, *Capital*, 11–16. Piketty notes that the theory that unfettered economic growth would eventually lead to an automatic correction of wealth inequality ultimately goes back to the economist Simon Kuznets, who first proposed the theory in 1955. Kuznets coined the phrase "growth is a rising tide that lifts all boats," and his theory became the prevailing economic position in the US during the Cold War. Part of the staying power of Kuznets' theory is the fact that Kuznets proposed that a bell curve would obtain such that wealth inequality would dramatically rise due to industrialization and economic development before tapering off and finally reducing down to much more equitable levels. For quite some time, this made the theory difficult to falsify. Advocates of the theory could always answer questions like the ones Eagleton brings forth in footnote 6 with the response, "Well, we just haven't hit the top of the bell curve yet. Wait for it." However, recent economic research has brought increased scrutiny on the data upon which Kuznets' theory was based. As Piketty puts it, "the magical Kuznets curve theory was formulated in large parts for the wrong reasons, and its empirical underpinnings were extremely fragile" (15). Especially damaging to Kuznets' theory is the fact that wealth inequality has ballooned in America, the country whose data was used to establish the equilibrium at the end of Kuznets' curve.

11. For a really disturbing look at this possibility, see Cavanaugh, *Being Consumed*, 39–43. Cavanaugh highlights the fact that death from overexertion is so common for Chinese sweat laborers that "the Chinese have even coined a word—*guolaosi*—for death from overwork" (41).

quite similar. This seems to point to the possibility that sweat labor exists in a sort of gray area on the boundaries of slavery. It may not be slavery in and of itself, but in many cases, it is dangerously close to qualifying.

Further, are consumer boycotts the only option to fix this problem? Among advocates of nonviolent resistance, the boycott is recognized as somewhat of a "scorched earth" option. It is quite a powerful tool.[12] So powerful, in fact, that boycotts require constant monitoring. In *any* boycott, the possibility exists that the worker could suffer more economic harm than the employer. Monitors of the boycott must be prepared to change tactics once this happens.[13] Few consumer boycotts of sweat labor are this coordinated. Could a boycott be successful if proper monitors were in place? Perhaps. However, as will become obvious later, I think organizing the laborers themselves may be preferable to a consumer boycott (though unions have certainly utilized consumer boycotts in the fight for better compensation and working conditions).

Why begin a chapter on economic rehabilitation by focusing on this issue? This is, after all, a work on rehabilitation from trafficking, not sweat labor. Are most organizations assisting in economic rehabilitation for survivors of human trafficking advocating for sweat labor as a corrective? Arguably no. However, many of them, while not openly championing sweat labor in the way that WuDunn and Kristof do, still rely on the same sorts of economic reductionism that is present in WuDunn and Kristof's way of viewing the plight of the poor in the developing world. This ends up skewing rehabilitation efforts by allowing NGOs to think that they can simply address economic rehabilitation through job skill training programs while ignoring very real forms of social domination that keep their clients in a state of economic exploitation after their trafficking. The purpose of this chapter is threefold: (1) to critique the ways in which the orthodox model offered up by Wheelan, Kristof, and WuDunn misleads economic rehabilitation efforts, (2) to offer up an alternative explanation

12. One of the most noteworthy examples of the boycott's power is the ending of the Apartheid regime in South Africa. An international boycott bankrupted the regime, forcing them to step down. For a brief history of the boycott, see Ackerman and DuVall, *Force More Powerful*, 335–68. Archbishop Desmond Tutu noted that the economic devastation from the boycott was so great that it prevented tribunals in the style of the Nuremburg Trials from being used to establish justice in the aftermath, as such tribunals would have been too expensive. This was one of many reasons why the Truth and Reconciliation Commission was chosen over a tribunal (Tutu, *No Future without Forgiveness*, 22–23).

13. Cartwright and Thistlethwaite, "Support Nonviolent Direct Action," 45–47.

for continued economic exploitation that takes in the realities of social oppression in modern rural India, and (3) to suggest an alternative solution to the problems addressed by Wheelan, Kristof, and WuDunn that is rooted in community and labor organizing and nonviolent civil disobedience.

The Myth of Skilled Labor

How does the picture that Wheelan paints above end up affecting the way anti-trafficking NGOs view economic rehabilitation? For starters, it turns out that the plight of workers in the developing world is not reducible down to the rather flat picture that Wheelan paints. It is not always the case that the poor are poor because they have no competitive advantage (i.e., they are "unskilled laborers"). Certainly, this may *sometimes* be the case, but describing the situation as Wheelan does above is painting with too broad a brush. And painting with too broad a brush leads to an oversimplified one-size-fits-all solution to a complex problem.[14] In the case of economic rehabilitation for trafficking survivors, that solution is job skill training. Take unskilled laborers, train them to perform skilled labor, and they will be able to acquire better jobs, better hours, better working conditions. Or they will be able to find a niche in the market where they can run their own business.

The problem is, the social workers I interviewed in Chennai told me that what they were finding among their clients was the exact opposite of what they would expect to find if the picture Wheelan paints is both accurate and complete. Here is what "Nisha" told me were her consistent findings when she performed strengths assessments (or "appreciative inquiries") on survivors of bonded labor:

> **Nisha:** One of the technique[s] that I use towards it is appreciative inquiry. And strength model, of course. You know, look into

14. This is a common critique of modern orthodox economic thought in general by theologians. Much of the fascination with the science of economics in our era is based upon its supposed ability to analyze and break down data in such a way that it can give a simple and straightforward "bottom line" solution to a complex problem, cutting through layers of social issues that are seen as too intractable to deal with directly. But what is simple can also end up being reductionistic. Few models are truly one-size-fits-all. For a more detailed version of this critique, see the discussion between Nancy Fox (an economist) and Steve Long (a theologian) in Long and Fox, *Calculated Futures*, 30–45.

> their strengths. Everybody, all of my clients, I totally believe that they come with a . . . what do you call it? Exclusive skillset. *And that is the reason also why they were chosen to become bonded. You understand? The owners understood their strengths.* Okay, the perpetrators understood their strength and totally used it for their benefit *but* left them—left all of my clients—without helping them to understand how wonderful they are with their skills. You know? How awesome they are with their skills. You know, helping them to understand those things has always been close to my heart. I totally help them to do that with the self-esteem part of it.[15]

In drastic distinction to Wheelan, Kristof, and WuDunn, Nisha and the other social workers claimed that her clients were falling into bondage not because they lacked a skillset and could thus only profitably perform unskilled labor. Instead, they were being targeted for bondage precisely *because* they were able to competently perform a very specific sort of skilled labor.

What skills did these survivors possess? "Naveen," another social worker who works with survivors of bonded labor, helpfully described a very specific sort of agricultural work that is passed down through the Irular tribe, namely rice cultivation. Rice cultivation requires a set of skills that take a considerable time to learn. In the case of the Irular, these agricultural skills are passed down through the tribe from generation to generation. In our interview, Naveen described in detail the skills necessary to dig out a rice paddy, to draw up its borders, to maintain those borders, to identify when the rice needs to be removed from its initial soil, relocated, and replanted, and to finally harvest the rice. Naveen was essentially describing a trade with a very specific body of wisdom and very specific practices that are not easily going to be learned within the space of say, a few months. Certainly, this is not a skillset that the higher-caste owners of the rice mills in which Naveen's clients were bonded have been able to cultivate themselves. Additionally, rice makes up a gigantic share of India's food economy. So, Naveen's clients are highly skilled laborers producing a product that is in very high demand.[16]

15. "Nisha," interview with the author, Chennai, India, November 7, 2014.

16. "Naveen," interview with the author, Chennai, India, November 12, 2014. Sandeep also verified Nisha and Naveen's statements ("Sandeep," interview with the author, Chennai, India, November 14, 2014).

Why then are they still often referred to as "unskilled laborers?" Part of the problem here seems to be that there is no one definition for what qualifies as "skilled labor" and "unskilled labor." Do these distinctions refer to the amount of time it takes to learn the type of labor in question? If this is the case, "unskilled" labor might take about a month to learn, "skilled" requires some sort of advanced educational program (perhaps two years or more), and "semiskilled" falls somewhere in between. On this definition, rice cultivation would be at least "semiskilled" if not "skilled." Or is the difference between "skilled" and "unskilled" a matter of wage level? Here, "unskilled" would mean low wages, "semiskilled" would mean medium wages, and "skilled" would mean high wages. On this definition, rice cultivation would be "unskilled," because it doesn't pay much. The gap between these differences in definition represents a problem for arguments like the one advanced by Wheelan at the beginning of the chapter. If wage level and education level are correlated, then there is no problem for Wheelan's argument. As he noted, "[unskilled laborers] are paid little by Western standards because they accomplish little by Western standards." However, if wage level and education level are not correlated, then the terms "skilled labor" and "unskilled labor" become mystifying: they obscure working conditions as they exist rather than illuminating them.

Caste and Exploitation[17]

If the problem is not a lack of skills, what is it that leads these highly skilled agricultural workers into bondage (and prevents them from earning a

17. At the outset of this section, it should be noted that there are two diabolical rhetorical strategies that Westerners have historically succumbed to when describing Hinduism and its role in the formation of caste. The first strategy is to present Hinduism as a monolithic cultural and religious system that is inherently socially and morally backward in comparison to Western religious and cultural sensibilities. The caste system is raised here as the primary piece of evidence, but certain issues involving the treatment of women are also brought up. Once this is done, the justification for colonialist intervention in the Indian subcontinent (in order to break up this unjust arrangement) is implicitly given. The second strategy is to offer an enthusiastic apology for Hinduism that too readily lets it off the hook for the formation of the caste system. This strategy fails to attend to the voices of Dalit liberationists who point squarely to the ways in which orthodox Hindu texts and institutions have served to bolster their oppression. In what follows, I have likely steered farther away from the danger of betraying Dalit liberationists than I have from the danger of betraying upper-caste anti-colonialist Hindus, due to the fact that the powers that be in India are trying far

living wage once they come out of bondage)? The caste system is by far the most obvious culprit. According to the staff members I interviewed at one NGO in Chennai, more than 99 percent of the bonded laborers they rescue are from one specific Adivasi tribe: namely, the Irular.[18] As an Adivasi group, the Irular fall below the caste system, and are therefore one of the groups most vulnerable to caste discrimination. Even after emancipation, caste discrimination continues to affect the survivor's economic status. This became painfully obvious when I accompanied Naveen on his home visits in rural Tamil Nadu. During one home visit, an Irular husband and wife reported that they tried to start their own tree-cutting business, but they were charged double the rate for the use of the grove they rented due to their Irular status.[19] The high costs of running the business eventually resulted in the business going under. The wife further reported that she rode a tractor as a job after that, but was fired by her employer for asking for her wages. She was replaced by a higher-caste member of the community. The husband, on the other hand, tried to use his familiarity with electronics to set up a stereo repair and home theater installation service. However, he felt he had to abandon the project because there was already a higher-caste man in the village community that

harder to narrate the ongoing plight of Dalits and Adivasis out of existence. However, I hope it is evident that my support for indigenous resistance movements and nonviolent civil disobedience that I am no supporter of colonialism. I likewise do not see the West as being morally and socially superior, given its own issues with race. And finally, Hinduism is so wildly internally variegated as to make any blanket condemnation of it virtually impossible; *any* statement made about Hinduism is going to be untrue for at least a few Hindu groups, even when it comes to beliefs concerning caste (see the elaboration I offer in the footnotes below). My concern in this section is not Hinduism per se, but caste. And it is impossible to talk in any depth about caste in India without talking about Hinduism.

18. "Ravi," interview with the author, Chennai, India, November 5, 2014. The NGO's target region doesn't extend much farther than the South Indian state of Tamil Nadu. In other areas of India, the Irular would not be the predominant survivors of bonded labor (since the tribe resides mostly in the south), but other groups also report a strong correlation between caste status and trafficking. According to Ravi, the National Commission on Rural Labor released a report back in 1993, which found that over 86 percent of all rescued bonded laborers from across India were either Dalits or Adivasis. At the time of our interview, there was no more recent study that was done on the same scale.

19. In India, "tree-cutting" businesses seem to predominantly provide wood to various customers (e.g., to serve as firewood). That is what this couple was doing. In the US, a "tree-cutting" business would likely be associated with landscaping. That is not what this couple was doing. The terminological difference initially confused me: I wondered why they had to rent a grove to carry out their business.

offered this service, and he did not want to risk competing with the man. It was difficult to tell from his description of the situation whether the man had exercised some political or social pressure to get him to quit the business or if he had simply internalized caste values to the point where he deferred to the higher-caste man without a struggle. It is also possible that both were the case.

For those unfamiliar with the Indian caste system, social scientists who study it describe it as the confluence of two different systems of social classification.[20] The first classification system divides Indian society into social groups known as *varnas*. Traditionally, there are four varnas: brahmins (the varna of priests and intellectuals), kshatriyas (the varna of warriors, politicians, and administrators), vaishyas (the varna of merchants, farmers, and economists), and shudras (the varna of laborers and artisans). The varnas are not only social categories; they are also theological categories. The existence of the varnas is given a theological justification in certain portions of Hindu scripture, most notably the *Manusmriti*, the *Bhagavad Gita*, and the *Rig Veda*. The Rig Veda contains a creation story which describes brahmins as being born from the mouth of God, kshatriyas being born from the shoulders of God, vaishyas being born from the thighs of God, and shudras being born from the feet of God, establishing an overt hierarchy with brahmins at the top and shudras at the bottom. There are also two social groups which are *avarna* or *chandala* (outside of the caste system): Dalits and Adivasis (referred to in government documents as "scheduled castes" and "scheduled tribes," respectively). Dalits have historically existed on the fringes of caste-based society, relegated to servile professions, and have been considered socially and ritually impure by those who do fit within the varnas (i.e., "untouchable"). Adivasis were not historically incorporated into caste-based society at all, and instead lived in independent tribal groups. However, in their interactions with caste-based society, they have been considered to have roughly the same social status as Dalits. This means that both groups have been historically subject to social and economic marginalization and exploitation, as well as physical, psychological, and sexual violence.

The second classification system divides Indian society into social groups known as *jatis*. Jatis designate both a family group and an occupation that family historically held. There are thousands (if not tens of

20. Rosen, *Essential Hinduism*, 39; Knott, *Hinduism*, 22; Flood, *Introduction to Hinduism*, 58.

thousands) of jatis. Quite frequently, a family's jati is indicated in their surname. For example, "Gandhi" designates a jati: it means "grocer."

Caste in India essentially results when jatis are fitted into the varnas. To stick with the example above, the jati "Gandhi" was typically historically seen to fall under the vaishya varna because grocers are involved with both commerce and agriculture. However, the fitting of the jatis into specific varnas is not always so neat. A family's jati is fairly stable. It is, after all, frequently indicated in their last name and the occupations each jati represents are generally easy to distinguish from each other. But in different regions of India, the same jati might be classified under different varnas. For example, a jati might be considered part of the kshatriya varna in northern India but considered part of the vaishya varna in southern India.

It should be noted that caste is a controversial topic in modern Hinduism.[21] It is not as though being Hindu automatically means that one fully supports the caste system. Anti-caste Hindus do exist.[22] Some

21. In fact, Hinduism is so internally variegated that nearly every assertion made in this section admits of counterexamples from within Hinduism itself. This has led some scholars of Hinduism to refer to it as "a conglomerate of religions" as opposed to a single, unified religion (see for example, Rosen, *Essential Hinduism*, 17). Other scholars of Hinduism find its center not in any shared set of religious doctrines, practices, or Scriptures, but in Indian nationalism. The modern *Hindutva* movement, founded by Vinayak Damodar Savarkar, comes to a similar conclusion, claiming the answer to the question "Who is Hindu?" can be found in a common heritage, a common nation, and a common culture. Other Hindus castigate Hindutva as a purely modern phenomenon with no traditional roots (see Bhatt, *Hindu Nationalism*, 77, 85). For a good short summary of the issues involved in defining the core of Hinduism, see Knott, *Hinduism*, 110–14. Still others claim that Hinduism has no center at all, claiming that, while there may be "Hindus," there is no "Hinduism" (see Sharma, "What Is Hinduism?," 6).

22. Some commenters put this in terms of a clash between "orthodox" or "brahminical" Hinduism on the one hand and "heterodox" Hinduism on the other. Some may object that use of "orthodox" and "heterodox" is simply yet another imposition of Christian terminology upon Hinduism, but the opposition is genuinely helpful to get some sense of how support for and resistance to the caste system have contributed to the proliferation of Hinduisms. Some forms of heterodox Hinduism have, for centuries, proliferated their own traditions to subvert the more dominant brahminical traditions. Some commentators would also point to the Hindu reformers of the past 150 years as additional examples of anti-caste Hinduism, but the degree to which the proposals of these reformers qualify as anti-caste must be evaluated on a case-by-case basis. For example, Gandhi is frequently cited as one such reformer, but he still adhered to a variety of brahminical Hinduism. As Flood points out, Gandhi still held out hope for "a society structured according to divisions determined by occupation, which Gandhi saw as the original, classical *varṇāśrama-dharma* of orthodox brahmanical Hinduism" (Flood, *Hinduism*, 260). While Gandhi did work toward the legal abolition

Hindus would say that the Hindu scriptures which describe the varnas played a historically important role in the development of Indian society but cannot be followed as an adequate guideline today.[23] Other Hindus believe that the varnas these texts describe were not originally meant as a description of rigid social roles, but something more akin to idealized spiritual states, virtues, or personality types.[24] As such, they were originally considered non-hereditary, and modern Hindus should return to this spiritual understanding of the varnas. Still other Hindus would argue that spiritualizing the varnas is simply an exercise in exegetical special pleading, given the clear reference to social roles that exist in these texts. As such, these Hindus would hold that the *Manusmriti* and other texts that describe the varnas should simply be excised from the Hindu canon; they are simply not Hindu scripture.[25] However, despite these alternative readings of Hindu sacred texts, it cannot be denied that (1) the caste system has been embraced by many Hindus throughout history, (2) the caste system still has religious advocates in India today, even despite the fact that caste discrimination is officially illegal, and (3) the texts mentioned above have been used to buttress the caste system.[26] Additionally, many

of untouchability in India, Dalit liberationists frequently accuse him of sanitizing an ideal caste system (a critique similar to the one Christian feminists levy against "love patriarchy"), which continues to contribute to caste oppression in practice.

23. This was the position of Dr. Krishnan, a Hindu advocate for Adivasi peoples and one of my interviewees (K. Krishnan, interview with the author, Chennai, India, November 20, 2014).

24. This is the interpretation favored by Steven Rosen (Rosen, *Essential Hinduism*, 40). Arvind Sharma also gives a species of this interpretation in the midst of a chapter challenging the typical interpretation of the varnas as a divinely ordained social system which is watertight and immutable (Sharma, *Classical Hindu Thought*, 132–80).

25. Knott gives the interesting example of a version of the *Ramayan*a which circulates among low-caste groups in South India in which Ravana is the hero and Rama is the villain (Knott, *Hinduism*, 92). This means that the roles are reversed from how they appear in the orthodox version of the Ramayana, and yet each character still represents the same value set that they represent in the orthodox version (i.e., Rama is characterized as an idealized brahmin). This shows that some Hindus have found it germane to edit the canon if the orthodox version of Hindu texts aid in the furtherance of the caste system. This seems to be easier in a religious tradition such as Hinduism than it is in one such as Judaism, Christianity, or Islam. For example, even though variations in canon exist in Christianity, "What counts as part of the Bible?" is a far more settled question in Christianity than "What counts as part of Hindu scripture?" is in Hinduism.

26. Flood points out that it is difficult to deny a clear social dimension for either the varnas or the jatis. Both are simultaneously social and ontological categories:

upper-caste Hindus who profess to eschew caste still benefit from the historic privileges their caste has conferred upon them, and as such do not embody an entirely "caste-blind" Hinduism. Caste biases even tend to work themselves into many scholarly works on Hinduism (by both Indians and Western scholars),[27] and as such non-Indian scholars who use these sources must be especially careful in using their work.[28] The problem is not, however, limited to Hindus; some Christians and Muslims in India have participated in these forms of oppression by incorporating caste into their communities rather than challenging the caste system. In fact, caste biases have even made their way into works of Indian Christian theology.[29]

In some schools of Hindu thought, the caste system plays a clear role in theodicy. Put more succinctly, karma determines caste. Those born into higher castes are being rewarded for just or righteous deeds in a past life, and those born into lower castes are being punished for unjust or unrighteous deeds in a past life.[30] Likewise, a person's dharma is also heavily determined by their caste. Dharma is a key concept in Hindu ethics that is often rendered in English as "duty," though that translation is clearly reductionist. Dharma is not only a guide for right conduct, it also names

"The term *jāti* refers not only to social classes, but to all categories of beings. Insects, plants, domestic animals, wild animals and celestial beings are all *jātis*, which shows that differences between human castes might be regarded as being as great as differences between different species. Members of a *jāti* share the same bodily substance, substances which are ranked hierarchically" (Flood, *Hinduism*, 59). As we shall see for *dharma* below, many schools of Hindu theology do not think of a person's being and social status as separate considerations: the two are frequently considered inseparable.

27. This may seem odd in the case of Western scholars, but it is often simply a matter of trusting your sources. If all of the sources a scholar of Hinduism reads reflect a brahminical perspective, their scholarship will also reflect a brahminical perspective.

28. For a good introduction that is charitable to Hinduism in general, but still rigorously interrogates Hinduism's role in the formation of caste, see Knott, *Hinduism*, esp. 80–93.

29. This is a common critique by Dalit Liberation Theologians (see for example, Nirmal, "Dalit Christian Theology," 537–41).

30. This view is expressed, for example, in the Chandogya Upanishad 10.7: "Those whose conduct here has been good will quickly attain a good birth, the birth of a brahmin, the birth of a kshatriya or the birth of a vaishya. But those whose conduct here has been evil, will quickly attain an evil birth, the birth of a dog, the birth of a hog or the birth of a *chandala*." The translation comes from Sharma, *Classical Hindu Thought*, 155, but I have changed the spelling of transliterated Sanskrit words to match the spellings I have used above (to avoid confusion).

a thing's nature: it is an inner principle that makes a thing what it is.[31] However the term is translated, dharma is clearly affected by social role. Men and women have different dharmas. A king has a different dharma than a farmer. This is why, in the *Bhagavad Gita*, Krishna bookends an extended discourse on the virtue of nonviolence with an admonition to Arjuna that he must go into battle and slaughter his cousins. His dharma as a prince demands that he do this.[32] Dharma fleshes out the content of the virtues. What it means to exercise the virtue of nonviolence depends upon your social role. And as such, some schools of Hindu theology find that caste provides clarity. It helps flesh out what dharma entails for each individual. Know your caste, know your dharma.

It should also be noted that Hindu scriptures used to buttress caste have a large cultural footprint in India. In my interviews, I asked multiple interviewees of different faith backgrounds to describe caste, and (practically to a person) they would immediately recount a version of the creation myth that describes the four varnas and their relationship to different parts of God's body outlined above. I am not sure that if I were to interview a group of American social workers of various faith backgrounds and ask if they could relate either of the two creation stories in the beginning chapters of Genesis that I would get similar results. Caste and its theological underpinnings are "in the water" in India in a way that cannot be ignored.

It is sometimes the case that one runs into Indian social analysts who claim that the caste system was once operative in India but passed away soon after caste discrimination became illegal. In truth, India is no more "post-caste" than America is "post-racial."[33] While there is some

31. As such, Rosen can say, "the dharma of the bee is to make honey, of the cow to give milk, of the sun to shine, and the river to flow" (Rosen, *Essential Hinduism*, 35).

32. Concerning Krishna's admonitions to Arjuna to put his doubts to rest and enter the battle, see Bhagavad Gita 2:2–3 and 18:59–73. Concerning Krishna's argument that it is the dharma of a kshatriya to "never retreat from battle," see 18:44. References to *ahimsa* (nonviolence) are numerous throughout the Gita. What I have given above is the orthodox Hindu interpretation of war in the Gita. There is also the mystic interpretation, which allegorizes Krishna's advice. On this interpretation, when Krishna tells Arjuna to destroy his cousins (the Kauravas), he is actually telling Arjuna to destroy the baser instincts that abide in his "lower self." On this interpretation, the Gita does not have a philosophy that justifies violence: it quickly leaves the battlefield behind to deal with the weightier matters of the inner self. This was Gandhi's preferred interpretation of the Gita. For a fuller treatment of both interpretations, see Diana Morrison's notes on the first chapter of the Gita in Easwaran, *Bhagavad Gita*, 50–51.

33. I draw the comparison because the discourse on caste in India sometimes

evidence that caste distinctions are lessened in very large Indian cities, the distinctions themselves still exist. And in the villages, caste is an extremely thick phenomenon. Social workers in India explained to me that most of the villages they work in are caste-striated, with brahmins living near the village entrance, moving down the caste hierarchy as you move toward the back of the village.[34] Their Adivasi survivors are forced out beyond the edges of the village, typically in the same area as the village graveyard (i.e., a space that is already ritually impure).

The fact that the caste system plays a major part in modern systems of slavery in India is by no means a new insight. Various studies focusing on slavery in India have repeated this point over and over.[35] It is so well-established that even someone who is only incidentally familiar with slavery in India may take this as simply belaboring the obvious. So why repeat the point here? The reason is that the economic analysis given by thinkers such as Whelan, Kristof, and WuDunn gives many NGOs the sense that caste can be largely ignored when doing economic rehabilitation among survivors. A focus on skills training can slowly chip away at their poverty and yield success stories among Dalit and Adivasi communities without directly challenging the caste system. Why would NGOs wish to avoid this? Three primary reasons came up in my interviews. Keep in mind that all three are predominantly *pragmatic* arguments that were given by individuals who worked for an organization that is ideologically anti-caste. It is not that these individuals want the caste system

---

mirrors the discourse on race in America. For example, not only does one occasionally run into the claim that India is "post-caste," one also occasionally runs into the claim that "reverse caste discrimination" occurs in India. This is the claim that policies designed to ensure that Dalits are equally represented in educational institutions and various sectors of the workforce are actually working to advance less-qualified Dalits over more-qualified high-caste individuals. The argument is structurally the same as the "reverse racism" argument against affirmative action in the United States. And much like its counterpart in the United States, it must ignore a mountain of social scientific evidence to the contrary in order to get off the ground.

34. "Sandeep," interview with the author, Chennai, India, November 14, 2014.

35. See for example Choi-Fitzpatrick, *What Slaveholders Think*, 45–49. See also the report cited by Ravi in footnote 18. Choi-Fitzpatrick explicitly comes to a conclusion strikingly similar to my central point here: "In other words, the economics of vulnerability are stark, but economics alone is insufficient to describe the complex interplay of debt and duty in the relationship between Tarun [a bonded laborer] and Aadi [a slaveholder]. Ideal social relations involve a fusing of debt and duty under the aegis of caste" (45).

to continue operating. Rather, these individuals think that they lack the power to address these problems effectively, given their current resources.

The first argument is that direct address of the caste system would be too resource and labor-intensive. Advocacy of various sorts would cost too much and move the anti-trafficking NGO away from the task of accomplishing their mission, which is to be more directly involved in addressing the day-to-day rehabilitative needs of bonded labor survivors. Lobbying and advocacy is costly and prohibitive. Job-skill training, on the other hand, is doable. In some cases, NGOs that were interviewed are working not only on rehabilitation, but also rescue of bonded laborers and prosecution of perpetrators. In such a case, resources are stretched even more thinly.

The second argument is that direct address of the caste system would be controversial and might be obstructed by government officials who are not anti-caste and are working with the NGO. This issue came up in my interview with Richard Ebenezer, when I was discussing with him a strategy change for IJM's legal team: they were starting to charge individuals under the SC/ST Atrocities Act rather than simply under bonded labor statutes.[36]

> **Richard:** So, booking them under that provision [i.e., the SC/ST Atrocities Act], it's seen as a threat for the perpetrator. And generally, we would consider the offence to be high-end. The police have a tendency to arrest them, given the flight risk involved in such cases. So that puts more pressure on the owners. On the perpetrators. To arrest them and keep them in jail. But in terms of why I said "mixed result," is, even though the law is good, the mixed result is this: there are opinions that the public—especially among some section of some castes of society—like especially the backward and most backward upper caste—say that this act is the most abused act. Because people use this act to harass people who belong to higher castes. So, this opinion, you will find it even among the investigating officials, who comes from all sections of the community. And even among the judges, who come from all sections of the community. So, this attitude of "Oh, you're bringing bonded labor under *that* category," under the Atrocities, can make the police do a poor investigation—poor quality investigation—and a very lethargic investigation,

36. The SC/ST Atrocities Act is a piece of civil rights legislation that was designed to criminalize mistreatment of members of scheduled castes (i.e., Dalits) and members of scheduled tribes (i.e., Adivasis) based upon their caste.

> and even the judge sitting may say, "Oh my god, these people! This case my mother told me . . ." With that sense of skepticism, they look at these cases.[37]

Note that Richard affirms the goodness of the law, but points to the need for governmental and societal opinions to change to effectively enforce it. Note also that Richard was not arguing that this strategy should not be adopted. On the contrary, he seemed to be in favor of pushing forward with it. But others in the NGO community I spoke to expressed a much more pessimistic outlook toward this strategy off the record, and for similar reasons.

The third argument is that it would be dangerous for the survivors themselves to directly challenge the caste system. This implicitly came up in my interview with Sandeep. At one point in the interview, I found myself having difficulties picturing how village structure related to the problems with rehabilitation his clients were experiencing. So, Sandeep came up with an idea:

> **Sandeep:** I can just show you, maybe. A pictoral.
>
> **Chris:** Yeah! That would be helpful.
>
> [*At this point, Sandeep goes over to a whiteboard hanging in the room and draws a circle on the board. He indicates the bottom of the circle with the marker*]
>
> **Sandeep:** This will be the main entrance. This is where the upper caste people live.
>
> [*Sandeep draws three horizontal lines through the circle, dividing it into quarters. He indicates the bottom quarter, near the entrance*]
>
> This is where the upper caste people live. As and when you enter through the streets, you can see the strata of people . . .
>
> [*Sandeep indicates successive quarters of the circle, each one representing a caste group, with the upper caste people living at the*

37. Ebenezer, interview with the author, Chennai, India, November 12, 2014. Again, this argument could be referred to as the "reverse caste discrimination" argument. Sandeep added here that a conviction under the SC/ST Atrocities Act includes reparation money to the victim, something in the ballpark of ₹22,000 (roughly $330 at the time of the interview). This additional money would help immensely with rehabilitation costs ("Sandeep," interview with the author, Chennai, India, November 14, 2014).

front of the village, and progressively lower castes living toward the back of the village. Sandeep then indicates the top quarter of the circle: the back of the village where the Dalits live]

. . . like the SC [i.e., Dalits] . . .

[*Above the diagram and to the right, Sandeep draws a snaking pathway from the village to an area outside the village. There he draws a diagram of an encampment. He points to the encampment with the marker*]

This is where mostly ST [i.e., Adivasi] people live. They need to.

Chris: Okay, so this would be like . . . [*Chris points to the outer edge of the circle*] When you enter into the village, would it actually be a walled structure? Or is that just a boundary?

Sandeep: This is just a picture. A boundary.

[*Sandeep points to the ST settlement on the diagram, then points to the front entrance*]

And mostly, these people would not be allowed to go through this way.

[*He indicates a path around the village*]

They need to go through this way.

[*He points to the main entrance once again*]

If they go through this way, they ask, "Why are they there? It's a sacred place!"

Chris: I see, so starting with the front, they go from higher caste to lower caste, and then the ST folks are even all the way back here.

[*Sandeep points next to the ST encampment*]

Sandeep: See, here will be the burial grounds. They will be just close to the burial grounds. Here they will have water reservoirs.

[*Chris points to the center of the village*]

Chris: And they won't be able to use the water source that's located here.[38]

38. Due to the fact that Dalits and Adivasis are seen as ceremonially unclean, they are traditionally forbidden from drawing from the primary village water source. If a Dalit or Adivasi person touches the water, it is seen as polluting the whole water source.

Sandeep: [*in agreement*] Yes.

[*Sandeep points back to the graveyard*]

They'll have to go here. Now there is a lot of social consciousness against caste discrimination. These Irular are allowed to come, because of education. But there are still stringent people who see caste as a big thing.

Chris: I see, so education in the villages is starting to change the minds of folks even in the upper castes, but there are folks that are . . . [*Chris searches for the right word*] "traditionalists." That are really trying to reinforce that.

Sandeep: Yeah.[39]

Sandeep was relating for me some difficulties that they were experiencing getting land pattas for their clients because the land they were living on was deemed "non-pattable" (a category for land that cannot be legally occupied). These difficulties included an incident where residents of the village made up counterfeit pattas simply so the land on the outskirts of the village wouldn't be occupied by the Irular. At one point during the interview, I became curious about what might happen if they tried to gain land pattas for plots of land located in the village itself:

Chris: How successful have you been in trying to relocate these folks [*points to the Irular settlement in the graveyard*] back into the village [*points to the center of the village*]?

[*Sandeep gives Chris a look of abject horror and shakes his head vigorously*]

Not so much? That wouldn't be safe?

Sandeep: *Never.* Yes. We have never done that.[40]

Sandeep's look of abject horror was triggered due to an awareness of the likelihood of caste-based violence resulting from such an act. Desiring to protect his clients from harm, he would never wish to provoke the villagers in such a blatant way.

If the caste system must be challenged to do effective long-term economic rehabilitation, what is the best way to do so? How might it be done effectively in a way that takes into account (1) limited NGO

39. "Sandeep," interview with the author, Chennai, India, November 14, 2014.

40. "Sandeep," interview with the author, Chennai, India, November 14, 2014.

resources, (2) the casteism of government officials, and (3) the safety of the survivors themselves? It turns out that some social workers in Tamil Nadu are already moving in a salutary direction here: they are starting to take steps to teach Irular communities how to organize. Social workers identify local leaders who can advocate for electricity, housing, land allotments, payment of the state-mandated reparation money owed to survivors of bonded labor, and other needs that their communities have. Interestingly, these social workers have started to move in this direction not necessarily because they have incorporated efforts to directly challenge caste into their mission. Instead, they are turning to organizing out of operational necessity. Each of the social workers that I interviewed had a personal caseload of 150 to 300 individuals. They were expected to move all of these individuals from rescue to rehabilitation in a very short period of time (in the case of one NGO, during a series of six one-hour long house meetings that took place over a period of two years). And as all of this is going on, new clients are being added to their caseload. To put it bluntly, managing such a caseload and expecting high outcomes from the rehabilitation process is simply not humanly possible. As such, clients constantly call these social workers with rehabilitative problems both large and small that emerge outside of their mandatory meeting times. One client lacks adequate housing for their entire family, with ten individuals sharing a thatched-roof hut that covers roughly two hundred square feet.[41] Another has been liberated for nearly two years and has not received the legally mandated reparation money necessary to start a new life.[42] Another is having difficulty making ends meet, and needs help ob-

41. Of course, it isn't possible to fit them all in at once. Most nights, most of these ten will be sleeping outdoors. Monsoon season is another matter, however. During the heavy rains, either all ten will attempt to squeeze into the home, or they will have to sleep in, say, the hallways of a local school while classes are not in session. Kadavul and the unnamed couple were living in situations like this, and Hannah alluded to it being a common problem among the survivors she worked with outside of our interview ("Kadavul," interview with the author, Chennai, India, November 6, 2014; unnamed couple, interview with the author, Channai, India, November 10, 2014).

42. Kadavul, Kumar, Vijaya, and Jaya all experienced this, and Hannah and Nisha testified that it was a common experience among the survivors they worked with ("Kadavul," interview with the author, Chennai, India, November 6, 2014; unnamed couple, interview with the author, Channai, India, November 10, 2014; "Hannah," interview with the author, Chennai, India, November 18, 2014; "Nisha," interview with the author, Chennai, India, November 7, 2014; "Kumar" and "Vijaya," interview with the author, Chennai, India, November 6, 2014; "Jaya," interview with the author, Chennai, India, November 10, 2014). This was possibly also the case for Latha and

taining a ration card and getting government-provided rice to feed their family.[43] Another lacks a land patta and is in danger of being pushed from location to location when setting up a home.[44] Another has a child who faces caste discrimination in school that is interfering with her studies.[45] Another knows that his former owner is still a free man, and he refuses to leave the house because his former owner is threatening to kidnap him, his wife, and his children, and press-gang them back into slavery.[46] Another is so traumatized by the abuse he suffered under slavery that he cannot bring himself to go back to the same type of work (say, brickmaking) that was performed on the compound on which he was enslaved.[47] Another is dealing with the trauma of sexual assault while enslaved and cannot find any counseling resources in her village to deal with it.[48] The list goes on.

No one social worker can be there to solve such a torrent of problems for three hundred individuals (especially when those three hundred people live in villages several hours' drive from the city where the social worker lives). Additionally, many of these social workers reported that a

Subramani ("Latha" and "Subramani," interview with the author, Chennai, India, November 10, 2014).

43. Kadavul did not complain about this particular struggle, but when speaking of his financial difficulties, it was very clear that he could really use a ration card ("Kadavul," interview with the author, Chennai, India, November 6, 2014). Hannah, Nisha, and Naveen all testified that securing ration cards was a big part of their work, and Hannah testified that it was frequently a struggle to procure one for her clients ("Hannah," interview with the author, Chennai, India, November 18, 2014; "Nisha," interview with the author, Chennai, India, November 7, 2014; "Naveen," interview with the author, Chennai, India, November 12, 2014).

44. This was the case for Kumar and Vijaya ("Kumar" and "Vijaya," interview with the author, Chennai, India, November 6, 2014).

45. This was the case for the unnamed couple (unnamed couple, interview with the author, Channai, India, November 10, 2014).

46. This was the case for the unnamed couple (unnamed couple, interview with the author, Channai, India, November 10, 2014).

47. No survivors testified directly that this was true in their case, but Pranitha Timothy claimed that some survivors she works with have struggled with this (Pranitha Timothy, interview with the author, Channai, India, November 11, 2014).

48. No survivors testified directly that this was true in their case, but Nisha claimed it was common among survivors she works with ("Nisha," interview with the author, Chennai, India, November 7, 2014). Pranitha Timothy did not make any claims about prevalence, but from anecdotes she shared during the interview, it is clear she has dealt with this issue among survivors on more than one occasion (Pranitha Timothy, interview with the author, Channai, India, November 11, 2014).

significant chunk of their time was dedicated to getting local government officials to comply with existing governmental policy on bonded labor. This should be expected to be the norm, not only because international literature has long accused the Indian government of a tepid response to human trafficking,[49] but also because government watchdog groups are necessary to provide accountability for state abuse or neglect in any modern democratic nation. Since social workers are overtaxed, pulled between offering direct services and advocating for the government to follow through on its commitments to bonded laborers, the only solution seems to be to give the survivors themselves resources by which to organize and advocate for rehabilitative services on their own. This takes the bulk of the work of government accountability off of the social workers and is far more efficient at dealing with the problem.

Finally, there are persistent questions about the efficacy of economic rehabilitation programs which rely solely on governmental intervention. Here the assessment of Austin Choi-Fitzpatrick is worth noting:

> Most government-led rehabilitations have focused on the simple disbursement of benefits rather than on a broader strategy of equipping former bonded laborers to advocate for their rights economically, politically, and socially. Subsequent analysis suggests that benefits alone have a high failure rate when it comes to sustainable rehabilitation (Government of India Planning Commission 2012) . . . While corruption and official apathy

49. During IJM's review of an earlier version of this publication, an email discussion occurred between myself and IJM management about the nature of the government's response to bonded labor in Tamil Nadu specifically. In the initial draft of my dissertation, I characterized the nature of the government's response to bonded labor as apathetic at best. IJM conceded that this was the case in 2014–15, but claimed that the government of Tamil Nadu had taken significant steps to enforce bonded labor in the past few years. Since there are questions about the efficacy of government intervention alone even when the government is living up to its policy promises (see Choi-Fitzpatrick's comments quoted above), this is actually a secondary concern. However, for those interested, here is a summary of the exchange: (1) Concerning the rescue of bonded laborers, IJM and an independent social worker (Hannah) were able to give clear and convincing examples demonstrating that the government of Tamil Nadu had taken significant steps forward in investigating bonded labor cases and granting release certificates to bonded laborers in the past three years. (2) Concerning perpetrator accountability, IJM gave an affirmation of improvement, but did not specify how this issue had improved. Meanwhile, other international organizations still report an extremely low conviction rate for bonded labor cases across India. (3) Concerning rehabilitation, IJM did not address whether or not the government's ability to provide rehabilitation funds in a timely matter had improved.

> are significant aspects of slavery's prevalence on the subcontinent, the persistence of bonded labor is the product of durable inequality rooted in the caste system . . . But the root of the problem is not a lack of resources for vigilance committees, or a lack of time or knowledge from magistrates, or an inability to identify bonded laborers, or a shortage of benefits for survivors or a shortage of lawyers to prosecute cases . . . There is strong evidence that the root of the problem is that India has yet to develop an indigenous commitment to "comparable humanity" for all of its citizens (Kara 2011, 12). The most superficial evidence of this failure is the institution of untouchability.[50]

In other words, getting the government to follow through on its promises to bonded laborers is good (even essential), but even when the government is performing optimally, it can only go so far. What is truly needed is for the survivors to organize. As the "Iron Rule" of organizing goes, "Never do for others what they can do for themselves."[51] The upshot of the rule is not to preclude any role for charity, mutual aid, or government assistance. It is to recognize that, in any act of organizing, "the mentor or coach needs to open up space in which individuals can act and grow and speak in their own voices."[52] People can deal with their problems far more efficiently directly, and feel empowered in doing so. All that they need is someone to teach them how to organize. Instead of leaning primarily on job skill training sessions which teach survivors job skills that will likely leave them still vulnerable to social and economic marginalization and exploitation, NGOs can run community organizing training sessions that teach survivors to advocate for themselves. So, what sort of skills would a community organizing training look to inculcate within survivors of bonded labor?

50. Choi-Fitzpatrick, *What Slaveholders Think*, 127–29. Choi-Fitzpatrick also notes that the nature of government intervention can vary substantially from administration to administration (as is true in any democracy). Thus, even if the government's response to bonded labor were sufficient *now*, there is no reason to believe that future administrations would never roll back the gains of the current administration. And with the rise of Hindu nationalism in Indian politics, there are serious storm clouds on the horizon when it comes to issues of caste equality (79–82, 90–91). If survivors know how to organize, it will help them weather the storms that accompany shifting political climates.

51. Stout, *Blessed Are the Organized*, 136.

52. Stout, *Blessed Are the Organized*, 136.

Grassroots Organizing

In the US, community organizing—sometimes referred to more generally as "grassroots organizing," especially when one is organizing among multiple communities—is often associated with the legacy of Saul Alinsky. Alinsky was a secular Jewish political theorist and community organizer whose most lasting legacy was the founding of the Industrial Areas Foundation (IAF), a coalition of religious and civic organizations aimed at producing political change from the bottom up (hence the "grassroots" label). At times, Alinsky's name has so monopolized the discourse that some have dismissed all things that go under the label "grassroots organizing" due to criticisms of Alinsky himself rather than any concrete critique of grassroots organizing methods. But in truth, grassroots organizing cannot simply be reduced to Alinsky's model of organizing or his theories concerning how political change occurs. Grassroots organizing has many different sources, and there are many different schools of organizing. Alexia Salvatierra and Peter Hetzel recognize this fact in their own grassroots organizing manual, tracing the sources of their own school of grassroots organizing through the Civil Rights Movement, the Labor Movement of the early 1900s, Mahatma Gandhi's philosophy of *satyagraha*, the People Power Revolution in the Philippines, the Liberation Theologies of Latin America, the Central American Sanctuary Movement, and the formation of the United Farm Workers by Cesar Chavez and Delores Huerta.[53] This cloud of witnesses includes those who were influenced by Alinsky, those who had never heard of Alinsky, and those who offered critiques of Alinsky. It also includes strategies that have worked in countries ranging from the US to India to the Philippines to South Africa to Argentina. Much of what follows in this section will also be an amalgamation of different schools of organizing. The account of grassroots organizing that follows is informed by students of Alinsky, union organizers, organizers associated with Clergy and Laity United for Economic Justice (CLUE), organizers associated with the national organizing network Gamaliel, and members of the Poor People's Campaign.[54]

53. Salvatierra and Hetzel, *Faith-Rooted Organizing*, 9–11.

54. My own personal experiences with grassroots organizing have come about by working with Milwaukee Inner-city Congregations Allied for Hope (MICAH), which is a part of Gamaliel, and with union organizing as a part of the Marquette Academic Workers Union (MAWU).

All of these various schools of organizing attempt to bring about social and political change. What distinguishes grassroots organizing from some other forms of political and social action is that grassroots organizing insists that the primary agents of change should not be political or economic elites, but rather everyday people who organize themselves to exercise political power. Many grassroots organizations do this by insisting that the voices of impacted people (those who are the most impacted by the policies the organization wishes to change) should be at the center of political activism. Many schools of organizing also emphasize the idea that new members ought to be recruited by appealing to their self-interest. "Self-interest" here is not synonymous with *narrow* self-interest or selfishness. It is rather the insistence that it is far easier to motivate people to get involved if they believe being involved in an organization will help them become who they want to become than it is to motivate people to get involved by guilting or shaming them. In fact, most grassroots organizations that stress the importance of appealing to people's self-interest also insist that, at some point in time, the organization will need to help them figure out how their self-interest connects to the common good. Salvatierra and Hetzel sum up all of these themes well in their own description of what they call "faith-rooted" organizing: "Faith-rooted organizing is a model built on a foundation of international strategies of system disruption and transformation for the good of the least among us and the common good."[55]

Most models of grassroots organizing start with face-to-face meetings. Face-to-face meetings are one-on-one meetings that occur between an organizer and a person in the community. The primary goal for the organizer during these face-to-face meetings is not to recruit the community member to the organization, but to simply listen to the concerns of the community member. This is quite different from models in which the organizer already knows what the issue is.[56] After enough face-to-face meetings have been conducted to get some idea of the relevant issues in the community, organizers try to gather interested community members into regular meetings. Depending on the model used, these gatherings might be referred to as "core teams," "organizing committees," "general

55. Salvatierra and Hetzel, *Faith-Rooted Organizing*, 11.

56. In the United States, the form of organizing driven by issues (rather than by listening to community members) is probably best exemplified by people with clipboards who stand on street corners or go door-to-door and greet people with "Excuse me, sir/ma'am. Do you have a moment today to talk about [insert issue here]?"

meetings," or "house meetings." Here is Jeffrey Stout's description of a house meeting conducted according to the IAF model:

> "House meetings" are small group discussions in which people exchange stories about their concerns. In these meetings people begin to discover that some of their own concerns resemble the concerns that other people have. The organizers and leaders who sit in on the sessions are able to continue the process of identifying potential leaders, while also taking note of whatever concerns arise repeatedly in house meetings throughout the area.[57]

As Stout mentions, leadership identification occurs throughout the process, as organizers are constantly looking for individuals who are dedicated enough to the cause to take up a leadership role.[58] Those individuals identified then go through a training process that helps them get oriented to the ins and outs of organizing. Once regular group meetings have been established, grassroots organizations can work on "cutting" (or "framing") an issue. Stories offered at house meetings are taken as expressions of the problem, and organizers and leaders begin to articulate a core issue that the group wishes to address, as well as a proposal for addressing it and strategies for implementing that proposal.[59] When an organization cuts an issue, it is usually taking on a smaller, more concrete issue that is somehow related to the larger issue it wishes to address. For example, WISDOM is a grassroots organization that is made up of faith-based and civic groups in Wisconsin. WISDOM has decided that it wishes to end mass incarceration in Wisconsin (given how that issue impacts the membership of the groups that make up WISDOM). Ending mass incarceration is a lofty goal, and one that cannot be accomplished all at once. So, one of the issues that WISDOM has cut is that it wants the State of Wisconsin to close three prisons that dramatically fail to provide any sort of meaningful rehabilitation for those incarcerated there.[60] This is clearly

57. Stout, *Blessed Are the Organized*, 42–43.

58. In grassroots organizing, "organizer" designates a paid employee of the community organization. "Leader" designates a volunteer involved with the same organization. "Leaders" may or may not be impacted people. If an organization has very few impacted people serving in leadership roles, however, this is usually an indication that something has gone horrendously wrong during the organizing process.

59. Stout, *Blessed Are the Organized*, 160.

60. Specifically, the prisons they wish to close are Milwaukee Secure Dention Facility (MSDF), Green Bay Correctional Institution (GBCI), and Waupun Correctional Institution.

a more concrete issue: one can determine whether or not the campaign has been successful simply by investigating if the facilities in question are still there and operating as prisons. It is also consistent with the overall aims of the organization, since ending mass incarceration will necessarily entail incarcerating fewer people.[61]

Once an issue has been cut, the organization begins to contact public officials and start to negotiate a change in policy. One way that grassroots organizations can ensure that public officials will be willing to negotiate with the organization and take a clear stance on its policy recommendations is by holding a public accountability session (which is a tool that is heavily utilized in the IAF model of organizing). Accountability sessions are held in a space controlled by the community organization, and public officials are invited to come and indicate their stance on the issue that has been framed. When the public official is asked to indicate their stance, they are specifically asked a "yes or no" question. This is to indicate whether the politician is committing to be an ally of the organization or not. If a public official refuses to answer "yes" or "no" and starts to give a speech, the organization (who is controlling the venue) promptly has their microphone cut off. The point of this exercise is not to humiliate the public official or to give them "a taste of their own medicine." The point of cutting off an official's mic is to force them to take a clear stand on the issue. This is important because one of the primary ways in which public officials try to defer making policy changes is either by giving vague promises of action[62] or by obfuscating the issue.[63] And most public officials are trained to give vague promises and obfuscating answers by engaging in speeches. Cutting off their mic prevents them from doing this. Public officials have plenty of other avenues to articulate

61. Most grassroots organizations add that a good issue for organizing is one that (1) is concrete, (2) is winnable, (3) is widely felt, (4) is deeply felt, (5) has a timeline, (6) has a target, and (7) advances the values and the narrative of the organization. This list was compiled from both trainings put on by WISDOM and from union organizing handbooks such as Bradbury et al., *Secrets of a Successful Organizer*.

62. "I would support such a measure" is perhaps the most common of political empty promises. It places the public official theoretically in the same camp as the organization, but conveniently avoids making any concrete promises of action toward making the policy a reality.

63. Public officials often do this by saying "you do not understand what you are asking" or "the issue is more complicated than you realize." This is one of many reasons why having directly impacted people in leadership roles in your organization is so important. They know *exactly* what the effects of the current policy are. It impacts them directly.

why they hold the position(s) that they do. What the organization needs from the official to proceed with their activism is either a clear "yes" of commitment or a clear "no" of opposition. If the organization needs to cut off the mic, "no" is the assumed answer. At accountability sessions, "scorecards" can also be kept to reveal how much a particular official has lived up to the commitments he or she has articulated in the past.

After a public official's commitment or opposition to the organization has been revealed, the organization can begin personalizing and polarizing the issue. Personalization is when the organizer identifies a clear decision-maker (e.g., the public official) who has the power to change the policy in question. Polarization occurs when an organization either identifies that decision-maker as an ally who has publicly committed to make the changes they want to see, or when the organization publicly denounces the decision-maker as a clear opponent who is either contributing to an ongoing injustice or neglecting to act in the face of a clear problem. Polarization is an art form, Stout contends, and a difficult one to master. It must be done with the conviction that an opponent today may be an ally tomorrow and vice versa (many schools of organizing endorse the rule "no permanent allies, no permanent enemies"). Hence, it is important to polarize in such a way that no permanent grudges are held, and organizations need to learn to skillfully depolarize after a major fight is either won or lost.

Once an issue has been polarized, an escalating calendar of actions can be taken against the decision-makers who are opposed to the policy change. Actions should ideally start small (such as by circulating a petition or asking supporters to call the decision-maker's office) and eventually build up to weightier and larger actions that might pressure the decision-maker to change the policy (such as holding public demonstrations or engaging in civil disobedience).

In my interviews, I found that social workers had already started teaching survivors some grassroots organizing techniques and identifying leaders to represent their communities before government officials. I introduced "Latha," one of these community leaders, back in chapter 2. Latha was able to meet with local government officials and negotiate several free services for her community based on their status as newly emancipated bonded laborers (such as free electricity). If social workers were to expand the training resources necessary for survivors to form their own grassroots organizations, survivor communities might gain the know-how to advocate for many of the services that they need themselves. This would make social workers' caseloads more manageable and would likely improve aftercare outcomes for their organizations. Additionally, social workers could now investigate the possibility of offering more specialized services, such as recovery services for former bonded laborers who have suffered through sexual violence. And finally, community organizing might provide the perfect opportunity for local churches to get involved in the work of survivor reintegration (a question that many local NGOs have been wrestling with). Local faith leaders could help identify and train leaders for the organization, give the Irular meeting spaces and locations to hold accountability sessions, serve as volunteers for the community organization to help with local issues that affect the Irular survivors, and join the survivors when they call for nonviolent civil disobedience against public officials who fail to support policies that would help survivors reintegrate.

The affirmation of a connection between grassroots organizing and nonviolent civil disobedience here is important to correct a common (although helpful) critique of many grassroots organizations. That critique is stated well by Drew Hart in his book *Who Will Be A Witness?* When commending various ways that the church might faithfully engage in the work of justice, Hart offers up four strategies: nonviolent resistance and struggle, social movement protest, organizing people power, and engaging in electoral politics.[64] The general sketch of grassroots organizing that I have offered up here fits squarely under "organizing people power." After giving a description of what organizing entails, Hart assesses its main strengths and weaknesses. Among its many strengths, Hart notes that grassroots organizing truly does help those who are on the margins realize that they have the power to make social and political change a reality, and it allows people to exercise power without giving in to the "top-down corrosive partisan platforms that are handed to society."[65] However, Hart notes that the primary weakness of grassroots organizing is that it sometimes is too dismissive of nonviolent protest. His critique here is worth quoting at length:

> Typically, one of its greatest weaknesses is its rigid approach, which is not usually adaptable or open to different methods or attentive to cultural moments. Organizers usually frown on protest movements. Since such mobilizing efforts are usually

64. Hart, *Who Will Be a Witness?*, 284.

65. Hart, *Who Will Be a Witness?*, 307.

> looking for a quick fix and are usually short-lived, and since they do not always empower communities to address their own list of specific concerns, they often have a bad reputation among organizers. Community organizations usually highlight the failures of protest movement to convince people of the value of structure and power-building found in organizing. Some of these critiques are legitimate concerns, but it can result in throwing the baby out with the bathwater. . . . Organizers do not usually engage in nonviolent disruption as a strategy, because they want to keep lines of communication open with the formal decision makers. However, there are times when the formal channels are broken or not working for more vulnerable and oppressed members of society. It is precisely in that moment that a willingness to seek change outside working with those at the top can be necessary.[66]

Hart offers this critique up not to dismiss organizing, but as a helpful corrective. In the end, he recommends a hybrid approach that blends all four strategies he outlines. And I bring up Hart's critique because I find it helpful. I do not think Hart's assessment has identified a weakness that is inherent in all forms of grassroots organizing. In my own experience with the more militant wing of the labor movement, I have seen labor organizers both adhere in a very disciplined way to the organizing method listed above while simultaneously engaging in forms of nonviolent civil disobedience in innovative and courageous ways. The same was true for Cesar Chavez in his involvement with the UFW. Chavez was trained in the IAF model of organizing, and he adapted the model for his own organizing while still engaging in nonviolent civil disobedience in tactically innovative ways.[67] So it is not the case that grassroots organizing inherently lends itself to a stance that precludes participation in protest. In fact, it may even be the case that the more intense varieties of nonviolent civil disobedience will require prior grassroots organizing to pull off. However, I think Hart has correctly identified a temptation many grassroots organizations have given into. And he is not the only one of my colleagues who has gotten involved with an organization that operates on the IAF model and has come back with the critique that the organization is far too hesitant to engage in actions that might burn bridges with the folks in power.

66. Hart, *Who Will Be a Witness?*, 307–8.

67. For an excellent short biography of Chavez that illuminates all of these aspects of his story, see Rhodes, "Union of the Spirit," 9–36.

I think at root the issue is that advocates of grassroots organizing sometimes forget their own best insights about the nature of power. Hart's critique could be fruitfully levied, for example, at Jeffrey Stout's account of grassroots organizing in his otherwise excellent book *Blessed Are the Organized.* One of the book's greatest strengths is that Stout is relentless in reminding his readers that the power that grassroots organizations wield ultimately comes from relationships built during face-to-face meetings. If a grassroots organization neglects face-to-face meetings, it will quickly find that its leaders are no longer able to credibly speak for those who they claim to represent. For this exact reason, Stout stresses that it is necessary for every grassroots organization to periodically reorganize by returning to face-to-face meetings. Stout holds up Ernie Cortez' recommendation that this process should preferably be repeated every two to three years.[68] So far, so good: all power ultimately comes from relationships. However, as one reads through the book, one gets the distinct sense that Stout believes the exercise of power is really predicated upon certain rights that a democratic order recognizes. For example, at one point he describes how the survivors of Hurricane Katrina were able to fight back against further displacement by the US government (from the Houston Astrodome to an unnamed location in Arkansas) with the following summary:

> This case makes clear how freedoms guaranteed by First Amendment [*sic*] clear space for democratic culture. It was by exercising the right to speak, to assemble, and to petition for the redress of grievances that the evacuees were able to create a public of accountability. And it was by treating the Astrodome's public address system as a *public* address system, as something they had a right to use, in the manner of a free press, that they were able to initiate the process.[69]

This makes it sound as though the power of these survivors' practices were dependent upon government recognition of their validity. This would suggest that even the ability to exercise people power ultimately comes from the state. No such dependence relationship exists.[70] To reiterate the

68. Stout, *Blessed Are the Organized*, 128.

69. Stout, *Blessed Are the Organized*, 79. Emphasis in original.

70. In fact, there are aspects of Stout's description of the event that suggest that the survivors of Katrina were able to exercise such power in the face of a lack of governmental recognition of these rights. The assistant fire chief in charge of relief efforts at the Astrodome even made a barely veiled threat of violence against the survivors:

view of power articulated by Gene Sharp in chapter 1, government officials receive power from the people they govern and not vice versa. This has been demonstrated remarkably well in the literature on nonviolent resistance, as forms of nonviolent direct action have been successful even at overturning autocratic regimes which fail to recognize such rights.[71] The structure of democracy does not give people the ability to exercise collective power. They have the ability to exercise collective power simply by virtue of being human and standing in relationship with other human beings.[72] This is not to say that formal recognition of the right to peaceably assemble has no effect. It may make things safer for those who exercise it, for example. But as Sharp highlights in his analysis, what is important for the exercise of nonviolent power is not government recognition of inherent rights (or even citizenship). Rather, what is important is managing the flows of obedience and disobedience to governmental authority. *That* is where power lies. The power to disobey rests within each person, whether the possibility of that disobedience is legitimized by the government or not.[73]

It may be unsurprising, then, that the last line of Hart's critique quoted above is true of Stout's account of organizing: it has little to say about how a community organization might seek change outside of working with those at the top. To be sure, Stout describes several acrimonious encounters between politicians and organizers, and he is clearly

"People are going to Arkansas. We have policemen here with guns and people are going whether they want to or not" (Stout, *Blessed Are the Organized*, 77).

71. This was the case in, for example, the Philippine Revolution (1986), the Iranian Revolution (1979), the Tunisian Revolution (2011), and the overthrow of General Maximiliano Hernandez Martinez in El Salvador (1944).

72. Sharp states this explicitly: "Ultimately, therefore, freedom is not something which a ruler 'gives' his subjects. Nor, in the long run, do the formal institutional structures and procedures of the government, as prescribed by the constitution, by themselves determine the degree of freedom or the limits of the ruler's power" (Sharp, *Power and Struggle*, 29).

73. Given that Stout is keen on viewing democracy as a tradition, Hobbesian versions of social contract theory might be to blame here, given their prominence in that tradition. The general idea in Hobbesian social contract theory is that peaceful society emerges after the state violently domesticates a primordial violence (a state of nature in which all people are out to dominate one another and in which life is "brutish, nasty, and short"). If you operate with that mythological understanding of how the world works, then violent state power comes as a precursor to and guarantor of the exercise of nonviolent people power. This is simply not how power works. Since nonviolent people power depends on the ability to disobey, it is simply always there, even without a state willing to clear the way for it.

on the side of the organizers. But Stout makes clear that he thinks the goal of grassroots democratic action is to "tame and civilize" elites.[74] Both Hart and Stout agree that the goal of grassroots organizing is to empower impacted people. But Stout additionally claims that another goal of grassroots organizing is to give us better elites. Those two goals can be in conflict, and they can suggest conflicting power analyses. I do not want to be misunderstood here: holding government officials accountable is a good thing. The problem is that Stout's overreliance on "taming" metaphors suggests that he sees the political landscape as analogous to a rural community overrun by wild horses. The horses (in this case, political and economic elites) are larger and stronger than the people in the community, and since they are wild, they go where they wish and behave how they wish without proper regard for others. But if the people band together, they can corral these horses, bit and bridle them, break them, and then train them. But fundamentally, the horses are the ones with the power: they are bigger and stronger than the people. People are only powerful insofar as they can make elites behave in such a way that they serve the community's collective interest. This unfortunate view of power might lead some to conclude that it is better to be an elected official than an organizer. After all, that is where the real power lies.

Luckily, this picture of political power is fundamentally flawed. Politicians don't generate their own power independent from the people. They aren't powerful because they're bigger and stronger than anyone else. They're powerful because lots of people are willing to do what they say. As soon as enough people are *not* willing to do what they say, they aren't any different from you or me. Nonviolent civil disobedience works not by appealing to a ruler's better nature and hoping that he has a change of heart, but by disrupting the myriad flows of power to that ruler and depowering him.[75] Pictures of political power like the wild horses one

74. Stout, *Blessed Are the Organized*, 94.

75. This corrects a common objection to "liberal pacifism" commonly advanced by the realist theologian Reinhold Niebuhr. Niebuhr held that "liberal pacifism" was an attempt to merge Christ's teachings against violent resistance to evil with the techniques of nonviolent direct action practiced by thinkers such as Mahatma Gandhi. Niebuhr thought this variant of pacifism was heretical, because it combined an overly optimistic view of human nature inherited from the Enlightenment with the teachings of Jesus Christ in the Sermon on the Mount. The type of pacifism Jesus preached, Niebuhr thought, was one of total nonresistance: Jesus held that one could not even engage in nonviolent resistance against an aggressor, because that would still be an attempt to exercise coercion upon the aggressor. This objection simultaneously misunderstands

just described forget that a president does not command an administration or a military in the same way that a horse commands its legs. In fact, any analogy that compares a body politic to a physical body seems to be subject to confusion of this sort. In any body politic, the administration or the military can itself engage in dissent even against those who hold the highest political offices. A horse's legs don't dissent against a horse in quite the same way. Sickness or injury may cause a leg to work improperly, but that really isn't the same thing as the leg joining others in coordinated disobedience against the horse based on a crystallization of conscience.[76] Many nonviolent protest methods recognize this possibility for internal dissent and attempt to cause members of the military and the administration to become disillusioned with and alienated from their commander-in-chief. In the history of nonviolent resistance, this can be as simple as convincing individual soldiers to disobey their superior officer when ordered to open fire on unarmed protestors (as was the case in the Egyptian and Tunisian revolutions of 2011) or as complex as convincing all branches of the local government to join with the people in resisting a policy issued by the national government (as has frequently occurred in sanctuary cities in the United States).

Holding a prescribed view of political power severely limits the tactical options of a community organization. As Hart points out, it can cause a community organization to be more concerned with getting elites on their side than with building power that could bring about changes that fundamentally run contrary to the commitments of the elite. It can also cause a community organization to dissuade its members from doing anything that might be considered breaking the law. This might be why, when Stout talks about power, he tends to talk about power that is

the Gospels and the nature of nonviolent direct action. It misunderstands the Gospels because Jesus clearly engages in at least two recognized methods of nonviolent direct action in every single one of the four Gospels (namely, in the triumphal entry and the cleansing of the temple). The triumphal entry is a form of public demonstration, the cleansing of the temple is a form of nonviolent occupation. Niebuhr's objection also misunderstands nonviolent direct action, because nonviolent direct action is not based in an overly optimistic view of human nature that thinks bad people will change their ways if you simply show them enough love and try to talk things out. While nonviolent direct action always leaves open the possibility that a ruler will change, that isn't what makes it *work*. What makes it work is the interruption of flows of obedience to that ruler, and this can be accomplished without the ruler's consent.

76. This is a phrase often used in both Catholic moral theology and the literature on conscientious objection (to military service). For a full description of what the phrase entails, see Allman, *Who Would Jesus Kill*, 54–57.

legally recognized (i.e., that is protected by the right to assemble, the right to petition public officials, etc.). This is far too great a concession for a power analysis. It should not be surprising that, if the people are unwilling to disobey public authorities and unjust laws, the resources for holding a specific authority accountable will be quite limited. The organizers Stout interviewed did speak of a virtue of disobedience; they spoke of the need to overcome that sense of deference that most of us are trained to feel toward authority figures.[77] But this virtue is severely curtailed if it is narrated as a matter of simply acting from within the confines of the space the state has carved out for you. Certainly, disobedience against a severely compromised authority might still be possible on this account of the virtue of disobedience, but it assumes that one still exercises this dissent from within the confines of the law. This is a way of thinking about civil disobedience that ignores the reality of the powers. It is good to wag one's finger at an official and tell them you won't take no for an answer. It is good to turn off their microphone. It is good to threaten not to vote for them. It is better to engage in civil disobedience. It is better to strike, to boycott, to obstruct administrative procedures, and to provide sanctuary for those whom the state labels "illegal." It is better to disobey unjust laws and policies than to simply threaten to reduce a person's re-election chances while obeying unjust laws and policies. Unfortunately, outside of a few campaigns that involved rallies, Stout covers no organizations that engage in nonviolent civil disobedience to accomplish their goals. For an adequate account of nonviolent civil disobedience, we will have to turn elsewhere.

If one is looking for a theological justification of nonviolent civil disobedience, there are few places better to start than Martin Luther King Jr.'s *Letter from Birmingham City Jail*. In that letter, he noted that the consensus view throughout the Christian tradition is that before you can answer the question "Should I follow this law?" you must first ask "Is the law just?" If the answer to this question is "yes," then a Christian is obligated to follow the law. If the answer to this question is "no," then a Christian is obligated to break the law (nonviolently).[78] The view that King argued against in the letter—the "White Moderate" view—holds

77. See for example, Stout, *Blessed Are the Organized*, 96 (quoting Carmen Anaya): "[We must learn] how to deal face-to-face with a politician and not humiliate ourselves or beg. We have the right to negotiate and tell him, 'You are not our patron—you are our servant.' This is very important."

78. King, "Letter from Birmingham City Jail," 293.

instead that the law ought never be broken or violated. It must be obeyed whether it is just or unjust.[79] If you do not like the law, then obey it until you gain enough power to change it in the legislature or the courts.[80] As King pointed out then, one of the major problems with this view is that it is fundamentally unable to make sense of the broader narrative of Scripture. Civil disobedience is a deeply ingrained part of the writings of the Exilic Prophets and the early Christian witnesses. The White Moderate view is incommensurable with that narrative because it claims that officials who punish those who follow God's law over human laws are in the right. In other words, it stands with Pilate over Jesus, Nero over Paul, and Nebuchadnezzar over Shadrach, Meshach, and Abednego. Indeed, many modern theologians (such as the late James Cone) have correctly pointed out that "to bear the cross" cannot mean simply to find suffering to be redemptive in and of itself. It means specifically to suffer *while standing in resistance to unjust powers*. Only this variety of suffering can be redemptive.[81] "To bear the cross"—the hallmark of Christian discipleship—means engaging in civil disobedience. It means this precisely because it was Jesus' acts of civil disobedience—namely the triumphal entry (a public demonstration) and the cleansing of the temple (a nonviolent occupation)[82]—that caused the Romans to take enough notice of him to send him to the cross. Those who claim that it is never acceptable to engage in civil disobedience are not only standing against this tradition, they are also claiming that it is never acceptable to be a disciple of Christ.

Sometimes there is no formal law standing in the way of rehabilitation for survivors of human trafficking. Instead, it may simply be a general governmental policy. We saw such a case earlier, where an Adivasi worker may have been directed by a local governing authority not to engage in direct competition with a higher-caste man who ran a stereo repair business. In this case, King's test still applies. Is the policy just? If it is, those under it are obligated to follow it. If not, they are obligated to

79. King, "Letter from Birmingham City Jail," 295.

80. The White Moderate view is undergoing considerable resurgence in our era. Nearly every time an ICE official is interviewed for a public news organization like NPR, I hear the view reiterated practically verbatim in an attempt to shut down any protest concerning US immigration policy.

81. Cone, *Cross and the Lynching Tree*, 150.

82. The two parenthetical statements are Gene Sharp's terminology for these sorts of actions.

break it (nonviolently), and the Christians around them are under an obligation to offer them support in doing so. Taking measures to hold political officials accountable to *all* the people they serve is a good step, but ultimately if negotiations break down, Adivasi peoples need to know that there are other means of exercising political power that don't depend on the official's approval.

If one is looking for a manual with descriptions of nonviolent civil disobedience tactics, by far the most comprehensive work is volume 2 of Sharp's *Politics of Nonviolent Action* (subtitled *The Methods of Nonviolent Action*). It was originally published in the mid-seventies, so many of its categories require updating, but I am unaware of any other resource that has matched it in terms of comprehensiveness. Far from being solely an academic work, versions of this publication have been utilized during actual nonviolent political movements (such as the revolutions in Tunisia and Egypt during the "Arab Spring" in the early 2010s). In it, Sharp catalogues nearly two hundred forms of nonviolent resistance.[83] Some of these methods are permutations of more well-known or classic forms of nonviolent resistance (such as the boycott, the strike, or the sit-in), while others may be more tactically restricted or less well-known (such as administrative shutdowns, the reverse strike, or protest disrobing). It is important to remember, however, that Sharp's work was not meant to be exhaustive, and other forms of nonviolent political action have been developed or discovered that could be added to his list (such as jury nullification).

As I mentioned before, there is no inherent reason why community organizations should not mobilize their constituencies for these types of nonviolent political action. Indeed, they seem to be perfectly equipped to do so. Methods of organizing such as face-to-face meetings and household meetings would also be ideal avenues for mobilizing nonviolent direct action. And many community organizations are rooted in local churches and other houses of worship, which have a vested interest (or at least, *ought to* have a vested interest) in forming their members in certain virtues. As Gandhi and King pointed out, formation in a specific set of virtues is absolutely necessary for any form of nonviolent political action. As King stated in *Letter from Birmingham City Jail*: "In any nonviolent campaign there are four basic steps: [1.] collection of the facts to determine whether injustices exist; [2.] negotiation; [3.] self-purification; and

83. Elsewhere, he numbers the list specifically at 198 (see Sharp, *Dictionary of Power and Struggle*, 330–38).

[4.] direct action."[84] A friend of mine once poignantly noted that many modern protest movements skip directly from step 1 to step 4. Negotiation and self-purification can easily become forgotten. The self-purification step King mentions is clearly an inheritance from Gandhi, and when Gandhi used the term, he clearly was referring to a process of forming participants in the virtues necessary to rightly engage in civil disobedience.[85] Again, community organizations are inherently concerned with negotiation, and houses of worship are inherently concerned with self-purification, so there is no necessary reason why dividing lines should be drawn up between organizing on the one hand and civil disobedience on the other. The two clearly were linked in King's own activism: "every town that invited King in to speak had already been organized."[86]

Is it realistic to expect that a powerless minority such as the Adivasi can engage in these forms of civil disobedience? It was somewhat frequently contended in my interviews that Indian NGOs are basically forced to use only those tactics that have explicit authorization by a governing authority, since Indian society is more communal and therefore less individualistic than American society. This is especially true in the villages. In a village setting, all conflicts are ultimately mediated through a panchayat (literally, "council of five"), the most local body of governance in most village settings. The panchayat system existed in India prior to the presence of Western colonial powers, and Gandhi stressed the re-establishment of the panchayat system as a method for local conflict resolution once India regained its independence.

The contention is that there is no avenue to defy the will of a panchayat because there is no "going it alone." "Mallika" expressed this opinion in her interview. She noted that the family of a sex trafficking survivor has no recourse to resist a panchayat's decision if the panchayat rules that a survivor must be cast out of the village because she was in the sex trade (and will not be moved by explanations that the survivor was not doing this willingly):

> **Mallika:** If the family gets to know [that the survivor was involved in the sex trade], then even if the family wasn't involved,

84. King, "Letter from Birmingham City Jail," 290.

85. This is clear in any of Gandhi's writings on satyagraha (his method of nonviolent resistance). For an excellent compilation of Gandhi's writings on satyagraha, see Gandhi, *Essential Writings*, 309–73.

86. Stout, *Blessed Are the Organized*, 267. Stout is himself paraphrasing a comment that Joan Bland made at a conference at Princeton on April 3, 2009.

> for the sake of honor, for the sake of the village. . . . They will not accept that girl. They will reject that girl. The stigma is too high. . . . Because a family . . . in our community, our culture, a family cannot subsist in a village setting without the village. They are not stand-alone. This is not like the Western society where you are not answerable to anybody, you do your own thing. In a village setting, especially in the rural areas, especially in smaller rural towns, and rural villages. Everybody knows what's happening in everybody else's house. It's an open community. So, you cannot hide these things. So therefore, it's not about everybody in just the family. I'm saying, then educate the village. Because the village has to accept the girl.[87]

Accordingly, the policy of Mallika's NGO is to not disclose what kind of work the survivor was doing while trafficked when the village gathers around to take her back in. But as Mallika indicates here, even that is a short-term solution: "You cannot hide these things." So, community education needs to take place.

Certainly, most forms of civil disobedience have very little effect if a single resister goes it alone. That is the point of forming organizations and building power through face-to-face meetings: most forms of nonviolent civil disobedience are only effective if people disobey collectively. One dissenter can be struck down. A hundred have to be negotiated with. Similarly, I don't dispute that any form of civil disobedience would need to be tactically tailored for an Indian village setting before I could suggest that the survivors I interviewed should engage in it. One does have to consider the differences between the American political landscape and the Indian political landscape before suggesting ways to exercise nonviolent political power. But of course, nonviolence is not foreign to India's soil. In fact, many advocates of nonviolent civil disobedience in America are influenced by Gandhi. One of the most noteworthy things about the sudden explosion of nonviolent revolutions in the twentieth century is that they emerged from rich back-and-forth conversations between East and West: Leo Tolstoy influenced Gandhi, who in turn influenced Howard Thurman, Jim Lawson, and others involved in the American Civil Rights Movement. Additionally, I want to challenge the idea that, the more communal a society becomes, the less plausible civil disobedience and governmental accountability become. In fact, the opposite may be true: Stout worries that American society is becoming too atomized to

87. "Mallika," interview with the author, Mumbai, India, September 17, 2014.

effectively hold its leaders accountable. This is a worry that is not unfounded. If you don't know your neighbors, you can't organize. And as Kalpana Mohanty points out, at certain points in history, the panchayats have acted not so much as a body for conflict transformation, but rather as a body that metes out harsh punishments that were not conducive to solving conflicts. In such times, rural Indians have taken it upon themselves to seek alternative ways of solving conflicts.[88] This indicates that resistance against panchayat authority at times when the panchayat is more interested in defending village honor instead of providing justice for survivors is very much possible.

Can such a small community succeed in achieving their goals in a village setting? One recent study suggests reasons to be hopeful. In their book *Why Civil Resistance Works*, political scientists Erica Chenoweth and Maria Stephan decided to test whether violent resistance movements or nonviolent resistance movements were more effective at meeting their stated aims.[89] They collected data for over two hundred violent resistance movements and one hundred nonviolent resistance movements that occurred between 1900 and 2006. They divided each movement up into three groups: successful, partially successful, and failed. Movements were divided into these groups based on their stated aims. Chenoweth and Stephan found out that the nonviolent campaigns were about 53 percent successful, 25 percent partially successful, and 22 percent failed. The violent campaigns were about 26 percent successful, 13 percent partially successful, and 61 percent failed.[90] That means that nonviolent resistance campaigns were successful or partially successful about twice as often as violent resistance campaigns. Additionally, nonviolent campaigns were trending upwards by decade (i.e., becoming more successful), whereas violent campaigns were trending downwards by decade (i.e., becoming less successful). Interestingly, they also stated that they have yet to find a regime that could stand against a nonviolent resistance movement in which 3.5 percent or more of the population is involved in sustained

88. Mohanty, "Nonviolence in the Hindu Tradition," 184–85.

89. According to the legend that circulates in peacemaking circles, the book was practically written on a bet. Chenoweth and Stephan met at a conference, and they got to talking about resistance movements. Chenoweth was the skeptic who didn't think nonviolence was a terribly effective way of bringing about change. Stephan was the true believer who thought that nonviolence could be an effective way to bring about change. So they decided to co-write and co-research this book. And due to its findings, Chenoweth now writes and speaks about the effectiveness of nonviolent resistance.

90. Chenoweth and Stephan, *Why Civil Resistance Works*, 9.

nonviolent resistance (in a lecture Stephan gave at Marquette University in April of 2017, she referred to this as the "magic number"). This means that nonviolent campaigns have been successful with a participation percentage of 3.5 *or less*.[91] So yes, while nonviolent resistance techniques are not a silver bullet that can always guarantee you the change you want, there is reason to be optimistic that even a small, marginalized group can push back against a panchayat and be successful

Local social workers are already about the business of teaching Adivasi survivors that being a part of a village setting does not automatically mean that one must always be obedient to authorities. The problem is that the caste system demands unquestioning obedience from lower-caste individuals toward upper-caste individuals, theologically reinforces the need for such obedience, and brutally punishes even the slightest act of disobedience. During the anti-exploitation educational sessions outlined in chapter 2, survivors are taught how to band together to resist being forced back into bondage by upper-caste employers. They are taught how to bring counterarguments against the sort of arguments that upper-caste employers will likely use to shame them into compliance. That is how one teaches the virtue of disobedience. That is also teaching a rudimentary form of organizing. And it is necessary because the caste system tries to beat disobedience out of Dalits and Adivasis from birth. Here is how Pranitha Timothy characterized one survivor's words upon graduating from her organization's rehabilitation program:

> **Pranitha:** Every two years, you have this graduation program for people who were rescued, so that we allow them to move on.

91. Numerous additional conclusions could be mentioned here. Chenoweth and Stephan also found that nonviolent movements were less likely to result in breakouts of future violence (e.g., civil wars) after the conflict was over. They also found that participation made the difference in success. The moral, physical, informational and commitment barriers are lower for nonviolent resistance than violent resistance, which leads to more participation for nonviolent resistance movements. Participation correlates with greater resilience, more tactical innovation, and greater civic disruption, all of which increase the possibility of success. Participants in nonviolent resistance movements were more likely to be seen by the opposition as trustworthy, leading to increased chances of the regime negotiating or making concessions. Perhaps most interestingly, Chenoweth and Stephan argue that nonviolence is inherently more egalitarian than violence. Most violent resistance movements throughout history have employed only men between the ages of eighteen and thirty-five (same as most militaries). Nonviolent resistance movements, on the other hand, pose no inherent barriers to participation for women, people under eighteen, and people over thirty-five. This also leads to greater participation.

> So, at one of the graduation meetings, I was shocked just looking at the group. They were so well-dressed and so happy, and all that laughing, and the kids are there, and a time of celebration. So, we were having speeches after speeches, and finally had the word of thanks by one of the clients. So, one of the leaders goes out, and I was expecting him to say, "Two years ago, look at where we were. And today, we have our children going in school, we have jobs, and . . ." That's not what he said. He went up, and he said, "Two years ago, did you imagine sitting on a chair?" And I just couldn't even imagine that, for them to sit on a chair meant everything. Like, that little that we gave them to sit on a chair. Which, I wouldn't even think twice. Like, for me, I didn't even think that they did not feel worthy enough to sit on a chair. To that extent, the community has actively oppressed them.[92]

Pranitha is speaking here about the caste requirement to physically sit lower than those who are above you in the caste system, to show them deference. I noticed this constantly in my bonded labor interviews: survivors I interviewed were constantly and reflexively trying to position themselves physically lower than myself to show deference. That is how thoroughly the obedience demanded by the caste system distorts bodies: it prevents them from even indulging in the small comfort of sitting in a chair. Prior to jobs, prior to education, prior to land ownership, a people with obedience so scarred upon their bodies need to learn to disobey. And they need to learn to disobey in a way that shows love for God, love for truth, and love for their neighbor. They have been taught the virtue of obedience. They need to discover the virtue of disobedience.

This process of discovery is difficult for most human beings, but it is even more difficult for those who are suffering under captive mentality. However, I see no reason why trainings oriented toward learning how to resist the caste system might not also incorporate elements meant to help overcome captive mentality. The Freedom Training I have referenced in both this chapter and in chapter 2 is a good model of a program which incorporates elements of both. As survivors are presented with an alternative view of justice and love that stands against the false views of justice and love presented to them by their captors, they can also be presented with what virtuous civil disobedience looks like. They can be taught to

92. Pranitha Timothy, interview with the author, Channai, India, November 11, 2014.

strike, to demonstrate, to occupy forbidden spaces, and to organize.[93] They could be given examples of others who have done this, and of the disciplines necessary to engage in those forms of civil disobedience. They could be introduced to thick philosophies of civil disobedience, such as Gandhi's program of *satyagraha.* Additionally, Freedom Training helps address the problem of community resistance to a survivor's newfound freedom by teaching them to find strength in numbers. By encouraging Adivasi survivors to band together to resist potential employers who may try to re-bond them, social workers are already moving along the lines needed to teach survivors safety precautions when engaging in any form of nonviolent resistance.

At the heart of all of this must lie forms of moral formation that allow for resistance, that ask Adivasi survivors not to stoop in the presence of others, but to disobey unjust laws and practices while preserving a posture of love for their enemies. And at times, it will be necessary to remember that enemies can come from without or from within the community. Dealing with those survivors who cross that line—who go back and forth from enslaved to enslaver, from abused to abuser, friend to enemy—will be the subject of the next chapter.

93. In Choi-Fitzpatrick's interviews, slaveowners express a great deal of fear that workers will learn to strike or unionize, and as such, they take great pains to isolate workers from each other in order to prevent this from happening (Choi-Fitzpatrick, *What Slaveholders Think*, 50). If workers were taught to recognize this, it would go a long way to empower them against exploitation.

Chapter 6

Justice

"BETH" IS AN ATTORNEY who has worked on the prosecution side of sex trafficking cases for many years. We meet one blazingly hot afternoon during monsoon season at a coffee shop in Mumbai. She's recently decided to step down from her position. She's disillusioned, and very frank about it. It's not so much that she doesn't believe in the necessity of the work anymore; she still wants to work to stamp out sex trafficking, just not from the prosecutor's bench. The problem is that she feels that she has spent far too much of her time prosecuting the wrong people. Few of the accused on the opposite side of the courtroom from her have been the politically connected heads of trafficking rings. Here is her description of one case that she worked:

> **Chris:** So, in this particular case, [the person arrested during the raid] was aware of the fact that there was sex on the premises, but he wasn't aware of the fact that it was illegal?
>
> **Beth:** Yeah. I don't know whether he had even thought about it, he was hardly 16 or 17 years old. He was the errand boy who would run out and get the coke and the drinks. So . . . [REDACTED] would arrest a lot of people who are just at that . . . who are [simply] *in* the brothel. Whereas the brains of the outfit are the people who are living off the fat of the land.
>
> **Chris:** Right, right.
>
> **Beth:** Yeah, in fact, even . . . Yeah, I don't think there was anyone who was so high up the chain. Most of those guys couldn't even afford their bail amounts. I remember once going to the CBI

[the Central Bureau of Investigation]—[we] did a case with the CBI—and I went to follow up, and the CBI official said, "Seriously? You think these are powerful traffickers? The guy cannot even afford a defense counsel."[1]

Arresting sixteen-year-old street kids that were hired as errand boys simply isn't justice. What would be just, Beth contended, would be targeting those who are actually making a substantial amount of money from the enslavement of others. While we were on the topic, I decided to ask her about another group that is commonly prosecuted in trafficking cases:

Chris: Have you also been seeing . . . I know 8 years ago, oftentimes you would see people in management in brothels who were formerly put out in the lineup and sexually exploited themselves . . . do you still see that happening 8 years down the line?

Beth: Yeah. So, many of these managers . . . I think the last . . . It was in [REDACTED]'s time, I think, we used to actually arrest some owners. Like in one case I remember, we actually arrested two very powerful brothel owners. But that was, what . . . four years ago? The last three years, most of those who were arrested were . . . I mean, you'd feel sorry for them, Chris.[2]

"Chitra," another attorney who works on sex trafficking cases, testified to encountering the same group:

Chris: Do you still find that happening in cases?

Chitra: Yes. Yes. In fact, we've had a case where, on the rescue operation, the brothel manager actually told us, "Where were you guys when I was being trafficked?" Yeah. So, it's quite sad, because most of these traffickers, most of these pimps and brothel managers—mostly in the brothel rescue situation—have themselves been girls and women who have been trafficked. And yeah, just being there, just being through the system has made them that brutal, where they're forcing other girls to prostitute. Hopefully, the next generation won't . . . Since all these rescues are happening, and the police have been very active in rescuing girls now, hopefully there won't . . . I just hope that this doesn't continue happening.[3]

1. "Beth," interview with the author, Mumbai, India, September 12, 2014.
2. "Beth," interview with the author, Mumbai, India, September 12, 2014.
3. "Chitra," interview with the author, Mumbai, India, October 13, 2014.

It can be horribly demoralizing to realize that, if you had raided the same space ten years ago, the person currently being hauled off to jail for trafficking minors would have been among the victims being sent to an aftercare home instead. Beth stated other reasons for walking away from the prosecutor's bench, but this seemed to wear on her the heaviest. She wasn't getting at the individuals who really benefitted from exploiting others in local human trafficking rings. She was catching former victims and clueless street kids instead.

What does one do with a person who has been both victim and perpetrator? What does one do with the enslaved person who helps the master enslave others? Such individuals have been a staple in many systems of slavery for centuries. What Chitra and Beth are running into on a regular basis is not a fluke; enslaved people of this sort are there by design. And yet, in my interviews, I could find no examples of rehabilitation services that were being offered to those who had played the roles of both victim and perpetrator at some point. Mona Almeida reported that her organization (Kshamata) once tried to do an outreach program for brothel madams who were involved in the trafficking of teenage girls (and who may have been trafficked *as* teenage girls themselves). However, the program fell apart due to funding issues. Few donors wish to expend resources to help traffickers reform, even if they first entered a trafficking ring as victims themselves.[4]

Enslaved people who cross the line from victim to abuser are left out of a great deal of anti-trafficking narratives. It simply seems easier to omit them. And as these individuals are omitted from the narrative, more and more campaign advertisements appear for legislators who promise to "bring the hammer down" on human trafficking, instituting tougher and tougher penalties for anyone involved in trafficking another human being. The intent is understandable, but I fear the effects may be rather unexpected. This middle class of enslaved person—this victim-perpetrator—is an integral part of systems of slavery for many reasons, but one of the primary reasons is to distance those higher up the chain from direct involvement in the day-to-day operations of slavery while still profiting from the enslavement of others. In other words, this class exists to shield the master from legal repercussions. Tougher laws may simply mean more victim-perpetrators. They will be deputized to bear

4. Mona Almeida, interview with the author, Mumbai, India, December 15, 2014.

the burden of imprisonment on behalf of the master. Slavery once again proves itself one step ahead of those who wish to resist it.

I do not, however, think that those who oppose slavery are without options on this point. There may be a way to continue to hold open the possibility of rehabilitation for victim-perpetrators without ignoring the fact that they have been complicit in causing harm to other human beings. And in doing so, there may be a way to remove them from play as an expendable resource for masters in the process. This will, however, require a move away from the "hammer" approach. It will require a turn toward a restorative view of justice.

What is restorative justice? For those unfamiliar with restorative justice processes, I will provide a brief overview of its advocacy over the last decade or so, starting with the insights of Howard Zehr, who is perhaps the most well-known advocate for restorative justice in America. This will include an overview of the theological insights that sparked the movement, as the restorative justice movement has long been seen as amenable to a particular Christian vision of justice. I propose to use the insights gained by the restorative justice movement to come up with some suggestions for how to proceed with rehabilitation for survivors of trafficking who have assisted in trafficking others. These suggestions will necessarily be extraordinarily tentative, as I could find no organizations even reaching out to this population, and I had difficulty even interviewing its members myself. As these suggestions are untested with this specific population, the model I will propose will doubtless need substantial tweaking. However, the severe shortcomings of the operative retributive justice model for dealing with this population mandate at least an attempt to procure justice in a different fashion. Because restorative justice puts a strong emphasis on naming the concrete harms that offenders inflict upon victims, it will be necessary to take a more in-depth look at this population of victim-perpetrators and their role within trafficking rings before moving on to a fuller discussion about restorative justice.

Enslaved Managers, Mestris, and Brothel Managers

How do victim-perpetrators come to occupy the positions they do in sex and labor trafficking rings? As we've already touched on above, in sex trafficking rings, this usually occurs when a victim reaches the point where she "graduates" from one role to another. In a brothel situation, this frequently means that customers have stopped requesting to have sex with her when they come to patronize the brothel (or are at least requesting her less often). This often happens when a victim reaches a certain age, and she is therefore seen as less desirable among brothel patrons, who have a general preference for younger victims. At this point, a victim realizes that she only has two choices, since long years in the sex industry have left her with few other employment options. The first option is to beg on the street, which is largely the same thing as choosing to go hungry. The second option is to go into a managerial position in the brothel. She now knows the interior workings of the brothel quite well, and she can use that knowledge to serve in a managerial role. Of course, if she serves any sort of managerial role in the brothel, this means that she will be taking part in the trafficking of other women in some shape or form. Many victims choose this option over begging on the street, arguing that it is what they need to do to survive.[5]

It must be noted that at nowhere in the course of this "promotion" does anyone up the chain (such as the brothel owner) lose anything in the way of return on their initial investment. In the role of sex worker, the enslaved person they bought who was once profitable has become unprofitable. And if she chooses to leave the brothel and go beg on the street, they gain no additional profit from her. However, the trafficking organization now finds new use of the enslaved worker in the form of cheap skilled labor if she transitions from sex worker to manager. Additionally, if local law enforcement does decide to raid the brothel, those who oversee the immediate operations of the brothel are the ones that are going to be arrested, since their role in the exploitation of enslaved workers in the brothel is much easier to establish than the role of individuals who are receiving money from the brothel. It is the manager who will take the fall. The master doesn't lose an enslaved worker, he gains an overseer and a buffer. This is not so much the liberation of an enslaved person followed by her deciding to become an enslaver herself, but merely a change in roles within an ongoing relationship of enslavement.

5. Nicholas Kristof and Sheryl WuDunn ran into a sex trafficking survivor named Momm who was in the process of making this transition in the course of their own research. The transition was halted when a government crackdown on sex trafficking forced the brothel she was working in to close (see Kristof and WuDunn, *Half the Sky*, 40). Eleanor Brown's study of female Cambodian sex traffickers found that many of them had been initially inducted into the trade as victims of commercial sexual exploitation themselves (see Brown, *Ties That Bind*).

In bonded labor in Southern India, the same crossing over of roles without experiencing liberation happens in the case of *mestris*. Mestris are bonded laborers who serve as overseers of other bonded laborers, recruiters of new bonded laborers, and hunters of runaway bonded laborers. In other words, they are enslaved workers who identify with the master over and against other enslaved workers. Pranitha Timothy described mestris as bonded laborers who had become fascinated with their masters and had earned their trust (harkening back to the description of captive mentality in chapter 2). And according to Pranitha, in any bonded labor situation, "the most cruel person is a co-laborer who's won the heart of the owner."[6] She went on to describe situations in which mestris would mercilessly beat and abuse laborers in order to gain their master's favor.

This may seem strange at first, but if Orlando Patterson's sociological analysis of slavery (given in chapter 1) is correct, the fact that mestris are unusually barbaric in their treatment of other bonded laborers is exactly what we should expect. To recap, Patterson argues that slavery is "the permanent, violent domination of natally alienated and generally dishonored persons."[7] In other words, there is a connection between violent domination and the loss of honor in systems of slavery. To lack honor (i.e., be enslaved) is to be violently dominated, to have honor (i.e., to be a master) is to violently dominate others. When mestris show unusual cruelty toward other enslaved workers, they are trying to ascend from the enslaved position to the master position. Because they cannot accrue honor themselves (and can therefore never truly ascend), they multiply their efforts out of desperation. The master, on the other hand, since his position is secure, exercises cruelty out of a desire for reaffirmation, rather than out of desperation for survival. This can mean that he may be laxer in his abuse than another enslaved worker attempting to ascend. It is much like watching two individuals climb two different slopes, one where the ground is dry, the other where the ground is coated with ice. A person climbing the icy slope might expend a lot of energy in an attempt to climb it, all while getting nowhere. Someone climbing the dry slope, however, can easily make slow but deliberate progress without panicking or straining themselves.

6. Pranitha Timothy, interview with the author, Channai, India, November 11, 2014.

7. Patterson, *Slavery and Social Death*, 13.

Unlike in sex trafficking cases, where brothel madams are treated unanimously as perpetrators, regardless of their trafficking history, mestris have frequently been treated as victims, but their former role complicates the rehabilitation process. At IJM, social workers confer with the community of bonded laborers being rescued, and they ask them whether or not they are willing to receive the mestri back into their community. If they agree to do this, then the mestri rejoins the community and is treated as any other community member so far as the rehabilitation process is concerned. If they do not agree to this, then the mestri is released on his own, and is dealt with separate from the rest of the rescued community. Raja's community decided to allow their mestri to rejoin their community, and he remembers their mestri going through the reintegration process just as any other person in the community.[8]

The fact that brothel managers and mestris go through this transition should be of no surprise to students of more ancient forms of slavery. "Overseers" or "managers" are common in many forms of slavery, and they are especially common in ancient Greco-Roman slavery. These individuals even make appearances in the parables of Jesus, the most prominent of which is probably the parable of the shrewd manager.[9] What is not always highlighted in treatments of ancient slavery, however, is the way in which a manager comes to identify with the master over and against his fellow enslaved workers. In ancient systems of slavery, the key role of the manager is to oversee the affairs of the household, and this entailed that they held a sort of mediate position in status and rank between the enslaved and the free members of the household.[10] In modern systems of slavery, this role is preserved for managers in both sex trafficking and bonded labor organizations. Since this mediate position is offered, managers often come to identify with the master over and against other enslaved workers. As such, given their managerial role, they may be particularly eager to participate in disciplinary action against other enslaved workers. Additionally, as enslaved workers themselves, managers have a unique insight into what techniques worked to assure their own

8. Raja, interview with the author, Chennai, India, November 12, 2014.

9. Those familiar with the scholarship on this parable might be aware that many NT scholars do not think that the shrewd manager was enslaved. I am more convinced by the arguments of Mary Ann Beavis, who argues that the manager is portrayed as enslaved (see Beavis, "Ancient Slavery," 37–54).

10. See Martin, *Slavery as Salvation*, 15–20, for the complexities of the "tiered slave structure" in the Greco-Roman household.

enslavement, and they use such methods (as well as shared cultural connections) to coax others into the system. As Pranitha mentioned, managers can also sometimes be used to hunt down and return workers who have fled from bondage.[11] This means that there are three unique classes of harm that managers are liable for when it comes to the treatment of their fellow enslaved workers: (1) they may be guilty of abusing fellow enslaved workers in the course of enacting discipline on behalf of their master, (2) they may be guilty of inducting fellow workers into slavery in the first place, and (3) they may be guilty of thwarting a fellow enslaved worker's attempt at gaining freedom.

Now that we've established who victim-perpetrators are, how they come to be, and what sorts of harms they inflict upon their fellow enslaved workers, let us turn to the much harder question: How do we deal with them? What does justice look like in their situation?

What Is Restorative Justice?

The restorative justice movement is usually traced back to the 1970s, when many individuals in a variety of countries began to articulate a feeling of dissatisfaction with the way in which crime is addressed in "Western" or "retributive" criminal justice systems. These individuals expressed doubts that the system adequately provided justice for all participants involved (victims, offenders, and community). The most well-known of the writings produced in this movement is probably Howard Zehr's *Changing Lenses*, which was originally published in 1990.[12] According to Zehr, there are many practices associated with a restorative view of justice, but all of them share a common thread: facilitated encounter between the victim and the offender.[13] Daniel W. Van Ness and Karen Heetderks Strong have expanded on this to argue that restorative justice has three focal concepts: encounter, repair, and transformation.[14] This is a good overview of what distinguishes restorative justice, so I will use Van Ness and Strong's three

11. Pranitha Timothy, interview with the author, Channai, India, November 11, 2014.

12. All citations of *Changing Lenses* in this chapter come from the most updated edition (listed in the bibliography).

13. Zehr, *Little Book of Restorative Justice*, 56.

14. Van Ness and Strong, *Restoring Justice*, 43–44.

focal concepts to guide what follows.[15] Advocates frequently contrast restorative justice with some other conception of justice, but again, what serves as the foil to restorative justice changes from advocate to advocate. Though there are issues with the contrast, I will frequently contrast "restorative justice" with "retributive justice," for reasons I will explain later.

First, restorative justice involves a facilitated encounter between victim and offender. In some cases, members of the community are involved as well. In all cases, trained professionals are involved, but they serve more of a support role to facilitate the encounter, rather than being the main players in the drama. This contrasts with the model preferred by most retributive criminal justice systems, where justice is meted out in the midst of a contest between proxy professionals. A prosecutor represents the state (or "society at large"), while a defense attorney represents the offender, and these professionals have a monopoly on participation in the process; neither the victim nor the offender play a substantial role (unless either is called as a witness, but even then, their participation is extremely limited). In a restorative system, the victim and the offender are the main players.[16]

15. Van Ness and Strong also articulate four "cornerpost values" of restorative justice. Each value comprises a chapter in *Restoring Justice*. Those values are:

1. *Inclusion: All affected parties are invited to directly shape and engage in restorative processes in response to crime.*
2. *Encounter: Affected parties are given the opportunity to meet the other parties in a safe environment to discuss the offense, harms, and the appropriate responses.*
3. *Amends: Those responsible for the harm resulting from the offense also take responsibility for repairing it to the extent possible.*
4. *Reintegration: The parties are given the means and opportunity to rejoin their communities as whole, contributing members rather than continuing to bear the stigma of harm and offense (Van Ness and Strong, Restoring Justice, 50).*

Since there is significant overlap here with the focal concepts of restorative justice, this overview does not explicitly cover them in as much detail.

16. As will be addressed later, this is not to say that prosecutors or defense attorneys have no place in a restorative justice system. They simply do not take the central role that they do in retributive justice systems. What is objectionable about the way prosecutors and defense attorneys participate in retributive systems is summed up ably by Amy Levad: "As crime becomes defined as an offense against the state rather than real harm caused to specific people, victims are marginalized from the legal process, unless they are useful as state witnesses. Offenders must disappear behind their lawyers because the adversarial legal process and the threat of severe punishment discourages their honesty about whether and why they violated the law. Communities become conflated with the state and have no voice other than the prosecutor's

To see how this is so, it may be helpful to refer to a specific restorative justice practice: victim-offender conferencing (VOC).[17] In one model of VOC, both the victim and the offender undertake a sequence of two to six meetings, during which a professional mediator is present to facilitate the process. To prepare for these sessions, professionals meet with the victim and the offender separately before bringing them together. During these separate sessions, mediators listen to how the crime affected each party, try to discern the needs of all parties involved, and try to prepare each party for the meetings they will have together. In the victim's case, these sessions focus on how the crime impacted the victim, what forms of grief the victim is going through, and what forms of reparation the victim would like to see the offender undergo. In the offender's case, the mediator attempts to build up the offender's capacity for empathy, tries to get the offender to assume a non-defensive posture in preparation for the meetings, has the offender guess at the concerns of the victim, and asks the offender what forms of reparation he or she thinks are appropriate. During these preparation sessions, forgiveness and reconciliation are not considered a mandatory part of the process, and the mediator is under strict training not to attempt to push either party toward those goals. To be sure, the goal of VOC is transformation of the conflict and the individuals involved, but there are many ways such a transformation can occur short of forgiveness and reconciliation. However, many professionals participating in VOC have attested that the desire for forgiveness and reconciliation arises in the vast majority of cases. And, it is most frequently the victim who introduces the topic, even in situations where they say they will never forgive the offender during the preparation meetings.

This brings us to the second focal concept in restorative justice: transformation. There are multiple forms of transformation that are sought after during VOC (or any restorative process). The main form of transformation desired is accountability; the offender must move to a place where she takes responsibility for her actions. "Accountability" is

in a courtroom hearing" (Levad, *Restorative Justice*, 95). What is objectionable under restorative justice is not the fact that prosecutors and defense attorneys have a place in the process. What is objectionable is the fact that their voices come to stand in for and override the voices of those most directly affected by the crime.

17. The description of VOC that follows comes directly from Ray Gingerich, a friend who was involved in this process when he was working as a probation officer in Austin, Texas. The description comes from a presentation he regularly (and graciously) agrees to give to the students of my Theology, Violence and Nonviolence class.

a word that is frequently used in justice contexts, but restorative justice advocates have a very specific understanding of what the term means. Under retributive theory, punishment and accountability are seen as synonymous. For example, an offender might be held accountable for stealing a laptop by being incarcerated for several years. Under restorative theory, punishment and accountability are not the same thing.[18] To use the same example, an offender might be punished (by incarceration) for stealing a laptop, yet never come to the point where he sees himself as responsible for the offense and for making reparations for it. He may continue to see the offense as something done out of necessity, or as an act that fundamentally did no harm to the victim or anyone else. He may continue to see himself as a victim of circumstance or of a justice system that is simply out to get him (and others like him). For advocates of restorative justice, most retributive systems are bad sources of accountability, because they usually forgo any process that might facilitate a transformation in the offender's attitude toward the offense. Instead, retributive systems usually simply trust that the punishment itself will foster accountability. Frequently, it does not.[19] Through a facilitated encounter between the victim and the offender, the offender can come to see the full extent of the damage done to the victim by the offense, and they can take steps toward taking responsibility for it. Of course, such encounters do not always result in the offender taking responsibility for their actions, but they at least provide an avenue where such a transformation might occur.

While getting the offender to take responsibility for the offense is the main form of transformation sought, other forms of transformation may

18. Zehr especially stresses this difference. See Zehr, *Little Book of Restorative Justice*, 24.

19. This is not to say that all advocates of restorative justice see no use for retributive considerations, or for punishment. For some advocates, if the perpetrator or victim is unwilling to take part in the process, then the typical adversarial courtroom process is the proper way to deal with the offense. Likewise, some advocates would say that, if the encounter breaks down at some point, or if the offender is unwilling to agree to a reparative plan, then the typical retributive process is the proper way to deal with the offense. Additionally, many restorative justice advocates (such as James Logan and Christopher Marshall) still see a place for "good punishment," even though they levy substantial critiques against the way punishment functions in the retributive system currently on offer. However, from a restorative standpoint, criminal justice systems that are unable to distinguish between punishment and accountability are seriously in danger of abandoning any rehabilitative or transformative element to sanctions applied against offenders.

also emerge during the encounter. For example, a victim's perception of the offender may change through the process, especially if the victim and offender had no prior relationship. Ray Gingerich (who was involved in restorative justice processes in Austin, Texas) frequently tells the story of a VOC process that he mediated involving a gas station owner who was robbed by a group of teenagers. The gas station owner came into the restorative process wanting to meet the "thugs" that robbed him. Through the process, he discovered that they were scared kids who made a series of bad decisions, not hardened criminals. He even offered one of them a job as an attendant after the process was over. The process of encounter had a transformative effect on how he viewed the offenders. This again stands in contrast to a retributive system, which tends to harden the roles each party plays in the conflict, and to reinforce initial perceptions. This is usually due to the fact that the victim and offender are simply silent observers of a courtroom drama that unfolds before them in which the attorneys that represent them are the main players. This gives each party little context for understanding each other's motives, thoughts, fears, etc. A facilitated encounter between victim and offender can often dispel the typical stereotyped roles that each person plays in this drama.

This brings us to the final focal concept in restorative justice: repair. In restorative justice, an offender is absolved of guilt by taking actions to make things right. This means that reparations are the primary sanction in restorative justice, rather than incarceration. Restorative justice advocates are split on the issue of incarceration. Some advocates would say that incarceration is incompatible with the values of restorative justice, and they would advocate for the abolition of prisons.[20] Other advocates

20. Even the term "prison abolition" is disputed. Some individuals who identify with the term express a moral opposition to all forms of incarceration, calling for the immediate closure of all prisons. Others who identify with the term call for a halt to any further production of prisons, and an extreme reduction in the number of current prison facilities. Others who identify with the term are opposed to the "prison-industrial complex," a diabolical confluence of prison production and corporate interests that leads to the pressure to lock more and more people up while reaping economic benefits from the resultant violence, community suffering, and public safety hazards that large-scale prison production yields. For the range of uses for the term, see Van Ness and Strong, *Restoring Justice*, 14–15. I would argue that being an advocate for restorative justice in the fullest sense implicitly commits someone to become a prison abolitionist in at least the latter two senses of the term, given that the prison-industrial complex and massive prison expansion are incompatible with the goals of a reparation-based system. Within the restorative justice camp, however, debate remains about whether the alternatives to incarceration on offer can deal with severely recalcitrant

of restorative justice believe that incarceration should not be the go-to sanction for any criminal justice system, but they hold that incarceration may be necessary in extreme cases. For either camp, it seems that there is now abundant reason to believe that an incarceration-centered system yields bad outcomes, including high operational costs, a tendency to create habitual offenders, and overall declines in public safety.[21] Powerful systemic critiques of incarceration-centered systems have also been levied, arguing convincingly that incarceration-centered systems are disproportionately used as a means of social control and oppression against the poor, Black people and other racial minorities, people with mental health problems, and other marginalized groups.[22] Systematic critiques of the economics of prison production have also been levied, pointing to the way in which large corporations of various sorts contribute to prison production, reaping large dividends off of the breakdown of minority communities which are over-policed and over-incarcerated.[23] In addition to these issues, advocates of restorative justice see moral problems with an incarceration-centered system on a more individual level: it often fails to secure perpetrator accountability, alienates the victim, and allows little chance for reform for the offender. Especially problematic here is the fact that, given the methods of control that are employed upon prison populations laid out in chapter 3, prison teaches inmates that manipulation is the norm in human relationships, especially between those in authority

and dangerous offenders (such as serial killers).

21. Cullen et al. "Prisons Do Not Reduce Recidivism," 48S–65S; Logan, *Good Punishment?*, 17–63. Logan paints a compelling portrait of a vicious cycle in mass incarceration in the US. Prisons are centers of manipulation and violence which teach inmates more profound forms of manipulation and violence. Hence, prisons produce criminal behavior. Then, public fear of crime, politicians who can advance their careers through "tough on crime" platforms, and corporations who can benefit economically from prison production cooperate to produce more prisons. This produces more crime, which produces more prisons, etc. However, Logan also notes that, even if one were to eliminate the manipulation and violence in prisons, the prison-industrial complex has developed to the point where it continues to expand regardless of whether the crime rate is increasing or decreasing.

22. Logan, *Good Punishment?*, 65–99; Levad, *Restorative Justice*, 1–7; Alexander, *New Jim Crow*; Davis, *Abolition Democracy*; Gottschalk, *Caught*. There is also the criticism (originating with Michel Foucault) that incarceration-centric systems create a "carceral archipelago" in which other major institutions (schools, etc.) take methods of social control from the prison and incorporate them. This critique was mentioned in Chapter 3 amid the discussion concerning Foucault.

23. Davis, *Are Prisons Obsolete?*, 84–108. This also serves to exacerbate the wealth gap in the United States discussed in the last chapter.

and those under authority.[24] Prisoners learn from these techniques and employ them upon others. Add to this the problems with reintegration experienced by prison inmates outlined in chapter 3, and a clear case can be made that incarceration should not be the norm for punishment. Yet in many criminal justice systems, this is exactly what has happened: incarceration rarely needs to be justified as a sanction, whereas any sanction other than incarceration (including reparations) is seen as a strange aberration in sentencing that requires significant justification.

In contrast, reparations include the victim in the criminal justice process and give the offender a chance to take responsibility and atone for wrongs done.[25] They also demonstrate to offenders that human relationships ought to be characterized by mutuality and responsibility rather than by manipulation. Reparations are simpler in some cases than others. For example, in the case of a stolen laptop, appropriate reparations would include returning the laptop or paying for a new one. Reparations need not be *limited* to this, but they should at least include this. In other cases, reparation plans are not so simple. This is because many forms of harm can be described but not quantified into any meaningful unit of value. To use an example of restorative justice methods on a much grander scale, the South African Truth and Reconciliation Commission (TRC) could draft no straightforward reparation plan to atone for the massive scale of the wrongs done by the apartheid regime during its time in power. Desmond Tutu has often said that the reparations that the TRC sought were much more symbolic, because the harm done to Black South Africans by apartheid cannot be quantified (say, into a straightforward dollar amount).[26] But then, retributive justice systems experience this problem with punishment schedules as well. Few retributive systems have claimed

24. Zehr, *Changing Lenses*, 43–44. Zehr also notes that these same obedience mechanisms serve as a barrier to reintegration. It is the rebellious inmates that have an easier time transitioning back into life outside of prison.

25. This is also why Ta-Nehisi Coates' "The Case for Reparations" needs to be taken much more seriously than it currently is in American public discourse (see Coates, "Case for Reparations"). Coates' proposal is extremely conservative: he merely wants a congressional committee to be formed to explore what reparations to Black Americans for centuries of systemic oppression might look like. He makes no hard recommendations himself. However, for restorative justice advocates, reparations are an essential part of any accountability and atonement process.

26. Tutu, *No Future without Forgiveness*, 61. However, it is possible to describe the harms done under the apartheid regime. For an extremely gruesome account of the atrocities committed by the regime, see Tutu, *No Future without Forgiveness*, 123–59. Here Tutu recounts the testimony given by offenders in front of the TRC.

that harm inflicted upon an offender must be exactly proportionate to the harm done to the victim. To use a classic example, there are no retributive systems on offer that advocate punishing a person convicted of rape by having that person raped themselves. So, it seems inevitable that all conceptions of justice are going to have this proportionality problem. However, restorative systems do have one benefit here over retributive systems, and that is that the victim is involved in the process of drafting a reparation plan for the offender. This reduces the likelihood that the sanction will be out of proportion with the harm caused to the victim, since the victim is involved. Pulling the victim out of this process increases the likelihood of disproportionate sanctions, since the severity of sanctions is being determined by those who have not been harmed by the crime. The victim is also more aware of what sorts of reparations will begin to repair the damage, even if those reparations are symbolic.[27] Symbolic reparations are more likely to be empty if they are divorced from the needs and desires of the victim.

Some advocates of retributive justice would argue that the presentation of retributive justice given above is a caricature. And to some extent, this is a fair criticism. There are a great many things that a restorative view of justice and a retributive view of justice have in common, and this can be lost if the contrast between the two views provided is too stark. To give some examples of just a few commonalities, both views share a desire for offender accountability, both share a desire to restore

27. As Amy Levad points out, retributive justice and restorative justice have differing conceptions of when the justice process is completed. Under retributive justice, "justice has been served . . . when offenders have completed a sentence proportional to their offense dictated by law." Under restorative justice, justice has been served when "the needs of all stakeholders of a crime have been met" (Levad, *Restorative Justice*, 133). The argument above is simply that the retributive standard of completion has a greater chance of being alienating, not only because affixing a number to a class of crimes always has a note of arbitrariness to it, but also because this standard fails to address, in numerous ways, the very real effects the system has on all parties involved. However, this is not to say that determining stakeholder needs in restorative justice processes requires no communal discernment. An individual victim may, for example, desire vengeance, but vengeance is not what they really need. This constitutes likely the strongest argument that restorative justice requires community involvement: the process is sometimes difficult to complete simply through facilitated encounter of victim and offender alone. For a much more in-depth discussion of what constitutes a "stakeholder need," and how the community can be involved to discern those needs in the work of various restorative justice advocates, see Levad, *Restorative Justice*, 133–42. For a general list of needs that must be addressed for all parties when any crime occurs, see Zehr, *Changing Lenses*, 188–209.

balance or right the wrong caused by an offense, both share a desire to see that the offender change future behavior, and both share a desire that offenders not be treated unjustly during punishment.[28] Additionally, many advocates of retributive justice do not have a problem with the inclusion of some restorative practices in the criminal justice system.[29] For these reasons, many advocates of restorative justice have changed their rhetoric based on this feedback. For example, when Howard Zehr began writing on the subject, he used "retributive justice" to describe the view of justice that served as a foil to his own. As time has gone on, Zehr has changed his views. He no longer describes retributive justice and restorative justice as polar opposites (he outlines them now on a spectrum from wholly restorative to wholly retributive), and he does admit that a retributive approach to justice may have its value in some cases. However, Zehr does still seem to view them as different ways of approaching questions of justice, and he rejects the sanction that serves as the ultimate expression of retributive justice (the death penalty) as clearly incompatible with a restorative justice approach.[30] Zehr now uses the term "Western criminal justice" to describe the view of justice that is under critique. However, this term is likewise misleading, since the view of justice he has in mind is found in the criminal justice systems of many non-Western countries as well (it is present in India, for example). Though the distinction is far from perfect, I have chosen to stick with Zehr's original opposition (restorative justice vs. retributive justice) for one crucial reason: there is a distinct difference in the role of pain and suffering between the two theories. As Zehr still points out,

> Retributive theory believes that pain will vindicate, but in practice that is often counterproductive for both victim and offender. Restorative justice theory, on the other hand, argues that what truly vindicates is acknowledgement of victims' harms and needs, combined with an active effort to encourage offenders to take responsibility, make right the wrongs, and address the

28. Van Ness and Strong, *Restoring Justice*, 51–53.

29. See for example, Robinson, "Vices of 'Restorative Justice,'" 384–91. Robinson argues that while restorative practices have clearly proved their usefulness, the only way to ultimately ensure that sanctions are just is if they are meted out based on what society decides an offender deserves. He believes the overall conceptual landscape of restorative justice conflicts with this conviction.

30. For more on this, see Zehr, *Little Book of Restorative Justice*, 74–82. I have yet to meet a restorative advocate that would differ from Zehr here; advocates of restorative justice seem to be completely ideologically opposed to the death penalty.

> causes of their behavior. By addressing this need for vindication in a positive way, restorative justice has the potential to affirm both victim and offender and to help them transform their lives.[31]

It is this view that pain is both necessary and sufficient to vindicate that marks off retributive justice theory as a distinct viewpoint.[32] Advocates of restorative justice, on the other hand, hold that vindication is a matter of accountability, not of pain. Of course, even under restorative justice, accountability is frequently painful. In fact, some critics of restorative justice allege that the pain inflicted may be greater amid the raw encounters that happen in restorative practices than the pain inflicted in a retributive courtroom or even in a jail cell. Overall, I find this critique difficult to believe. Prisons are violent places, and sexual violence is especially rampant behind prison walls.[33] Restorative processes simply do not admit themselves of the same kinds of regular abuse. But in some rare cases, it may well be the case that going through a restorative process would be more traumatic than a stint in prison, and this is why advocates of restorative justice insist on both securing informed consent from all participants beforehand and preparing those parties carefully before they meet with each other. However, treating pain as an inevitable byproduct of the process rather than as the catalyst and goal of the process makes a significant difference. And as such, the shift in focus from pain to accountability under restorative theory does make several differences in the actual practice of criminal justice. For example, it makes encounter and reparations central to the justice process, rather than incidental, as outlined above.

A related criticism of restorative justice is that it is simply impractical to replace the current criminal court system on offer (in both the United States and India) with restorative practices such as victim-offender conferencing, sentencing circles, and reparation plans. The adversarial courtroom approach will still be necessary in cases where guilt is disputed. Some advocates of restorative justice readily admit this. However, they do question what processes ought to be the norm and what processes

31. Zehr, *Little Book of Restorative Justice*, 59.

32. Advocates of retributive justice frequently use the language of "deserts" more than "pain," but the result is essentially the same: the offender deserves the pain he endures at the hands of the justice system, and that pain serves to vindicate.

33. For a particularly graphic testimonial from a victim of sexual violence in prison, see Logan, *Good Punishment?*, 210–13.

ought to be reserved for extreme cases. In fact, in the United States, the criminal justice system already operates with the understanding that only in rare cases is a trial actually required. There is widespread recognition that criminal trials *cannot* be the norm; they are too resource intensive to be used in every case. However, this does not mean restorative processes have become the norm in American criminal justice. Instead, plea bargaining has become the norm. And there are many critiques of this system on offer. Most importantly, the plea bargaining system on offer seems to be used in many cases to coerce individuals who may be innocent of a crime to plead down to a lesser charge.[34] It would be far preferable in a great many cases to rely on a restorative process rather than coerce a defendant into a plea deal.

The Indian system faces a similar problem. In the Indian system, the possibilities for the coercion of innocent defendants are taken much more seriously than in the American system. For example, in the Indian system, a confession is only admissible in court if given directly in front of a judge. This is due to the recognition that the police could use various means to coerce a confession out of a defendant.[35] However, this has

34. The podcast *Serial* recently highlighted how problematic this system can be by following the case of a woman in Cleveland who was assaulted (sexually and physically) by a hostile crowd in a bar. When a police officer attempted to break up the melee, in the confusion, the woman accidentally struck the officer in the face. Though the woman was clearly on the receiving end of abuse, the police officer ended up arresting her and charging her with assaulting a police officer (a felony). The officer made no other arrests. The woman ended up pleading guilty to disorderly conduct (a misdemeanor) to avoid a trial. In the end, she was harassed by officers, spent four nights in jail, had to pay almost $1300 for a bond and court fees (because she plead guilty), and had to make over twenty trips to the justice center to clear things up. Bizarrely, everyone interviewed except the woman (including her defense attorney) saw this outcome as evidence that the plea system was working the way it should (Koenig, "Bar Fight"). The same podcast series also highlighted the problematic practice of "stacking" charges (charging, say, eight felonies with slightly different wording for a single criminal act). Presenting such an impressively thick set of charges is an attempt to make the accused look like a habitual offender even if this is their first run-in with the justice system; it is a way of subtly signaling to juries that a defendant is probably guilty of *something*, even if the prosecution cannot prove all of the charges. The result is that defendants are more likely to accept a plea deal, even if innocent, because juries are more likely to convict (Koenig, "Pleas Baby Pleas").

35. Indeed, one of the issues with police corruption in a city like Mumbai is that the police will resort to torturing suspects in custody to secure a confession. I have personally witnessed Mumbai police officers do this. However, if documentation of this practice in print from interviews with police and tortured suspects is desired, see Mehta, *Maximum City*, 143–44, 161–65, 176–77, 183–88, 197, 240. Chitra did testify,

led not to widespread criminal justice reform or to a turn to restorative practices, but rather to a maintenance of the old retributive system with lower outcomes. To put it more precisely, the prosecution rate in India is extremely low. In 2006, the anti-trafficking NGO I worked for operated with the understanding that, while our office's conviction rate was higher, a 2 percent conviction rate in trafficking cases was the norm across India. To be clear, that meant for every fifty trafficking cases heard by the court, only one resulted in conviction.[36] From my more recent interviews, it seems that the rate is a bit higher than this, but still not ideal. However, the attorneys I interviewed also suggested that the conviction rate in criminal cases seems to be extremely low across the board.[37] The reason for this seems to be that the Indian criminal justice system runs on the assumption that it is far better for a guilty defendant to go free than for an innocent defendant to be put in jail.[38] However, a turn to restorative

however, that police brutality toward suspects has decreased since she started the work in the mid-2000s ("Chitra," interview with the author, Mumbai, India, October 13, 2014).

36. When it comes to labor trafficking, the rate may be even lower. NGO workers in Tamil Nadu reported that the overwhelming majority of cases ended in acquittal. And when a conviction did occur, the sanctions for the perpetrator were frequently insubstantial. Frequently in bonded labor cases, the penalty for being found guilty of a bonded labor offense is to stand in the back of the room until the court adjourns for the day (Ebenezer, interview with the author, Chennai, India, November 12, 2014; "Anika," interview with the author, Chennai, India, November 13, 2014). This matches with the findings of the International Trade Union Federation, whose recent report to the International Labour Organization (in 2018) reported a conviction rate of around 7 percent for cases reported by vigilance committees across India between 2006 and 2015. See International Labor Organization, "Observation (CEACR)."

37. "Beth," interview with the author, Mumbai, India, September 12, 2014. The 2021 Trafficking in Persons (TIP) Report claims that the overall acquittal rate for all forms of trafficking remains quite high (73 percent) and that zero convictions or prosecutions were reported for 2021 (see US Department of State, "2021 Trafficking in Persons Report: India").

38. Richard Ebenezer stated the Indian principle this way: "Bail should be the rule and jail should be the exception" (Ebenezer, interview with the author, Chennai, India, November 12, 2014). It's a principle I've heard quoted by more than one Indian attorney over the years. That's better than the reverse (that jail should be the rule). However, holding bail as the standard still presumes an incarceration-centric system, just one that is more hesitant to apply a sentence because of the realization that it may result in locking up an innocent person. Further, bail-centric systems have their own problems, as they are frequently used as a mechanism to incarcerate indigent defendants while allowing wealthy defendants to move about freely.

practices might result in better outcomes while preserving the laudable insight in the Indian system that incarceration is hardly an ideal standard.

One final criticism of restorative justice is important to note: it is often thought that restorative processes will work better for less serious offenses (such as drug violations) than for more serious offenses (such as violent crime). This is an important assumption to consider because, if true, it would render this entire chapter superfluous. Restorative justice might be a topic germane to the modern discussion on criminal justice reform more generally, but it would hardly be appropriate to discuss in a work on human trafficking if it does not work in serious cases. In fact, this is exactly the assumption that most restorative justice advocates began with when they tried implementing restorative practices in the American criminal justice system. However, subsequent research has suggested that the exact opposite is true: restorative practices seem to have better outcomes in cases involving more serious offenses than in cases involving less serious offenses. The oft-quoted study that established this is Lawrence W. Sherman and Heather Strang's *Restorative Justice: The Evidence*.[39] The study itself is an overview of thirty-six other studies which compared two similar populations, one of which received a restorative justice intervention, the other did not. Sherman and Strang found that restorative justice interventions frequently had better outcomes in cases involving violent crime than cases involving property crime. Other important findings of the study are ably summarized by Van Ness and Strong in this handy bullet-point list:

1. Crime victims who receive restorative justice do better, on average, than victims who do not, across a wide range of outcomes, including post-traumatic stress.
2. In many tests, offenders who receive restorative justice commit fewer repeat crimes than those who do not.
3. In no large-sample test has restorative justice increased repeat offending when compared with criminal justice.[40]
4. Restorative justice reduces repeat offending more consistently with violent crimes than with less serious crimes.

39. A summary version of this study can be found in Sherman and Strang, "Restorative Justice," 292–319.

40. Again, different advocates of restorative justice use different foils for it. Here, it is opposed with "criminal justice," which basically denotes the system currently on offer in the countries studied.

5. Diversion from prosecution to restorative justice substantially increases the odds of an offender being brought to justice.
6. Restorative justice does not conflict with the rule of law, nor does it depart from the basic paradigm of the common law of crime.
7. Restorative justice can do as well as, or better than, short prison sentences, as measured by repeat offending.
8. Restorative justice reduces stated victim desire for revenge against offenders.[41]

The outcomes found in Sherman and Strang's study continue to be verified by others.[42] The evidence is now out there. Not only can restorative justice produce better outcomes than the alternative system, it can do so in cases which involve unspeakable violence. This is more than enough reason to attempt to apply its principles and practices in cases of human trafficking, and especially in the cases of victim-perpetrators. However, there may still be some lingering moral and theological doubts from Christian readers of a more retributive bent. Even if restorative justice practices produce better outcomes, is it consistent with what the Bible says about the nature of justice? As it turns out, the restorative justice movement has thickly theological roots. And it is to a discussion of these roots that we will now turn.

A Theological Justification of Restorative Justice

On a theological level, advocates of restorative justice processes see them as more open to the teachings of Jesus concerning forgiveness, reconciliation, repentance, and peace. Zehr himself is a Mennonite, and the eighth chapter of *Changing Lenses* lays out a theological defense of a restorative view of justice, arguing that it is more germane to the majority view of justice laid out in the Hebrew Scriptures and the New Testament than a retributive conception of justice. To some readers, this may seem like a strange claim, since there are several Christian groups who claim that the *lex talionis* ("eye for an eye") serves as a summation of a biblical view

41. Van Ness and Strong, *Restoring Justice*, 53–54.

42. See for example the list in Van Ness and Strong, *Restoring Justice*, 60n19. See also the articles that run from 257–353 in Johnstone, *Restorative Justice Reader*.

of justice. On its face, the *lex talionis* does seem quite retributive. Here is Leviticus' version of the principle:

> Anyone who takes the life of a human being is to be put to death. Anyone who takes the life of someone's animal must make restitution—life for life. Anyone who injures their neighbor is to be injured in the same manner: fracture for fracture, eye for eye, tooth for tooth. The one who has inflicted the injury must suffer the same injury. (Lev 24:17–20)

However, five things should be noted here. First, there is a growing consensus among scholars of the Torah that "the *lex talionis* is neither as central to biblical justice nor as vengeful in meaning as many people think."[43] What leads many scholars to this conclusion is the application of the principle within the Torah. It is neither consistently nor primarily applied in a retributive fashion. One can see this even in the brief passage above, where the prescribed remedy for taking the life of a neighbor's farm animal is *restitution*. If the principle were meant in a clearly retributive fashion, the punishment for killing a neighbor's cow would be that the offender's own cow is killed.

This is also the case in one of its two parallels (Exod 21:23–24), which states the *lex talionis*, then goes on to apply it in various cases of personal injury. Interestingly, in many of these cases, Exodus calls for reparations instead of a retributive interpretation of the principle. In fact, the two verses that directly follow the presentation of the "eye for an eye" standard explicitly dismiss a literal application of the principle. Here is the passage in context:

> But if there is serious injury, you are to take life for life, eye for eye, tooth for tooth, hand for hand, foot for foot, burn for burn, wound for wound, bruise for bruise.
>
> An owner who hits a male or female slave in the eye and destroys it must let the slave go free to compensate for the eye. And an owner who knocks out the tooth of a male or female slave must let the slave go free to compensate for the tooth.

These verses present the "eye for eye, tooth for tooth" standard, then call not for taking the offender's eye or tooth, but to have the offender grant restitution to the injured party (in this case, by giving them their freedom). J. David Pleins argues that these verses demonstrate that "eye for an eye" was never actually meant to describe a prescriptive retributive

43. Marshall, *Beyond Retribution*, 78.

justice standard. "Eye for an eye" is not so much a *command* as it is a *limit*. It expresses the allowable limitations of retributive justice, but proffers restitution as a better alternative.[44] Christopher Marshall agrees that the *lex talionis* does indeed serve this function, but he argues that its purpose in the Torah is much more expansive than this. Marshall argues that the *lex talionis* "is applied not as a law of equivalent retribution, but as a way of underlining the seriousness of certain offenses and of expressing the principle of moral equivalency."[45] In other words, the harsh punishment described is *expressive*, not *prescriptive*. It is intended to serve as an expression of moral and legal theory. Striking a pregnant woman and causing her to miscarry is morally equivalent to murder (the case under consideration when the *lex* is applied in Exod 21), as is blasphemy (the case that bookends the presentation of the *lex* in Lev 24), as well as false testimony in a capital case (the case under consideration when the *lex* is presented in Deut 19). The principle was never intended to be literally applied.

At first, this argument may sound like special pleading on the part of restorative justice advocates, but interestingly, two very different sets of biblical interpreters from outside of the restorative justice movement have reached the exact same conclusion, and for completely different reasons. The first set of biblical interpreters is the rabbinic sages. In the Babylonian Talmud (b. Sanh. 71a), the rabbis exegete a particularly troublesome bit of legislation concerning capital punishment in Deut 21:18–21, namely the execution of a "stubborn and rebellious son" who is both "a glutton and a drunkard." If putting one's own son to death for dissolute living sounds barbaric to the modern reader, rest assured that it did for the rabbis as well.[46] The rabbis end up amplifying the conditions under which this sentence is carried out to the point where the son has to eat and drink more than humanly possible in a single sitting in order to meet the legal requirement for "glutton" and "drunkard." The Talmud concludes that "there never has been a stubborn and rebellious son, and there never will be one in the future, as it is impossible

44. Pleins, *Social Visions of the Hebrew Bible*, 53 (and especially n36).

45. Marshall, *Beyond Retribution*, 82. This seems to be the reason why the rabbinic sages interpreted "eye for an eye" to entail "monetary compensation." For a good overview of rabbinic passages that offer up this interpretation, see Milgrom, "Lex Talionis and the Rabbis," 48.

46. If the father in the parable of the prodigal son (Luke 15:11–32) is meant as a stand-in for God, then Jesus apparently believed that God would find it barbaric as well.

to fulfill all the requirements that must be met in order to apply this *halakha*."[47] In the very next sentence, the Talmud goes on to ask, "And why, then, was the passage relating to a stubborn and rebellious son written in the Torah?" This is a cogent question: why would God give a law that is impossible to apply? The Talmud answers: "So that you may expound upon new understandings of the Torah and receive reward for your learning, this being an aspect of the Torah that has only theoretical value." The law is given not to be literally applied, but to push the student of the Torah so that they become better at legal theory. The second group of biblical interpreters are modern scholars who have compared the dictates of the Torah to laws that appear in law codes from other nations in the ancient Near East (such as the code of Hammurabi). James Barr argues the emerging consensus from much of this scholarship is that ancient Near Eastern law codes often prescribe horrendous punishments that were not intended to be carried out literally. The intent of such prescriptions is simply to underscore the seriousness of the offense.[48] Marshall notes that in the Torah, the *lex talionis* seems even more theoretical than it does in other ancient Near Eastern law codes, because, unlike those other law codes, the Torah does not lay down the process for appointing a court executioner or mutilator who is to carry out the sentence.[49] So here we have two very different sets of interpreters claiming a merely theoretical place for "eye for an eye," one due to the difficulties it produced in casuistic application,[50] and one due to a study of how legal rhetoric functioned in ancient Near Eastern culture.[51]

47. Much like the term *torah*, *halakha* can be rendered "law," "ordinance," "way," or "teaching."

48. Barr, "Ancient Biblical Laws," 28–29.

49. Marshall, *Beyond Retribution*, 81.

50. In fact, the rabbis' insights concerning difficulties in application go beyond this. In the Babylonian Talmud (b. B. Qam., 84a), the rabbis point out that a literal application of the *lex talionis* would frequently fail to be equitable, even under retributive standards. The rabbis trot forward a few exceptional cases in which application of the standard would fail to be equitable (e.g., "What if a blind man put out another person's eye?"), before moving on to a much more general and serious consideration. In a world without antibiotics, amputation can lead to serious infection, which can lead to sepsis, which can lead to death. What if a court were to apply "eye for eye" literally in a case where one person chops off the hand of another person? And what if the victim lives, but the offender contracts sepsis when the court imposes amputation upon the offender in retaliation? If this occurs, then the court would have punished amputation with death, which would be inequitable retribution.

51. See also Ezek 20:23–26. Here Ezekiel gives a slightly different argument than

The final place in which "eye for an eye" is invoked (Deut 19:20–21) is worth looking at in some detail. Here "eye for an eye" is applied specifically in situations where false testimony is given in court. The false witnesses become liable to the punishment meted out to the defendant based on their false testimony. Interestingly, this context also makes Deut 19:15–21 one of the most important passages that serves as a *check* on a heavily retributive criminal justice system. Many casual modern readers of Deuteronomy (or the Torah in general) perceive it as heavily retributive because it describes so many capital offenses, far more than even most modern advocates of capital punishment are comfortable with. While it is true that capital punishment is the epitome of a purely retributive system of justice, Deut 19:15–21 establishes a standard of evidence so high that it actually seems to function as a *ban* on the application of capital punishment in practice. The standard is this: "One witness is not enough to convict anyone accused of any crime or offense they may have committed. A matter must be established by the testimony of two or three witnesses" (v. 15). It has long been recognized within the Jewish tradition that having two or more eyewitnesses is a standard of evidence so high that it almost bars capital punishment altogether.[52] It should be noted that most convictions under capital punishment statutes in the US go forward to a conviction on a much lower standard of evidence than this (usually circumstantial or forensic evidence is sufficient to secure a conviction). Very few capital convictions are secured on the basis of direct evidence from *one* eyewitness, let alone two. The most famous discussion in the Jewish tradition that reaches the conclusion that the

---

either the rabbis or modern biblical scholars, but one that still entails that some laws of the Torah were never meant to be literally applied. Here Ezekiel claims that, because Israel failed to follow God's good statutes in the wilderness, God proceeded to give Israel other statutes that were "not good" and could not be put into practice. Why? "In order that I might horrify them" (v. 26)!

52. In fact, there are two stories in the extended canon of Christian Scripture that suggest that some ancient Jews thought the two witnesses requirement entailed such a high standard of evidence that, for at least some offenses, it was actually suspicious if the prosecuting agent was able to *meet* it. Those two stories are the story of Susanna in the Greek edition of Daniel (which is not in the Jewish or Protestant Bible but is included as the thirteenth chapter of Daniel in Catholic and Orthodox Bibles) and the story of the woman caught in adultery (John 8:1–11). In both cases, the expert on the law (Daniel in the first case, Jesus in the second) thinks it suspicious that those accusing the woman of adultery were able to procure two witnesses to the event, so he throws the question of guilt back on the accusers. After all, how many times in history have two or more people just happened upon an act of adultery in progress?

standards of evidence in the Torah basically preclude capital punishment can be found in the Mishnah (m. Mak. 1:10):

> A Sanhedrin which imposes the death penalty once in seven years is called murderous. Rabbi Eleazar ben Azariah says, "Once in seventy years." Rabbi Akiba and Rabbi Tarfon say, "If we were on the Sanhedrin, no one would ever be put to death."[53]

The discussion begins with the presumption that it is the fault of the court if it enforces the death penalty. A Sanhedrin (the highest Jewish court in the land) which enforces capital punishment too frequently is to be labeled "murderous." But how frequently is too frequently? The consensus is that even one execution in a seven year period is too frequent. By that standard, there are more than twenty US states with criminal courts that would be labeled "murderous" as of the time of this writing. But some rabbis go beyond this. Rabbi Eleazar ben Azariah says that even one enforcement of capital punishment in a *seventy*-year period should be enough to label the court "murderous." But Rabbi Akiba (who is frequently recognized as the weightiest voice in the Mishnah) and his colleague Rabbi Tarfon are completely against the idea of capital punishment altogether.[54] Akiba and Tarfon realize that a heavily retributive standard may be *expressed* quite frequently in the Torah, but high standards of evidence seem to outright prohibit its *practice*. All of these complexities put together suggest that to say that the Torah is retributive is severely reductionist. A far more complex vision of justice is present.

53. It should be noted that the Mishnah is among the oldest of the rabbinic corpus, with critical scholars dating parts of its written material as far back as the second century. And, as Shaye J. D. Cohen has helpfully established, some (though by no means all) of the legal practices prescribed in the Torah are far older than this (see Cohen, "Judaean Legal Tradition," 121–43). It is likely that Jesus was far from alone among the legal experts of his age in his unwillingness to actually carry out the forms of capital punishment suggested in the Torah. The anti-capital punishment view might even have been made more palatable by the fact that, under Roman rule, the Sanhedrin was forbidden from carrying out the death sentence. This is why, during the trial of Jesus, Pilate is ultimately the only person with the legal power to sentence him to death.

54. To give full disclosure, the passage in m. Mak. 1:10 actually ends with the opinion of Rabbi Simeon ben Gamaliel: "So they would multiply the number of murderers in Israel." Simeon is articulating the typical deterrence argument in favor of capital punishment; he is arguing that Akiba and Tarfon's anti-capital punishment stance would lead to more murderers running around Israel. But the inclusion of Simeon's opinion only reinforces the argument I have made above. The legal opinion which dissents from the majority is usually placed exactly where we find Simeon's opinion: at the end of the discussion. Simeon's full-throated advocacy of the death penalty is a fringe view among the rabbis, not the consensus opinion.

Second, the principle of "eye for an eye," is explicitly singled out by Jesus as a provisional or lower standard in the Sermon on the Mount:

> You have heard that it was said, "Eye for eye, and tooth for tooth." But I tell you, don't react violently against the one who is evil. If anyone slaps you on the right cheek, turn to them the other cheek also. And if anyone wants to sue you and take your shirt, hand over your coat as well. If anyone forces you to go one mile, go with them two miles. Give to the one who asks you, and do not turn away from the one who wants to borrow from you. (Matt 5: 38–42)

It is important to note that the Sermon on the Mount is the most substantial commentary Jesus gives on the Torah in any of the Gospels. It gives us more insight into how Jesus interpreted the Torah than any other extant record we have of his life and teachings. Given the fact that Jesus does not see himself as invalidating the Torah here (see Matt 5:17–20), his words are usually taken as a deepening of what the Torah requires. For example, he asks his disciples to exhibit a higher form of righteousness than even "the Pharisees and teachers of the law" (v. 20). Jesus is saying that "eye for an eye" is a significantly lower standard of justice than the standard he is advocating.[55] As such, even if "eye for an eye" were to be taken in a retributive sense (as it sometimes has been), those who follow Jesus should take "eye for an eye" to be an incomplete standard of justice, one surpassed by a form of justice which is not characterized by violent retribution. Some commentators (in line with Pleins' argument above) reinforce this point by pointing out that in some cases, "eye for an eye" can stand as a limit on the use of excessive violence in righting wrongs. It can help to prohibit the all-encompassing desire for revenge that we sometimes experience when someone has wronged us. "Eye for an eye" at least holds that you cannot kill a person for putting out one of your eyes, or that you cannot kill an offender's entire family in retribution for a murder committed solely by the offender. Limited retribution is better than unlimited retribution.[56] However, "eye for an eye" can still be inter-

55. See Hays, *Moral Vision*, 94–101; 324–27 for the more extended argument about Jesus heightening or intensifying the requirements of the Torah.

56. Zehr refers to unlimited retribution as the "Law of Lamech," which is named after the individual mentioned in Gen 4:19–24. The standard of retributive justice Lamech establishes is as follows: "I have killed a man for wounding me, a young man for injuring me. If Cain is avenged seven times, then Lamech seventy-seven times." The contrast between Lamech's words and Lev 24:17–20 (and its parallels) is striking.

preted in such a way that capital punishment is seen as a viable option, and as such can be taken as an affirmation that violence and pain are both necessary and sufficient to vindicate. And for those reasons Jesus holds that the standard needs to be surpassed entirely.

Third, there are other standards of justice in the Hebrew Bible that are more prominent than "eye for an eye" (even without reference to Jesus intensifying the dictates of the Torah). It has long been noted that the most common Hebrew concepts relating to matters of justice (*shalom*, *tzedakah*, and *mishpat*) are far more holistic than the way their English counterparts (most often "peace" and "justice") are commonly employed.[57] *Shalom* itself means "completeness" or "wholeness," and goes beyond a lack of conflict to a sense of rightness with God and all parts of creation. It is also God's intention for all of creation, the driving goal of God's redemptive work in the world (which in itself is an outpouring of God's *tzedakah*).[58] *Shalom* is also what was violated with the entry of sin, death, and oppression into the world. And of course, the form in which God's redemptive work in the world takes is called covenant. God covenants with all of creation, but the more particular form of the Covenant which includes the Torah is reserved especially for God's chosen people Israel. And when Israel violates the Covenant, *shalom* is broken. The prophets then call on Israel to "do justice";[59] to return to the practice of the Torah and the right relationships it imagines. The Prophets held that God sent the people of Israel and Judah into exile because they refused to do this, and especially because the kingship had become so inherently corrupt that it had to be eliminated. But if covenant justice were retributive, things would have ended there. By sending Judah into

---

It may even be the case that the compilers of the Torah meant for the two standards to be compared, and thus rendered them in similar language. Zehr also notes that the story of Cain and Abel (to which Lamech refers above) makes it difficult to reduce the Torah's standard of justice down to "eye for an eye," since the story ends with God intervening to protect the world's first murderer from the death penalty. See Zehr, *Changing Lenses*, 151, for this discussion.

57. See for example, Zehr, *Changing Lenses*, 133–45; Marshall, *Beyond Retribution*, 45–53; Burns, "Jewish Ideologies of Peacemaking," 87–89.

58. The prophet Isaiah explicitly makes a connection between the three concepts: "Then justice [*mishpat*] will dwell in the wilderness, and righteousness [*tzedakah*] abide in the fruitful field. The effect of righteousness will be peace [*shalom*] and the result of righteousness, quietness and trust forever" (Isa 32:16–17, translation provided in Marshall, *Beyond Retribution*, 49).

59. E.g., Mic 6:8.

exile, justice would have been satisfied. The exile would be the end of the story of God's relationship to God's people. But *shalom* had not yet been restored. And the Hebrew Bible affirms that God has an attribute called *hesed* (covenant faithfulness). God is faithful to the Covenant even when Israel is not. And God deals with God's people out of *hesed*, not out of any abstract concept of what God's people *deserve*. And so, God intended to restore that *shalom*, and the Prophets operated with the understanding that the story would continue.[60] They looked forward to a day when God would end the exile, restore a remnant of God's people, and the terms of the Covenant would be so deeply internalized that they would be written on the hearts of all (Jer 31). Only then would *shalom* be restored. The story of God's Covenant with Israel reveals that ultimately, pain does not vindicate. Only accountability, transformation, and restored relationship can vindicate.

Fourth, as alluded to above, a restorative conception of justice is more open to Jesus' teachings on forgiveness and reconciliation than is a retributive conception of justice. Perhaps the most famous example of this is Jesus' response to Peter when Peter asks, "How often should I forgive?" Jesus' response is "seventy-seven times" (Matt 18:21–22).[61] The number is clearly symbolic. It asks for the constant openness to transformation in one who sins. It asks for the willingness to forgive an unlimited number of times. Jesus exhibits this openness to unlimited forgiveness in Luke when he prays for the people who put him to death: "Father forgive them, for they know not what they do" (Luke 23:34). And he exhibits it again in Acts when he chooses Paul, the most notorious persecutor of his disciples, to serve as his apostle to the gentiles (Acts 9:1–22). Marshall notes that Jesus' teaching on forgiveness is noteworthy not only for its scope, but also for its significance in the kingdom of God. Jesus "makes

60. Marshall also makes this connection, but with an eschatological twist: "In exilic and post-exilic writings, especially in Deutero-Isaiah, God's righteousness becomes the ground and content of an eschatological hope for the ultimate revelation of divine power to vindicate Israel's trust and lead all nations to acknowledge God's cosmic lordship" (Marshall, *Beyond Retribution*, 52). He additionally notes that, when the prophets employ forensic metaphors (i.e., of a lawsuit God brings against Israel), the law court imagined takes a restorative approach to justice (Marshall, *Beyond Retribution*, 51).

61. The Greek phrase is *hebdomēkontakis hepta*. Some translators prefer "seventy times seven," but Jesus is probably putting forward a subtle reference to (and inversion of) Lamech's standard in Gen 4:24. Lamech offered "seventy-sevenfold" (i.e., unlimited) vengeance, but those in God's kingdom must offer "seventy-sevenfold" (i.e., unlimited) forgiveness.

the readiness to forgive others a condition for appropriating the forgiveness of God."[62] This idea is invoked in the Lord's Prayer ("forgive us our debts, as we also have forgiven our debtors"),[63] in the Sermon on the Plain ("forgive, and you will be forgiven"),[64] and it is the moral of the parable of the unforgiving servant ("this is how my heavenly Father will treat each of you unless you forgive your brother or sister from your heart").[65] This should not be taken in a transactional sense: we will only "earn" God's forgiveness if we agree to "pay" our own forgiveness. Instead, Jesus is merely noting the reciprocal interplay inherent in forgiveness in the kingdom. As Marshall puts it,

> Because of the reciprocal nature of forgiving mercy, it is simply not feasible for its recipients to keep it selfishly for themselves. They are compelled, by the very nature of the reality itself, to channel it on to others. When they stubbornly refuse to do so, they block the flow, so to speak, and consequently cease to be beneficiaries themselves. They close themselves off to the continuing experience and benefits of God's mercy. God goes on being forgiving, just as the sun goes on shining. (It cannot do otherwise.) But it is still possible to remove oneself from the liberating power of this mercy, just as it is possible to hide oneself from the sun and lose its benefits.[66]

One final note is important here. As discussed before, restorative justice interventions do not *mandate* such radical forgiveness. Facilitators are given explicit instructions not to even bring up the topic of forgiveness, so as not to pressure victims into feeling that it is the goal of the process. After all, forcing forgiveness or pressuring a victim to move to it too quickly would defeat the process, and it would be unjust to the

62. Marshall, *Beyond Retribution*, 73.

63. Matt 6:12; Luke 11:4.

64. Luke 6:37.

65. Matt 18:35. Some readers critique this parable as ultimately self-contradictory. Marshall puts the critique quite succinctly: "Jesus urges unlimited forgiveness, but the king in the parable does not grant forgiveness even a second time, never mind seventy-seven times" (Marshall, *Beyond Retribution*, 77). As discussed in chapter 3, Jesus' parables frequently compare God to a litany of evil characters. Not all of them are meant to be taken univocally, as a transparent window into the life of God. The comparison is meant to be provocative, and naturally (as Marshall notes) the parable breaks down if pressed too far.

66. Marshall, *Beyond Retribution*, 76.

victim.[67] However, because restorative practices encourage transformation, it is always possible for the kind of forgiveness Jesus asks of his disciples to arise as a byproduct.[68] Restorative practices are perpetually *open* to forgiveness without *mandating* it.

Fifth and finally, the New Testament contains a pervasive critique of the entire Roman justice system, which was heavily retributive. Whereas many interpreters argue that the authors of the New Testament have nothing to say about how a criminal justice system ought to run, Marshall astutely points out that the New Testament gives its readers a very thick view of criminal justice "from the underside."[69] The authors of the New Testament almost unanimously assume that the broader Roman and Judean justice systems do not, in fact, dispense real justice. They offer the critique of a people who are the criminal justice system's victims, rather than its beneficiaries. Not only this, but their critique especially points out the myriad ways in which a retributive system whose primary mechanisms are incarceration and capital punishment can go horribly wrong. And far from offering an occasional critique about specific officials within the system, their critique takes its aim at all of this system's

67. As Greg Jones puts it, there are two dangers one must avoid when speaking of forgiveness. The first danger is turning forgiveness into a "cheap therapeutic" concept. This makes forgiveness into a purely internal and private affair which demands no social transformation (i.e., no unlearning of vicious habits and no communal struggle for healing). The second danger is the "eclipse" of forgiveness, where violence ultimately has so strong of a hold on our lives that forgiveness becomes impossible. Here there is no unlearning of violence on the part of offenders, and no healing from violence on the part of victims. There is only the cycle of violence which continues unabated (Jones, *Embodying Forgiveness*, esp. 35–98). Though I would resist labeling the first danger as "therapeutic" so as not to contribute unnecessarily to mental health stigma (which, as I mentioned before, is a problem in both the US and India), I would agree that he has characterized the two most common dangers concerning forgiveness correctly. Retributive systems which expel all considerations of reform in favor of retribution and incarceration fall headlong into the latter danger. A restorative system which mandated forgiveness on the part of the victim would fall headlong into the former danger.

68. As Emmanuel Katongole and Chris Rice have put it, "there is no reconciliation without conversion" (Katongole and Rice, *Reconciling All Things*, 151). Restorative justice focuses on fostering the sorts of transformation or conversion that must occur prior to forgiveness. It does not assume that forgiveness and reconciliation are givens that will necessarily follow, but it is not surprising if conversion and transformation do lead to forgiveness and reconciliation.

69. Marshall, *Beyond Retribution*, 9.

constituent parts, including the courts, police forces, and prisons.[70] The idea that such a system will inevitably see Jesus as a criminal features extremely prominently in Jesus' ministry, and figures heavily in the theology of the evangelists.[71] Luke probably offers the best summary of this position: "The kings of the earth took their stand, and the rulers have gathered together against the Lord and against his Messiah" (Acts 4:25). In other words, the most impressive, developed, expansive judicial system in the world looked upon God made flesh, decided he was a criminal, and killed him. That should be enough to give most advocates of a "law and order" Christianity pause. Most importantly for our purposes, however, is the fact that the release of prisoners was an important part of Messianic expectation. As I mentioned in chapter 3, Jesus wholeheartedly embraced this aspect of the Messiah's mission in his ministry:

> The Spirit of the Lord is upon me, because he has anointed me to bring good news to the poor. He has sent me to proclaim release to the captives, and recovery of sight to the blind, to let the oppressed go free, to proclaim the year of the Lord's favor. (Luke 4:18–19)[72]

70. For an excellent treatment of this critique of the Roman judicial system in the New Testament, see Marshall, *Beyond Retribution*, 12–16. For our purposes, a briefer analysis will have to suffice. Matt 5:25–26; Luke 12:57–59; 1 Cor 6:1–7; and Jas 2:6 stand out as the most explicit warnings to believers not to involve themselves with these sorts of justice systems, whether Roman or Judean. Jesus names visiting those in prison among the works of mercy, implicitly calling attention to how frequently unjust imprisonment occurs (Matt 25:36). In all four Gospels, the lack of justice in Jesus' hearings before Herod, the Sanhedrin, and Pilate is particularly telling (Matt 26:57–68; 27:11–26; Mark 14:53–65; 15:1–15; Luke 22:66—23:25; John 18:19–24; 18:28—19:16), as is the depiction of police brutality meted out by the Roman guard upon Jesus at his crucifixion (Matt 27:27–31; Mark 15:16–20; Luke 22:63–65; John 19:1–3). All four evangelists present Pilate as willing to execute a man he knows to be innocent of inciting a violent rebellion while simultaneously letting a man he knows to be guilty of the exact same crime to go free (Matt 27:15–22; Mark 15:5–15; Luke 23:13–25; John 18:39–40), suggesting that the way the Roman system dispenses justice is fundamentally arbitrary. Luke's subtle yet pervasive presentation of the lack of justice in both the Judean and Roman justice system throughout the book of Acts is particularly sublime, and it can be seen almost any time the apostles are arrested and arraigned in front of a magistrate in the book (Acts 4:1–22; 7; 12:1–5; 16:16–40; 17:16–34; 19:21–41; 24–26).

71. E.g., Matt 26:55–56; Luke 22:37; John 18:30–32. Once again, in Matt 25:36, Jesus exhibits a "real presence" among those in prison.

72. Jesus is reading from Isa 61:1 and using Isaiah's words as a sort of mission statement for his own ministry. For other examples of this theme in the prophets, see Isa 42:6–7 and Zech 9:11–12.

The fact that Jesus was named among criminals and saw the release of prisoners as part of his public ministry should give pause to any advocate of an incarceration-centered system. It is likely that Jesus would still find himself numbered among those who suffer under a system of mass incarceration, rather than among its beneficiaries.

Having surveyed the theological arguments for a turn to a restorative system, let us now consider what its implementation might look like in the case of victim-perpetrators in human trafficking cases.

How Might a Restorative Approach Help with Victim-Perpetrators?

As mentioned previously, there are no organizations I know of working on rehabilitation for victim-perpetrators, and it is difficult to find research on them or even to gain access to them for research purposes. However, there are reasons to believe that a restorative approach would be beneficial for this population for several reasons. Again, restorative practices are untested with this population, and so all proposals here should be taken with the expectation that quite a bit of tweaking will need to occur. Hold them as suggestions rather than as dogmatic pronouncements.

The first issue is that the rhetoric concerning trafficking statutes seems to be stuck on a "the harsher, the better" approach. The most popular justice reform suggested among advocates is simply to extend prison sentences for offenders. If a trafficking conviction currently mandates five years in prison, push for legislation that will make it ten. If a conviction currently mandates ten years in prison, make it twenty. The argument for such reforms (implicitly or explicitly) is deterrence. Harsher penalties will dissuade traffickers. The problem with all forms of deterrence thinking, as Zehr pointed out thirty years ago, is that deterrence only works among populations that perceive that they have the freedom to choose otherwise.[73] Harsh sentences do not work to deter those who see their lives as propelled largely by forces beyond their control. One might argue in response that there is always an alternative to living life as a part of a trafficking ring, but the question is about what the agent's *perception* is, not about the real existence of viable alternatives. A mestri or brothel madam will likely feel they have no choice but to accept the promotion within the trafficking organization if the only other option they perceive

73. Zehr, *Changing Lenses*, 60.

is risking starvation, homelessness, or the organization's wrath. Harsh trafficking sentences may work to deter those higher up the chain in the organization who were never enslaved themselves. However, rather than deterring them from profiting by enslaving people, it may simply deter them from taking part in the direct operations of the trafficking ring. They may multiply the number of victim-perpetrators they use to shield themselves from prosecution. So, harsher trafficking sentences may actually work to multiply the number of victim-perpetrators a trafficking organization turns to for promotion.

Some at this point might ask how accountability is to be secured. Again, insights from restorative justice are salutary here. Requiring a victim-perpetrator to go through a reparation plan would bring recognition to the fact that they did very real damage to the lives of others by inducting them into slavery. It might even help to recruit them in anti-slavery efforts. If an offender recruited bonded laborers to a brick kiln during his tenure as a mestri, why not require that he help secure the release of other laborers bonded from another brick kiln (or in another industry entirely)? If an offender managed trafficked women in a brothel, why not require that she point out other brothels that she worked with to help community leaders halt their operations? Or if she is a member of a trafficking ring and she reports to people higher up than herself, why not require that she disclose who these individuals are?[74] Alternatively, reparations may entail that an offender help with the rehabilitation of another survivor. In the current system in India, the state bears the burden of reparations for bonded labor survivors. As previously noted, under Indian law, all survivors of bonded labor who receive a release certificate are entitled to ₹20,000. In cases where a conviction for their perpetrator is secured, survivors are entitled to ₹100,000 or more. This practice is,

74. In America, this is a common practice referred to as "turning state's evidence." In India, Beth, Chitra, and other attorneys inform me that it is not commonly practiced ("Beth," interview with the author, Mumbai, India, September 12, 2014; "Chitra," interview with the author, Mumbai, India, October 13, 2014). It may even be controversial (as it sometimes is in the US) because it can seem like one is letting the offender off the hook for the crime in exchange for a few bits of information. This is not necessary if incorporated into a reparations plan. Reparation plans often include multiple requirements for the offender. The interaction need not be reduced to a simple tit-for-tat plea deal where the defendant is granted immunity from prosecution in exchange for testimony against another. Again, in restorative justice, the goal is for the offender to take responsibility for harms done. In this case, turning state's evidence could simply be one requirement in a list of reparations which allows an offender to demonstrate that they are willing to accept responsibility for the offence.

oddly enough, both in line with and at variance with restorative practice at the same time. It is not fully in line with restorative principles since it does not yet require reparations by the offender. But it is in line with restorative principles in that a restorative view of justice entails different levels of guilt and can admit that state or societal complicity in an offense does frequently occur. So, state payment of reparation money is acceptable on a restorative view of justice, but a restorative view of justice would ultimately wish to incorporate reparations made by the offender, as well. Some interviewees testified that it was a good thing that this reparation money is furnished by the state rather than the offender, because it would take too long for guilt to be assigned in a criminal trial, and survivors of bonded labor have very immediate physical needs (as we saw in chapter 2).[75] But this is a false binary: it need not be *either* the state that pays reparation money *or* the offender. It could be both. An initial payment by the state could meet some of the survivor's initial needs, and a later payment by the offender could be part of the offender's reparation plan. This would work out especially well if, as one interviewee argued, the ₹20,000 amount is no longer sufficient.[76] Of course, in the case of mestris, they will leave a state of bondage just as poor as the other survivors, so such a payment might not be feasible. However, there are other ways a former mestri can contribute to the rehabilitation of another survivor. They could, for instance, agree to help the survivor build a house with the reparation money they receive from the government. If money is not feasible, contributions of labor or more symbolic gestures could be substituted as part of the reparation plan.[77]

75. According to Richard Ebenezer, the *minimum* time for a bonded labor case involving criminal charges to come to trial is three years (Ebenezer, interview with the author, Chennai, India, November 12, 2014). The *average* time is somewhere in the five- to six-year range.

76. "Manav," interview with the author, Chennai, India, November 18, 2014. Manav's argument was that the ₹20,000 amount was determined quite some time ago, and the number hasn't been adjusted to keep up with inflation in India. Again, the rehabilitation funds have been raised to ₹100,000 or more, but only in rare cases where a conviction is secured.

77. Payment plans are common in some reparation plans when an offender is in a fiscal bind, but in the case of mestris, care should be taken not to open up an avenue for re-trafficking. If a mestri is put on a payment plan, this will essentially entail new debt. And remember that debt is how bonded labor cases normally begin. If the former mestri accrues new debt and cannot secure gainful employment, he may end up re-bonding himself to discharge the new debt.

The inclusion of a reparation plan will also help eliminate the binary that Raja's community faced when they had to decide between receiving their mestri or not. Again, under the current rehabilitation system, freed bonded laborers are asked whether they are willing to receive the mestri back into the community or not. Without a restorative intervention, the choice often seems like the only two options are forgetting the offense or submitting the mestri to exile. Restorative interventions which include a reparation plan to mestris provide a third way forward, one which neither simply requires that the offense is forgotten nor cuts the mestri off from the rest of his people and forces him to fend for himself for the rest of his life.

A reparation plan might also assist the offender in getting help as well. Since the offender will likely still suffer residual trauma (and perhaps some vestiges of captive mentality) from their own period of enslavement, one of the terms of the reparation plan might be that the offender must undergo TFCBT or some similar program. A reparation plan that includes both elements of rehabilitation incorporated in earlier chapters and obligations that must be paid to any individuals victimized would strike a balance between treating a victim-perpetrator wholly as an offender or wholly as a victim, since these individuals exist in the complicated space where they are both at the same time. Transformation for a victim-perpetrator entails both developing a willingness to bear responsibility for their actions, as well as developing an openness to a life beyond slavery. For a brothel madam who was trafficked, she must be willing to make amends for assisting in the trafficking of other women, as well as submitting them to violent discipline, rape, and torture. But she must also be open to rehabilitation; she must see a possible life where she is neither enslaved nor enslaver. Similarly, for a mestri, he must take responsibility for betraying his fellow workers by tricking them into bondage for his master, as well as by beating and breaking their bodies in a feeble attempt to ascend to a position of mastery. But he must also be willing to work toward a world without bonded labor, which means breaking the chains of slavery that remain in his own soul as much as it means helping break the chains of slavery upon others. Extending the possibility of rehabilitation to these individuals is not only the best way to assure that justice is extended to all, it may be the only way to strike out against the trafficking organizations that create victim-perpetrators. After all, if the studies linking incarceration to repeat offending have taught us anything, it is that a victim-perpetrator who is extended no rehabilitation options is likely to simply return to a trafficking organization once they are out of prison. And Sherman and Strang's findings suggest that a victim-perpetrator who receives a restorative justice intervention would be less likely to repeat their offenses than one who does not. To extend the possibility of restoration to them is to take soldiers out of the enemy's armies. To break the spell of captive mentality on them is to starve out the power that is slavery.

But what about captive mentality on the victim's part? Is it safe to put a sex trafficking survivor in a face-to-face encounter with their brothel madam (or, for that matter, their pimp)? What if the survivor is still in some way fascinated with their former captor? What if the offender can convince them that they still love them and still have their best interests at heart? Might a facilitated encounter be an avenue for re-trafficking down the line? This is indeed possible, and it is the reason why face-to-face encounters would need to be handled on a case-by-case basis. It may be necessary for a counselor to assess whether a willing survivor might be vulnerable to the effects of captive mentality before greenlighting a face-to-face encounter. Advocates of restorative justice have long recognized that power imbalances still exist in some cases between the victim and the offender, even after the offender has been arrested and incarcerated. In such cases, face-to-face encounter between the victim and the offender should not proceed.[78] Instead, surrogates are preferable.[79] What this would entail would be that a victim of the same *class* of offense meets with the offender, rather than the person whom the offender directly harmed. In this case, it might entail going forward with the encounter with a trafficking survivor unfamiliar to the offender who is willing to stand in for the victim. This would alleviate the problem,

78. I would not, for example, recommend that a face-to-face encounter should occur between Jyothi (the survivor whose story appears in the introduction) and her father (if they were both still alive). He clearly continued to hold power over her that would likely subvert the whole intention of facilitated encounter. But simply because a face-to-face encounter with her father would be unwise does not necessarily mean a face-to-face encounter with her madam would be unwise. Such decisions would need to be made on a case-by-case basis by trained facilitators in conjunction with input from social workers involved in the survivor's case.

79. Zehr, *Changing Lenses*, 206–8; Zehr, *Little Book of Restorative Justice*, 67. Zehr also counsels for special safeguards in the case of domestic violence situations (Zehr, *Little Book of Restorative Justice*, 50). Those safeguards would likely apply in many trafficking cases, as well.

especially if a willing surrogate can be found who has already been through a rehabilitative program that includes counseling.

Could a facilitated encounter reopen old wounds for a survivor? Could it serve to re-traumatize them? Again, Sherman and Strang's findings are that this is usually not the case. Victims who participate in a restorative justice intervention have better outcomes on average than those who do not. This includes an overall lower amount of post traumatic stress. Of course, facilitators would need to be well-trained to recognize the forms of trauma survivors go through, and to be aware of ways that that trauma might be triggered throughout the process. This is one of many reasons why the facilitator meets with both parties separately before bringing them together. The facilitator's job in these meetings with the offender is to both assess and to help increase the offender's capacity for empathy. If the offender shows no capacity for empathy, the meeting between the two parties does not go forward. The process is actually far more cognizant of a survivor's trauma than is a typical courtroom setting. Survivor testimony is heavily sought after in the courtroom, because it provides one of the best forms of evidence for securing a conviction against a trafficker. And the adversarial nature of cross-examination can serve to re-victimize a survivor, since it is a defense attorney's job to poke holes in the survivor's story. There is abundant survivor testimony available as to how traumatic the experience can be. Horror stories abound of defense attorneys attacking survivors' credibility, sexual history, motivations, and character in open court. For decades now, survivor advocates have been pushing for reforms to the system that will protect survivors on the stand, including closed testimony in a judge's quarters, where only the judge and the survivor are present. In sex trafficking cases in Mumbai, this is now the norm.[80] However, the process can still be extremely draining for the survivor if court officials do not have proper sensitivity training. The risk is far lower for re-victimization in a restorative justice intervention since this adversarial environment is taken away. The survivor gets the chance to tell their story uninterrupted, to name the harms done to them, and to articulate their desires going forward. The process is victim-centered, and as such, the survivor sets the agenda. Their testimony is not an obstacle for the other side to overcome, but a truth to be received. Thus, if it is seen as acceptable to submit a survivor to the testimony process in court,

80. "Mallika," interview with the author, Mumbai, India, September 17, 2014. Mallika did note, however, that she still does run into occasions where this procedure is not followed, and the judge makes a survivor testify in open court.

how much more so should it be seen as acceptable to give the survivor a chance to participate in a restorative process?

A restorative approach might also help with the abysmal prosecution rate found in both sex trafficking and labor trafficking cases. As previously, mentioned, Sherman and Strang found that a diversion from prosecution to a restorative justice intervention substantially increased the odds of an offender being brought to justice. Most justice systems are much more willing to carry out a restorative justice intervention with two willing parties than they are to incarcerate a person who is possibly innocent (and with good reason). And it is interesting how much even the offer of a restorative justice intervention increases an offender's willingness to cooperate. To return to the Truth and Reconciliation Commission in South Africa, Archbishop Tutu recounts that there were individuals who were granted amnesty by the TRC who had also been previously acquitted of atrocities by South African criminal courts. The TRC found that many of its amnesty applicants severely perjured themselves in court, but openly admitted to atrocities in front of the Commission. The very format encouraged honesty, because the deal was that amnesty would be granted on the condition that the individual fully disclosed what they had done in public (and would bear the public sanctions that resulted from such a disclosure). In contrast, the very format of the retributive justice system encouraged dishonesty, and as such, led to a lack of convictions. Tutu says this was the case because they were not incentivized to disclose the atrocities they had committed, and there was not enough evidence to find them guilty beyond a reasonable doubt.

> In many of the cases which came before the commission, the only witnesses to events who were still alive were the perpetrators, and they had used the considerable resources of the state to destroy evidence and cover their heinous deeds. The commission proved to be a better way of getting at the truth than court cases.[81]

South Africans faced a stark choice: try a (limited) restorative justice intervention,[82] or stand by and watch as the truth was buried under a mountain of acquittals. Given the situation in the Indian criminal justice

81. Tutu, *No Future without Forgiveness*, 23.

82. I add "limited" here because the TRC definitely incorporated *encounter*. It is less clear that it always incorporated *reparations*. And whether *transformation* will ultimately result is a question which haunts South African politics more with every passing election.

system, it seems that anti-trafficking advocates are faced with the same choice. With as low as the conviction rate is, the choice is not between a restorative justice intervention and a retributive justice intervention. The choice is between a restorative justice intervention and an acquittal.

Finally, to return to the story I started with, a restorative approach would also help avoid the key issue that caused burnout in Beth's case: grabbing up all individuals on the premises and charging them with trafficking offenses, regardless of what their level of involvement is. Again, part of the encounter process is to name the harms done by the offender, and if the person arrested is a teenager who runs out to get drinks for guests, it will be difficult to articulate what the concrete harms done to the victim are. If this cannot be done, the person arrested will be quickly ruled out during the process. A turn to restorative justice practice will not only help secure just treatment of the accused, but it will help reduce burnout for advocates like Beth and Chitra. Because God knows we need people like Beth and Chitra. And we need to assure that, after the years of tireless work that they put in, they can still feel right about what they are doing at the end of the day.

For those who are still skeptical, I would encourage at least attempting some limited restorative processes. In restorative justice interventions in the US (as infrequently as they occur), if both parties do not agree to a restorative intervention (or if the restorative process breaks down), the case defaults back to the old retributive system. The same could be done in trafficking cases. Again, I would hope for greater changes to the system than this, given the revelations about incarceration that have arisen amidst the current conversation on criminal justice reform in the United States. But small steps toward restorative justice are preferable to none at all.

Of course, exactly none of this will be easy. We are talking about making amends for a set of actions that are fundamentally unjustifiable, of trying to find reparation plans for an incalculable amount of damage done, of transforming hardened individuals who have had years of practice making themselves indifferent to the suffering of others, and of facilitating difficult conversations between victim and offender that will be painful, trying, and risky. But then, the criminal justice process is already plagued by these problems. Any attempt at finding justice in the wake of a practice as evil as slavery is going to have these difficulties. And there is enough data that suggests it is at least worth trying a victim-centered approach which simultaneously allows the offender to try to make things right. And again, none of this is set in stone. Restorative practices will need to be attempted, evaluated, refined, and re-attempted. But hopefully some of these suggestions will help to address a problem and a population that, as of this writing, few anti-trafficking organizations have been willing to address.

CONCLUSION

What Remains

THE PENULTIMATE QUESTION I always asked my survivor interviewees was simply, "Are you free?" I asked them the question without any further introduction or explanation, not wanting to guide their response in any predetermined direction. Many were taken aback by the question, unsure of how to respond to it. Some responded with a "yes," and then ironically proceeded to list off all the ways in which they continued to experience forms of harassment, oppression, or physical need. Others responded with a dismissive or enthusiastic "yes," as though the answer were obvious and could not have been otherwise. No one responded with a "no." Very few responded with a complex answer such as "in some ways yes, in some ways no," or "not yet, but I'm on my way there."

It isn't an easy question to answer, even for someone who has never been enslaved and will never likely be enslaved. This is perhaps the reason why aftercare specialists came up with the maxim I referred to earlier: "rehabilitation looks different for every survivor." Rehabilitation is a many-faceted phenomenon that is difficult to reduce to a checklist because freedom is a many-faceted phenomenon that is difficult to reduce to a checklist. While this maxim is indeed a valuable thing to keep in mind, there are some general recommendations on how aftercare ought to be approached that emerged from the testimony of the survivors and the aftercare providers interviewed for this book. Some of these recommendations are already being implemented by some NGOs. Some are being implemented by almost no one, and they will likely require revision as new difficulties in implementation arise. Some are ideal recommendations that may be criticized as too resource-intensive to pull off anytime soon. Others may be feasible, but there is currently no political or social will to pull them off in a thoroughgoing way. Others are much smaller-scale changes that are quite doable provided the willpower exists to carry them out. If one of the proposed large-scale proposals seems out of reach, try a smaller change first. We will start with the large-scale recommendations and work down to the more small-scale ones. Let us refer to the changes that will require more willpower, action, and time as "ultimate" recommendations, and the ones that can be implemented more readily "proximate" recommendations.

Ultimate Recommendations

Concerning the problem of captive mentality: A full-scale turn to Trauma-Focused Cognitive Behavioral Therapy (TFCBT) to deal with the aftereffects of slavery. TFCBT seems to work well largely because its therapeutic approach and psycho-educative aims give survivors a better footing to articulate how it was that their former masters wronged them. It gives them a basis to understand how the love and justice their masters offered them while in captivity were false forms of love and justice. Additionally, the basic education in forms of abuse will help especially with identifying and intervening in forms of domestic violence that occur within rehabilitating bonded labor communities. Extending TFCBT to survivors of bonded labor as well as survivors of sex trafficking may be especially helpful to bonded labor survivors who have suffered forms of sexual violence, given TFCBT's roots in dealing with PTSD resulting from sexual abuse.

Concerning institutional aftercare for sex trafficking survivors: A thick aftercare chain which includes both group homes and "after-aftercare" communities that allow sex trafficking survivors to find support networks even after moving out of closed homes. These homes may be closer to the group home model (such as NGO X), or they may experiment with various intentional community models (closer to L'Arche or the Catholic Worker).

Concerning economic rehabilitation for bonded laborers: Training survivors in forms of organizing and civil disobedience that will directly confront caste-based economic disparity and political marginalization. Slaveholders seem to particularly fear the strike, so a thoroughgoing education on how strikes are organized, variation in forms of strikes, and how to respond to efforts on the part of owners to bust strikes should be included. It must be recognized that there is no silver bullet economic solution (such as job skill training) which will allow rehabilitation to proceed without directly confronting the realities of caste. To quote King, "constructive, nonviolent tension . . . is necessary for growth."[1] Caste tension is not created by the outcaste who disobeys; it is created when an upper caste person puts his foot on the outcaste's neck. The outcastes who engage in civil disobedience are merely bringing that tension to the surface so that it can be dealt with.

Concerning enslaved overseers and restorative justice: A shift from retributive justice practices to restorative justice practices. This would include making reparations the normative sanction for offenses rather than incarceration, as well as the implementation of some model of facilitated encounter between victim and offender (whether that be victim-offender counseling, sentencing circles, or some other model). Shifting in this direction would put more power in the hands of survivors, since they often are marginalized by a more retributive system. It would also provide recognition that formerly enslaved overseers have done other formerly enslaved workers considerable harm, and it is their responsibility to mend that harm to the extent that such a thing is possible. And yet, a turn to restorative justice practices also recognizes that formerly enslaved overseers ought to be given a chance at rehabilitation as well.

Proximate Recommendations

Concerning the problem of captive mentality: If practitioners of TFCBT are rare (or too expensive), any program which gives survivors a basic education in forms of abuse would be better than nothing. Such educational programs should emphasize that love is emphatically not compatible with violence. Additionally, requiring aftercare professionals to undergo trauma-informed care trainings is necessary to avoid reactivating trauma while giving care. For Christian churches involved in aftercare, a fuller theological education concerning the nature of God (and the analogous language the Christian tradition uses to describe God) will go a long way to disestablishing ideas that (1) the former master is God, and (2) God is akin to a big slaveholder in the sky. Fuller theological education will also help remind Christian survivors and Christians giving care that perfect

1. King, "Letter from Birmingham City Jail," 291.

love and perfect justice are shown forth in Jesus Christ's nonviolent politics of resistance against the powers and principalities, which culminates in accepting the way of the cross. Forms of love and justice that ask a survivor to accept abuse to uplift a master are false forms of love and justice.

Concerning institutional aftercare for sex trafficking survivors: Prison architecture for aftercare facilities (e.g., stone walls with razor wire, bars or gates behind which inmates are locked in at night) must be abandoned. Corporal punishment for disciplinary purposes must be abandoned. Shame-based disciplinary measures must be abandoned. These disciplinary regimens do not constitute enough of a break from the control mechanisms present under slavery, do not adequately aim at rehabilitation, and can serve to push a survivor back into bondage. Timetables are acceptable (and perhaps even necessary) provided they are used to pull survivors off of the master's time and not to institute a new form of control. Monitoring survivors is acceptable, and is especially necessary during the initial months after rescue. However, it must be remembered that the goal is to move survivors to points of more and more responsibility in their community and greater and greater forms of freedom. Regular forms of encouragement for survivors must be implemented into the schedule of the aftercare home because survivors will experience regular crisis periods.

Concerning economic rehabilitation for bonded laborers: Aftercare providers should give formal recognition that a lack of job skills does not always lie at the root of a former bonded laborer's economic marginalization. Training programs should be implemented to teach survivors community organizing skills so that they can push for benefits mandated under law. The less social workers have to work to get the government to provide services it has promised, the more time they can devote to deeper forms of aftercare (such as counseling, skills assessments, educational placements for children, and the trainings listed under the ultimate recommendations section).

Concerning enslaved overseers and restorative justice: Aftercare services already provided to survivors should be extended to formerly enslaved overseers who are incarcerated under the current retributive system (such as counseling and therapy services, as well as transitional housing and job skill training for alternative forms of employment should they ever be released). This is not only to give them a chance to rehabilitate like other formerly enslaved people, but to take expendable resources out of the hands of trafficking rings, as a mestri or brothel madam who comes out of the retributive justice system may simply go back to their old masters upon release.

Questions for Further Research

Even with all of the myriad topics this book has covered, many questions remain as to how to best address the numerous moral and theological problems faced by survivors once they are freed. The following is merely a representative list of questions that could not be addressed in this book due to a lack of either data, space, or my own expertise.

Concerning slavery itself: Are there rules of thumb that can be followed for identifying how slavery is about to undergo change? What is the relationship between slavery and incarceration? Why do these two practices seem to appear in tandem so often?

Concerning captive mentality: What sorts of programs or therapy rubrics might help to combat the effects of captive mentality other than TFCBT? Would logotherapy[2] be beneficial? How does one even begin to respond to the questions survivors have about why a good God would allow them to suffer so? What would a biblical education that incorporates the insight that all language about God is analogous look like among various Indian Christian groups?

Concerning institutional aftercare: Can a monastic model ever properly train a survivor in the right kinds of *dis*obedience? Is stability necessary for "after-aftercare" homes? Can any guidelines or rules of thumb be provided for how churches can help these institutions flourish?

2. This is a therapy rubric that arose out of the work of the psychiatrist and Holocaust survivor Victor Frankl. It seeks to help survivors find meaning amid their suffering. Pranitha Timothy mentioned in her interview that she was starting to turn to it more in her work with survivors of human trafficking. On first blush, I think this is an interesting suggestion, since it may help the survivors find meaning in their lives that isn't dependent upon their former master. However, I didn't encounter a thick account of a logotherapy rubric for survivors in my interviews, and I don't have much expertise on the method. I imagine that a theological treatment of such a rubric would have to offer a thick discussion of theodicy (how it is that a good God can allow suffering in the world).

Concerning community organizing and civil disobedience: What would an expanded training program for survivors look like in rural South India that includes trainings on how to organize? What would an educational program that trains survivors in nonviolent resistance look like? What would a formation program that teaches the virtue of disobedience look like? What might a heterodox analysis of economic rehabilitation for survivors of human trafficking look like?[3]

Concerning restorative justice: What new problems might victim-perpetrators face if they are extended rehabilitative services? What would a training program for restorative justice facilitators look like? How might a restorative justice approach be implemented for offenders who are not victim-perpetrators? What sorts of changes would have to be made to any model of facilitated encounter that includes these individuals?

Concerning other topics: How do Christian groups in India communicate some of these theological values and practices in ways that would be viable to survivors of other religious traditions?[4] How can we assure that survivors are taking the lead in any of these areas (rather than each area merely remaining the purview of non-survivor academics and experts)?

It is my hope that subsequent abolitionists will be willing and able to dive into some of these questions.

The vigilance necessary to form the virtues and continue the practices of a truly abolitionist society is great, greater indeed than perhaps many groups in the nineteenth century were able to muster. Frederick Douglass' call to remain ever attentive to the ways that slavery will reassert itself remains sound counsel. It is likely slavery will be with us for a good long while yet. Not everyone can resist its siren song. The promise of godhood, at least over an individual human life, is far too tempting.

3. "Heterodox" here means economically heterodox (i.e., written from a different perspective than the neoliberal orthodoxy which produces problematic economic analyses like the ones critiqued in chapter 5). I would settle for *any* heterodox perspective, really. It could be socialist, anarchist, Marxist, feminist, distributivist, or anything else.

4. I assume that the answer here cannot be by translating them into "objective," "rational," "universal," "secular," or "natural law" terms. It may be the case that all of those terms have their proper place. But when it comes to using them as a medium to communicate between different religious traditions, all of them become Trojan horses of one species or another. I suspect a deeper conversation must be had about both the agreement and disagreement that exists between *specific* aspects of two different religious positions. After all, this is what members from within the same religious tradition have to do when they experience tension or disagreement.

We may destroy one of slavery's forms. We may fracture it such that it has to move underground for a while. But it will continue to reappear, rebranded as something else. It will continue to prowl around like a roaring lion, ready to devour the vulnerable. Yet this does not make the abolitionist cause a fruitless one. It does not make the work of rehabilitation for survivors a fruitless one. It calls instead for greater discernment, greater attention, and greater endurance. For in the end, slavery's days really are numbered. Christ has come in victory, putting all powers, even slavery, under his feet. One day, that victory will come to fruition, every chain will be broken, and slavery will be no more. In the meantime, the fostering of abolitionist virtues and practices will be necessary for all who seek, like Christ, to resist the power that is slavery. May the day of slavery's demise come, and come soon.

Bibliography

Ackerman, Peter, and Jack DuVall. *A Force More Powerful: A Century of Nonviolent Conflict*. New York: Palgrave, 2000.

Aland, Barbara, et al., eds. *Novum Testamentum Graece*. Stuttgart, Germ.: Deutsche Bibelgesellschaft, 2012.

Alexander, Michelle. *The New Jim Crow: Mass Incarceration in the Age of Colorblindness*. New York: The New Press, 2012.

Alexis-Baker, Andy. "Violence, Nonviolence, and the Temple Incident." *Biblical Interpretation* 20 (2012) 88–92.

Allman, Mark J. *Who Would Jesus Kill? War, Peace, and the Christian Tradition*. Winona, MN: St. Mary's, 2008.

Alter, Robert. *The Art of Biblical Narrative*. New York: Basic, 2011.

Appiah, Kwame Anthony, and Martin Bunzl, eds. *Buying Freedom: The Ethics and Economics of Slave Redemption*. Princeton, NJ: Princeton University Press, 2007.

Athanasius. *The Life of Anthony and the Letter to Marcellinus*. Translated by Robert C. Gregg. New York: Paulist, 1980.

Augustine. *Augustine: Political Writings*. Edited by E. M. Atkins and R. J. Dodaro. New York: Cambridge University Press, 2001.

———. *City of God*. Translated by Henry Bettenson. London: Penguin, 1984.

———. *Expositions on the Psalms 51–72*. Translated by Maria Boulding, OSB. New York: New City, 2001.

Bales, Kevin. *Disposable People: New Slavery in the Global Economy*. Los Angeles: University of California Press, 2000.

Bales, Kevin, and Zoe Trodd. *To Plead Our Own Cause: Personal Stories by Today's Slaves*. Ithaca: Cornell University Press, 2008.

Bales, Kevin, et al. *Modern Slavery: The Secret World of 27 Million People*. Oxford: Oneworld, 2009.

Balthasar, Hans Urs von. *The Glory of the Lord: A Theological Aesthetics*. Vol. 7. Edinburgh: T. & T. Clark, 1982.

Barr, James. "Ancient Biblical Laws and Modern Human Rights." In *Justice and the Holy: Essays in Honor of Walter Harrelson*, edited by D. A. Knight and P. J. Peters, 21–33. Atlanta: Scholars, 1989.

Basil of Caesarea. *Letters*. Vol. 2, *186–368*. Translated by Agnes Clare Way, CDP. New York: Fathers of the Church, 1955.

Batstone, David. *Not for Sale: The Return of the Global Slave Trade—and How We Can Fight It*. New York: HarperOne, 2010.

Beavis, Mary Ann. "Ancient Slavery as an Interpretive Context for the New Testament Servant Parables with Special Reference to the Unjust Steward (Luke 16:1–8)." *Journal of Biblical Literature* 111 (1992) 37–54.

Berkhof, Hendrikus. *Christ and the Powers*. Translated by John Howard Yoder. Scottdale, PA: Herald, 1962.

Bhatt, Chetan. *Hindu Nationalism: Origins, Ideologies, and Modern Myths*. New York: Berg, 2001.

Bird, Michael F. "Inerrancy Is Not Necessary for Evangelicalism Outside the USA." In *Five Views on Biblical Inerrancy*, edited by James R. A. Merrick and Stephen M. Garrett, 145–73. Grand Rapids: Zondervan, 2013.

Blackmon, Douglas A. *Slavery by Another Name: The Re-enslavement of Black Americans from the Civil War to World War II*. New York: Random House, 2008.

Bradbury, Alexandra, et al. *Secrets of a Successful Organizer*. Brooklyn: Labor Notes, 2016.

Brown, Eleanor. *The Ties That Bind: Migration and Trafficking of Women and Girls for Sexual Exploitation in Cambodia*. Phnom Penh: International Organization for Migration, 2007.

Brown, Henry Box. *Narrative of the Life of Henry Box Brown*. New York: Oxford University Press, 2002.

Brueggemann, Walter. *The Prophetic Imagination*. Minneapolis: Fortress, 2001.

Brueggemann, Walter, and Tod Linafelt. *An Introduction to the Old Testament: The Canon and Christian Formation*. Louisville: Westminster John Knox, 2012.

Burns, Joshua Ezra. "Jewish Ideologies of Peacemaking." In *Peacemaking and the Challenge of Violence in World Religions*, edited by Irfan A. Omar and Michael K. Duffey, 83–106. Malden, MA: Wiley Blackwell, 2015.

Campbell, Douglas A. *The Deliverance of God: An Apocalyptic Rereading of Justification in Paul*. Grand Rapids: Eerdmans, 2009.

Cartwright, John, and Susan Thistlethwaite. "Support Nonviolent Direct Action." In *Just Peacemaking: The New Paradigm for the Ethics of Peace and War*, edited by Glen Stassen, 42–56. Cleveland: Pilgrim, 2008.

Cavanaugh, William T. *Being Consumed: Economics and Christian Desire*. Grand Rapids: Eerdmans, 2008.

———. *Migrations of the Holy: God, State, and the Political Meaning of the Church*. Grand Rapids: Eerdmans, 2011.

Chenoweth, Erica, and Maria J. Stephan. *Why Civil Resistance Works: The Strategic Logic of Nonviolent Conflict*. New York: Columbia University Press, 2011.

Chirichigno, Gregory C. *Debt-Slavery in Israel and the Ancient Near East*. Sheffield: Sheffield Academic, 1993.

Chittister, Joan. *The Rule of Benedict: Insights for the Ages*. New York: Crossroad, 1992.

Choi-Fitzpatrick, Austin. *What Slaveholders Think: How Contemporary Perpetrators Rationalize What They Do*. New York: Columbia University Press, 2017.

Coates, Ta-Nehisi. "The Case for Reparations." *The Atlantic*, June 2014. https://www.theatlantic.com/magazine/archive/2014/06/the-case-for-reparations/361631.

Cohen, Shaye J. D. "The Judaean Legal Tradition and the *Halakah* of the Mishnah." In *The Cambridge Companion to the Talmud and Rabbinic Literature*, edited by Charlotte Elisheva Fonrobert, 121–43. Cambridge: Cambridge University Press, 2007.

Cone, James. *The Cross and the Lynching Tree*. Maryknoll: Orbis, 2013.

Coulter, Michael L., et al. *The Encyclopedia of Catholic Social Thought, Social Science, and Social Policy*. Lanham, MD: Scarecrow, 2007.

Cullen, Francis T., et al. "Prisons Do Not Reduce Recidivism: The High Cost of Ignoring the Science." *The Prison Journal* 91 suppl. (2011) 48S–65S.

Cunningham, David S. *These Three Are One: The Practice of Trinitarian Theology*. Malden: Blackwell, 1998.

Davidson, William, trans. *The William Davidson Talmud*. https://www.sefaria.org/texts/Talmud.

Davis, Angela Y. *Abolition Democracy: Beyond Empire, Prisons, and Torture*. New York: Seven Stories, 2005.

———. *Are Prisons Obsolete?* New York: Seven Stories, 2003.

———. "From the Prison of Slavery to the Slavery of Prison: Frederick Douglass and the Convict Leasing System." In *The Angela Davis Reader*, edited by Joy Davis, 74–107. Malden: Blackwell, 1998.

Day, Dorothy. *Loaves and Fishes*. Maryknoll: Orbis, 1997.

Dear, John. *The God of Peace: Toward a Theology of Nonviolence*. Maryknoll: Orbis, 1994.

Dever, William. *Who Were the Early Israelites and Where Did They Come From?* Grand Rapids: Eerdmans, 2003.

Douglass, Frederick. *Narrative of the Life of Frederick Douglass, an American Slave, Written by Himself*. San Francisco: City Light, 2010.

———. "The Need for Continued Anti-Slavery Work." In *The Life and Writings of Frederick Douglass*, edited by Philip S. Foner, 4:577–80. New York: International, 1955.

Dreher, Rod. *The Benedict Option: A Strategy for Christians in a Post-Christian Nation*. New York: Sentinel, 2017.

Dubler, Joshua, and Vincent W. Lloyd. *Break Every Yoke: Religion, Justice, and the Abolition of Prisons*. Oxford: Oxford University Press, 2020.

Du Bois, W. E. B. "The Spawn of Slavery: The Convict Lease System of the South." In *Dubois on Reform: Periodical-Based Leadership for African Americans*, edited by Brian Johnson, 84–91. Lantham: AltaMira, 2005.

Eagleton, Terry. *Why Marx Was Right*. New Haven: Yale University Press, 2012.

Easwaran, Eknath, trans. *The Bhagavad Gita*. New Delhi: Penguin, 1996.

Edwards, Jonathan, et al. *Jonathan Edwards' Sinners in the Hands of an Angry God: A Casebook*. New Haven: Yale University Press, 2010.

Ellul, Jacques. *The Ethics of Freedom*. Translated by Geoffrey W. Bromiley. Grand Rapids: Eerdmans, 1976.

Elshtain, Jean Bethge. "Augustine." In *The Blackwell Companion to Political Theology*, edited by Peter Scott and William T. Cavanaugh, 35–47. Malden, MA: Blackwell, 2004.

Finn, Daniel K. *Faithful Economics: 25 Short Insights*. Minneapolis: Fortress, 2021.

Flood, Gavin. *An Introduction to Hinduism*. New York: Cambridge University Press, 1996.

Foucault, Michel. *Discipline and Punish: The Birth of the Prison*. Translated by Alan Sheridan. New York: Vintage, 1995.

———. *Power*. Translated by Robert Hurley et al. New York: New Press, 2000.

Fry, Timothy, ed. *RB 1980: The Rule of St. Benedict in Latin and English with Notes*. Collegeville, PA: Liturgical, 1981.

Gandhi, Mahatma. *The Essential Writings*. Edited by Judith M. Brown. Oxford: Oxford University Press, 2008.

Garnsey, Peter. *Ideas of Slavery from Aristotle to Augustine*. New York: Cambridge University Press, 1996.

Gerassi, Lara B., and Andrea J. Nichols. *Sex Trafficking and Commercial Sexual Exploitation: Prevention, Advocacy, and Trauma-Informed Practice*. New York: Springer, 2018.

Glazek, Christopher. "Raise the Crime Rate." *n+1* 13 (2012). https://nplusonemag.com/issue-13/politics/raise-the-crime-rate.

Gooding, Chris. "Judgment, Sex Trafficking, and Bonded Labor." In *The Routledge Companion to Christian Ethics*, edited by D. Stephen Long and Rebekah Miles, 289–99. Routledge Religion Companions. New York: Routledge, 2023.

Gottschalk, Marie. *Caught: The Prison State and the Lockdown of American Politics*. Princeton: Princeton University Press, 2014.

Gregory, Brad. *The Unintended Reformation: How a Religious Revolution Secularized Society*. Cambridge: Belknap, 2012.

Gregory the Great. *Dialogues*. Translated by Odo John Zimmerman. New York: Fathers of the Church, 1959.

Gutting, Gary. *Foucault: A Very Short Introduction*. New York: Oxford University Press, 2005.

Hart, David Bentley. *The Experience of God: Being, Consciousness, Bliss*. New Haven: Yale University Press, 2013.

———, trans. *The New Testament: A Translation*. New Haven: Yale University Press, 2017.

———. *That All Shall Be Saved: Heaven, Hell, and Universal Salvation*. New Haven: Yale University Press, 2019.

Hart, Drew G. I. *Who Will Be a Witness? Igniting Activism for God's Justice, Love, and Deliverance*. Harrisonburg, VA: Herald, 2020.

Hays, Richard B. *The Moral Vision of the New Testament: A Contemporary Introduction to New Testament Ethics*. New York: HarperCollins, 1996.

Hays, Sophie. *Trafficked: My Story of Surviving, Escaping, and Transcending Abduction into Prostitution*. Naperville, IL: Sourcebooks, 2013.

Hector, Kevin W. *Theology without Metaphysics: God, Language, and the Spirit of Recognition*. New York: Cambridge University Press, 2011.

Hegel, G. W. F. *Phenomenology of Spirit*. Translated by A. V. Miller. New York: Oxford University Press, 1977.

Herman, Judith. *Trauma and Recovery*. New York: Basic, 1997.

Hopkins, Dwight N. "Slave Theology in the 'Invisible Institution.'" In *Cut Loose Your Stammering Tongue: Black Theology in the Slave Narrative*, edited by Dwight N. Hopkins and George C. L. Cummings, 1–32. Louisville: Westminster John Knox, 2003.

International Labor Organization. "Observation (CEACR), adopted 2018, published 108th ILC session (2019)." https://www.ilo.org/dyn/normlex/en/f?p=1000:13100:0::NO:13100:P13100_COMMENT_ID:3958308.

Janzen, David. *The Intentional Christian Community Handbook: For Idealists, Hypocrites, and Wannabe Disciples of Jesus*. Brewster, MA: Paraclete, 2013.

Jennings, Willie James. *The Christian Imagination: Theology and the Origins of Race*. New Haven: Yale University Press, 2010.

Johnson, Elizabeth. *She Who Is: The Mystery of God in a Feminist Theological Discourse.* New York: Crossroad, 1992.

Johnson, Luke Timothy. *Sharing Possessions: Mandate and Symbol of Faith.* Philadelphia: Fortress, 1981.

Jones, L. Gregory. *Embodying Forgiveness: A Theological Analysis.* Grand Rapids: Eerdmans, 1995.

Jones, Serene. *Trauma and Grace.* Louisville: Westminster John Knox, 2009.

Kaiser, Walter C., Jr. *The Old Testament Documents: Are They Reliable and Relevant?* Downers Grove: InterVarsity, 2001.

Kara, Siddarth. *Sex Trafficking: Inside the Business of Modern Slavery.* New York: Columbia University Press, 2009.

Katongole, Emmanuel, and Chris Rice. *Reconciling All Things: A Christian Vision for Justice, Peace and Healing.* Downers Grove: InterVarsity, 2008.

King, Martin Luther, Jr. "Letter from Birmingham City Jail." In *A Testament of Hope: The Essential Writings and Speeches of Martin Luther King, Jr.*, edited by James M. Washington, 289–302. New York: HarperCollins, 1986.

Kirk-Duggan, Cheryl. *Exorcizing Evil: A Womanist Perspective on the Spirituals.* Maryknoll: Orbis, 1997.

Knott, Kim. *Hinduism: A Very Short Introduction.* New York: Oxford University Press, 1998.

Koenig, Sarah. "A Bar Fight Walks into the Justice Center." *Serial: Season 3* (podcast), September 20, 2018. https://serialpodcast.org/season-three/1/a-bar-fight-walks-into-the-justice-center.

———. "Pleas Baby Pleas." *Serial: Season 3* (podcast), October 11, 2018. https://serialpodcast.org/season-three/5/pleas-baby-pleas.

Kraybill, J. Nelson. *Apocalypse and Allegiance: Worship, Politics, and Devotion in the Book of Revelation.* Grand Rapids: Brazos, 2010.

Kristof, Nicholas, and Cheryl WuDunn. *Half the Sky: Turning Oppression into Opportunity for Women Worldwide.* New York: Vintage, 2009.

———. "Two Cheers for Sweatshops." *New York Times Magazine*, September 24, 2000.

Krugman, Paul. "Hearts and Heads." *New York Times*, April 22, 2001.

Lederach, John Paul. *The Little Book of Conflict Transformation.* New York: Good Books, 2003.

Lehner, Ulrich. *Monastic Prisons and Torture Chambers: Crime and Punishment in Central European Monasteries, 1600–1800.* Eugene, OR: Cascade, 2013.

Levad, Amy. *Restorative Justice: Theories and Practices of Moral Imagination.* El Paso, TX: LFB Scholarly, 2012.

Lloyd, Rachel. *Girls Like Us: Fighting for a World Where Girls Are Not for Sale.* New York: HarperCollins, 2011.

Logan, James Samuel. *Good Punishment? Christian Moral Practice and U.S. Imprisonment.* Grand Rapids: Eerdmans, 2008.

Long, D. Stephen. *The Perfectly Simple Triune God: Aquinas and His Legacy.* Minneapolis: Fortress, 2016.

———. *Saving Karl Barth: Hans Urs von Balthasar's Preoccupation.* Minneapolis: Fortress, 2014.

Long, D. Stephen, and Nancy Ruth Fox. *Calculated Futures: Theology, Ethics, and Economics.* Waco: Baylor University Press, 2007.

Longman, Tremper, III. *How to Read Exodus.* Downers Grove: InterVarsity, 2009.

MacIntyre, Alasdair. *After Virtue*. Notre Dame: University of Notre Dame Press, 1984.

Marshall, Christopher D. *Beyond Retribution: A New Testament Vision for Justice, Crime, and Punishment*. Grand Rapids: Eerdmans, 2001.

Martin, Dale B. *Slavery as Salvation: The Metaphor of Slavery in Pauline Christianity*. New Haven: Yale University Press, 1990.

McCloskey, Deidre. *The Bourgeois Virtues: Ethics for an Age of Commerce*. Chicago: University of Chicago Press, 2007.

Meeks, M. Douglas. "Economics in the Christian Scriptures." In *The Oxford Handbook of Christianity and Economics*, edited by Paul Oslington, 3–21. New York: Oxford University Press, 2014.

Mehta, Suketu. *Maximum City: Bombay Lost and Found*. New Delhi: Penguin, 2004.

Milgrom, Jacob. *Leviticus*. Minneapolis: Fortress, 2004.

———. "Lex Talionis and the Rabbis." *Biblical Research* 12 (1996) 16, 48.

Mohanty, Kalpana. "Peacemaking and Nonviolence in the Hindu Tradition." In *Peacemaking and the Challenge of Violence in World Religions*, edited by Irfan A. Omar and Michael K. Duffey, 178–99. Malden, MA: Wiley Blackwell, 2015.

Myers, Ched. *Binding the Strong Man: A Political Reading of Mark's Story of Jesus*. Maryknoll: Orbis, 2008.

Nirmal, Arvind P. "Towards a Dalit Christian Theology." In *An Eerdmans Reader in Contemporary Political Theology*, edited by William T. Cavanaugh et al., 537–52. Grand Rapids: Eerdmans, 2012.

O'Loughlin, Michael J. "Internal Report Finds That L'Arche Founder Jean Vanier Engaged in Decades of Sexual Misconduct." *America*, February 22, 2020. https://www.americamagazine.org/faith/2020/02/22/internal-report-finds-larche-founder-jean-vanier-engaged-decades-sexual-misconduct.

Pandey, Geeta. "Calling Your Husband by Name for the First Time." *BBC News*, July 28, 2017. http://www.bbc.com/news/magazine-40745343.

Patterson, Orlando. *Slavery and Social Death: A Comparative Study*. Cambridge, MA: Harvard University Press, 1982.

Phillips, Elizabeth. *Political Theology: A Guide for the Perplexed*. London: T. & T. Clark, 2012.

Piketty, Thomas. *Capital in the Twenty-First Century*. Cambridge: Harvard University Press, 2014.

Pleins, J. David. *Social Visions of the Hebrew Bible: A Theological Introduction*. Louisville: Westminster John Knox, 2001.

Popovic, Srdja, and Raphael Mimoun. "How to Beat the Islamic State through Non-Violence." *Foreign Policy*, March 14, 2016. https://foreignpolicy.com/2016/03/14/how-to-beat-the-islamic-state-through-non-violence.

Purnell, Derecka. *Becoming Abolitionists: Police, Protests, and the Pursuit of Freedom*. New York: Astra, 2021.

Raboteau, Albert J. *Slave Religion: The "Invisible Institution" in the Antebellum South*. New York: Oxford University Press, 2004.

Rambo, Shelley. *Spirit and Trauma*. Louisville: Westminster John Knox, 2010.

Ramelli, Ilaria L. E. *The Christian Doctrine of Apokatastasis: A Critical Assessment from the New Testament to Eriugena*. Boston: Brill, 2013.

Rawick, George P., ed. *The American Slave: A Composite Autobiography*. Vol. 7, *Oklahoma and Mississippi Narratives*. Westport, CT: Greenwood, 1972.

Rhodes, Daniel P. "In the Union of the Spirit: Cesar Chavez and the Quest for Farmworker Justice." In *Can I Get a Witness? Thirteen Peacemakers, Community Builders, and Agitator for Faith and Justice*, edited by Charles Marsh et al., 9–36. Grand Rapids: Eerdmans, 2019.

Richardson, Elaine. *PHD to Ph.D.: How Education Saved My Life*. Anderson, SC: Parlor, 2013.

Rist, John M. *Augustine: Ancient Thought Baptized*. New York: Cambridge University Press, 1994.

Robinson, Paul H. "'The Virtues of Restorative Processes, the Vices of Restorative Justice.'" In *The Restorative Justice Reader*, edited by Gerry Johnstone, 384–91. New York: Routledge, 2013.

Rosch, Eleanor. "Peace Is the Strongest Force in the World." In *Peacemaking and the Challenge of Violence in World Religions*, edited by Irfan A. Omar and Michael K. Duffey, 142–72. Malden: Wiley Blackwell, 2015.

Rosen, Steven. *Essential Hinduism*. Westport: Praeger, 2006.

Rosenblatt, Katrina, and Cecil Murphy. *Stolen: The True Story of a Sex Trafficking Survivor*. Grand Rapids: Revel, 2014.

Rowe, C. Kavin. *Early Narrative Christology: The Lord in the Gospel of Luke*. New York: de Gruyter, 2006.

———. *World Upside Down: Reading Acts in the Greco-Roman Age*. New York: Oxford University Press, 2009.

Ruether, Rosemary Radford. *Sexism and God-Talk: Toward a Feminist Theology*. Boston: Beacon, 1993.

Salvatierra, Alexia, and Peter Hetzel. *Faith-Rooted Organizing: Mobilizing the Church in Service to the World*. Downers Grove: InterVarsity, 2014.

Sanders, Cheryl J. "Liberation Ethics in the Ex-Slave Interviews." In *Cut Loose Your Stammering Tongue: Black Theology in the Slave Narrative*, edited by Dwight N. Hopkins and George C. L. Cummings, 73–96. Louisville: Westminster John Knox, 2003.

Shankar, Jogan. *Devadasi Cult: A Sociological Analysis*. New Delhi: Ashish, 1990.

Sharma, Arvind. *Classical Hindu Thought*. New Delhi: Oxford University Press, 2000.

———. "What Is Hinduism?" In *The Study of Hinduism*, edited by Arvind Sharma, 1–19. Columbia: University of South Carolina Press, 2003.

Sharp, Gene. *The Politics of Nonviolent Action, Part One: Power and Struggle*. Manchester: Extending Horizons, 1973.

———. *The Politics of Nonviolent Action, Part Two: The Methods of Nonviolent Action*. Manchester: Extending Horizons, 1973.

———. *Sharp's Dictionary of Power and Struggle: Language of Civil Resistance in Conflicts* New York: Oxford University Press.

Shelley, Louise. *Human Trafficking: A Global Perspective*. New York: Cambridge University Press, 2010.

Sherman, Lawrence W., and Heather Strang. "Restorative Justice: The Evidence." In *The Restorative Justice Reader*, edited by Gerry Johnstone, 292–319. New York: Routledge, 2013.

Simon, Marcel. *Verus Israel*. Translated by H. McKeating. New York: Oxford University Press, 1986.

Smith, James V. "Benedictines." In *The Dictionary of Historical Theology*, edited by Trevor A. Hart, et al., 63–65. Grand Rapids: Eerdmans, 2000.

Spierenburg, Pieter. *The Prison Experience: Disciplinary Institutions and Their Inmates in Early Modern Europe*. Amsterdam: Amsterdam Academic Archive, 2007.

Stout, Jeffrey. *Blessed Are the Organized: Grassroots Democracy in America*. Princeton: Princeton University Press, 2010.

Stringfellow, William. *The Politics of Spirituality*. Philadelphia: Westminster, 1984.

Surin, Kenneth. *Freedom Not Yet: Liberation and the Next World Order*. Durham: Duke University Press, 2009.

Taylor, Dennis E. *We Are Legion (We Are Bob)*. New York: Ethan Ellenberg Literary Agency, 2017.

Taylor, Mark L. *The Way of the Cross in Lockdown America*. Minneapolis: Fortress, 2001.

Thomas Aquinas. *Summa Theologica*. Translated by Fathers of the English Dominican Province. 5 vols. Westminster, MD: Christian Classics, 1981.

Tutu, Desmond. *No Future without Forgiveness*. New York: Doubleday, 1999.

US Department of State. "2021 Trafficking in Persons Report: India." August 5, 2021. https://www.state.gov/reports/2021-trafficking-in-persons-report/india/.

Vanier, Jean. *Community and Growth: Our Pilgrimage Together*. New York: Paulist, 1979.

———. *Jean Vanier: Essential Writings*. Edited by Carolyn Whitney Brown. Maryknoll: Orbis, 2008.

Van Ness, Daniel W., and Karen Heetderks Strong. *Restoring Justice: An Introduction to Restorative Justice*. Waltham, MA: Elsevier, 2015.

Vitale, Alex S. *The End of Policing*. Brooklyn: Verso, 2017.

Walker, David. *Appeal to the Coloured Citizens of the World*. Edited by Peter P. Hinks. University Park: Pennsylvania State University Press, 2000.

Ward, Benedicta, trans. *The Desert Fathers: Sayings of the Early Christian Monks*. New York: Penguin, 2003.

Wheelan, Charles. *Naked Economics: Undressing the Dismal Science*. New York: Norton, 2010.

Wilkinson, Fred T. *The Realities of Crime and Punishment: A Prison Administrator's Testament*. Springfield, MO: Mycroft, 1972.

Williams, Rowan. *On Christian Theology*. Malden: Blackwell, 2000.

Wilson, A. N. *My Name Is Legion: A Novel*. London: Hutchinson, 2004.

Wilson-Hartgrove, Jonathan. *New Monasticism: What It Has to Say to Today's Church*. Grand Rapids: Brazos, 2008.

Wink, Walter. *Engaging the Powers: Discernment and Resistance in a World of Domination*. Philadelphia: Fortress, 1992.

———. *Jesus and Nonviolence: A Third Way*. Minneapolis: Fortress, 2003.

———. *Naming the Powers: The Language of Power in the New Testament*. Philadelphia: Fortress, 1984.

———. *Unmasking the Powers: The Invisible Forces That Determine Human Existence*. Philadelphia: Fortress, 1986.

Wright, Gavin. *Slavery and American Economic Development*. Baton Rouge: Louisiana State University Press, 2006.

Wright, N. T. *The Challenge of Jesus: Rediscovering Who Jesus Was and Is*. Downers Grove: InterVarsity, 1999.

Yoder, Carolyn. *The Little Book of Trauma Healing*. New York: Good Books, 2005.

Yoder, John Howard. *The Politics of Jesus*. Grand Rapids: Eerdmans, 1994.

Yong, Amos. *In the Days of Caesar: Pentecostalism and Political Theology*. Grand Rapids: Eerdmans, 2010.

Zehr, Howard. *Changing Lenses: Restorative Justice for Our Times*. Harrisonburg, VA: Herald, 2015.

———. *The Little Book of Restorative Justice*. New York: Good Books, 2015.

Zelazny, Roger. *My Name Is Legion*. London: Faber & Faber, 1979.

Zimmerman, Yvonne C. *Other Dreams of Freedom: Religion, Sex, and Human Trafficking*. New York: Oxford University Press, 2013.